Intelligence Operations

Intelligence Operations

Understanding Data, Tools, People, and Processes

First Edition

Erik Kleinsmith

American Public University System

cognella®

SAN DIEGO

Bassim Hamadeh, CEO and Publisher

Mary Jane Peluso, Senior Specialist Acquisitions Editor

Alisa Muñoz, (Senior) Project Editor

Christian Berk, Production Editor

Emely Villavicencio, Senior Graphic Designer

Greg Isales, Licensing Associate

Natalie Piccotti, Director of Marketing

Kassie Graves, Vice President of Editorial

Jamie Giganti, Director of Academic Publishing

Cover image copyright© 2019 iStockphoto LP/shulz.

Printed in the United States of America.

cognella® | ACADEMIC PUBLISHING

3970 Sorrento Valley Blvd., Ste. 500, San Diego, CA 92121

Dedicated to my wife, son, and daughter.

Brief Contents

Detailed Contents

Foreword

In my early days as an Army leader, I thought that intelligence was somebody else's job. Frankly, I didn't think much about the intelligence process, I simply wanted someone to concisely and definitively deliver information to me about the weather and terrain and, oh by the way, tell me precisely where our enemies were and what they were doing. I expected to be a recipient, a customer of intelligence, not a participant in the intelligence process.

In the mid-1990s, as a Lieutenant Colonel commanding an infantry battalion in Germany, I first met (then) Captain Erik Kleinsmith, our battalion's S-2, the intelligence staff officer. Erik began to educate me (ever so gently and respectfully given the difference in our positions in the rigid hierarchical structure of the U.S. Army!) on my responsibilities in the intelligence process.

He would complicate my life by asking questions like, "Why do you want to know that? What decisions will that information affect? What will you do with that piece of information? What resources are you willing to commit to obtain that bit of information?" At first, I wasn't too happy with Erik's approach. I just wanted him to give me all the information I requested and I wanted it *now*! Slowly, Captain Kleinsmith started to wear me down; started to make me understand that, as the decision-maker, I had a critical role in the intelligence process and it wasn't just to demand current, tactical information.

In *Intelligence Operations: Understanding Data, Tools, People, and Processes*, Erik Kleinsmith shares his 30+ years of experience in the intelligence community in a refreshing, logical, and easily understandable way. While this book can certainly be read from front to back, its organization and structure also makes it a handy reference for continued use by decision-makers in both government and the private sector. Given his background as a military intelligence officer, Erik's writing has a distinct military flavor. But, this book is not exclusively for military intelligence personnel. Rather, the issues and principles addressed in *Intelligence Operations* have wide applicability in business, local governance, and most other meaningful endeavors.

I especially like the way the author has clearly outlined learning objectives in the chapters, and offers some thought-provoking questions for the reader to contemplate or for the academic instructor to pose to her/his students.

This common sense approach makes *Intelligence Operations: Understanding Data, Tools, People, and Processes* a valuable resource for academics and practitioners alike.

When applied effectively, the processes and activities outlined by Erik can be of immeasurable benefit to the decision-maker. Using the techniques suggested herein, senior leaders and intelligence professionals are likely to achieve better outcomes for their organizations and do so with less friction and wasted effort. Working together, the leader and the intelligence staff can more rapidly and more effectively assess the environment in which they are working, identify threats and opportunities, and greatly improve the likelihood of success, no mater whether on the battlefield or in the arena of commercial competition.

Intelligence Operations: Understanding Data, Tools, People, and Processes is timely and relevant. But, it also describes many timeless themes and principles, which will long outlast the latest trends. Erik Kleinsmith has crafted a guide which is of immediate value to the military professionals, the business leaders, and to those engaged in government activities from federal to local levels. Those who read, understand, and apply what Erik has described will have significantly improved their chances for success.

—GEN Carter F. Ham (ret.)

Introduction

Throughout my career I've periodically been asked by friends and colleagues how to start a career in intelligence. While I am not sure I would have always answered it this way, but after over 30 years in the intelligence business my answer is now always the same, "Do something else first."

As a profession, intelligence goes beyond a job, occupation, or career since it involves substantial training and education as well as certain certifications. It can also include required security clearances. Often unstated, intelligence as a profession relies heavily upon other areas of knowledge and experience. From military to finance, experience in other areas provides the profession with a greater depth of knowledge and insight for the predictive analysis that sets intelligence apart from other analytic careers.

As a result, intelligence is more of an accession profession, routinely relying on people who have experience and expertise in other walks of life and who have decided to use that expertise to understand and overcome enemies, adversaries, and competitors.

My own path into intelligence, like many others, started with the military. While I had been interested in studying my opponents since childhood through role-playing and war-gaming, being commissioned out of Purdue University's ROTC program as an Army Lieutenant in 1988 started me on that path. The experience I received as an M-1 Tank platoon leader and later as a reconnaissance scout platoon leader was invaluable as I transitioned into intelligence and took on the roles of an intelligence officer for an infantry battalion and armor brigade, as a counterintelligence company commander, and in my final role position in the Army as the Chief of Intelligence for the Army's newly created Land Information Warfare Activity.

Unfortunately, learning how to be an intelligence professional was much more elusive than I would have imagined it would be for other professions. Attending an eight-week transition course and a five-month officer advanced course for new Army captains at Fort Huachuca, Arizona, taught me the basic concepts and processes needed for tactical intelligence, but beyond that there were few opportunities to improve knowledge and expertise in the actual tasks and responsibilities I would be expected to perform. I spent a lot of time looking for ways to learn more on my own. I dove into war and strategy gaming and changed my approach in reading military histories, using an intelligence and predictive analysis perspective as I went through one source after another.

From my own studies, I found that the preponderance of intelligence-specific books and literature could be grouped into one of five categories: the history of spies and spying, U.S. intelligence within the national level agencies, analytic techniques, doctrinal manuals and regulations, and a newest category—anecdotal experiences—also known as "I was there" books. Not to detract from these sources, as most are excellent reading, there was still not much available in the way of laying out the issues and considerations that an intelligence officer would have to tackle during operations. My book is my attempt to fill that gap.

Intelligence Operations is a book about the various aspects, issues, challenges, and solutions that can be found in every type of intelligence operation. It is presented in an academic format much like a textbook, but it is not intended to be kept solely within the academic environment. It is meant as a guide to be read, studied, referenced, and applied in the midst of ongoing operations. In this way, it is not meant solely for the academic mind as much as it is meant for the operator and practitioner of intelligence. Whether used in the creation of a new capability from scratch or in seeking to improve an existing operation, this book is designed and organized to help in the review, planning, and management of intelligence operations, no matter the level or the environment.

An idea that sounds good on paper or in theory but cannot be recreated or adapted to actual operations is not worth much. This book attempts to present many issues in a way that can be tailored and applied to any operation. Throughout my time in intelligence, I have been able to capture many lessons learned from both my successes and mistakes. Much of what I've included in the book is based on the understanding that intelligence operations are similar to many other types of operations and yet have many unique aspects. The concepts, lists, figures, and charts presented within this book are my own but are a presented and explained in a way that fosters discovery and discussion. They are meant to be understood, used, broken, adapted, and ultimately improved and applied in a way that best fits the particular operation or requirements of the reader.

The 12 chapters of *Intelligence Operations* follow a fairly logical flow and invite the reader to look at the various aspects of intelligence from a broader perspective than they may have been trained or used to in the part. The reader is first introduced to the many defining concepts associated with intelligence as well as the main subject of intelligence, i.e., the threat. This broader perspective approach continues in looking at the community of intelligence, revealing where intelligence is actually practiced as well as what defines and characterize intelligence operations themselves.

From this point, the remainder of the book follows two concurrent themes: First, it covers each of the four components critical to every intelligence operation, i.e., the data, tools, people, and then processes. Then, various operational and analytic processes are looked at in more detail in the final four chapters; as much of what intelligence does involves a variety of processes from the time the requirement is understood to when a response is delivered to the supported customer.

To get the most out of this book, there are few additional points that the reader should consider:

- Many of the ideas and concepts presented here are simplified versions of reality. Instead of trying to reinvent concepts and terms like the Intelligence Cycle, I've instead presented them as they are being practiced in operation. Many of the ideas, concepts, and processes presented here are not so much new ways of doing business as they are attempts to more accurately capture and codify the current realities of the business.

- I spent a major part of my career in military intelligence and still retain a military-like approach to my ideas of intelligence today. While I've made a deliberate attempt to present intelligence ideas and concepts for universal application, many of them will have a military feel to them. Many of these areas discussed here are foundational and therefore applicable to intelligence operations in any environment.

- Several of these topics I've written about have been developed over several years and can be found in courses I've developed and taught for Army Intelligence, Defense Intelligence, and Homeland Security members. I've given credit to colleagues or external sources who have created original versions or adaptations of processes shown, but each of these has been developed by myself through my own experience and instructional design efforts.

- As an avid board, miniature, and video gamer, I understand that the best games are often those with simple rules that are able to capture complex strategies. Unfortunately, many intelligence processes, both operational and analytic in nature suffer from overcomplications. Throughout my career, I've found myself simplifying many complex topics in order to get to the heart of their intended purpose. If I was going to apply, explain, or train other in them, this was a critical requirement. In this book, I've taken great care to codify many ideas and processes in a simplified manner so that the reader can more easily adapt them to their own intelligence operation or organization.

- Instead of quoting some doctrinal or scholarly source, I've presented many of the terms and definitions related to intelligence in this book from my own perspective. In doing so, I have used terminology that is similar to other traditional or more widely known processes already in use elsewhere, but it is important for the reader to understand and form their own opinions regarding these terms. In the same vein, I've also deliberately avoided acronyms. While they are used to simplify commonly held concepts and terms, they often lead to confusion when used across different professional cultures.

- Finally, it is unfortunate to have to address this explicitly, but intelligence isn't about political correctness and neither is this book. While I strive in my writing to exclude, or at least reduce, any comments, ideas, or examples that are politically charged, there will undoubtedly be a topic or subject of discussion that will offend someone. Data, information, and intelligence products are routinely used by bad and evil men and woman to support their illegal, immoral, and malicious operations. In discussing intelligence as a way to defeat the threats to a supported customer, I am not advocating death or destruction or the use of immoral and horrific tactics and strategies to do so—far from it. This book is intended to strengthen the intelligence operations of those good people who look upon intelligence as a noble and necessary cause so that others may live their lives in security and freedom.

This book was made possible because of the generosity of American Military University (AMU) and the insightfulness of Cognella Publishing among other great qualities both institutions possess. I am relatively new to the academic world and sincerely appreciate the help and guidance I received from several great people within AMU and Cognella during my writing. I am also in awe of the sacrifice and support of my wife Susan, my son Ethan, and my daughter Olivia. I am forever grateful for their understanding of the long hours spent to create this book, and I am inspired by their faith in me throughout this journey.

Erik Kleinsmith

Chapter 1

The Art, Science, and Business of Intelligence

Learning Objectives

After completing this chapter, you will be able to:

- ▸ Understand the operational definition and primary purpose of intelligence.
- ▸ Understand several of the roles intelligence provides to serve the primary purpose.
- ▸ Be familiar with the various perspectives and aspects of intelligence and why they exist.
- ▸ Be familiar with the foundational principles and rules that exist within every intelligence operation no matter what type.

Intelligence Is for the Customer

To most of the world, the faces of intelligence are a group of men whose names all start with the letter J: James Bond, Jason Bourne, Jack Ryan, Jack Bauer, and Jack Reacher. The perception of intelligence as a profession has been shaped by the entertainment industry. Fantastical fiction in the movies and on television has created a perception of intelligence as an intriguingly fast-paced and deadly world of men and women who live on the edge day in and day out. All of these Js give the world the impression that intelligence is all about spying, intrigue, explosions, high-speed chases (car, motorcycle, train, aircraft, speed boats, gondolas, zip lines, etc.), femmes fatales, sniper scopes, and jumping from roof tops to helicopters. A good spy movie only needs to follow a simple formula of a renegade bad guy who must be thwarted by the resident good guy who in turn also happens to be imperiled as a maverick by their own organization. Add in a couple of shapely vixens, an elderly or geeky technical expert, and a secret darkened room with about a dozen analysts who never need sleep and can pull up any piece of information in the world within seconds, and the rest of the story writes itself.

1

FIGURE 1.1   Sean Connery as James Bond—007, filming the movie *Diamonds Are Forever*, 1971

It seems obvious to point out, but like many other aspects of our lives, the business of intelligence presents a much more complex picture. It involves data, tools, people, processes, organizations, budgets, centers, laws, regulations, and, unfortunately, politics. It also involves many other fields of study such as psychology, sociology, criminology, geography, topology, logic, and mathematics. What tends to get lost in the business of intelligence is the entire reason why the intelligence profession exists—to support someone else and their decisions. Intelligence not in support of a customer is worthless.

The reality of intelligence, like most any other professional outside of the Hollywood caricature, is much more mundane, repetitive, and bureaucratic. While a small fraction of intelligence professionals live like Hollywood spies for a small fraction of their careers, the rest of the intelligence world is filled with the daily business of collecting information, processing it, analyzing it, and delivering any new knowledge from that analysis to a customer in order to assist in their decision-making processes. It can be rote, academic, and just like any other profession—boring at times. The most significant difference between intelligence and other analytical professions is that intelligence is about understanding our competitors, adversaries, and outright enemies, i.e., our threats.

Defining Intelligence

Intelligence has multiple definitions depending on the perspective. Academically, intelligence can mean the ability to acquire and apply knowledge as well as the ability to use reason, logic, and learning in understanding the world. In other perspectives, intelligence can mean an ability to conceptualize complex concepts or an ability to mentally adapt to changing information or environments. Intelligence is measured in terms of an intelligence quotient or IQ, and described for computers and automation in terms such as artificial intelligence or AI. Using the common vernacular, someone who possesses intelligence is referred to as smart, wise, gifted, or genius, while someone who lacks it is described derisively as a dolt, dullard, imbecile, moron, or numbskull.

Like the academic perspective, *intelligence in an operational sense is about acquiring and applying knowledge, but more specifically it is about learning and understanding the threats to a supported customer through the collection and analysis of relevant information*. It's about recognizing these threats, finding them, predicting their actions, and then helping to reduce, mitigate, defeat, or, in some cases, destroy them. From this perspective, intelligence is defined more by what it does than what it is.

What makes intelligence confusing to the outsider or layman is that even in the operational sense, the word "intelligence" is used to describe several things—all related to each other. To put it succinctly:

- Intelligence **Is a Product:** It is the result of taking data, information, and created knowledge about the threats that a customer faces. It is delivered, disseminated, posted, shared, and presented in order to assist in their decision-making processes.
- Intelligence **Is People:** It is the name given to teams, sections, units, activities, agencies, organizations, and businesses of personnel who work to support customers with analysis and advice about their threats.
- Intelligence **Is a Process:** It is the methods, procedures, and techniques used to collect, process, analyze, produce, and deliver analysis about threats.
- Intelligence **Is a Business:** Intelligence assets offer goods (products) and services (threat analysis) to their customers just like any other business. It is therefore subject to many capitalistic principles such as supply and demand and competition.[1]

There are two common threads to each of these perspectives. One of them is that each is related to the *threat* which, as explored in more detail in Chapter 2, is a fairly broad term and subject to different interpretations. One misperception of intelligence is that a threat can only be lethal or militant by nature and therefore only a concern at the national or strategic levels of our society. While most academic sources of intelligence address threats within the narrow scope of national security, the reality is that the fundamental steps found in the intelligence process are conducted in virtually every aspect of society. To those who must understand and overcome their enemies, adversaries, and even competitors, collecting, analyzing, and making decisions based on what they know about them is commonplace.

The other common thread is the purpose of intelligence—and that is to support a customer/consumer. Intelligence is nothing by itself. It doesn't defeat the enemy or apprehend

---

1   Assets can refer to any intelligence organization, unit, individual, or capability such as a collection platform or analytic tool.

FIGURE 1.2   What is left of the south tower of the World Trade Center in New York City stands like a tombstone among the debris and devastation caused by the September 11 terrorist attack. U.S. Navy photo by Journalist 1st Class Preston

the bad guy. It doesn't seize or hold key terrain. It doesn't develop a new product that will outpace the competition. In order for it to be effective, it must be in the hands of someone who has the capability to effectively use it—i.e., the customer.

The customer, also known as the decision-maker or consumer of intelligence, can be anyone who needs to have a better understanding about the environment around them and the threats they face, whether in real space or cyberspace, in lethal or nonlethal environments. A customer could be a military commander, another analyst, a police chief, a corporate executive, a sports coach, a lawyer, an investigator, an operational planner, or anyone else who needs analysis conducted about someone who opposes them. Intelligence personnel dedicate their time to understanding and assessing the various threats to their customers so that they in turn can spend more time managing and leading the entire operation. While everyone does a degree of their own analysis, history has proven the success of dedicating someone in an organization specifically toward collecting information and gaining an understanding about our threats, what they're capable of and, most importantly, what they intend to do.

While intelligence customers have historically been limited to only national, political, military, and federal law enforcement organizations, it is no longer an exclusive club. Intelligence has its roots in antiquity, but it's only been recently recognized as a critical need for organizations to succeed in everyday life. As explained in more detail in Chapter 3, those that have recognized the need to understand and mitigate perceived and real threats have grown exponentially in number and in the diversity of their business over the past 20 years.

The Primary Purpose and Roles of Intelligence

Through each of the different lenses that intelligence is viewed, the conduct of intelligence must appear to the layperson as a complex set of disparate operations, each conducted in a unique manner depending on the customer, against different threats, and within different environments. After all, there are significant differences between tactical military, law enforcement, and business or competitive intelligence operations; the threats, their organizations, techniques, and targets all differing significantly from those in other areas. Yet, the fundamental reason behind *what* intelligence does and *why* it is conducted, i.e., its purpose, is universal.

In the context of building or improving an intelligence capability within an organization, intelligence's *primary purpose above all others is to provide information and analysis of the threats, adversaries, enemies, or competition in support of a customer.* Looking at this purpose statement in more detail reveals three basic components: the importance of supporting a customer; the focus on the threats to their operations; and the roles intelligence plays in collecting, analyzing, and defeating these threats. These three things are what make intelligence unique as both a profession and a business.

Providing information and analysis to a customer involves some sort of deliverable, either in the form of a tangible product or a presentation of some sort, e.g., a briefing, wargame session, or informal Q&A. These deliverables to a customer will take three basic forms. Articulating this in a 1995 paper in the Central Intelligence Agency (CIA) publication, *Studies in Intelligence*, Jack Davis defines the analytic mission of intelligence is to provide policy and decision-makers, i.e., customers, with facts, findings, and forecasts.[2] Using a more current lexicon, these deliverables can be best described in the following manner, ranked in order of complexity and difficulty from lowest to highest:

1. Information: Conducting basic information from various sources with little to no analysis to a customer. Keeping them informed about the situation and significant events relating to the threat within their operating environment.
2. Assessments: Supporting the customer with analysis based on available data and information regarding their threats. Going beyond the baseline of sourced information into order to generate knew knowledge and likewise considerations for the customer.
3. Predictions: Conducting more complex analysis for the customer by extrapolating available information to predict future threat dispositions and actions. Can be geared for both short and long future time periods.

While the purpose and basic functions of intelligence are similar no matter the environment, intelligence support in practice can mean something different to each type of customer. Much of this is dependent on both their past experiences and future expectations of intelligence support.

Besides simply offering products and presentations, intelligence has to provide a benefit to a customer. In other words, intelligence must play an important role in support of a customer in order for them to turn to their asset time and time again. For those policy- and decision-makers who do not either understand or trust intelligence, their supporting asset has failed to prove their worth.

The specific roles that intelligence plays for each individual customer is often defined by stated or unstated customer requirements depending on what is needed at any given time. For some, intelligence is required to simply have a better understanding of the situation, while for others it is needed to predict and either mitigate or counter impending threats. For others still, intelligence is required to assist them achieve their objectives over a threat or threats that are actively working against them.

The roles intelligence plays in support of a customer can be best articulated in four ways:

1. **Providing Increased Situational Awareness:** While policy-makers are usually responsible for taking complex subjects and articulating perspectives and

---

2   Davis, Jack. (1995). Facts, findings, forecasts, and fortune-telling. *Studies in Intelligence, 39*(3), 25–30. Retrieved from https://www.cia.gov/library/center-for-the-study-of-intelligence/csi-publications/csi-studies/studies/davis-pdfs/facts-findings-forecasts-and-fortune-telling-davis-1995.pdf

opinions into directives, instructions, and standing orders relating to these subjects, decision-makers are usually responsible for carrying out operations, directing personnel and actions in the process. Both of these types of customers benefit from intelligence personnel, who can dedicate themselves to identifying, understanding, and articulating the key features of their environment so that they may spend their time weighing their decisions and policies among many other factors.

2. **Providing Accurate and Timely Indications and Warnings:** Besides providing a customer with awareness of their current situation, intelligence also plays an important role by continually watching a given environment and the threats present within that environment. Intelligence personnel look for indicators in the form of movements, meetings, actions, events, and other changes in the disposition of the various threats and in the process identifying those key changes that are important enough for a decision-maker to be notified of a future impending action against them.

3. **Actively Countering Threats:** A small portion of the intelligence world is directly involved in countering the actions of a customer's threats. Counter-intelligence operations are designed to nullify or mitigate efforts of the threat to conduct their own intelligence or other covert actions. It is carried out by counter threat specialists and agents, and often requires the support of intelligence analysis themselves.

4. **Supporting Operational Objectives:** The main objective of intelligence operations is to provide information and analysis that supports a decision-maker's ability to successfully carry out their own missions and operations. This is where the variety and uniqueness of customer missions will distinguish one intelligence operation from the next. Consumers of intelligence could require support in order to defeat an enemy military force. They could also need it to predict the future criminal actions of a gang and possibly prevent them. They also simply need intelligence in order to win their next football game, or get a jump on the competition in the commercial arena. Customer objectives are generally categorized as those that help to advance the customer and their organization and those that seek to defeat or nullify threats and obstacles to achieve success.

If an intelligence organization, operation, or center cannot identify a direct link between their efforts and support to a customer in one of these four areas, they can be deemed ineffective from the outset. This may seem ridiculous to mention, but intelligence, like other operations, can be overcome by events, lose focus, or simply outlive their usefulness to their primary and secondary customers.

In order to better understand the relationship between the categories of deliverables and the roles intelligence plays for a customer, Figure 1.3 helps to visualize the following statement: Intelligence delivers information, assessments, and predictions in support of a customer in order to provide increased situational awareness, accurate and timely indications and warnings, counter threats, and support their operational objectives.

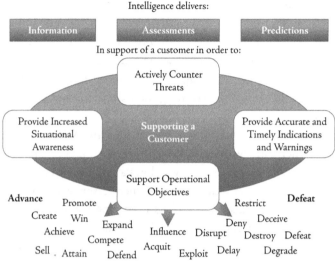

FIGURE 1.3   The roles of intelligence

The Intelligence Business

For those who spent most of their intelligence careers within the government or military, the idea that intelligence is a business may seem a distant concept. After all, most military, law enforcement, and other government intelligence operations enjoy a persistent status as a monopoly. Expanding the aperture to include intelligence operations in the commercial environment reveals an environment that is strikingly similar to a competitive market space.

As already established, intelligence serves to support a customer. With no customers, it is ineffective and a waste of resources for whoever is funding it. In serving their customers, intelligence assets provide goods and services not only to their primary customer but also to others who would have use of it. Instead of making a profit in dollars, most intelligence assets are paid in trust and advocacy, while intelligence personnel are rewarded with accolades and advancement in the long term. The higher the quality of the deliverable, the more respect they receive. Those who do not earn or lose the trust of their customers eventually find their analysis unread and disregarded.

This view of intelligence as a business helps to highlight the importance of the supported policy and decision-maker as a customer. To serve them, intelligence assets involve a myriad of people, organizations, centers, and processes. From a business perspective, intelligence assets provide both goods and services to a customer the cost of which is determined by associated labor, equipment, materials among other indirect costs.

In macro sense, the overall need for intelligence to support a growing number of customers has resulted in the rapid expansion of intelligence operations far beyond the borders of the intelligence community. We are now a society that collects information and analyzes data on just about everything. The Information Age, getting out of its adolescent years, has become more than just a rapid expansion in the availability of information; it's been an expansion of people and tools that can and want to do something with that information.

Analysis of threats to a given customer or organization is just one of the new capabilities brought about by recent advancements in information technology. It is now available to virtually anyone who has recognized their need of it. Analysis of enemies, adversaries, and competitors has always taken place; it's just not always recognized as intelligence gathering.

From balloons to satellites, spies, radars and sensors, unmanned aerial vehicles, and even computer scripts and web crawlers, the race to gather information about threats knows only the limits of today's technology and self-imposed legal and moral restrictions. The commercial sector is not immune. Sports teams have their scouts. Businesses conduct intelligence from both competitive and protective postures. Corporations gather information about their competition. Some companies simply provide information as their primary service. There are even entire businesses that exist solely for collecting information and conducting analysis on anyone a paying customer desires. The size and scope of the national intelligence community is enormous with funding measured in the tens of billions of dollar annually. And yet the private and commercial sector is poised to overtake the size and scope of the intelligence community within a generation.

The Intelligence Profession

Of course, the ubiquitous act of analyzing information is not unique to the intelligence profession. There are countless other lines of work that have to support decision-making processes with in-depth collection and analysis of relevant information. What makes the professional of intelligence unique in this regard is that it is about analyzing threats, whether they are threats to national security, public safety, or commercial success. No other profession is about analyzing threats as its primary purpose.

Intelligence analysis is much more difficult than any other type of analysis because it is one of the only forms of analysis where the subject doesn't want to be understood. Enemies, adversaries, and competitors actively resist the efforts to collect and analyze information about them. They go to great lengths to keep others from knowing what they would prefer remain secret. They hide it, guard it, and conceal their intentions. They attack the means of collecting it. It seems trivial to point this out, but there is an ageless, multibillion dollar industry in operation every day trying to gather as much information from persons who are also spending billions of dollars trying to ensure no one collects it.

Protecting information about capabilities, vulnerabilities, motivations, and objectives, and methods of operations range from simple security procedures to deceptive and outright deadly measures. There are currently 90 stars on the memorial for fallen heroes at CIA headquarters in Langley, Virginia, as a testament to how dangerous the business of intelligence is. As Jimmy Dugan, played by Tom Hanks in the 1992 movie, *A League of Their Own*, says, "If it was easy, everyone would do it. The hard … is what makes it great."[3] Intelligence can be a truly hard and dangerous profession simply because of the lethality of the threats from the people who are being spied upon.

Besides focusing on adversaries, what also makes intelligence unique is that it is also about making predictions. Conducting analysis to determine what happened is the investigator's job; their primary purpose is to make sense of what happened after an event, such as a crime that has already occurred. Investigative analysis is based upon known facts and events that have already happened. The investigator fills in the blanks of information with their own analysis in order to paint the most complete picture possible. Criminal investigations start with the understanding that nothing can change or influence something that has already taken place. The ultimate result of an investigation is to tell a story or reach a logical conclusion of a particular event or storyline. Like intelligence, this requires assembling as many relevant facts as possible and filling in the gaps with logic and conjecture.

Instead of telling a story of what happened, it is the job of intelligence to determine what's going to happen. Instead of an assembly of facts and logical thought processes against those facts, intelligence requires an extrapolation of facts and logical thought in order to assemble and present some certain future scenarios among almost limitless possibilities. Since it is the job of many customers of intelligence to deny, degrade, disrupt, defeat, or destroy (among other effects upon) our adversaries, many of their decisions depend heavily upon being able to know what the bad guys are going to in the near and distant future. Intelligence about their enemies helps them to plan their own actions accordingly.

Intelligence relies much more heavily upon analysis and prediction than criminal investigations simply because intelligence tries to deal with predicting the future using the same information that an investigator already has. The more the intelligence personnel can inform their customer about the future of a given threat, scenario, or environment, the better decisions the customer is inclined to make in facing or shaping that future. While there are never any guarantees against bad decisions, it's the job of intelligence to do everything in within its capacity to minimize the guess work of their customers.

Understanding Intelligence Through Its Disciplines

Much of intelligence is divided into different areas or disciplines that are in turn defined by how they collect data and information. The wide variety of methods and means for acquiring either raw data or information can be categorized fairly easily as they contrast significantly from one another. Human collectors rely on personal contacts and handheld imagery, while satellites, radar, drones, and other technical equipment, i.e., collection platforms, provide a host of other types of data from overhead imagery to radio waves and electronic signatures.

---

3   Retrieved from http://www.moviequotes.com/fullquote.cgi?qnum=1766

These methods have enough of a distinction from each other that they can help to delineate budgets, organizations, and personnel/career specialties. These disciplines have their names shortened to similar-sounding acronyms collectively known as the INTs. Each INT denotes how a particular piece of intelligence was derived from a type of source. For example, a large amount of intelligence data is collected through the signals of our threats; radio waves, cell phone and Internet traffic, electronic emissions, and even heat signatures reveal information about our threats. Intelligence derived from this type of information is called Signals Intelligence or SIGINT.

Learning and understanding how each of these specialties works help to paint a comprehensive picture of the entire intelligence profession as a whole. There are six broad categories in total along with two additional specialties: counterintelligence, which is instead defined by its mission, and all-source intelligence, which is an amalgamation of all the others, sometimes referred to as Fusion Intelligence (Chart 1.1).

CHART 1.1   The Intelligence Disciplines

Intelligence discipline	Description and subcategories
SIGINT	Signals intelligence includes COMINT (communications), ELINT (electronic), FISINT (foreign instrumentation signals) intelligence
HUMINT	Human intelligence includes collection from persons (sources), interrogations, debriefings, documents, and media exploitation (DOCEX)
GEOINT	Geospatial intelligence includes imagery (IMINT) and collection of other geospatial information
MASINT	Measurements and signature intelligence includes collection of electromagnetic, radiation, radar, and radio frequency data
OSINT	Open-source intelligence includes collection from print literature (newspapers, magazines, brochures), the Internet, media broadcast and pretty much any information that is available publicly
TECHINT	Technical intelligence includes information obtained from "reverse engineering" a piece of equipment or scientific data
CI	Counterintelligence actions and operations designed to keep our threats and enemies from conduct all of the other INTs on us; not really a true collection discipline, but an operation that relies on the other disciplines, especially HUMINT to be conducted effectively
ALL-SOURCE	The fusion of all of the above disciplines into a comprehensive product; all-source intelligence is more well-rounded than intelligence derived from a single discipline or source, but also more general in nature

Much of the world of intelligence, i.e., the National Intelligence Community or IC is organized around these INTs. Organizations such as the National Security Agency (NSA) and the National Geospatial Agency (NGA) were created to specifically handle SIGINT and GEOINT, respectively. While each of the above INTs can be found in almost every intelligence organization in some form, these INTs serve as a common set of boundaries for many of our national intelligence operations, including budgets, personnel, training, suborganizations, doctrine, mission sets, and scientific developments.

All-source analysts have general knowledge of all types of intelligence as well as more skills in terms of how best to integrate the sources. They can therefore be found almost everywhere within the community, especially at the tactical level, as they specialize in combining one or more of the other disciplines and presenting them together into a fused product.

Is Intelligence an Art or a Science?

After starting with a basic idea of what intelligence is and why it is needed, another way to understand it is to understand the dichotomy of thought surrounding it. Among both academics and practitioners, there is disagreement between as to whether it should be looked upon as an art or a science. A simple online search will reveal several sources of opinions, including my own, that swing from one side of the argument to the other.[4] If these two perspectives are arranged on a linear spectrum, each opinion offered will fall somewhere toward one side or another. Many arguments are vehement that intelligence is either purely one or the other. As Figure 1.4 shows, each of these perspectives are described by a series of criteria that have similar opposing criteria associated with the other side.

For those who view intelligence as an art, the intelligence profession and intelligence analysis are something akin to mastering some form of artistic expression such as playing an instrument, painting, or dancing. All of the tools and data are simply raw materials that mean nothing until they are in the hands of master who can makes sense of it, allowing it to take shape in the form of an intelligence estimate or assessment. Intelligence products are simply ways to capture that expression allowing the analysis to be codified into a workable record of someone's thought process. Moving these assessments are emotive logic and subconscious levels of thought with bare instinct and fuzzy math and mental scenes playing out in the analysts mind.

On the other end of the spectrum is the perspective that intelligence is more of a science than an art. Intelligence deals in the business of data and information as a commodity. Everything about intelligence, from the technical methods used to collect it to the mathematical and methodical ways to parse, tag, store, retrieve, and visualize it, involves math and information technology. The processes used to analyze information and create a new set of knowledge from it involve logical, structured, proven, and repeatable analytic techniques, much like scientific inquiry. Quantity is more of a priority than quality of information as all analysis is based on hard data, not hunches or gut feelings.

Many people within the intelligence profession are drawn toward those aspects of it that best fit their perspective. Those with a more scientific bent tend to be drawn to the more technical areas of intelligence such as SIGINT, IMINT, GEOINT, and TECHINT. Those who approach intelligence from a more artistic/humanities-based perspective tend to be drawn more to areas such as HUMINT or counterintelligence.

---

4   Kleinsmith, Erik A. (2016). Is intelligence an art or a science. *Public Safety* Retrieved from https://inpublicsafety.com/2016/05/is-intelligence-an-art-or-a-science/

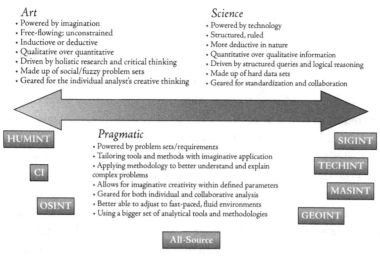

Art
- Powered by imagination
- Free-flowing; unconstrained
- Inductive or deductive
- Qualitative over quantitative
- Driven by holistic research and critical thinking
- Made up of social/fuzzy problem sets
- Geared for the individual analyst's creative thinking

Science
- Powered by technology
- Structured, ruled
- More deductive in nature
- Quantitative over qualitative information
- Driven by structured queries and logical reasoning
- Made up of hard data sets
- Geared for standardization and collaboration

HUMINT   SIGINT
CI   TECHINT
OSINT   MASINT
GEOINT
All-Source

Pragmatic
- Powered by problem sets/requirements
- Tailoring tools and methods with imaginative application
- Applying methodology to better understand and explain complex problems
- Allows for imaginative creativity within defined parameters
- Geared for both individual and collaborative analysis
- Better able to adjust to fast-paced, fluid environments
- Using a bigger set of analytical tools and methodologies

FIGURE 1.4   Intelligence as art versus science

In the purist's mind, these two perspectives are diametrically opposed to one another and therefore completely incompatible. The reality is that the perspectives of most intelligence professionals and their customers will fall somewhere in between the two. This pragmatic approach acknowledges that intelligence involves science and technology to be sure, but it also involves creative and critical thinking skills as well as tapping into and effectively harnessing the emotional and subconscious ways we solve problems and make decisions as human thinkers.

For this reason, intelligence can be seen as an art, powered by science. The greatest paintings in the world may be artistic masterpieces, but they still required the mastery of pigments and dyes; the same is with the musician's use of sound and its scientific properties or dancers and their ability to master muscle use and timing. Intelligence should be viewed in the same way—using information technology to gather and mold data and information in a way that the analytical artist can then mold it into an effective tool for decision making. The beauty of intelligence is in the eye of that which it was created to support—the customer.

In taking a more pragmatic, art powered by science, approach those looking to learn about or understand intelligence better are given two lenses or perspectives to assist them. First is that the sometimes overwhelming amount of technology available and required by intelligence professionals should be viewed at as means to an end. Information technology along with databases, collection systems, and visualization tools does not make an intelligence operation.

Only the effective use of these things by the right people using the right processes to create the right responses for their customers can be called an effective intelligence operation. Intelligence doesn't exist for the sake of intelligence, and the tools and data are no exception to this. When learning about intelligence-related technology as a student or evaluating it as an operator, the intelligence professional should be able to link the particular technology and its role in benefitting the analyst and greater operation in their fulfillment of customer requirements. If the technology provides no increased or otherwise tangible benefit, it is useless.

Second is that hunches are not a sign of a great and artistic intelligence analyst. Hunches, gut feelings, the force, or some other unseen hand-guiding analysis are sometimes attributed to an ability of good analysts to piece together, extrapolate, or connect the dots when there is not enough information to validate their assessments. Too often, this type of analysis is portrayed in movies and television as a protagonist who can see beyond what everyone else does in solving the main problem or challenge.

Unfortunately, hunches are indicators of an analyst either guessing, not conducting proper analysis, or analyst's inability to articulate why they came up with their assessments. Of the three, the latter is most likely. On average, intelligence analysts are not known as great communicators as many of them lean toward introversion. Their ability to clearly state and present their analysis using public speaking skills is a persistent challenge of

Lessons in Intelligence:
Intelligence as a Horizontal Profession

I joined the American Public University System (APUS) and their associated American Military University (AMU) in Spring 2015. I was very familiar with the school as the alma mater of my master's degree as well as serving on their Industry Advisory Council or IAC for a few years during my previous job. I was hired onto the university's outreach team where I spent my first weeks learning about the academic environment.

With intelligence as my assigned area of responsibility or what we termed a vertical, other verticals within our team were Law Enforcement, Fire and Emergency Management, and Commercial and Military; each one labeled to help define and categorize the organizations we would coordinate and partner with. One of the first tasks I identified was to develop an outreach and marketing plan for the intelligence and security market. Although my fellow law enforcement, military, and commercial vertical leaders each had several directors responsible for different sections of their own verticals, I was starting out alone. Since I had already studied and mapped out the intelligence community as a community of practice (see Chapter 3), I already had a baseline to work from.

In formulating a plan, it didn't take me long to realize that my approach would have to be much different than what I was learning about the other verticals. While there are a handful of intelligence-specific organizations at the national level, the majority of intelligence professionals work in an organization designed to do something else. A few of my new colleagues also knew this and were concerned that as the new guy I would be treading into their territories. To alleviate their concerns, I briefed my plan to several of them, asking them to look at intelligence as a horizontal, not a vertical. I wasn't concerned with meeting with the head of a particular military command, police department or company, just the intelligence personnel within the organization. This went a long in establishing working relationships with my new colleagues as also inspired me to write my first article for our school blog, InPublicSafety.com sharing this new map with our students.[1]

---

1   Kleinsmith, Erik A. (2015). Intelligence work expands beyond the core intelligence community (and so should your job search). *Public Safety*. https://inpublicsafety.com/2015/08/intelligence-work-expands-beyond-the-core-intelligence-community-and-so-should-your-job-search/

intelligence leadership. There are many structured analytic techniques available for virtually every kind of intelligence analysis, and each of them can be adapted to a given problem set given a good imagination combined with logical reasoning.

Intelligence as Required by the Customer

It is important to know that these abstract perspectives, while key to an understanding of the field, are not in the forefront of what drives the day-to-day of intelligence work. Ideally, customer requirements drive almost everything about intelligence, and it is their perspective that becomes the most important for defining how intelligence operations are conducted on a day-to-day basis.

Customers are generally categorized by six factors, each of which represents an aspect of their operating environment.

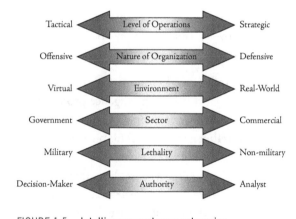

FIGURE 1.5   Intelligence customer categories

Using these aspects, a commander of an infantry battalion in the U.S. Army would be a tactical, offensive, real-world, government, and military decision-maker. Conversely, the head of cyber security for a major U.S. defense contractor such as Lockheed Martin or Northrop-Grumman would be a strategic, defensive, virtual, commercial, and nonmilitary decision-maker. A single change in any category can likewise dictate significant changes to the type of intelligence that is required. Because every customer can be defined in these general terms, their intelligence requirements will mirror these categories. Supporting intelligence must be cognizant of which type or types of customers they routinely support and define, refine, and tailor their operations accordingly.

Just like the wide variety of customers, not all individuals who are drawn into intelligence are the same. The aspects of the customer and their associated environment will also tend to draw in different types individuals, each motivated for different reasons as they follow their personal and professional goals and objectives in life. Intelligence personnel can range from muddy boots military analysts to academic deep-thinkers. There are those who view intelligence as just a job or career while others go so far as to view it as a profession, noble in their support of others but menacing in their goal of defeating an enemy. Much of what molds the individual who works in intelligence is their sense of belonging and ownership they have created toward the profession.

Ten Simple Rules for Understanding Intelligence

Understanding intelligence may seem daunting from the outset. This is because of the overwhelming unique rules and challenges present within each customer and requirements along with their unique ways of doing their business within the various operating environments. A more feasible approach would be to strip away all of these unique descriptors and get down to the fundamental characteristics that all intelligence operations share. Besides the fact that they all conduct the Intelligence Operations Process in support of a customer in the same general manner, there are several other rules that each operation is governed by—no matter if they are in support of a national decision-maker, local police chief, or combat commander:

1. **Intelligence Is for the Customer:** As the opening for this chapter, this is the golden rule that intelligence professionals should never lose sight of. Providing intelligence to support someone else is the entire *raison d'être* or reason why intelligence exists. Any business that forgets its customer is doomed to fail and intelligence as a business is no different. Intelligence produced for the sake of the intelligence asset has often been referred in the community as a self-licking ice cream cone by frustrated analysts and collectors. In other words, intelligence is not the end state; it must always contribute to something else. Success of intelligence is measured in terms of the success of a customer's operation, not by self-congratulation or adulation.

2. **Information Is Not Intelligence:** Neither is data. While information can simply be collected, intelligence is something that must be produced through proper collection and analysis. Simply regurgitating information does not guarantee intelligence will be gleaned about a particular threat. Someone has to look at the information and study it in order to create a new set of knowledge, i.e., conduct analysis of it in order for that information to be of any use to the decision-maker. They then must package and present that information in a way that us usable by a customer for their own use.

3. **There Is No Such Thing as Perfect Intelligence:** This is primarily because no one person will ever have 100% of the information about a particular subject. Our environment clouds, distracts, hides, obscures, and generally makes it impossible to have an adequate amount of information the analyst needs to make a completely error-free picture of what's going on. Even if information were perfect, the human mind is only capable of processing limited amounts of information at a time. Consequently, there is no such thing as a perfect intelligence assessment regarding a particular scenario or situation. The quality of intelligence is therefore rated according to its timeliness, accuracy, reliability, and relevancy among other criteria set by a supported customer.

FIGURE 1.6   Intelligence acronym word cloud

4. **Intelligence Loves Acronyms:** Intelligence as a profession, much like the military, is plagued by abbreviations, acronyms, and buzzwords that simply do not make any sense outside of the community. Perhaps most egregious is to find an acronym that contains another acronym inside of it. To intelligence and military professionals, acronyms can help simplify the day-to-day language within the community, but to the rest of the world it can seem like a different language altogether, making it difficult for the layman or outsider to effectively engage in it. It is therefore critical for outsiders to understand the particular language used by their support intelligence personnel just as it is important for intelligence personnel to be cognizant while using it among others.

5. **Intelligence Is Not About Spying on Our Friends and Neighbors for Personal Gain:** While it's certainly acceptable to try to understand our friends and neighbors, it's only acceptable to do it with information that is already available to everyone. Practicing intelligence within a strict moral code is critical in separating the profession from stalking, trolling, or invading someone's privacy. Witnessing your neighbors argue on their front lawn is acceptable and probably unavoidable; peering through their windows is unacceptable (and illegal). There are parallels across the intelligence industry. Doing nefarious things online or with nonpublicly available data is also not acceptable and borders on criminality. You can spy on enemies, but the basic idea behind the right to privacy and what constitutes publicly available information is different in America as it is in the rest of the world. Intelligence operations, if not restrained by rules and regulations, must be guided by principles and ethical conduct.

6. **Intelligence Is Predictive, Not Historical:** It's not about telling a story or explaining the past; that's the job of the historian and investigator. Although understanding the past of a particular subject is a large part of our work, intelligence is about

extrapolating that the same information used by the investigator and predicting what could and will most likely happen in the near and far future. Customers of intelligence make their decisions and create policy based on what they think their threats are going to do in the near and far future. Predictive analysis comes with an associative set of terms such as almost certain, likely, possible, etc. because they are based on estimates with assigned percentages. Intelligence personnel need to understand this language as well.

7. **Intelligence Is Part of Operations, Not Separate:** Intelligence doesn't occur in a vacuum or a sequestered portion of an organization. No magical barriers should separate intelligence work from those that it supports. Cultural, budgetary, and parochial factors continuously push and pull intelligence into its own world and this pressure must be continuously resisted. The vision of intelligence professionals simply throwing something over a wall hoping it's what the customer needs is simply a waste of time and resources. To be successful, intelligence processes have to be pushed and pulled out of the realm of the intelligence professionals and integrated into overall operations, not as a concurrent but separate operation.

8. **Intelligence Is about Learning:** It's about taking actions to collect information and studying threats, enemies, adversaries, or competitors. Effective intelligence analysts should be spending a majority of their time that involves learning about threats. Ineffective organizations are those where analysts spin their wheels doing mundane tasks. Microsoft PowerPoint is perhaps the most prolific productivity tool that is counterproductive in undisciplined hands; a great tool to express thoughts and ideas, turned into a weapon of mass distraction by organizations that require analysts to spend more time on presentation than on learning and analysis.

9. **Intelligence Is a Competitive Business:** As outlined already, intelligence is like any other commercial industry in that it provides a service by taking raw information and turning it into intelligence as its commodity. Its product is perishable, flawed, and incomplete, but a valuable product is highly valued by a customer. Intelligence organizations, even within the federal government, are part of the larger business community that affects and is affected by similar market-based forces as any other industry. Analysts compete with other analysts for recognition, respect, and advancement, while programs compete with other programs over personnel, priorities, and funding. Understanding some basic market-based principles will go far in helping to understand why certain intelligence organizations behave the way they do.

10. **Politics Ruins Intelligence:** Just as it ruins sports, entertainment, business, and the media, injecting politics into intelligence assessments and products is a guarantee of eventual failure. There are too many recent episodes of intelligence failures due to politics from body counts in Vietnam to weapons of mass destruction in Iraq. When political ideology skews or takes priority over logical analysis, the resultant product is likewise skewed with bias and misperceptions. Avoiding politics is difficult for intelligence because of their close proximity to

each other. Intelligence managers and leaders who wish to remain professionals must take constant and active measures to identify, reduce, and mitigate the effects of politics throughout their entire operation.

What's important to understand about these rules is that they are likely to persist in some form or another for the foreseeable future. Thinking of intelligence as a business, e.g., is something very new to this line of work, but the patterns and characteristics of market-based principles have always been present.

For this reason, learning about intelligence and thinking about how to create or improve a viable operation requires a better understanding of just how intelligence has evolved into its current state as both a profession and a business. The most effective approach to this is in understanding the customer and their threats and how their evolution has been the primary driver for intelligence.

Summary

Intelligence is about acquiring and applying knowledge, but more specifically it is about learning and understanding the threats to a supported customer through the collection and analysis of relevant information. It is a product, a process, people, and a business. It is unique as a profession and is perceived as both an art and a science. Intelligence performs several roles and functions, but what is most important is to understand its primary purpose is to support a customer, be it a commander, director, analyst or some other decision-maker.

Key Summary Points

+ Intelligence in an operational sense is about acquiring and applying knowledge, but more specifically it is about learning and understanding the threats to a supported customer through the collection and analysis of relevant information.
+ The primary purpose of intelligence is to provide information and analysis of the threats, adversaries, enemies, or competition in support of a customer. To do this, it performs several roles.
+ Understanding intelligence involves understanding the different perspective from which intelligence is viewed including academic, disciplinary, business, and customer perspectives.
+ While specific intelligence operations will vary dramatically from each other, there are several foundational principles and rules that remain constant.

Discussion Questions

- As intelligence is for the customer, what are some of the effects that could take hold within an intelligence organization or operation that loses sight of this primary purpose?
- In discussing the primary purpose of intelligence, which characteristics are the most important and which are the most often overlooked by intelligence professionals?
- In viewing intelligence as a business, what market-based forces most easily apply and how do they affect the nature of intelligence operations?
- Besides the 10 rules listed here, are there any additional rules that can be expressed in a way so that they would apply to every type of intelligence operation?

Figure Credits

Chapter 2

Competitors, Adversaries, and Enemies
Today's Threats

> This is another type of war, new in its intensity, ancient in its origins—war by guerrillas, subversives, insurgents, assassins ... seeking victory by eroding and exhausting the enemy instead of engaging him.
>
> John F. Kennedy, 1962[1]

Learning Objectives

After completing this chapter, you will be able to:

- Recognize what constitutes a threat.
- Identify recent key events that have been the catalyst for the evolution of threats.
- Describe the terms associated with several military theories of how wars would be fought in the future and how threat groups have similarly evolved in response.
- Discuss the commonalities that all asymmetric and unrestricted threats share.

The Complex Threat

Intelligence, most commonly associated with spying and espionage, has traditionally been thought of as a sport of kings, meaning its practice has been restricted to nation-states or national military powers. We too have thought of our threats in this light—as enemies of our country, whether they were an army, navy, guerrilla, or spy. Thanks to several different factors, including

---

1   President Kennedy's address at graduation exercises of the U.S. Military Academy, Public Papers of the Presidents, Kennedy, 1962, p. 453.

technology and our growing ability to harness and use information, our threats and those we support in making decisions about our threats are evolving rapidly.

Today's reality is that every individual has threats: threats to our business; threats to our community; threats to our team's drive toward a championship; and threats to our rights as individuals, which are best thought of as threats to our lives, our liberty, and our pursuit of happiness. Our threats are no longer only military or deadly enemies. Now they can also be seen as adversaries, competitors, or simply our opponents in some form or fashion. Once violence is removed as a qualification for a threat, virtually every other aspect that defines our adversaries, competitors, and opponents are strikingly similar.

Defining a Threat

When we try to define threat without including violence, the definition becomes much broader. Nonviolent threats are those against which we collect information, analyze that information, and make predictions on future moves. For instance, political candidates conduct opposition research on each other. Police investigators read and analyze graffiti to understand a gang's self-declared territory and predict changes in the status quo on the street. Football teams watch and analyze video and injury rosters of the other teams in preparation for a game. Corporations want to know what their competitors are up to—what products or services they are developing, how they plan to increase sales, and how they keep costs down for a healthy bottom line. They must also protect trade secrets, developing technologies, and other articles of proprietary information.

Even gamers use the basic processes of intelligence as part of their hobby. From competitive to casual players of video, board, or role-playing games, gamers study which strategies they can use for their game, which strategies are available to the other player or players, and counterstrategies they must keep in their pocket in case their opponents make certain moves. Whether they are trying to beat an evil boss powered by a program's artificial intelligence (AI) or trying to run up their kill/death (K/D) ratio in a player-versus-player (PVP) battle, gamers must spend time understanding how their adversaries fight; what patterns they display; and how to counter, pre-empt, or exploit these patterns.[2]

While these decisions are nonlethal or nonmalicious, the processes we use to understand, predict, and outplay our opponents are strikingly similar to what national-level or military decision-makers use to defeat our enemies. One of the main differences between conducting intelligence operations against our strategic and national enemies and all other types of threats is the priority and relative amount of resources we pour into the effort.

---

2   The kill/death (KD) ratio in multiplayer first-person shooter games is one of the several statistics that many video games track for players. In this case, a KD ratio is the number of player opponents you've killed compared to the number of times you've been killed and is normally expressed as a number like 0.95 or 1.2. Anything higher than 1.0 means you've killed more players than the number of times you have been killed. Depending on how much a person plays a given game, both the kills and deaths can go up to tens of thousands.

FIGURE 2.1   Intelligence processes are commonly used in gaming

Outside of national or military decision-making, it's not in our nature to refer to our efforts to understand and predict the next steps of our adversaries as "intelligence." We call it scouting, templating, or getting a jump on our competition and participate in worst-case, predictive, vulnerability, forensic, investigative, market, and competitive analyses.

It is, likewise, not our nature to label our adversaries and competitors as formal threats, since the name connotes something deadly and sinister. We tend not to think of a group of people we are just trying to overcome in a courtroom or in the marketplace as a threat. Whatever term we use for our threats such as enemies, adversaries, competitors, and opponents, we can more easily understand all of them by their shared characteristics.

By starting with a more broad-based view of what a threat is and who practices intelligence, we can begin to see the validity in studying intelligence as art (powered by science) as well as a profession. No matter what your threat is, or what part of society you are in, your threats, adversaries, competitors, and opponents share several common aspects. Understanding what these common aspects are is critical to understanding and planning for what you want to do about your threats.

A Brief and Recent History of Today's Threats–Evolution and Revolution

Threats can evolve. Certain factors are attributed to every form of evolution, and our threats, along with other aspects of intelligence, are no different. While we can postulate in what direction our threats will evolve in the future, it cannot be done effectively unless we understand the factors that have contributed to past evolution of our threats. Analyzing these influential factors gives us a starting point (today) and an expected future trajectory, and it can help us to identify many of the common characteristics that all of our threats share.

While there are several factors that have contributed to where we are now, we can arguably point to three crucial events that have influenced the evolution of today's threats: the First Gulf War, the Cold War, and 9/11. Each of these events is within the realm that is arguably the most significant catalyst for the change in world history, i.e., warfare. While it might not seem that these events could be tied to the rise of hackers, religious extremism, or even organized crime, the effects of these events were the beginning of the rapid evolution of our enemies into the ones we are facing today both on and off the battlefield.

The Destruction of Saddam Hussein's Army

The First Gulf War (1990–1991) was one of the most lopsided victories in military history. What started as a brazen grab by Saddam Hussein to invade and annex the oil-rich country of Kuwait and rename it as Iraq's 19th province resulted in a smack down of epic proportion. After a little more than 5 weeks of aerial bombardment and only 100 hours of ground combat operations, the United States and its coalition partners removed Iraq from Kuwait and reduced the world's fourth largest army to a shattered remnant.[3] Even more dramatic was the fact that we achieved the liberation of Kuwait with losses on par with the heroic defense of the Alamo in 1836.[4]

The main problem with the Iraqi strategy was the underlying assumption that they could seize and defend Kuwait with the same strategy that they had used in the Iran–Iraq War that ended just three years earlier. Indeed, many losing armies fight the previous war instead of the one before them.

Waged from September 1980 until August 1988, the Iran–Iraq War shared many of the same characteristics of World War I: grinding trench warfare, waves of assaulting infantry, massive artillery barrages, and even the use of gas and other chemical weapons against both soldiers and civilians. Iraqi national leaders and military commanders thought that by recreating their defenses against the Americans and coalition partners would be a grinding bloodbath punishing them until their resolve fled.

In his plan for Kuwait in 1990, Saddam fortified the Kuwaiti–Arabian border with an extensive, yet static defensive belt of trenches, minefields, bunkers, and improved fighting positions. This defense incorporated several Iraqi Army divisions, supported by artillery and a further reserve of the Iraqi Army's best and most loyal units of the Republican Guard. Commanding from his headquarters in Baghdad, Saddam believed his army could absorb the coalition's attacks and then unleash the Republican Guard-armored units in a counterattack from the north and northwest. Apparently forgetting the lessons from

---

3 Knights, Michael. (2005). *Cradle of conflict: Iraq and the birth of modern U.S. military power*. Annapolis, MD: United States Naval Institute Press. p. 20. ISBN 978-1-59114-444-1.

4 The United States incurred 113 combat deaths, 145 deaths due to accidents, and 35 were lost to friendly fire. Losses at the Alamo are estimated between 182 and 207 American and Texan deaths depending on the source.

FIGURE 2.2   Iraqi civilian and military vehicles north of Kuwait City along the "Highway of Death" after the Desert Storm, 1991

World Wars I and II where the French Army prepared to fight the Germans according to how the Germans fought previously, Saddam saddled himself with the tactics and equipment of previous wars.

Unfortunately for Saddam, the Americans didn't bring their last war's military to the fight. Instead, they brought a military honed by Cold War strategy and tactics: a massive array of overwhelming firepower paired with state-of-the-art technology. After more than a decade of soul-searching since the Vietnam War and the Cold War, the U.S. military had become a leaner, meaner, and professional fighting force backed by massive and agile logistical capabilities Heading the largest coalition of forces assembled since World War II, U.S. military superiority was evident from the start of the bombing campaign and continued through the destruction and flight of the Iraqi Republican Guard. From the outset, it was evident that United States and several coalition partners had vastly superior vehicles, aircraft, ordinance, and information systems. All these systems were manned by a professional and volunteer force facing off against an Iraqi Army filled with conscripts.

A fitting epitaph to the Iraqi Army was Highway 80, the main road leading from Kuwait City northward toward Iraq. As Iraqi forces fled Kuwait before the onslaught of U.S. Marines, coalition air power caught many of them along this road, blocked their escape with precision strikes and proceeded to destroy the traffic jam over the next several hours. Highway 80 and its continuation Highway 8, leading from Kuwait into Basra, Iraq, where the massacre ensued took on the moniker "Highway of Death," as scores of Iraqis simply died there, or got out of the vehicles and fled on foot to escape the carnage. News reports showed hundreds of military and stolen commercial vehicles destroyed or abandoned; a fitting monument to Saddam's tragic mistake.

Information Technology Goes to War

The First Gulf War and the resulting destruction of the Iraqi Army was the first war where information technology played a critical role in the success of the United States and our allies. The introduction of Global Positioning Systems (GPS) enabled U.S. forces to maneuver far out into the often featureless areas of the deep desert. Night vision devices (NVDs) allowed United States and coalition forces to see via either passive or thermal means, enabling our forces to maneuver in and engage a blinded enemy in pitch-black conditions. Use of air- and space-based intelligence platforms effectively allowed U.S. and allied commanders to "see" the battlefield with unparalleled clarity while Iraqi forces were enshrouded with the chaos brought about by precision strikes targeting their radar assets and communications.

One U.S. collection platform in particular, the Joint Surveillance Targeting Attack Radar System (JSTARS), was an airborne collection system. Even though it was still in development, two of these aircrafts were able to warn the U.S. commanders of the large movements of Iraqi ground forces.[5] In particular, these advanced radar systems were able to detect and report on the movements of the Iraqi Republican Guard, Saddam's elite force that was held in reserve as part of his plan to launch them as a counterattack. This force was targeted heavily during the allied air campaign and then partially destroyed in several engagements by the U.S. Army VII Corps and our British Allies as it tried to flee our forces.

The Whole World Was Watching

Media coverage of the buildup of allied forces during both phases of the First Gulf War, Desert Shield, and the violence of Operation Desert Storm was unprecedented. Americans and the world were able to follow the daily events from political and strategic maneuverings of the Bush administration down to the movement of units into the Southeast Asia theater of war and the daily numbers of air strikes flown against Iraqi positions.

This media access to war was rigorously controlled by coalition forces, and focused on providing coverage of the thrashing Iraq received as Desert Shield turned into Desert Storm. Video of precision-guided "smart" bombs showing the impotence of Saddam's air defenses and hardened bunkers were anecdotal of the war's overall tone.

Thanks in part to this intensive coverage, the entire world was able to witness how dominant the American military had become as the world's only remaining superpower. U.S. weapon systems far outperformed the primarily Soviet-equipped Iraqis and showed the rest of the world who were similarly armed that their militaries were suddenly antiquated.

In addition, the success of such an audacious U.S. plan of attack showed how a volunteer force lead on the ground by professional noncommissioned officers (NCOs), and junior officers could easily outfight a more autocratic force of mostly conscripts whose operational control was closely held at only the highest levels. Armies with equipment and force organization similar to the Iraqis seemed to be outdated overnight.

---

5 Tagg, Lori. (2015, January 16). *JSTARS plays critical role in Operation Desert Storm.* Retrieved from https://www.army.mil/article/141322/JSTARS_plays_critical_role_in_Operation_Desert_Storm

FIGURE 2.3　Joint STARS depicting Ground Moving Target Indicators or GMTI from overhead imagery

A Revolution in Military Affairs

In terms of military studies, the First Gulf War was a showcase of the success of techni-cally advanced firepower coupled with information technology. To U.S. military planners, this was a complete validation in the belief that advanced technology was bringing about dramatic changes to military operations in terms of how we are able to organize, equip, and fight wars. Coined as the Revolution in Military Affairs or RMA, this theory centered on the idea that warfare periodically goes through a huge sweeping change on how it is conducted, usually brought about by the introduction of a new technology.

Past examples of military revolutions include the horse stirrup, gun powder, and the airplane. In this most recent case, the deemed agent of change was information technol-ogy along with major increases in weapons and stealth capabilities. New areas where we could wage war effectively included information operations that included such strategies as deception, psychological operations, and electronic warfare along with other strategies that were defined in terms of the technical superiority that would allow precision strikes, dominating maneuver, and space warfare.[6]

One aspect of this type of military thinking was the idea that having a massive amount of firepower no longer ensured victory in war, but having that firepower along with state-of-the-art data collection and communications technologies would increase the effectiveness of firepower manyfold.

Information technology was identified as a critical "combat multiplier" for this reason.[7] Countries with the resources to equip their military with the latest weapons augmented such capabilities as tracking the enemy at night and/or from the orbit, disrupting their communications networks, and deceiving or destroying their command and control centers could allow their forces to defeat a numerically superior foe.

Cold Warfare

Superior technology and its influence on U.S. military organization, strategy, and doctrine over the past decades can be tied back to the U.S. experiences from the Cold War. From the end of World War II until the early 1990s, the United States and our North Atlantic Treaty Organization (NATO) allies squared off against the Soviet Union and their Warsaw Pact members over the control of Europe and the world. While not a full-blown open conflict, both sides worked against each other's interests through proxies and third parties that included both nation-states such as Cuba and Nicaragua and non-state actors such as the various Palestinian and Leftist European terror groups that proliferated in the 1960s and 70s. In this way, the Communist East and the U.S.-dominated West struggled and maneuvered through a series of confrontations in every major theater from Budapest to Korea and from Afghanistan to Vietnam.

It would have been a doomsday scenario if the Cold War during those decades ever went "hot, meaning a full-blown lethal conflict involving opposing armies." Open conflict with the Soviet Union and its Warsaw Pact allies in Europe was commonly referred to as the impending Third World War. If war were to start, the most common scenario envisioned was that it would start with a massive blitzkrieg-type invasion of West Germany by the Soviets and their Eastern European allies. This scenario reached a crescendo in the mid-1908s through fictional novels such as *The Third World War: The Untold Story* by General Sir John Hackett (1982), *Red Storm Rising* by Tom Clancy (1986), and *Team Yankee* by Harold Coyle (1987). Tabletop wargames and even the computer gaming industry also featured World War III as the next great conflict yet to happen.

In all versions of this scenario, the West was most certainly outnumbered in terms of fighting men and equipment. To reinforce the relatively small number of units kept in Europe throughout the Cold War, the U.S. military would have to traverse the globe through a contested Northern Atlantic Ocean. Besides the United Kingdom and West Germany, the United States could rely on little help from the rest of Europe. The NATO

---

6   http://www.au.af.mil/au/awc/awcgate/ssi/stratrma.pdf

7   http://defencejournal.com/2000/sept/military.htm

FIGURE 2.4   U.S. and Soviet tanks face off at Checkpoint Charlie, Berlin, October 1961

was a more fractured organization than the Warsaw Pact with many of its members either incapable or unwilling to maintain a large conventional military presence despite the threat looming just beyond their eastern horizon.

To overcome these challenges, the power of the free market gave the United States and the West some distinct advantages. The most prominent advantage was the rapid advance of technology that capitalism fostered through economic competition. As the Eastern Bloc economies of the Warsaw Pact stagnated under the crush of socialism and communism, the entrepreneurial climate enjoyed by the United States and the West spurred decade after decade of technical advances, and the military applications of these new technologies became a critical part of our plan to fight as an outnumbered force.

As a result, the American view of war shaped the idea that while we may be outnumbered in tanks, ships, aircraft, and other weapons, each of our weapon systems could be and would have to be far superior to our communist counterparts. Use of the latest weapons and information technologies would allow for new strategies and tactics in fighting, including changes to how we organize our units, logistics, intelligence, etc.

U.S. forces, bolstered by the best technology and equipment in the world were also better led, not necessarily by our Army commanders, but also by junior officers and strong NCO corps, something many communist and Third World armies completely

Platoon Kill Battalion

As an M-1 tank platoon leader near the end of the Cold War, I experienced the Army's reliance on technical superiority first hand as we practiced a drill called PKB or "Platoon Kill Battalion," where each tank platoon in my battalion had to plan and run a battle drill on how we would stop and destroy an attacking motorized rifle or tank battalion—our four vehicles defending against an enemy numbering some 30 vehicles in all. As frightening as this may sound, this was the expectation and we all understood our life expectancy could be extremely short in this type of fight if it weren't for the 60-ton turbine-powered behemoths we rode into battle.

My platoon of four tanks prepared our temporary defensive positions in advance. We put out markers 2,000 and 1,000 meters out to measure when the advancing unit would be in the range of our tank's main guns. We rehearsed sectors of fire to ensure each tank had its own targets to destroy first and also rehearsed when we, whoever survived the initial contact, would need to pull back to alternate positions as we prepared to be overrun. The attack commenced with the sight of the dust signatures from a much larger force in the distance. As the opposing force reached our first set of markers, I gave the order to engage; all four tanks moved into position exposing our turrets. The first two shots from each tank "destroyed" the first eight vehicles of the mass advancing towards us; their amber lights flashing as a kill. The rest of the engagement was a blur of dirt and smoke as we ran through our crew drills engaging as many targets as possible.

While understanding that this was just a training exercise, the realization that hits you middle of the engagement was that we were preparing for the real possibility that someday we would be required to fight this way using real sabot rounds killing a very real enemy without much hope of surviving the day. While the doctrinal term for this type of fight was called "defend in place" missions, tankers and cavalry scouts would frequently refer these scenarios as "die in place" missions.

lacked. This force would be the bulwark against any all-out attacks from the East and would also provide a strong deterrent from occurring in the first place.

In addition to the Revolution in Military Affairs theory that became relevant from the 1970s to the 1990s, other military theories also came into favor such as *Network Centric Warfare* and *Full Spectrum Dominance*. Network Centric Warfare involves the use of information technology as one of the most important strategies in warfare. Full-Spectrum Dominance focuses on the military's need to dominate all aspects of both the physical battlespace and the infosphere (cyberspace and the electromagnetic spectrum). This dominance requires maintaining the free flow and access to required information networks while denying the enemy theirs.[8] In each of these cases, the rapid advancement

---

8   Alberts, David S., Garstka, John J., Frederick P. Stein, Frederick P. (2000). *Network-Centric Warfare: Developing and Leveraging Information Superiority* (2nd ed.). CCRP Publications. Retrieved from http://

of technology—and most importantly—information technology was the primary driver for changes in how we expected to fight future wars.

These Cold War theories were bolstered by the result of the First Gulf War, along with several other military successes as a validation of firepower combined with leading-edge technology. Another operation that reinforced them was the relative success of U.S. involvement in the Balkans during the latter half of the 1990s. During the Kosovo War (1998–1999) in particular, the United States used advanced weaponry to launch a sustained air campaign against Serbian positions without having to risk putting ground troops into combat, also known as "boots on the ground." As a result, we were able to influence the outcome in favor of Kosovo's semi-independence without suffering a single U.S. military casualty. It was an ideal little war from the United States' perspective, because our risks were minimal due to our superior technology.

Other quick victories followed against forces who thought they could match U.S. military prowess or who didn't have any other alternative at the time. In the fall of 2001 almost immediately after the 9/11 attacks, the Afghan United Front (also known as the Northern Alliance), with the support of U.S. and UK special operations and air support, were able to take control of Afghanistan in a matter of weeks; something the Soviets were never able to achieve after eight years of occupation during the 1980s.

Two years later during Operation Iraqi Freedom, the United States' war-fighting capabilities were again able to make quick work of Saddam Hussein's military driving up from Kuwait as part of the second largest international coalition since 1945. The iconic images of Saddam's towering statue being ripped and toppled from its base by a U.S. M88A2 Recovery Vehicle were a real and vivid reminder of the folly of taking the U.S. on military force versus military force.

While these victories were not without their detractors, the idea that technology would be the key to the next apogee of military science was the logical next step in the evolution of U.S. military dominance. In many ways it was. From an American perspective, the belief that this was the future of fighting in the world helped to align our strategies toward maintaining the preferred and current status quo. The United States' ability to perennially maintain a large, technically superior military ahead of our adversaries was a virtual guarantee that we would remain the dominant world power for the foreseeable future.

The only problem with this theory was that much of the rest of the world didn't accept as the inevitable status quo, especially our enemies.

Changing the Definition of a Battlefield

From our enemies' perspective, Saddam Hussein demonstrated how squaring off against the United States on the conventional battlefield would prove to be a one-sided fight.[9]

---

www.dodccrp.org/files/Alberts_NCW.pdf

9   As a young Armor Lieutenant assigned to an M-1 Tank Battalion during the First Gulf War, other junior officers and I would joke that after the war, the Army was going to erect a statue of Saddam Hussein

FIGURE 2.5   M1 Tanks from the 2nd Battalion 77th Armor Regiment during winter maneuvers, Fort Carson Colorado, 1989

Even during the Vietnam War, the conventional U.S. military never lost a "battle of any consequence."[10] As of 2018 we maintain an annual defense budget that is larger than the next seven countries combined.[11] American military power is truly a premier global force. Saddam did not learn this lesson, deciding it was better to provoke the U.S. and Coalition forces into a second war just 12 years later, resulting in his overthrow and eventual execution.

Unlike Saddam, our more competent adversaries understood U.S. military power, and as a result decided to look to other ways of engaging with United States. Their answer wasn't in trying to outspend us in military technology. We had demonstrated to the Soviets during the Cold War that this was an impossible task. Instead, our adversaries simply turned to strategies that took advantage of their strengths and capabilities.

Many of our adversaries found they could successfully attack U.S. interests by doing it in a more oblique manner, or rather, asymmetrically. In doing so, their strategies dragged us into many other realms of conflict: economic, psychological, social, and cyber. This meant employing attacks and stratagems beyond the conventional battlefield. This could include hit

---

at the entrance to Fort Knox, Kentucky, home of the Army's Armor School. The plaque on his statue would read "Saddam Hussein, Savior of Armored Warfare, 1991."

10   [Westmoreland] *Speech by General William C. Westmoreland* before the Third Annual Reunion of the Vietnam Helicopter Pilots Association (VHPA) at the Washington, DC Hilton Hotel on July 5th, 1986 (reproduced in a Vietnam Helicopter Pilots Association *Historical Reference Directory Volume 2A*). https://www.vhpa.org/stories/Westmoreland.pdf

11   http://www.pgpf.org/chart-archive/0053_defense-comparison

and run or bombing attacks, assassinations, hijackings, or planting a malicious virus. Many of these attacks were more effective against the United States and most Western democracies because of their ability to influence public opinion through the open nature of our society.

By going outside what could be considered the traditional definition of military conflict, the aperture of engagement could be opened up to a much wider spectrum. In essence, they were leveling the field of conflict by redefining its parameters.

One of the key lessons our adversaries learned could be pulled from the First Gulf War itself. Taking a critical look at the U.S. military victory, two Colonels in the People's Liberation (Chinese) Army published a book called *Unrestricted Warfare* in 1999 that took a keen interest in U.S. military performance during a decisive foray into Kuwait and Iraq. Colonels Qiao Liang and Wang Xiangsui claimed that the First Gulf War heralded a functional change in how warfare should be viewed:

> If we acknowledge that the new principles of war are no longer "using armed force to compel the enemy to submit to one,s will," but rather are "using all means, including armed force or nonarmed force, military and non-military, and lethal and non-lethal means to compel the enemy to accept one's interests."[12]

As explained by the authors, taking the realm of conflict outside the boundaries of the battlefield (also known as battlespace and operating environment in military doctrinal terminology), our enemies have successfully discovered ways to harm the United States without the risk, cost, or most probable failure of going toe to toe against our military in a traditional fight.

Further in their study, the authors of *Unrestricted Warfare* give great credence to the saying "fight the fight that fits your weapons, not the enemy's." In other words, you shouldn't try to fight the type of war for which you are not equipped. Instead, you should be looking to what weapons and other capabilities you do have and use those, including weapons that are not military weapons at all. In our adversaries' eyes, the United States is the richest country in the world and can always afford the most expensive and "high-tech" weapons.[13] That doesn't mean everyone else has to fight against those kinds of weapons. When you remove the restriction of warfare occurring on the physical battlefield, you will find that you have more "weapons" at your disposal.

Since the First Gulf War, the United States suffered several examples where conventional military might was offset, countered, and mitigated by an asymmetric threat. Places such as the World Trade Center (1993), Mogadishu (1993), Khobar Towers (1996), Nairobi and Dar es Salaam (1998), and Aden, Yemen (2000) showed that despite their military prowess, the United States could be attacked successfully several times within a span of eight years. To be successful, these attacks required a capability that could be employed

---

12   Liang, Qiao, & Xiangsui, Wang. (1999, February). *Unrestricted Warfare*. Beijing: PLA Literature and Arts Publishing House.

13   Liang, Qiao, & Xiangsui, Wang. (1999, February). *Unrestricted warfare* (p. 24). Beijing: PLA Literature and Arts Publishing House. Retrieved from http://www.c4i.org/unrestricted.pdf 30 Sep 2017.

against a U.S. weakness, and many of these weaknesses were found outside of the battlefield. Minor attacks such as shooting down a U.S. Army Black Hawk helicopter and dragging the bodies of the crew around on television gave the enemy the ability to affect U.S. public opinion and therefore could impact U.S. policy at the strategic and national levels.

The most glaring attack against the United States on 9/11 that took 2,977 innocent lives shocked America to the emerging and growing threat from a non-state group, Al Qaeda. Osama Bin Laden's terrorist organization sacrificed 19 terrorists, and spent between $400,000 and $500,000.[14] As a result a relatively small and desegregated but fervent and educated non-state organization was able to cause damage worth approximately $55 billion related to the death toll and physical damage along with another $123 billion harm due to the economic impact of its attacks.[15] These were also catalysts for dramatic changes in the U.S. policy, restructuring the U.S. government toward security and prevention, and going to war to defeat Al Qaeda along with a return to Iraq to overthrow the regime of Saddam Hussein.

Omnipresent Warfare Means Omnipresent Threats

Military theory and doctrine is a robust field of study. For several millennia, strategic thinkers have studied, practiced, taught, and written about warfare. These commanders and theorists include recognizable names such as Sun Tsu, Miyamoto Musashi, Napoleon, Carl Von Clausewitz, Erwin Rommel, Mao Zedong, and BH Liddel Hart. The nature of warfare, when described in the last century especially, has been given a variety of descriptors including asymmetric, asynchronous, complex, guerrilla, idiosyncratic, irregular, low-intensity, total, and unrestricted war. The origins behind each of these terms serve to highlight the various perspectives of those who use them as well as the specific strategies and tactics employed while waging war.

Depending on the time period, the prevalence of one term over the other has fallen in and out of favor over the years. For example, guerrilla warfare is a Spanish word for "Little War" and was made popular during Napoleon Bonaparte's occupation of Spain from 1808 until 1814. Terror, terrorists, and terrorism can trace their beginnings slightly further to the Jacobin Reign of Terror from 1793 to 1794 at the height of the French Revolution. Both terrorism and guerrilla warfare have become part of our vocabulary for such a long time that there are literally dozens of definitions for each of them.

Asymmetric warfare is noted as a conflict where the opponents are imbalanced, with one side having a distinct advantage over the other, usually in terms of conventional military power. The side with the disadvantage must turn to capabilities and tactics that take advantage of what strengths they do have to engage their foe.

---

14   National Commission on Terrorist Attacks upon the United States, Appendix A: The Financing of the 9/11 Plot, page 131.

15   Shan Carter and Amanda Cox, One 9/11 Tally:$3.3 Trillion; New York Times, Published: September 8, 2011. http://www.nytimes.com/interactive/2011/09/08/us/sept-11-reckoning/cost-graphic. html?mcubz=1

While each of these types of warfare is expressed as a subset or implies an exception to "normal warfare," "normal warfare" really doesn't exist. There has never been a battle that was completely balanced, fair, or fought using rules that everyone agreed to follow in perfect weather on featureless terrain. There has never been complete symmetry in any way between the opposing forces. Leonidas had a narrow pass to aid in his stubborn defense against the Darius III's invasion, Rome had their legions, Napoleon had his maxims, Rommel had his Atlantic Wall, and Patton had Rommel's book.[16]

Warfare is inherently more complex than the simple notion of two armies meeting each other on a field of battle to determine right there and then who will be the victor by force of arms. Whether conflict has been an open warfare or not, there has always been unconventional strategies and tactics employed in every struggle. There are no such things as the abstract sterile and balanced environment akin to a game of Chess. Indeed, after looking at warfare and conflict in this way, the notion of a conventional battle is more of a myth than the more specific types of unconventional warfare listed above.

What makes things even more confusing to students of military history and doctrine is that while there is a general description included with each term, there is no one universally agreed-upon definition for any of them. As with many military theories, there is a plethora of sources, quotes, and perspectives for each of these terms. Even the U.S. government has multiple definitions for terrorism.[17]

Our threats today are mostly less than a generation old and yet their tactics and techniques in attacking us are not new at all. Terrorism, deception, sabotage, propaganda, economic warfare, insurgency, and biological warfare are among other strategies (except for cyberwarfare) that have been used successfully since the beginning of time. Because of the current age we live in, our threats and their attacks are now more visible and damaging to us as they can now reach us anywhere we live, work, and play. So while the Industrial Age may have brought about the scourge of Total War where every resource at a nation's disposal was required to wage it, the Information Age has ushered in the concept of Unrestricted War where the spectrum of war expanded even further from our military and industry into just about every part of our society and even personal lives.

Because our notions of warfare have changed and expanded over the last century, we need to take a much more appropriate view of what defines our threats. Perhaps a better way of thinking about this is not to look at our threats as going off the traditional battlefield, rather that our battlefield has expanded to the point that everything and everyone can be involved or affected by it in some way.

---

16   Allen, Lee. (1979). Publishers Note in Rommel, Erwin. (1979). Attacks (p. v). Vienna, Virginia: Athena Press Inc.

17   Libaw, Oliver. (2001, October 11). How do you define terrorism? Retrieved from http://abcnews. go.com/US/story?id=92340&page=1

A Broadened Perspective of Our Threats

By shattering the traditional notion of what could be considered a battlefield, we must also broaden our perspective on what and who our threats are and what strategies they can use. To a policeman, a cyber defender, or a security professional, understanding military terms like asymmetric and unrestricted warfare may not seem that important, but these concepts are critical to understanding the threat that they face in their professions.

Part of what has propagated the myth that threats to our way of life are the problem of the military and homeland security folks only has been the success of these very same people. While 9/11 touched all Americans (who are old enough to remember it) on an emotional level, the current generation of Americans has been relatively spared the violence and horrific toll of war since then. While our military fights around the world and our national intelligence and public safety communities support these efforts here and abroad, the rest of us are at the Apple Store. Unfortunately, we cannot expect this insular nature of living to go on forever. In the coming years, the next complex threat will take the fight to new heights involving all of us.

Even the U.S. military has indirectly acknowledged that our threats have expanded beyond the battlefield. Using their own terminology, they've attempted to capture it within their realm of understanding by broadening their use of the term "battlefield." Many years ago, the term battlefield changed to battlespace in the lexicon of their manuals. Subsequently, the term battlespace has evolved into "operating environment." Each change has broadened the scope of what the military felt should be consider as an area of conflict.

To engage our threats we must come to the realization that our threats operate in areas not necessarily related to national security, and their targets are not always in the political-military spectrum. They operate in our airports, malls, hotels, and movie theaters. They use our banking system, our schools and universities, and our infrastructure. They live in our neighborhoods, shop where we shop and use all the same technologies we take for granted on a day-to-day basis. As already stated our threats aren't just our enemies. They are also our adversaries, competitors, and opponents.

Understanding Threat Strategies

Arguably, the threat groups we face are defined and often labeled by what they do. Terrorists naturally practice terrorism and guerrillas obviously practice guerrilla warfare. While many of these groups overlap in terms of the strategies they employ, it's important to have an understanding of these strategies in order to understand the groups that employ them.

Perhaps the most basic way to introduce yourself to the most common strategies is to define them using two criteria: whether or not they are violent and whether or not they are illegal. Both of these are fairly subjective terms.

Determining whether or not a threat strategy is violent is fairly straightforward. For purposes of analysis, a strategy that causes harm or death to a person or persons qualifies as violent. Indeed, strategies employed by military forces or terrorists require violence or the threat of it as part of their operations. Other strategies that do not require violence,

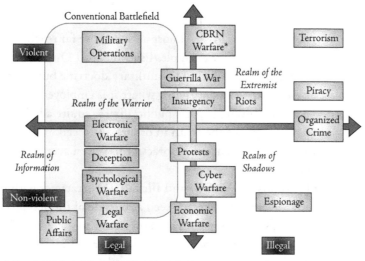

Conventional Battlefield

Violent	Military Operations
	CBRN Warfare*
	Terrorism

Realm of the Warrior

Guerrilla War

Realm of the Extremist

Insurgency   Riots

Piracy

Electronic Warfare

Organized Crime

Realm of Information

Deception

Protests

Realm of Shadows

Psychological Warfare

Cyber Warfare

Non-violent

Legal Warfare

Economic Warfare

Espionage

Public Affairs

Legal

Illegal

* Chemical, Biological, Radiological, Nuclear Warfare

FIGURE 2.6   Threat Strategy Matrix

but may cause it indirectly or as a secondary or unintended effect, like psychological operations or deception, are still considered nonviolent for the purposes of analysis.

Much more problematic is in determining whether or not a strategy is legal or illegal. In order for a strategy to be considered illegal it had to be in violation of some sort of law or societal norm. Much of this can because for debate. Laws could include domestic federal or civil laws, international treaties, or laws of nature, humanity, or what's acceptable to our society. Different interpretations of this is truly where the cliché "One man's terrorist is another man's freedom fighter" comes from.

Using these two criteria, we find the most common criteria will fall into one of the four quadrants. In some cases strategies can straddle two quadrants depending on the perspective and specific actions with each strategy a group may employ, which is shown in Figure 2.6.

For ease of understanding, each of these quadrants can be labeled as the following realms of conflict: The Realm of the Warrior, the Realm of the Extremist, the Realm of Information, and the Realm of Shadows:

+ **Realm of the Warrior—Violent and Legal:** This realm is dominated by the conventional battlefield. The struggles of nations are typically thought of in this realm, as open warfare has always been the most significant catalyst in the history of human events. This realm included heavy force-on-force contact between conventional armies. While paramilitary forces may seek to exist in this realm as a validation of their success, this goal is not always achieved and if so, only on a temporary basis for most guerrillas or insurgents.

+ **Realm of Information—Nonviolent and Legal:** With many of these strategies accepted as part of military operations, this realm contains many that do not require violence to succeed. Many of the strategies within this realm are conveniently grouped within the military as either Information Operations (IO) or Information Warfare (IW). Almost of them have far reaching applications outside of the military. For example, Psychological Operations (PSYOPS) has a codified definition within U.S. military doctrine but is known as propaganda or even fake news depending where it is employed. While deception is lying to achieve a given purpose, public affairs require a believable truth or at least believable *spin* of the truth in order to succeed. These strategies are almost entirely legal because their practice has been accepted as part of our society today.

- **Realm of Extremists—Violent and Illegal:** The strategies within this realm are inherently violent and generally seen as outside of the accepted norms of a significant part of society. Again this is a subjective area as suicide bombers that are abhorred in one part of society are seen as heroes and martyrs in another. Being unable to achieve success either on the battlefield or through other accepted channels, terrorists, guerrillas, insurgents, pirates, rioters, gangs, and crime syndicates have chosen to take more extreme routes to further their goals, all of which involve a certain degree of violence. Terrorism in particular includes bombings, assassinations, kidnapping, and hostage taking each with varying expectations for casualties and risks to the attackers.

- **Realm of Shadows—Nonviolent and Illegal:** This is the realm of both covert and clandestine operations. The difference between these two terms is that while the former conceals the identity of the operative, the latter conceals the fact that the operation was even carried out. Espionage, cyberwarfare are strategies that go to great lengths to hide the perpetrator, the most successful of which are completed before the victim has any realization that something nefarious has happened. While some of these operations can be included into national strategies, for the most part they violate some sort of legal system—either domestic or international. By using a simple model like the Threat Strategy Matrix, intelligence analyst as well as military theorists can more easily understand the commonalities of seemingly disparate threats. This understanding in turn provides a sound basis for profiling many of the more complex aspects of these threats and support the development of plans to mitigate and counter them.

Threat Commonalities and Patterns

Each of the threats outlined in Figure 2.6 is worth studying in its own right, both for general understanding and for predictive analysis. Each threat has its own idiosyncrasies that make it distinctive from the others.

Some strategies could fall into more than one realm in the chart above. Their employment takes on aspects of both legality and illegality and some can be both violent and nonviolent. These distinctions may be minor or trivial as today's threats can employ or be defined by several different strategies making them a more hybrid type of a threat. For example, drug cartels could practice terrorism, economic war, as well as many other actions related to organized crime such as extortion, money laundering, and outright theft. So, while all terrorists are criminals in their actions, not all criminals are terrorists. Furthermore, peaceful protests may be a fundamental right in the Western society, but there is a truly fine line between peaceful protests and violent riots, and the difference between the two can be breached in a matter of seconds, succumbing to a spark that lights that fire.

It is important to understand when looking at the list below is that these strategies are inherently asymmetric, i.e., employed in a way that is traditionally seen as what is considered traditional warfare. By their nature, they operate under a different set of rules which are important for analysts to understand. The six most common rules for today's asymmetric threats will generally apply to all threats, but each type of threat will have many others that an analyst can identify:

The Six Rules for Understanding Asymmetric Threats

1. **The Rule of Inequality:** The traditional balance between two opposing forces is disparate and unequal for a variety of reasons. This balance can be between military forces, economic assets, or any other contested area. This imbalance is unacceptable to one side or the other and often unavoidable. In order to either level up the playing field or gain the advantage, other strategies and tactics must be used by the side that is at a distinct disadvantage to fight according to the terms dictated by the dominant force.

2. **The Rule of Capability:** Every threat organization has strengths and advantages that can be molded into capabilities to use against an adversary. These capabilities, including strategies, tactics, techniques, or technologies, are somewhat unique to the lesser-strength force. Forces that don't appear to have asymmetric capabilities possibly haven't recognized their own strengths and advantages or don't appear to be using them as capabilities. It's also possible they have cleverly hidden that capability. Don't be fooled; every organization has them.

3. **The Rule of Vulnerabilities:** Threat tactics, techniques, and other strengths can only be considered as capabilities if they can be employed against a related weakness in an adversary. In turn, a weakness should then be considered a vulnerability if an adversary has an ability to exploit it or take advantage of it. Every organization has weaknesses, but they aren't vulnerabilities unless an adversary has something that can take advantage of that weakness. Asymmetric capabilities and strategies can be military, economic, political, psychological, and information technology or cyber-related. Keep in mind, if your adversary doesn't have a corresponding vulnerability, your capability isn't worth much. A six-month-old computer virus doesn't mean much to a corporation with the latest network defenses.

4. **The Rule of Adaptability:** A successful enemy worthy of any consideration somehow figures out the keys to Rules 2 and 3. That is, they successfully identify

what strengths and capabilities they possess, and are able to use them against an adversary's weakness and vulnerabilities. In some cases, just the threat of using them can be enough to elicit a favorable response from an adversary. To continually do this over time, the same strategy and tactics can't be attempted over and over in the same way; successful enemies are adaptive and can learn from the changes their enemies have made since their last successful attack. Strict adherence to doctrine and inflexible paradigms are keys to failure for anyone in a conflict or competition.

5. **The Rule of Similarity:** No matter the type of threat or a group that employs asymmetric strategies, they all share similar characteristics of a group. Every group can be collected against, analyzed, and profiled. This can be done by adapting various analytic approaches. There is no need to discard all the analytic methods used for one threat just because the next one may have different goals and objectives, or employ asymmetric strategies differently. Terrorists, gangs, guerillas, insurgents, organized criminals, even hacker groups are all made up of people and because of this they can all be patterned, analyzed, and predicted using similar methods that you may already be familiar with.

6. **The Rule of No Rules:** Except for the above-mentioned rules, asymmetric strategies do not generally follow the agreed-upon rules. They are unrestrictive in nature. They are not bound by time, the real or virtual world, or geopolitical boundaries, and they are not limited by the range of a weapon system. They also tend to disregard domestic or international laws, treaties, societal norms, or social conventions. They are only bound by the limits of the strategist's imagination and the advantages he is able to identify and use against his adversary.

Looking into the tool bag of actions of a threat group reveals an almost limitless number of strategies that can be considered. In line with the six rules presented previously, the only limitations are those that are considered within the capabilities of the group that can target a vulnerability of their adversary and can be conducted within any other self-imposed parameters in the executor such as the law, morals, or accepted societal norms. The only final limitation is the imagination of the executor themselves.

A key thing for the analyst to keep in mind with all of these strategies is that they are simply actions to achieve a goal or objective. They are not a mysterious phenomenon where we must throw out all the analytic techniques that have been used on a conventional threat in the past. The use of certain strategies may appear to be illogical, random, or senseless to the victim or analyst, but to the perpetrators, they most certainly are not. They are all conducted for a specific reason or purpose. Even the lone actor, possibly operating with some sort of mental deficiency or illness has a reason behind their acts. They will just appear to make no sense to the rest of the world.

Also key to analyzing these strategies is that some of the groups that are associated with them by one name or another will actually employ several of them concurrently and simultaneously. These groups are known as hybrid threats. Even more complex is the threat group that is linked to other groups through some type of formal or informal relationship; each group practicing its own strategies, following their own goals and objectives in the process. While we recognize the problems of terrorism, nuclear proliferation, rogue states, and cyberwarfare, it seems logical not to combine them with organized crime, gangs, or hackers, since the American approach is to handle these threats with law enforcement instead of military assets. While the approach is sound, it reinforces a myopic and distinctly separate view of our threats.

This difficulty is further reinforced by the natural way that we organize ourselves to handle intelligence. This is partly because of the similar ways we separate our intelligence, homeland security, and law enforcement organizations to combat our threats. We even do this with our funding of these organizations. Different types of organizations have different sets of customers and even are funded through different "colors of money" depending on their parent organizations. Each are therefore tied to different requirements and in some cases in reporting their results and effectiveness.

The boundaries that we've set between military and domestic law enforcement do not matter much to the terrorist or hacker nor are they bound to follow our rules of war, jurisdiction or any other type of boundaries or limits (see rule 4 above). It is also not something that is set apart from traditional conflict. Any in-depth study of war, terrorism, or a particular type of threat strategy will most certainly show a tangle of asymmetric and conventional ties within it. There is simply no way to cleanly separate open war, crime, terrorism, cyber, and drugs, from each other, especially when dealing with threats that are deeply intertwined within all of them.

To become an expert in counterterrorism for example, the intelligence analyst must be well-versed in international finance, ideologies, socioeconomics, communications, and weapons technology as just a start to the number of topics they will eventually become familiar with.

In reality, asymmetric threats, warfare, and strategies are not separate from traditional military conflict—they are an integrated part of it; always have been and always will be. Every conflict in our past has had asymmetric or nontraditional strategies as a significant part of the outcome. No matter where you may be as an intelligence analyst—either in military, law enforcement, or even in a for-profit or not-for-profit company—understanding your threats involves a baseline understanding of where they came from and their baseline commonalities before you can effectively get into the details of your specific threats.

Summary

Today's threats are the product of recent decades of evolution. This evolution is in part due to the rapid and increasingly technical advances of U.S. military power as demonstrated on several battlefields in the last few years. The most persistent threats have been carried out by entities who have successfully adapted to this environment. These groups have been able to identify strengths, capabilities, and associated strategies, allowing them both to survive as well as continue to engage the United States and other similar nation-states despite their relative weakness militarily and economically.

While the study of today's threats may seem daunting, complex, or simply too chaotic to apply rules of reasoning, the key to understanding these threats is to understand that all of them operate within a focused set of rules. These rules, along with other identified commonalities and patterns can be identified with proper research and analysis. If today's threats can be analyzed, the can be templated, predicted, and countered with the right assets. The next key for intelligence analysts is to understand their own operating environment to include their mission and their customers, and the data, tools, people, and processes at their disposal.

Key Summary Points

- Our threats today are not a new phenomenon, but they are the result of an evolution that has been molded by key events and the rapid increase in capabilities associated with information and other technologies.
- Several key events that have pushed our adversaries to look beyond the battlefield to engage the United States include the results of the Cold War, the demonstration of the U.S. military's might during the Gulf Wars and other operations, and significant asymmetric successes such as 9/11.
- To gain a baseline level of understanding, all threat strategies can be categorized as either violent or nonviolent and legal or illegal. This has allowed us to identify one of four distinct realms where threat strategy can be found.
- While asymmetric threat strategies are different, there are some commonalities within all of them that can be identified to help the analyst.

Discussion Questions

- Besides the three major catalysts (the Cold War, the First Gulf War, and 9/11) for the evolution of today's threats, what other catalysts were significant in recent threat evolution?
- Why is there no single agreed-upon definition for many asymmetric threats and strategies such as terrorism or cyber warfare?
- What is the most accurate description or label to assign to today's threats? Does unconventional, unrestrictive, omnipresent, ubiquitous, or some other term fit better than the term symmetric?
- What additional rules for understanding asymmetric threats could be added to the six rules presented in this chapter?

Figure Credits

Fig. 2.1: Copyright © 2017 Pixabay/Olichel Adamovich.

Fig. 2.2: Source: https://commons.wikimedia.org/wiki/File:Operation_Desert_Storm_-_Abandoned_Vehicles_1991.jpg.

Fig. 2.3: Source: https://commons.wikimedia.org/wiki/File:GMTI_JSTARS.jpg.

Fig. 2.4: Source: https://commons.wikimedia.org/wiki/File:US_Army_tanks_face_off_against_Soviet_tanks,_Berlin_1961.jpg.

Chapter 3

The Once and Future Intelligence Community

The necessity of procuring good intelligence is apparent and need not be further urged—All that remains for me to add is, that you keep the whole matter as secret as possible. For upon Secrecy, success depends in most Enterprises of the kind, and for want of it, they are generally defeated, however, well planned ...

Gen. George Washington, 1777.[1]
[Letter to Colonel Elias Dayton, July 26, 1777]

Learning Objectives

▸ After completing this chapter, you will be able to:

▸ Understand the evolution of U.S. intelligence along the respective paths of national, law enforcement, and military intelligence.

▸ Recognize the six major factors that are currently changing the face of U.S. intelligence today.

▸ Discuss the map of today's intelligence community to include the characteristics of each concentric ring.

▸ Execute a bottom-up approach of the intelligence community from a specific position.

Spies: Inquire Within

Understanding intelligence as both a community and a practice is a daunting task. To the layman or outsider, the community is so large and complex that it appears to be unknowable in its entirety. To know of all the programs, directorates, offices, divisions, operations, and functions is simply impossible

---

1   General George Washington in a letter to Colonel Elias Dayton, July 26, 1777. Retrieved from http://www.access.gpo.gov/intelligence/int/int022.html

for one person. Even an insider such as the Director of National Intelligence or DNI could never know about every separate effort, operation, or program that falls within their area of responsibility. Compound this difficulty with the fact that the practice of intelligence is no longer constrained to the federal government, but has now extended to state and local levels and even into the commercial sector.

Understanding the intelligence community is especially difficult because of the way it is generally taught—i.e., from the top-down. Many intelligence and security students learn about the intelligence community starting with a high-level overview of its structure at the national level and then go into the details of each of the U.S. Intelligence Community's (IC) 16 members. They learn the missions, roles, and functions of each agency, followed by an understanding of how each agency relates to a broadly defined mission subject area—like international terrorism or the most current conflict. This approach presents the IC as a massive, complex, dynamic, interconnected (and some would even say bloated and redundant) collection of organizations.

While learning about the intelligence community from a top-down approach, it is important to link it to national security priorities and objectives, understanding that the way the IC actually operates on a practical level requires a different approach. Approaching this community from the bottom-up helps the working professional gain a more unique and personal perspective, starting in their own foxhole and expanding out from there. From their own position within an intelligence organization, their learning extends to their colleagues, associates, and specific parts of other organizations where they personally have a connection or actively conduct the most work.

This bottom-up approach is similar to the way most people learn about other massive organizations. Take, e.g., how a soldier learns about the Army. Their learning starts with the makeup of the squad along with roles and responsibilities. That knowledge is then used to go up the chain of command by using units at one level as building blocks for units at the next. In this way, a young soldier or military student learns about the organization, mission, and functions of more complex military formations such as platoons, battalions, regiments, and so on.

Learning about, such as, massive intelligence landscape using either of these methods can be more difficult if it requires the learner to understand the intelligence community without the background and history of how it came to be. Included with this history are the critical events and factors that have shaped it along with way. By studying the historical origins and evolution of intelligence, the student can pick up a simple set of concepts that will help them understand the intelligence community's complex organizations and relationships in the proper context.

The way the U.S. Intelligence Community is organized, operates, and imbues a certain associated culture is tied to American history, our military, and law enforcement traditions. It is also tied to our approach to the balance between security and civil liberties. It's not always been a smooth evolution with many fits, starts, and errors along with way.

Our Humble Beginnings

> Where-ever their Army lies, it will be of the greatest advantage to us, to have spies among them.
>
> General George Washington, 1777[2]

Intelligence operations in America are older than America itself; from scouting and reconnaissance missions of rangers and light infantry regiments during the French and Indian Wars to George Washington's extensive spy network in and around Boston and New York and throughout the American Revolution. Called the second oldest profession, the pace of evolution of U.S. spying and intelligence work has varied greatly over the course of our history.[3]

From the start, American intelligence during our colonial period was as rough as the frontier and practiced almost exclusively by rank amateurs. Washington himself understood that intelligence was important as an offset to the British military's superiority. His spy ring was similar to the rest of the Continental Army in that it attracted patriots with next to no formal training or experience in intelligence.

For example, one of Washington's favorite spies was Benjamin Tallmadge, a dragoon officer and former Yale classmate of Nathan Hale. Tallmadge was the son of a Connecticut churchman and was noted for his "delicate" physical features.[4] Joining the continental army after Hale's betrayal, capture, and execution in 1776, Tallmadge organized the Culper Spy Ring to report on British operations in and around their occupation of New York City in 1778. Eventually Tallmadge

FIGURE 3.1   Benjamin Tallmadge was the leader of George Washington's Culper Spy Ring during the American War of Independence

---

2   Bakeless, John. (1998). *Turncoats, traitors & heroes.* New York: Da Capo Press.

3   Numerous intelligence source cite our business as the second-oldest assuming we all know the first.

4   Rose, Alexander. (2006, May) *Washington's spies: The story of America's first spy ring* (p. 4 and illustration). New York: Bantam Books.

became Washington's Chief of Intelligence and was later elected to the U.S. House of Representatives.

With no proper intelligence training or doctrine in existence, Tallmadge broke from the more tactical and less risky methods of using military reconnaissance to understand British army dispositions and plans. His preferred methods of gathering intelligence through covert agents and sympathizers with cover stories who were living in the midst of British held areas ran afoul of his immediate superior, General Charles Scott, who had relied upon military reconnaissance in the form of scouts and uniformed dragoons. Washington's acceptance of Tallmadge's type of active collection only came when he became unsatisfied with the intelligence he was getting from Scott's more traditional methods.[5]

Washington's awareness of the importance of intelligence during the American Revolution was not enough for it to become an essential element in establishing the security of a new country. After the war concluded, intelligence gathering assumed its earlier status as "a gentleman's game" with an emerging American military tradition that would relegate intelligence to a relatively unimportant position for much of the next century. Two key factors in this tradition were central in the relatively slow evolution of intelligence in the United States. A primary factor was the overall American approach to fighting wars. This can be best summed as: Don't go out looking for a war, but once involved, use overwhelming military and economic might for a victory and a quick return home. The U.S. military generally followed this pattern through several early conflicts prior to and throughout our involvement in both world wars. Only three times have Americans ever fought a war for longer than 5 years: the American Revolution (8 years),[6] the Vietnam War (roughly 12 years), and the War on Terror (8+ years). We unilaterally declared an end to the last war but as recent attacks in Europe and in the United States have shown, it is arguably ongoing today.

The other significant factor was the United States' geographic position in the world. While a young America was relatively weak in many strategic areas, we had no significant threats just across our borders. We had sparsely populated Canada to our north and relatively weak threat from Mexico to our south. We also had and two great big oceans to our East and West that allowed us grow almost unfettered by the geopolitical machinations of older, more developed powers of the day. The overarching need for a robust intelligence and spying apparatus against our immediate threats was not seen as necessary.

Much of our early history, therefore, suggests that U.S. intelligence was attended to only when considered a necessity. When Americans didn't think we needed it, its evolution and growth stagnated. The way Americans fought wars did not lend itself to a long-term sustainable capability in either collection or analysis.

In light of these factors, the first 75 years of American history occurred without any notable operation or capability that could reasonably be called intelligence. If it did exist, it lived predominantly within our military. One notable instance during the

---

5   Ibid, pp.77–78.

6   Starting in 1775, major combat operations in America during the American Revolution ended in 1781 after 6 years. The Treaty of Paris officially ended the war in 1783.

Mexican–American War, waged from 1846 to 1848, was the U.S. Army's march on Mexico City led by General Winfield Scott. Scott was aided by reconnaissance missions conducted by small mounted detachments. One of the most notable commanders of one of these detachments was a young Captain Robert E. Lee.[7]

Intelligence, spying, and covert missions certainly increased during the American Civil War, but again, no network that could be called an intelligence organization survived it in any permanent sense. Intelligence in support of law enforcement was simply nonexistent during America's early years. While the U.S. Secret Service was created in July 1865, its original primary purpose was to catch counterfeiters and later anyone who perpetrated fraud against the government.

FIGURE 3.2   Robert E. Lee as a younger officer after the Mexican–American War. Drawn from an 1850 photograph

Another 20 years had to pass before the creation of the Military Information Division in the Army's General Staff. This small section of one officer and four clerks was placed within the Adjutant General's Office. The purpose of the Military Information Division was to collect and catalogue information on other countries that would be of use to the U.S. military. This included geographical and political information of several countries in the event of war or some other necessity. Within a few years it had grown to 52 officers, 12 clerks, and 16 attaches.[8] Thanks to this small group, information collected about Cuba proved invaluable during the Spanish–American War.[9] This arrangement stayed in place for another two decades until the creation of the General Staff's Second Section in 1903—now known as the Army G-2. What is interesting to note here is the implied use of analysis as a specialized part of MID's functions even though intelligence as a function capability continued to flounder over the next decade. It took a World War to solidify intelligence as a permanent staff function within the Army and another to create a national intelligence structure.[10]

---

7   Eisenhower, John S. D. (1989). So far from god (pp. 312–313). New York: Doubleday Books.

8   Federation of American Scientists. (2007, January 21). *History of military intelligence.* Retrieved from http://www.fas.org/irp/doddir/army/miotc/mihist.htm

9   Ibid.

10   Finnegan, John Patrick, & Danysh, Romana. (1998). *Army Lineage Series. Military Intelligence* (p. 4). Washington, DC: Center of Military History, United States Army.

Three Paths of Intelligence Evolution

The best way to understand intelligence's evolution from this point is to separate it along three paths of development: intelligence for military purposes, national and political intelligence, and intelligence in support of domestic security and law enforcement. The pace of evolution between these three areas was remarkably different. As slow as the development of intelligence capabilities for military purposes was up to this time, it was decades ahead of the other two.

Intelligence in support of law enforcement was never really part of the U.S. lexicon until the 20th century. While the U.S. Secret Service can trace its origins back to the American Civil War and the Pinkerton Agency, it wasn't until 1908 that the U.S. Department of Justice created the Bureau of Intelligence, an organization that evolved into what we now know as the Federal Bureau of Intelligence or FBI. Organizations such as the Law Enforcement Intelligence Unit (LEIU) and the International Association for Law Enforcement Intelligence Analysts (IALEIA) were not created or incorporated until 1956 and 1981, respectively. Evolution of intelligence in this sector either took place within agencies at the national level like the FBI or DEA, or took place within each state, local, or tribal agencies. It was neither standardized, coordinated, integrated with each other until 9/11 identified the need for fusion centers.[11]

Intelligence for the purpose of protecting the United States and its national and foreign interests developed on par with law enforcement as it was left up to whims of diplomatic circles. The statement that best personifies the state of foreign political intelligence during this period comes from U.S. Secretary of State Harry Stimson who stated that, "Gentlemen do not read other gentleman's mail." Stimson used this as his explanation for shutting down MI-8, the state department's code breaking office in 1929.[12] While national and domestic security intelligence capabilities were still in their incubation stage, the development of the military intelligence continued its evolution into a more permanent capability.

FIGURE 3.3   Allan Pinkerton, President Lincoln, and Major General John A. McClernand after the Battle of Antietam during the American Civil War, 1862

---

11   Carter, David, Chermak, Steve, Carter, Jeremy, & Drew, Jack. (2014). Understanding law enforcement intelligence processes. *Report to the Office of University Programs, Science and Technology Directorate, U.S. Department of Homeland Security* (p. 3). College Park, MD: START.

12   Kahn, D. (2004). *The reader of gentleman's mail: Herbert O. Yardley and American Intelligence* (p. 98). New Haven, CT: Yale University Press.

Comparatively speaking, intelligence in support of military operations evolved out of necessity at a much faster pace than intelligence in support of law enforcement or national objectives. Operational and tactical level intelligence—i.e., intelligence about specific and relatively smaller scale operations—was increasingly needed on the battlefields of the late 19th and early 20th centuries, but then set to a lower priority in the relative calm of peacetime. World War I provided a small acceleration in this development as U.S. forces arriving in Europe found their operational and tactical level intelligence capabilities lagging behind British and French allies.[13]

As a result, the U.S. military intelligence began a process of evolution over the next eight decades that pushed intelligence information, operations, and personnel to lower and lower levels within the respective military formation. Intelligence as a specialty wasn't created to decentralize and localize their support by placing intelligence officers within combat units all the way down to division, brigade, and even the battalion level. Analysis of threats and enemy intentions took place as part of military operations conducted by staff sections internal to their own units.

For national and law enforcement intelligence, the growth and emergence of a structure similar to what was happening within the U.S. military was anecdotal at best. Analytical cells or departments at the national and department levels simply did not exist as the exclusive, segregated, or specialized three-letter agencies that we know today.

World War II and the Cold War—Codification and Centralization

What use are they? They've got 40,000 people over there reading newspapers.

President Nixon referring to the CIA
as quoted in Spying for America[14]

Both World War II and 9/11 each brought about abrupt changes to the evolution of U.S. intelligence. One of the primary reasons is that they both began with massive intelligence failures—i.e., the surprise attacks on Pearl Harbor and on New York/District of Columbia/Pennsylvania, respectively. In 1941, the Japanese were able to achieve a strategic surprise in an attack that all but crippled the U.S. Pacific fleet. By a stroke of luck, U.S. Aircraft Carriers were at sea and were saved from the same fate as many of our other ships. And while no military combat units were targeted on 9/11, the damage caused, both from an economic and also a psychological standpoint, was enormous. For both attacks, we had indications or warnings but these alarms could not be heard over the din of the daily intelligence business.

The immediate remedy after the disaster at Pearl Harbor was the creation of the Office of Strategic Services (OSS) in June of 1942. Created at the behest of

---

13   Finnegan & Danysh, Ibid, 4.

14   Lathrop, Charles E. (Ed.). (2004). *The literary spy* (p. 340). New Haven, CT: Yale University.

FIGURE 3.4   The USS Arizona burns and sinks during the Japanese attack on Pearl Harbor, December 7, 1941

William J. Donovan, President Roosevelt placed the OSS within the military, more specifically the Joint Chiefs of Staff. Its purpose was to provide information and analysis as well as covert and clandestine operations to defeat the Axis powers on a global scale. OSS agents operated in every theater and conducted missions of great risk and importance to the allied war effort. To fill the ranks of the Research and Analysis section of the OSS, Donovan recruited heavily from Ivy League professors including the head of the section, William L. Langer.[15] This fact is something of an eyebrow raiser given the climate of academia toward federal service today. This centralization of collection, operations, analysis, and counterintelligence was a watershed moment in U.S. intelligence history, but it was only the beginning.

Following World War II, the need for a more permanent national intelligence organization was well recognized. One lesson learned was that the U.S. could no longer afford to revert to an isolationist stance and be blind to external threats. Oceans would no longer provide our first line of defense in age of the Aircraft Carrier and Nuclear Weapons. The appearance of an Iron Curtain over Europe as coined by Winston Churchill in 1946 sealed the perception that the United States faced a more persistent threat of communist

15   Odom, William E. (2003). *Fixing intelligence* (pp. xiii–xiv). New Haven, CT: Yale University.

expansion in both Europe and around the world intelligence was increasingly seen as that new first line of defense, providing the eyes, ears, and shadow warriors of the Cold War. Even before the end of World War II, Donovan and others were working with President Truman on plans for a "peacetime intelligence agency."[16] The result of which was abolishment of the OSS in September 1945 followed by the creation of the Central Intelligence Agency as part of the National Security Act of 1947.

The creation of the CIA propelled our national intelligence gathering at an incredibly fast pace. One of the catalysts of growth was need for consolidation and centralized control of existing capabilities. New organizations were created in succession as a way to better structure the more specific and often technical aspects of national intelligence operations. The National Security Agency was created in 1952 as a consolidation of all intelligence-related signals and communications at the national level. Nine years later, the National Reconnaissance Office (NRO) was created as an agency jointly operated by the Air Force and CIA. Its primary mission was to consolidate and organize the development and deployment imagery collection systems such as aircraft and satellites.

Also in 1961, the Defense Department consolidated its national and strategic intelligence function within the Defense Intelligence Agency (DIA). Imagery interpretation needed this same sort of restructuring and the National Photographic Interpretation Center or NPIC provided the solution that same year. Later in 1996, the NPIC became the National Imagery and Mapping Agency as a further consolidation and since 2004 has been renamed once again as the National Geospatial-Intelligence Agency (NGA).

Without going into the specifics behind the missions and functions of each of these organizations, it is important to understand the trend that took place as the intelligence community formed itself for the Cold War environment. Instead of changing the structure of the entire community every few years, newly created organizations were simply added to the existing structure.

As well as attaching new organizations, the intelligence community grew internally as its definition became inclusive of each branch of military service as well as existing domestic and law enforcement organizations such as the Department of Energy, Department of Treasury, and FBI. Even after the end of the Cold War, the intelligence community continued to add new members. As recent as February 2006, the then Director of National Intelligence, John Negroponte, welcomed the Drug Enforcement Administration into the intelligence community as its 17th member.

The Rise of the Machines–Intelligence Gets Technical

A series of events that occurred during the Cold War helped spur the increasing use of technology in intelligence gathering. The launching of the Soviet satellite Sputnik in 1957 and the United States responding with its first satellite, Explorer I in January 1958 marked an early harbinger of things to come. Another key milestone was the use

---

16   Prados, John. (1986, 1996). *President's secret wars* (p. 15). Chicago, IL: Elephant Paperback.

FIGURE 3.5   Lockheed SR-71 Blackbird

of U2 reconnaissance that demonstrated that the Soviet Union was installing offensive nuclear missiles in Cuba, a mere 90 miles away from the coast of the United States. In December 1964, the newly developed SR-71 became the fastest aircraft on the planet. Able to achieve Mach 3 with a cruising altitude of 80,000 feet, the Blackbird could survey 72 square surface miles and evade enemy missiles fired at it by simply speeding up.[17] Also not to be overlooked was the November 1985 Microsoft launch of a computer program intended as a graphical user interface for MS-DOS—called Windows.[18]

These and countless other milestones are as important in the history of U.S. intelligence as any international crisis or spy arrest. As technology provided a catalyst for the evolution of the threats, it also was as much a part of the evolution of intelligence as any single cataclysmic event.

The primary emphasis of intelligence-related technology development throughout the Cold War was in collection systems and platforms. The United States spent enormous

17   *SR-71 blackbird history, Pacific Coast air museum.* Retrieved from http://pacificcoastairmuseum. org/2002Site/aircraftPCAM/SR_71/SR71_History.asp

18   Bellis, M. The unusual history of Microsoft Windows. *About.com: Inventors.* Retrieved from http:// inventors.about.com/od/mstartinventions/a/Windows.htm?rd=1

amounts of money on satellites, unmanned aerial vehicles (UAVs), photoreconnaissance systems, among other initiatives. As the Cold War carried on, technical solutions were seen as an increasing part of our overall strategy of keeping tabs on communist adversaries. From a competitive standpoint, our appetite for technology gave the U.S. collection capabilities no other country could match. As our collection capabilities advanced, more and better hard data for analysts was the result.

As the U.S. Intelligence Community employed new types of collection systems, they also created new categories of intelligence information. Intelligence from monitoring signals, communications, and electronic signatures were dubbed SIGINT, COMINT, and ELINT, respectively. Our capabilities in IMINT or imagery intelligence went far beyond hand-held cameras as it grew to include aerial (air-breathing) and satellite (non-air-breathing) platforms. Information derived from other aspects of a target such heat signatures and other emissions were classified as MASINT or measurement and signature intelligence. The importance of intelligence technology was such that entirely new agencies were created around these categories. Agencies like the National Security Agency (NSA), National Imagery and Mapping Agency (NIMA) (now known as the National Geospatial-Intelligence Agency or NGA), and the National Reconnaissance Office (NRO) were borne out the desire to create parochial ownership of each "INT." These new organizations were created from emerging collection capabilities, codified and attached to the U.S. Intelligence Community structure.

Through the remainder of the Cold War, this brick-by-brick building method for the U.S. Intelligence Community proved to be a success. Technical intelligence showed its worth in its ability to gather information from behind the iron curtain where human collection had been stymied. Technical platforms provided information about the number of strategic bombers, locations of ICBM and submarine sites, and even indicators of activities such as nuclear weapons testing. This information was critical to national-level decision-making that needed an accurate understanding of our adversaries' capabilities and intentions. The more technology-aided intelligence, the more the intelligence community relied upon technology as its preferred way of doing business.

As covered in Chapter 2, this dominance of technology reached its peak of success from 1990 to 1991, during the First Gulf War. Here, U.S.-led coalition forces reduced the world's fifth largest army to next to nothing in the space of 41 days with fewer U.S. combat deaths than we suffered at the Alamo (148–179 respectively).[19, 20] This feat was repeated 12 years later during the Second Gulf War in 2003 when a smaller and even more technically advanced U.S.-led coalition was able to invade Iraqi again, only this time with the goal of unseating the Saddam Hussein regime and destroy their perceived capabilities

---

19 *Taken from the unfinished war: A decade since desert storm.* Retrieved from http://www.cnn.com/SPECIALS/2001/gulf.war/facts/gulfwar/

20 Approximated from several sources as cited by "Casualties at the Siege of the Alamo." Retrieved from http://www.geocities.com/the_tarins@sbcglobal.net/adp/history/1836/the_battle/the_texians/casualties.html

in creating weapons of mass destruction. U.S. tanks rolling into Baghdad were covered by U.S. media with as much vigor as they covered military operations in the First Gulf War despite the claims of "Baghdad Bob" and the Iraqi Ministry of Information saying the opposite on Iraq's state run media outlets. The intelligence community, created for the contest between the East and the West seemed perfect for kicking a thug dictator out of a small country like Kuwait.

Advantages to technical intelligence were numerous. Satellites and aerial reconnaissance platforms were seen as timelier than human sources and without nearly the same amount of risk. Why spend months to years trying to build a vulnerable spy network inside an enemy country when a simple flyover will answer the question? Technical collection was also cleaner than human methods. It not only provided hard data versus subjectively written reports, but did so without forcing us to associate with the scoundrels, rogues, and other criminals so often associated with the more human aspects of intelligence. Another perceived benefit to technical intelligence is that it was perceived to be more resistant to deception and other forms of human error. As a result, the United States invested more and more into these areas of intelligence relying more and more upon technical solutions to our intelligence problems. Costs in terms of monetary outlay were only a minor factor.

Unfortunately, our pursuit of technical capabilities for intelligence came at the expense of the more traditional—and critical—capabilities such as human and counterintelligence. Using operatives and spies, while great fodder for movies, proved in reality to be a dirty business. HUMINT by its nature is conducted in the shadows through both clandestine and covert operations. The very nature of human-based intelligence means that successes are rarely publicized, while failures tend to get aired out for everyone to see.

The naïve beliefs or near perfection that often accompanies technological gains took hold in the intelligence arena as well. Rarely was a collection system held to blame for an intelligence failure. Machines were pristine, did what they were told, and did so without bias, apprehension, or a parochial/political agenda in mind. If there was a problem, user error was generally considered to be at fault. But errors in HUMINT were handled quite differently. A number of Congressional hearings in the 1970s aired publicly some dirty laundry. The Rockefeller Commission, the Church and Pike Committees, and the Murphy Commission were all investigations into possible illegal activities within the CIA during the mid-1970s. The 1987 Iran–Contra affair in which covert operations illegally conducted arms sales to Iran in order to secretly fund Contras in Nicaragua both embarrassed the Reagan Administration and contributed to a general skepticism about the use of HUMINT.

Over time, the failures of HUMINT during the Cold War became a festering wound. Not only were congressional hearings front page news, repeated revelations that some of our own spies had turned traitor further damaged its reputation. The exploits of spies like Aldrich Ames, Robert Hanson, and Edward Snowden did untold damage to not only our immediate national interests, but also severely damaged our national confidence in the use of humans to conduct intelligence operations. No technical collection platform ever turned traitor or could be blackmailed for a past indiscretion.

As a result, the United States placed an ever-increasing reliance on collection through technology and downgraded the importance of almost all forms of human-based intelligence. Since many of the technical programs were within the U.S. Department of Defense (DoD), their internal intelligence agencies became more and more dominant at the national level. As our reliance on technology grew, our ability to conduct human-based intelligence suffered what amounted to a wholesale gutting.

The Peace Dividend That Gutted Army Interrogation Units

As a U.S. Army Military Intelligence (MI) officer in the mid-1990s, I saw results of our aversion to human-based intelligence first hand. During that time, someone way above my pay grade decided to deactivate several of the Army's interrogation companies. This reduction was seen as part of the "peace dividend"—the false perception that we could save money on defense and intelligence since we no longer faced any serious national-level threats. Normally, these interrogation companies were found at the corps level with a primary mission to provide HUMINT through direct contact with cooperative sources, and if necessary, interrogation of noncooperative sources.

The intelligence unit that I was a member of from 1996 through 1998 had one of these interrogation companies. When I arrived to the unit in April 1996, the 165th MI battalion was in the middle of peacekeeping operations in Bosnia. I was amazed to learn upon arrival that the battalion's interrogation company was in the process of deactivating—in the middle of operations no less. I remember standing on the coal blackened ground of our base camp in Lukavac, Bosnia, for the deactivation ceremony late that spring. The soldiers and officers of the battalion watched incredulously as the battalion commander LTC William Caniano, and the Interrogation company commander, CPT Alex Cochran presided

FIGURE 3.6   Portion of the INSCOM Detention Training Facility (IDTF) on Camp Bullis, Texas

over the roll up of the company guidon for the last time. The soldiers that were in the company were rolled into the battalion's counterintelligence company. I took command of that company a few weeks later. Throughout my time in command, the leftover interrogators would slowly rotate out of my company without any replacements.

The memories of that day stayed with me for several years along with the opinion that the Army was making a huge mistake in phasing out interrogators at the tactical level. My opinion was validated in 2006 when as a program manager for Lockheed Martin I took over an interrogation instructor and roleplaying contract as part of my training program in 2008. Situated at a brand-new mock-up detention training facility at Camp Bullis, Texas, my instructors were tasked to train up four newly created battalions of army interrogators along other units who rotated through their facility on a regular basis. Thanks to notorious instances such as the mistreatment of detainees at Abu Ghraib, Iraq, the Army had learned the peace dividend lesson the hard way.

The downside to this approach started to become apparent until after the First Gulf War when the U.S. military ventured in force into Somalia in 1993 and the Balkans in 1995. While imagery platforms such as satellites, reconnaissance aircraft, and the first UAVs could identify large troop movements, signal collectors could monitor communications patterns, they could not penetrate the decision cycle or the motivations held in the minds of our adversaries. In Somalia in particular, one of the biggest shortfalls was the lack of linguists in our military who could speak Somali.[21] In these environments where human-based collectors and counterintelligence were more effective than any technical collection system, we found ourselves with scant resources and those resources we did have were being stretched thin in a relatively short amount of time.

9/11 Through Today–Decentralization Through Information

The term "intelligence community" was first coined by Lieutenant General Walter Bedell Smith as early as 1952.[22] As the nation's 4th Director of Central Intelligence (DCI), Smith was describing how his responsibilities were much larger than just the head of the CIA. Simply put, he was responsible to the president for all intelligence operations at the national level whether they were conducted by the CIA or another agency. Codified under Title 10 of U.S. Code, it is now the largest, most well-funded, and arguably complex collection of intelligence organizations in the world.

---

21   Bullock, Major Harold E. *Peace by committee: Command and control issues in multinational peace enforcement operations*. Retrieved from http://www.fas.org/man/eprint/bullock.htm

22   We the People of the CIA ... The First Community DCI: Walter B. Smith, Featured Story Archive. Retrieved from https://www.cia.gov/news-information/featured-story-archive/2007-featured-story-archive/first-community-dci.html

The U.S. Intelligence Community today is defined as "a federation of executive branch agencies and organizations that work separately and together to conduct *intelligence activities* necessary for the conduct of foreign relations and the protection of the national security of the United States."[23] Executive Order 12333, originally created during the Reagan Administration, details six primary objectives to the IC related to collection, processing, and disseminating intelligence as well as other activities.[24] It consists of 17 member organizations including the Office of the Director of National Intelligence or ODNI, as shown in Chart 3.1.

CHART 3.1   The U.S. National Intelligence Community

Office of the Director of National Intelligence	
Air Force Intelligence	Army Intelligence
Central Intelligence Agency	Coast Guard Intelligence
Defense Intelligence Agency	Department of Energy
Department of Homeland Security	Department of State
Department of the Treasury	Drug Enforcement Administration
Federal Bureau of Investigation	Marine Corps Intelligence
National Geospatial-Intelligence Agency	National Reconnaissance Office
National Security Agency	Navy Intelligence

The organizations listed above were created to provide support to our national decision-makers and our military. These customers have been served by the intelligence community for decades without any major shifts to their structure or mission set.

Today's intelligence community of practice is a larger and much more diverse network of organizations and people. Outside of the "Core" 17 agencies, the majority of intelligence is conducted in an almost totally unconstrained and unregulated environment. It is a community whose development has been driven by a variety of factors, including our customers, our threats, and various market forces. It is also a community where the line between who is an intelligence analyst or operative and who is not has been slowly blurred beyond recognition over the past 20 years.

While it's inaccurate to say that 9/11 was the single watershed event that has reshaped the intelligence community, the magnitude of this event as an intelligence failure is as dramatic as the sinking of the Titanic. Both were catastrophic and arguably preventable, but only in hindsight do we now know that both tragedies were the result of a series of failures, not just one pivotal mistake. While the intelligence community was just beginning to evolve away from its Cold War paradigm prior to 9/11, this tragedy revealed that

23   The definition of the intelligence community was taken from http://www.intelligence.gov/1-definition.shtml.

24   Executive order 12333, http://www.archives.gov/federal-register/codification/executive-order/12333.html

many of these changes had either taken intelligence in the wrong direction or had not gone far enough.

Perhaps even more tragic than the failures preceding 9/11 was the failure to paint an accurate picture of Saddam Hussein's Weapons of Mass Destruction or WMD program in 9/11's aftermath. Because of the politically charged bias surrounding all these issues, the damage to the U.S. Intelligence Community's reputation has been significant and will last for decades to come. Much of the damage to their reputation has been self-inflicted in the form of internal second-guessing and calls for radical reorganization at all levels.

In this shadow the intelligence community continues its evolution, but perhaps more dramatically is the revolution taking place within the intelligence community of practice. Neither the structure nor the place where intelligence is practiced at the national level or within the rest of our society looks anything like the intelligence community of September 10 2001. While the evolution of intelligence during the Cold War leaned toward centralization and a reliance on technical collection capabilities, there are several distinct factors that have changed intelligence into the much more desegregated and commercialized community of practice that exists today.

Intelligence is now appearing in virtually every sector of our lives and the need for and practice of intelligence is expanding faster than the traditional community structure can accommodate.

While these factors have had a subtle impact over decades of our history, they've become more prominent with exponential impact that information technology has had over the past few years. Each of these factors is intrinsically related as a chain of effects in the order listed in Chart 3.2.

1. The Intelligence Environment Is Changing

The intelligence environment is no different from other environments in that change is a constant. The three most influential environmental changes for the business of intelligence has been technology, the availability of information, and as a result of the previous two, our threats. The same technological advancements of the information age that our threats have taken advantage of have also changed our efforts at finding and fixing them. Technology and the availability of information has brought about increased capabilities, but has also brought several unintended consequences. In short, technology has allowed everyone to get into the analysis game.

The U.S. investment in technology during the Cold War not only brought about a great increase in capabilities, but also exposed some vulnerabilities. One obvious result was a dependence on the technologies themselves. Anyone who has been unable to access the internet for a day realizes how difficult it can be to do tasks that used to be routine and simple. In addition, with the rapid advancement in collection systems and platforms came a robust stream of data and information flowing into intelligence centers for the analysts. This exponential growth in the amount of available information quickly overwhelmed most intelligence centers' ability to handle all of it effectively. Information that took hours

Breaking the 1.44 Megabyte Barrier

As an army officer who grew up at the tactical level, I was shocked in 1996, when a briefing I was working on had a single slide that was too large to fit on a 3.5" floppy disk. I couldn't believe my bosses actually needed something so graphically intensive (read: cheesy) that one slide needed to be larger than 1.44 megabytes. Even more absurdly, this happened as my unit was deployed to Lukavac, Bosnia, in the middle of peacekeeping operations. We were working out of the abandoned offices of a coal processing facility, aptly named Gotham City by the soldiers. We ended up breaking the graphics up from that one slide onto multiple disk and them reassembled them for the briefing on in another basecamp.

Four years later, I along with one of my chief warrant officers were deleting 2.5 terabytes of Able Danger data as required by intelligence oversight regulations. This amount of information equates to roughly 1,736,000 floppy disks. We now measure information not by the number of credible reports we have available, but by how much memory our reports take up.

to days to collect during the Cold War is now available in minutes to seconds. Instead of analysts being starved of information, they are now drowning in it, overwhelmed by the amount of information available and coming at them. Information that was strictly controlled prior to the information age is now a cheap commodity.

From an analytical perspective, then, the tools to support analysis were not developed on par with the ability to collect information. In the past, analysts wished that they could spend more time analyzing information rather than trying to research and collect it. Now analysts are wishing they can spend more time analyzing information rather than organize, manage, and sift through it. Collection(?) systems and data mining tools have often revealed that they already own some critical piece of information—they just have to find it within their own databases.

2. Intelligence Customers Are Changing

While intelligence professionals like to think that they do all the thinking about our enemy for the decision-makers, the reality is that most of today's customers of intelligence make their decisions based upon their own analysis. They do it every day. They read their own sources or in most cases, rely upon research conducted by staffers. Looking something up on the internet aka "Googling" is now an elementary skill. With so much information that is available to decision-makers that wasn't a generation earlier, it only makes sense that our decision-makers are drawn to doing their own collection and analysis, albeit to the degree that their time and skill allows. Technology, as it has changed the intelligence environment for both intelligence professionals and our threats, has also changed our customers.

CHART 3.2   How Intelligence Customers Are Changing

- There are a lot more customers at lower levels and in more diverse organizations.
- Customers are involved in more dynamic, fast-paced, and fluid operations.
- Customers have higher expectations of what intelligence can do.
- Customers are more impatient for information and/or analysis.
- Customers want to do more of their own analysis.

More and more intelligence is now being required by people who didn't think they needed it when the structure of the intelligence community was created. With complex threats that now have the ability to affect just about every part of our society, many decision-makers are just waking up to the realization that they need to know more about the world around them, including our threats and adversaries. Decades prior, our threats were perceived as coming from a state and confined to national and military arenas of competition. Even terrorism has been historically perceived as a foreign problem or at least was not an issue that needed to be dealt with domestically. This perception has radically changed only recently. Organizations that didn't think they needed intelligence have now found the absence of it unacceptable.

Intelligence customers have expanded not only in number, but in the diversity of their professions. Lawyers, law enforcement agencies, local police, and sheriff offices need intelligence. State governments, municipalities, airlines, port authorities, multinational corporations, schools and universities, power plants, nonprofit organizations all do. As our enemies have made it to our shores and have infiltrated our society, everyone has a vested and even personal interest in understanding the threats, their objectives, targets, and capabilities.

The U.S. Intelligence Community has responded to these new demands as it has in the past: With new organizations and a new focus to the existing structure, they've expanded only enough to cover their traditional customers, i.e., those within the U.S. military or within the Federal Government. When 70 percent of the U.S. Intelligence Community's budget goes to private contractors, it means the ranks of the various agency employees are filled with contractors and private consultants.[25]

The intelligence community's core agencies just do not have the capacity to handle the explosion of new customers. Who gets what information and intelligence products is no longer a matter of technology, it's a matter of prioritizing the analyst's time and resources. The number of actual requirements today is so far outside the IC's core capabilities that they've simply been unable to satisfy everyone. While the debate continues within the core agencies of whether the military operator or the national decision-maker has the priority, everyone else who needs intelligence is ranked as a lower priority if considered

25   Priest, Dana, Censer, Marjorie, & O'Harrow, Robert, Jr. (2013, June 12). Private contractors play key role in U.S. intelligence work. *The Seattle Times*. Retrieved from http://www.seattletimes.com/nation-world/private-contractors-play-key-role-in-us-intelligence-work/

at all. Even long-standing customers have changed what they want, how much they want, and how fast they want it.

Intelligence customers, both new and old, have been spoiled by inaccurate portrayals of intelligence. This in part thanks to the Js of Hollywood: James Bond, Jason Bourne, Jack Ryan, and Jack Bauer. Recent fiction books, movies, and TV shows have a tendency to skew our perspectives of what intelligence can and cannot do. In these works, intelligence is shown as a sexy, fast-paced, technologically savvy, and an incredibly efficient profession. Need to track a terrorist through the streets of Washington, DC, or Tangiers? Just ask the intel guys. Want to watch a covert take down of a terrorist training camp live? Just move a satellite over with the same ease as it takes to use a game controller. Having trouble with an international criminal? Don't go to the Justice Department. The NSA has an elite squad of commandos ready to do your dirty work for you—i.e., when they aren't chasing down autistic kids who've inadvertently broken their codes.[26]

For the press, it's just the opposite. Combine intelligence operations with the competitive nature of the media as a business and the results are pretty predictable. Stories that make it into the media are usually those that portray failures, leaks, and alleged abuses of power, whether they were committed by intelligence professionals or not. Throughout the Global War on Terror there have been untold number of intelligence successes from the thwarting of terrorist attacks to the pinpointing and capture of Iraqi thug Saddam Hussein. Sadly, the only thing that resonated in our media is Abu Ghraib,

Unlearned Lessons from Able Danger

The Able Danger story is just a typical example of this. When the story first broke in the summer of 2005, many of us involved hadn't talked about it with each other or with anyone else for years. Able Danger got traction in the press because of the fantastic allegations of conspiracies, cover-ups, and bureaucratic bungling. While I agree with the bureaucratic bungling part, from my perspective the majority of these stories were nonsense. Yet, they continued to be promoted by people who didn't have any clear details about what actually happened. The real story that I've tried to promote myself is that Able Danger was actually about how the right data, tools, people, and analytical process could have actually done some great things. Once the thread turned into a good news story, it ceased to become a story. Able Danger is not a singular anomaly in this sense. It happens all the time in the news. If it bleeds it leads, everything else is just an opinion of what happened.

---

26   This last premise was the scenario played out in the 1998 movie, Mercury Rising, starring Bruce Willis.

WMD, WikiLeaks, and the failure to catch Mohammed Atta & Company prior to their fateful flights.

The net result of the media and Hollywood's fantastic portrayals is a pervasive misperception about what intelligence can and cannot do. Even without these works of fiction, the realities of intelligence capabilities are being skewed daily. Just the idea that the core 17 intelligence agencies with a budget nearing $60 billion a year assumes we have the ability to watch everywhere both mile wide and mile deep.[27]

Not only has the technology changed the customer's perception of intelligence collection capabilities, it has also created a misperception of intelligence's ability to create refined products.

Intelligence customers know that the Information Age is upon them just as intelligence professionals do. Both surf the Internet. Both download maps and imagery to their phones or tablets. With relatively little effort, both can have access to information far beyond what an entire agency could provide to them 20 years ago. What changes the paradigm the most is that intelligence customers can now do these things more easily—i.e., without intelligence analysts holding their hands.

That being said, consumers of intelligence want more. Because information is more readily acceptable, intelligence customers want more of it and they don't want it to be held back in order to let the analyst filter and package it with their biases. To them, raw information on time is better than perfectly presented information that is late. They want intelligence faster, with more pictures in brighter colors. Any way that makes it easier and faster for them to gain knowledge about the subject for the decisions is considered optimal.

In many cases the difference between vetted intelligence products and preliminary analysis is lost on intelligence customers. They no longer care if it has the CIA "slam dunk" stamp of approval on it. A smart, trusted analyst from any organization will do, even better if they are within their own organization because they can have a say in the types of intelligence products they need. Being able to reach out to a non-vetted intelligence section for tailored and timely intelligence is an easy trade versus a distant but well-resourced agency.

Intelligence customers want to do their own analysis when convenient. It's human nature to think and study our environment and surroundings. Intelligence analysts have no more a monopoly on analyzing our threats than the major media outlets have on determining what news is important to their consumers.

3. Intelligence Requirements Are Changing

As intelligence customers have changed, they've driven changes in the kinds of intelligence they've wanted. As a general rule, intelligence is being asked to be more responsive, timely, and specifically focused toward individual customers than ever before. While the U.S. l Intelligence Community is based upon customer service, it operates within

---

27   http://intelligencecommunitynews.com/odni-requests-57-7b-in-appropriations-for-fy-2018/

somewhat rigid structures and business models and is constrained by national-level priorities, resources, and intelligence oversight rules. This is not true for the entire community of practice.

Think about the resources required to create and almost constantly update the most popular news sources. Fox News, CNN, and even ESPN employ dozens of writers, graphic artists, web designers, network engineers, anchors, consultants, content editors, and salesmen who as a group are posting articles and streaming information in real time on their websites no matter what time of day it is. Their websites contain an incredible amount of data available for the visitor to maneuver where they want. Now think about the ability of an intelligence section of, say, a dozen analysts to produce the same amount of original content and make it available to their customers in such an easy manner. It's just impossible.

These kinds of shortfalls are typical of a community that is being asked more and more questions about our world and our threats that we just don't know about and are not either prepared to find answers for everyone. There are only so many number one priorities. As much as we don't want to admit it, the intelligence community is market driven. Intelligence customers, through their requirements, drive every part of intelligence. As these requirements have changed, their effect on the various characteristics in how intelligence is conducted has become permanent.

An Example of Circular Reporting

During my tenure as chief of intelligence for LIWA, one of my analytical teams received a Request For Information (RFI) from one of our Field Support Teams or FSTs deployed to Kosovo in support of our peacekeeping efforts there. This FST was looking for information about the specific electric grid including where the power lines were in the surrounding area. The type and detail of information the team needed was so specific that none of my analysts could find an answer using our databases and research methods.

Accordingly, we sent the request up to the national-level community to see if the big three-letter agencies had anything. Our request went to DIA who also couldn't answer it. DIA personnel sent our request to one of their subordinate organizations, who in turn sent it to their collection teams on the ground in Kosovo. When DIA personnel in Kosovo received the request, their answer was that this request required too much of a diversion to their regular mission and they would not be able to satisfy the request. Their response went back through DIA to my analytical team, and back to our FST on the ground in Kosovo. It turned out that the DIA team in country that denied the request was just a few tents over from our team. While trying to use the proper channels, our FST found it was easier just to use the in-house assets on the ground.

CHART 3.3 Cold War Versus Modern Intelligence Characteristics

Intelligence Characteristic	Cold War Model	Current Model
Analytic focus	Situational awareness Predictive analysis	Situational awareness Predictive analysis Support to operations
Operational pace/tempo	Days—weeks—months	Days–hours: as soon as possible
Established priorities of work	Top-down: from National Security Council to agencies	Bottom-up: set by customers at all levels
Work environment	Structured, stable	Fluid, dynamic, chaotic
Analytical products	National intelligence estimates, periodic briefings/read files	Intelligence Summaries (INTSUMS), Situational Reports (SITREPs), key reads, verbal briefs
Type of intelligence	All-source, vetted, refined	More raw intelligence, repackaging, individual vetting
Analytical divisions and specializations	Separated, stovepiped into disciplines and parochial interests, protected, specialized	Some specialization, stovepiping, generalists with limitations

The main pattern of each characteristic shows a compression between national/strategic level and the operational/tactical level intelligence support. Prior to the information age, the types of intelligence support at these two levels were separate and distinct from each other. As operational and tactical infrastructure evolved at a faster pace because of the pressing needs of the war fighters, strategic level capabilities and resources have gradually shifted to supporting current operations versus long-range planning and vision. As a result, the operational/tactical way of doing business in the intelligence world now dominates the community across several areas.

It's not just the war fighter in the middle of operations that needs responsive and tailored "actionable" intelligence; anyone working operations in the military, government, or commercial sectors that can be affected by terrorism, crime, and other asymmetric threats does as well. In responding to these changing requirements, the intelligence community has retooled its priorities to the operational levels.

The Warfighter Is the First Priority

Providing an information brief on a strategic topic, writing a National Intelligence Estimate (NIE) or preparing a situational file full of background information may have satisfied our customers in the past—but no longer. Evolving intelligence at the national level, support to the war fighter has been elevated to a top priority over all types of intelligence requests. Military operations and personnel that conduct them are directly supported by intelligence people and capabilities with much more importance than general support to non-DoD customers. After all, the returns and impacts of this type of intelligence are dramatic and decisive with immediate feedback. Intelligence for the purpose of only providing situational awareness or background information for decision-maker not in the midst of a high stakes and high visibility operation has fallen to the second tier of importance and priority.

While technology has allowed a tremendous amount of information to be collected and processed, it has also allowed for the passing of more information to the lowest levels. Instead of making the standard tasks easier and faster, intelligence customers have increased their requirements and now expect better information in higher quantities from the same people. This has translated into expectations that intelligence will provide much more than the information that intelligence customers can easily get themselves. They want more insight, and original analysis rather than regurgitation of some news story.

Unfortunately, analyzing raw information in order to produce intelligence takes time. It is this time that is no longer available in many operations. Intelligence customers at the operational and tactical levels cannot afford to spend waiting on an in-depth analytical answer from intelligence personnel who need that time to collect, process, analyze, and produce a product for them.

4. Intelligence Requirements Are Overloading the Structure of the Current Intelligence Community

> Not a single item in our trillion-dollar arsenal can compare with the genius of the suicide bomber—the breakthrough weapon of our time. Our intelligence systems cannot locate him, our arsenal cannot deter him, and, all too often, our soldiers cannot stop him before it is too late.
>
> Ralph Peters 2006, *The Counterrevolution of Military Affairs*[28]

Building upon the idea that the intelligence environment has changed, intelligence customers and their requirements have also changed. What has not changed significantly is the overall structure or hierarchy of the national intelligence community. The most recent creation of DHS and ODNI represent a consolidation and addition to the community, respectively, but they are not so revolutionary that the structure of this community has been altered in any serious way.

The history of U.S. intelligence is full of many successes that we will never know of. Unfortunately, we know of many failures, some of them spectacular. Many of these can be laid more squarely on the intelligence community—rather than with our customers. Often times, U.S. intelligence capabilities were beaten by simple deception, cunningness, and the ability of the U.S. enemies to keep their intentions hidden until too late. From an asymmetric stand point, they were able to exploit weaknesses despite the strengths United States had in military, or in economic and financial resources.

Many failures of intelligence are not the fault of the analyst at all. In many of these cases, the decision-maker was presented with an accurate picture of the enemy, but simply made the wrong decision. Even when presented with the best intelligence available, it is unjustified to blame intelligence when the policies or communications fail. Failure to portray an accurate picture is intelligence's fault and rightly so. Making the wrong decision is not and pointing

---

28   Peters, Ralph. (2006, February 6). *The counterrevolution of military affairs. The Weekly Standard*, 11(20).

fingers at the intelligence community in these instances does nothing to learn and improve our operations. With the figure-pointing that inevitably follows any significant intelligence failure, accusations are merely indicators of largely underlying problems. Sometimes the problem is properly identified and fixed; sometimes only the symptoms are remedied.

Ralph Peters, a former military intelligence officer and well-known columnist on national security affairs hit the nail on the head with his assessment that the intelligence community will never meet the expectations of our customers. Why? Because in his view, their expectations are unrealistic. While he claims that the intelligence community can be improved, the thing that needs to change the most is that "our fantastic expectations must be lowered to a level in accord with our present and potential capabilities."[29]

In some cases, the U.S. Intelligence Community actually helps to propagate false expectations. Intelligence officials, those who deem themselves "visionaries" within an intelligence agency or organization will claim that their intelligence program, software, suite of tools, collection platform, and network of collaboration will revolutionize the previous paradigm. All too often what the intelligence community delivers is something different altogether. In the meantime, that visionary has since moved on to another duty station or position leaving his vision half-baked or broken at best. Until the intelligence community provides realistic expectations themselves, they will always be seen as delivering one failed promise after another to an increasingly skeptical customer.

In reality, many of these skeptical intelligence consumers are looking more and more to their own organizations for intelligence support. Instead of buying the smoke and mirrors of some far away agency, they are looking at what resources they have, what could be available given today's technology, and how they could move themselves to the front of the line in terms of a priority customer for analytical products dedicated to their problem sets and requirements. The same pattern of evolution that has taken place in military intelligence almost a century ago is now taking place everywhere else.

5. Analysis Is Moving Outside of the Intelligence Community

> So instead of asking "Does DIA have a better counterterrorism analyst than we do?" he said, units are motivated to get their own so they won't have to coordinate, they can get their product out faster, and can build strength in their stovepipe.
>
> Sebastian Abbot quoting John Gannon,
> former CIA Deputy Director for Intelligence.[30]

---

29   Peters, Ralph. *Our strategic intelligence problem.* Retrieved from www.realclearpolitics.com/articles/2006/08/our_strategic_intelligence_pro.html

30   Abbot, Sebastian. (2006, July 28). The outsourcing of US intelligence analysis. *News21.* A journalism initiative of the Carnegie and Knight Foundations. Retrieved from http://newsinitiative.org/story/2006/07/28/the_outsourcing_of_u_s_intelligence

Given this overwhelming need for intelligence-related information and the inability of the current national structure to satisfy the requirements from the expanding customer base, it's no wonder that the business of intelligence is becoming everyone's business.

Decision-makers within every sector of our society are coming to the realization that more and more intelligence is need to support their operations. It has to come from somewhere. One approach is to turn to a massive well-established industry that has been in operation for several decades. The United States arguably has the best intelligence apparatus in the world successfully providing intelligence to national-level decision-makers, military campaigns, and security operations with a few (albeit glaring) mistakes. Others, though have chosen to conduct intelligence analysis themselves rely upon a combination of the intelligence community, their own data, and what's available in the public domain for information.

Creating an *effective* intelligence capability within any type of non-intelligence organization can be a very expensive undertaking. There are costs associated with hiring or contracting the right people, getting access to the right data, and buying (and integrating) the right tools. These startup costs are both steep and recurring for what in essence is analyzed information.

The national intelligence community provides an already established architecture to support a wide variety of customers with quality analysis that meets vigorous vetting standards prior to dissemination. So why, then, are intelligence customers doing their intelligence—often at greater expense? The answer lies in the difference between *having* intelligence support and *owning* intelligence support.

By creating their own intelligence analysis capability in-house, decision-makers become the number one customer at all times. They get to set what the intelligence priorities are, establish when you want it, and at what intervals. Instead of waiting for a product to get thrown over the proverbial wall to them, they have the ability to interact with the both the collectors and the analysts throughout the Intelligence Cycle.

Thanks to information technology, the gap between homegrown intelligence and what the national intelligence community can provide in terms of quality and quantity is closing every year. If a non-intelligence organization has access to classified information, this gap is even smaller. Decision-makers who have their own intelligence assets or capability are also the final authority on whether or not the intelligence their own organization has created has met their requirements. With national-level intelligence created for national-level customers, one size has to fit all.

Organizations that have relied upon solid intelligence analysis from the national-level intelligence community are still there. But what they want is changing more so today than ever before. Add to this an expansive customer base far beyond what could have been imagined even a decade ago and you have a logical conclusion. The consumers of intelligence are creating their own capabilities. In applying this to a program management model, having their own internal intelligence shop allows decision-makers/owners to determine the quality, the speed at which it is provided, and how much it will cost to run such a shop within their group.

Not only are traditional intelligence customers creating their own assets, but the newer customers are as well. They are standing up their own intelligence centers. They are creating their own intelligence divisions, hiring their own analysts, collecting their own information, and disseminating their own products. Intelligence operations, something that used to only occupy the imaginations of most Americans, are now being performed by an exponentially growing number of us. Because analysis needs people, many organizations are realigning their investigators, agents, officers, and other personnel normally associated with operations into analytical roles. "Instead of putting four more police officers on the street" they ask, "why don't we dedicate a couple of people to analysis so that they can step back, identify patterns of these crimes, profile the individuals involved and show us how to make our criminal investigations more efficient and properly focused?" In a world of limited resources, having a few analysts can be as cost effective as an entire office full of investigators.

So, while the intelligence community undergoes reform after reform, vision after vision, reorganization after reorganization, the business of intelligence has slipped beyond its bureaucratic and parochial barriers.[31]

6. The U.S. Intelligence Community Is Evolving into a More Diverse and Expansive Community

> First thing we must do is know this: We are, all of us and each of us, part of the new U.S. defense. We are all soldiers now. We have been drafted by history. And we must be watchful and protective soldiers.
>
> Peggy Noonan, *Wall Street Journal*, November 2, 2001;
> in response to the attacks on 9/11.[32]

This last factor is actually the result of the first five. The business of intelligence is no longer just the business of the U.S. Intelligence Community, it's everyone's business. Thinking about threats, how they can affect operations, disrupt lives, and endanger people and assets affects nearly every organization. Intelligence has escaped the confines of national government as it is no longer just the job of a few select intelligence professionals sitting in classified facilities with multitudes of information coming across their screens.

The U.S. Intelligence Community, its structure, personnel, collection and data mining assets, and its massive analytical capabilities, is the best in the world. It does what's it's supposed to do—provide intelligence support for our national security and foreign relations along with the key decision-makers at those levels. The intelligence community of practice is vastly larger than that as it includes all sectors where intelligence is practiced.

---

31   Clift, A. Denis. Intelligence in the internet era. *CIA Studies in Intelligence*. Retrieved from www.cia.gov/csi/studies/vol47/no3/article06.html

32   Noonan, Peggy. (2001, November 2). We're all soldiers now: Survival tips for the new war. *Wall Street Journal*.

Mapping the Intelligence Community of Practice (ICOP)

It is virtually impossible to visualize or map out what this community of practice actually looks like using traditional line and block chart or similarly traditional hierarchical models. One of the reasons for this is that those who are practicing intelligence in our society no longer exclusively trace themselves back to the U.S. Intelligence Community. So, instead of trying to visualize the 16-member agencies and the Officer of the Director of National Intelligence (ODNI) at the head of a vast and expanding structure, it is easier and more accurate to visualize today's intelligence community as a series of concentric rings that group together entities that share common characteristics for how they *practice* intelligence (see Figure 3.7).

In this map, the 16-member agencies of the U.S.Intelligence Community along with the Office of the Director of National Intelligence are not the entire community of practice. While they are strictly defined in terms of U.S. Executive Order 12333, the business and practice of intelligence is a much larger world. In terms of its age, resources, structure, and stability of as the leader of U.S. intelligence, it should be considered the core of a rapidly expanding community of intelligence practitioners.

While its emergence was slow prior to 9/11, the ring just outside of the Core 17 grew rapidly as in the years following the Al Qaeda's dramatic attacks. These are the low-density IC members. Organizations within this ring are either relatively new or have a relatively intelligence role, function, or capability. Intelligence capabilities within these organizations are considered low-density in that they take the form of sections, directorates, or subdivisions inside these organizations. These sections exist to support their own organization as a primary mission while support to the larger intelligence community is secondary.

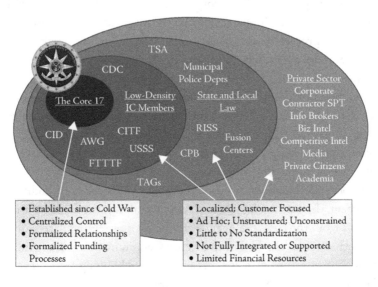

FIGURE 3.7   Today's intelligence community

From an official command and control perspective, almost every organization within the low-density IC member ring can trace its authorities and responsibilities back to one of the Core 17 organizations. The intelligence function within them is seen as much more remove from the U.S. Intelligence Community proper. Many of the intelligence personnel within these of the members of these organizations do not necessarily consider themselves as an integrated part of the intelligence community; their identity primarily leans toward their own organization first.

The ring contains organizations that conduct intelligence at the state, local, municipal, and tribal levels. Because of this the focus of intelligence, here is in direct support of law enforcement, emergency management, and homeland security missions. Organizations within this realm specifically do not trace back to the U.S. Intelligence Community even though they may coordinate with and benefit from it. The predominant types of organizations are police departments at various levels from the state down, but can also include state and regional fusion centers with a more refined or regional focus of their efforts.

The outer ring is perhaps the largest, most unconstrained, unregulated, and as a consequence, undefined. This ring includes commercial businesses, nonprofit organizations, and even private citizens conducting intelligence on their own. It also includes the study of intelligence through schools and universities.

This outer ring exists because of the need for intelligence in understanding threats to the business, success, or survivability of organizations in this environment. As discussed in the previous chapter, these threats aren't necessary deadly enemies, but they are adversaries and competitors—again taking a more broad-based view of what constitutes a threat.

Businesses practice competitive intelligence for several reasons. From a protective standpoint, these businesses need to safeguard their physical assets, their properties and equipment. They also need to protected their employees, intellectual property, and processes to conduct their business. From this perspective, the critical components businesses need to protect are the same critical components that make up an effective intelligence operation: data, tools, people, and processes.

In academia, intelligence has been codified in various curriculums. For a majority of programs, intelligence studies are found within other programs ranging from homeland or national security, political science, criminology, or even some of the harder sciences such as geographic studies. For an over $50 billion industry at the U.S. Federal Government alone, it is amazing that there are only a few schools that teach intelligence as a stand-alone degree conferring program.

While the core of this community operates in a relatively structured, codified, and regulated environment, the outside rings do not. As a general rule, the further the organization on this chart is from the core intelligence group, the more unregulated, unstructured, and unstandardized it is. The U.S.l Intelligence Community and all organizations that trace back to it are governed by a congressional oversight along several oversight regulations. Organizations in the outermost rings are under no such parentage. Oversight rules, budgetary reviews, ethics panels, or any other methods to regulate the conduct of intelligence operations are simply nonexistent in commercial or private organizations.

While there are privacy laws in the United States and elsewhere, the unrestricted nature of the Internet make enforcement of these laws extremely difficult.

The Bottom-Up View of the Intelligence Community

Despite the need to understand the intelligence community from the ground up, the concentric map of today's intelligence community still requires a top-down view. This concentric map was created by positioning entire organizations as the pieces in the puzzle. While it's important to understand the intelligence community at the national level, for the both working professional and student, their intelligence community is a community of practice rather than a collection of federal entities. To them, their community is where intelligence is conducted as both operation and business. Understanding in detail about some other intelligence operations over the horizon in some other part of the community isn't going to help their operation. Their more immediate need is to know about their own foxhole and what's going on to their immediate surroundings. A bottom-up view of the intelligence community is shown in Figure 3.8.

As stated earlier in this chapter, to learn about the intelligence community from a bottom-up approach, intelligence professionals must use the bottom-up or an inward–outward approach, starting with an understanding of their position and working your way out from there. Once they have an understanding of their roles and responsibilities, which will most likely be dictated or assigned, intelligence professionals should then learn about how their position fits within their section or division within an organization.

Going outward and upward from their position, intelligence professionals should learn the various roles and responsibilities at each level to include those that are both specified

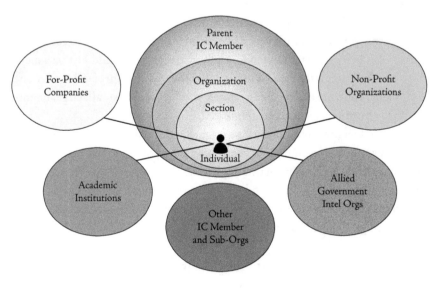

FIGURE 3.8   Bottom-up view of the intelligence community

and implied. This is important because understanding at each level helps to define several aspects important to functions and requirements of a specific position such as primary and secondary customers, supporting assets and resources, legal authorities and restrictions, and analytical requirements among others.

From there the entire community that is in close proximity to the intelligence professional and their organization should be learned well enough so that it is clear who they need to work with, how responsibilities may overlap or compliment, where they will get their data, and other critical aspects of the individual position. The rest of the community will remain somewhat blurred, but learning all of it is both impossible and not necessary for them to do their job and understand their mission and operating requirements.

From this point, intelligence professionals can then much more easily gain an understanding where their organization fits within the rest of the intelligence community. From an organization's perspective, where it fits within the community affects almost every aspect of operations: mission and operational responsibility, customers and production requirements, chain of command and reporting responsibilities, intelligence oversight and legal restrictions, and of course—funding. Many other professional networks, including combat units, police and fire departments, and even sports teams are learned in the same way; why should intelligence be any different?

Unlike the military or similar organizations that have a high degree of standardization, most intelligence organizations have little in the way of standardization. Instead, many are organized according to required functions, requirements, and individual vision and imagination. This can present quite a challenge, especially in an organization that changes its internal structure every couple of years for what would seem to be random, political, or some other capricious, personality driven reasons. Learning about your intelligence community therefore is best done from within an organization and it must be revisited periodically.

In gaining an understanding of where the intelligence professional and their organization fits in the world, the result is of a like-minded community that is relevant to their efforts. This can be an actual drawn out or physical map or it could just be a mental picture. This, in effect, is intelligence community from individual professional as a network of your personal contacts and working relationships. It can be small, large, or enormous depending on the criteria is used to define it.

The U.S. Intelligence Community is so large that not a single person, even at the most senior levels has an understanding of everything going on in it.[33] While no intelligence professional really must accomplish this impossible task, it is only after having the context of the individual position, section, and organization within the larger intelligence community can intelligence professionals more effectively begin to look at the other critical aspects of intelligence operations.

---

33   Priest, Dana, & Arkin, William M. (2010, July 19). A hidden world, growing beyond control. *Washington Post*. Retrieved from http://projects.washingtonpost.com/top-secret-america/articles/a-hidden-world-growing-beyond-control/

Summary

The practice of intelligence is as old as the ages, and has been part of the American story since our beginning days. U.S. intelligence has evolved along three different paths, national-political, military, and law enforcement. Today, based on the changing technology, threats, and customer requirements, intelligence is a diverse and desegregated community that has expanded beyond what is thought of as the traditional intelligence community, appearing in every facet of society. The map of where intelligence is conducted is as diverse as the threats within each of society's segments. Understanding today's intelligence community is best if seen as a map where the members of the national intelligence are merely the core of a greater community of practice that includes low-density members, state and local governments, and law-enforcement and the private sector, the latter being perhaps the largest and most significant sector of growth over the past 30 years.

Key Summary Points

+ While many students learn about the U.S. Intelligence Community from a top-down approach, it is critical for those professional to also learn about their own community from a bottom-up or inward-outward approach.
+ U.S. intelligence is as old as the first days as our nation. U.S. intelligence traditions have mirrored our military traditions in that up until World War II, it was developed by necessity. Any significant steps forward were temporary and fleeting as a particular conflict ended.
+ After World War II, U.S. intelligence—like our military industrial complex—became a permanent structure.
+ As the Cold War continued new organizations that were largely based on collection technologies were simply added to the existing structure.
+ In most recent years, several key factors have influenced the evolution of what could now be considered today's intelligence community of practice.

    1. The intelligence environment is changing.
    2. Our customers are changing.
    3. They now have new expectations and requirements.
    4. Intelligence requirements are overwhelming the structure of the current intelligence community.
    5. Analysis is moving outside of the intelligence community.
    6. The U.S. Intelligence Community is evolving into a more diverse and expansive community.

+ In order for intelligence professional to more effectively understand the myriad of challenges affecting their operation, they must create their intelligence community, starting with their own position, their section, and their organization within the context of who they work with on a regular basis.

Discussion Questions

+ What were the primary evolutionary factors and revolutionary events that have molded the U.S. Intelligence Community into what it looks like today?
+ In what ways has advances in Information Technology served as a catalyst for the continuing evolution of the intelligence community?
+ What are the major differences between the U.S. Intelligence Community and the intelligence community of practice detailed in Figure 3.7?
+ How does understanding the Intelligence Community from a top-down versus a bottom-up approach help the intelligence professional?

Figure Credits

Fig. 3.1: Source: http://www.the-athenaeum.org/art/detail.php?ID=22665.

Fig. 3.2: Source: https://commons.wikimedia.org/wiki/File:Robert_E._Lee.jpg.

Fig. 3.3: Source: https://commons.wikimedia.org/wiki/File:PinkertonLincolnMcClernand.jpg.

Fig. 3.4: Source: https://commons.wikimedia.org/wiki/File:USSArizona_PearlHarbor_2.jpg.

Fig. 3.5: Source: https://commons.wikimedia.org/wiki/File:Sr71_1.jpg.

Fig. 3.6: Mark Stanley, "IDTF," 2019.

Fig. 3.7a: Source: https://inpublicsafety.com/2015/08/intelligence-work-expands-beyond-the-core-intelligence-community-and-so-should-your-job-search/.

Fig. 3.7b: Source: https://commons.wikimedia.org/wiki/File:United_States_Intelligence_Community_Seal.svg.

Chapter 4

Intelligence Operations and Centers

Learning Objectives

After completing this chapter, you will be able to:

▸ Understand what intelligence operations and intelligence centers are along with their differences.

▸ Be familiar with the most common challenges for all intelligence operations.

▸ Understand the three main functions of an intelligence center along with their varied configurations.

▸ Be familiar with the four pillars of every intelligence operation.

Similar Uniqueness

One of the pitfalls within the mindset of intelligence professionals is the tendency for some to think that their intelligence operation is unique to other operations. Their organization may be the only one conducting intelligence for a specific operation or they may be using bleeding-edge technology tools that are being developed or improved by software engineers on a daily basis. They may also be the only organization that is focused on a particular target or that produces a set of required intelligence products.

Because of the focus of their mission, the customers they support, or the type of analysis they conduct, many, especially more senior professionals, can fall into an intellectual trap where they believe their operation is so completely different than all other intelligence operations that the foundational elements of a successful operation simply don't apply to them. Simple requirements, standards, and procedures don't need to be followed.

A typical statement aligned with this sort of mindset would be, "We're different than everyone else because of the type of intelligence we have to produce. The rules everyone else uses don't really apply to us." In other words, because their operation is so specialized or has unique aspects to it, they don't need to operate using the same methods that everyone else does.[1]

In reality, no intelligence operation is completely unique as there are inescapable commonalities and standard operating procedures (SOPs) that apply to everyone. For starters, whether they are in one of the large standing federal trigraph agencies, out on the periphery of the U.S. Intelligence Community, or somewhere not even in what would be considered the IC such as the commercial world, each intelligence operation serves the same baseline purpose as all the others—that of collecting, processing, analyzing, and presenting their findings in support of someone else, e.g., the customer. All other common features exist in intelligence operations because of the primary mission to support someone else.

What *is* unique to an intelligence operation is the particular customer, mission, capabilities, and operating practices and procedures. An operation may access different data, use different sets of tools, or even have a different physical look than other intelligence operations, but the foundational functions required to turn incoming information into analyzed intelligence that will support a customer's decisions cannot be escaped. An operation may be unique in many respects, but these aspects of the operation have an inescapable similarity to every other intelligence operation.

To support the customer, every intelligence operation must have four aspects that are in effective working order. These four "pillars" are data, tools, people, and processes. Along with the other aspects of intelligence operations, these pillars vary according to several external factors, but overall each of them must be functioning, and more specifically, functioning together in order to guarantee successful support.

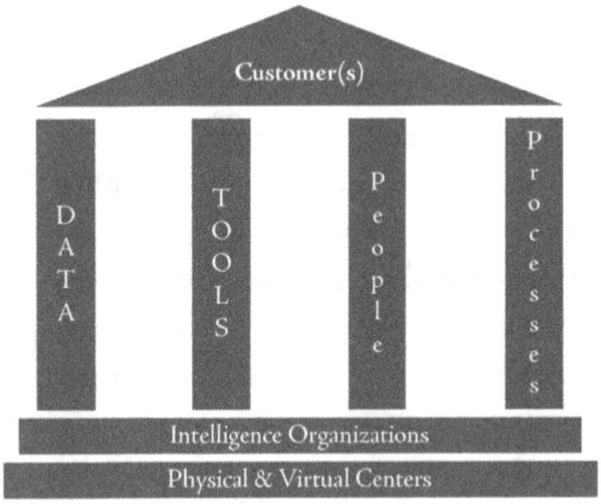

Finally, two more aspects that all intelligence operations use to function are the process of intelligence itself—also known as the Intelligence Cycle—and a center of operations. Like a car or aircraft engine, the Intelligence Cycle is a fairly straightforward baseline process all intelligence operations must generally follow in order to function. The center on the other hand can be a combination of a physical facility or facilities and some sort of virtual presence or network that helps to tie the four pillars together. As much as the Acropolis

FIGURE 4.1   Common elements of all intelligence operations

---

1   This was a paraphrased response to an informal training needs assessment I was conducting for a customer while a defense contractor with a midsize company. The manager in question was using the interview to impart to me that they didn't need any formal training program, their software engineers could teach their analysts everything they needed to know right on the operations floor.

diagram is somewhat a cliché in business and academic circles, the simplicity of this model fits well for intelligence operations.

Again, every intelligence operation is going to have different looks to each of these elements. They must be different because their customers and the environment they operate in are different. The intent here is to provoke some issues and ideas that will help develop specific plans and solutions.

Semi-Interchangeable Terms: Intelligence Centers and Intelligence Operations

For clarity, an intelligence center is normally the single physical space where the business of intelligence takes place, whereas an intelligence operation (or Intel Op) is the function of intelligence, i.e., what happens at an intelligence center or elsewhere. For example, a single intelligence center can be on multiple floors, in different parts of the same building, or be located across several buildings in close proximity to each other. Any further subdivision or distance constitutes multiple centers. Each can fall under one intelligence operation at one time or another. An intelligence operation, on the other hand, can refer to operations within a center, an intelligence section, branch, division, directorate, or any other intangible capability. An intelligence center generally refers to a geographic location, whereas an intelligence operation is a function that can be conducted in one or multiple locations.

In terms of personnel, an intelligence center can have between 4 (like a single tactical vehicle) and 4,000 persons (spread out over a large or several large facilities). They can keep business hours or operate on a 24-hour cycle. There will most likely be areas of specialization within the center, but the personnel in the center as a whole will share a common mission and purpose, serving one or more related operations at a time.

As a subset of intelligence operations, intelligence collection is also an operation in itself as it involves a complex set of processes, techniques, and tradecraft to collect data, information, or finished intelligence as a feeder for further analysis and production. It often runs persistently and concurrently to analysis and is externally and independently run. Analysts rely upon both incidental and directly collected information without regard to their specific mission sets.

Challenges to Intelligence Operations

Intelligence operations are like any other business operations—fraught with challenges to its efficiency. Every single intelligence organization, unit, or center has its strengths while also being beset with inefficiencies. Often times these inefficiencies rule the day. The primary reason for this is many intelligence managers understand intelligence, but not "the business" of intelligence.

When using the term business, intelligence must be looked at as a service-oriented operation that provides analysis and information as a commodity to its customers.

The success of this service depends on the efficiency of the operation, the timeliness and quality of the product, and ultimately the satisfaction of the customer. Each intelligence operation operates in a nascent and skewed marketplace with various customers seeking intelligence and information support from the available customers.

Much has been written and spoken about the failures of intelligence, especially in the last few years. Key decisions that shaped the direction of national security have been torn apart by our nation's pundit class and Monday morning quarterbacks, often with an accusing finger directed at intelligence and the part it has played. Indeed, bad intelligence is the result of many mistakes decision-makers have made, but where many of the critics of intelligence are wrong is where they tend to lay blame on faulty analysis. In most cases, it's not the analysis itself that has been the source of the failure as much as the failure in the management of intelligence operations.

Failure can also be rightly attributed to the decision-maker who makes the wrong decision based upon good intelligence, but that's not the correct focus. In the words of one of my most respected commanders, "Intel never gets to say, 'Told ya so.'"[2] So, while near-perfect intelligence cannot guarantee the right decision or a successful operation, it's not the job of the intelligence professionals to spend time pointing fingers at every operational failure.

Intelligence operations are meant to give the analyst a purpose, mission, and working environment so that they do their job, which is quite simply to conduct analysis. Where the operational challenges lie, therefore, is not necessarily with the individual but with how analysts are organized, empowered to do their work, and how the process of intelligence is supposed to work across a functioning organization. By looking at intelligence failures and where they most likely occur, here are some of the top challenges of intelligence operations:

CHART 4.1   Key Challenges to Intelligence Operations

1. Physical location, layout, and architecture
2. Repetitive tasks
3. Leadership and management
4. Organization and operating processes
5. Training and professional development
6. Understanding who is the customer
7. Analytical culture
8. Budget
9. Parochialism and stagnation
10. Current ops versus long-range planning

---

2   As the new intelligence officer of a mechanized infantry battalion, my battalion commander, the then LTC Carter Ham let me know this during a training battle in which the opposing force followed the template created before the battle, but our unit planned for them to do something different. Being right in intelligence is worthless if you can't convince your supported decision-maker that your analysis is sound.

Going into these challenges in a bit more detail:

1. **Physical Design and Layout:** A majority of intelligence operations take place in an area or facility that was not originally designed for intelligence, especially operations that relyheavily upon the latest technology. Analysts make the best of cube farms, refurbished basements, repurposed buildings, operational command and control centers, and even tactical vehicles that were designed for some other purpose. Since there is little that can change this dilemma, the best approach is to ask what can be done to tailor operations in the given environment. Added to the physical complexities is the architecture put in place for receiving, organizing, storing, and retrieving pertinent data and information. Much of it was suited for systems that have since been outdated by newer technologies.

2. **Repetitive Tasks:** A large majority of intelligence and investigative work involves repetition. Think of it this way: Watch a criminal investigation show like *CSI* or *Law & Order.* Take out all the drama and "sexiness." Now watch the same episode eight times in a row. That's what one shift can be like working in an intelligence center. Repeat for every shift in a week and almost every week in a month and you get the idea what some of the most repetitive intelligence work is like. While intelligence may look different in each agency or organization—as I've mentioned throughout this book—the basic process of collecting, processing, analyzing, producing, and disseminating remains consistent no matter how "high speed or low drag" the operation is. Analysts who get to take on a new task that involves learning as a large part of it are more apt to be more imaginative, motivated, and energetic. Analysts who spend day after day looking at the lines of data, signal traffic will quickly become bored and apathetic.

3. **Leadership and Management:** Or rather, poor leadership and management. Command climate represents one of the largest and persistent complaints of analysts. Many complain about feeling like mushrooms or, in their words, being fed feces and left in the dark. Common complaints range from nonexistent communications to a general lack of feedback or appreciation for their work. In a very simplistic sense, great analytical skills do not equate to skills in management and leadership. Analysis is an introverted sport. As a workforce, analysts require adequate situational awareness, guidance, and vision, as well as avenues for their ideas, complaints, and solutions. Want to know if an organization is successful in meeting these requirements? Look at their attrition rate. If it's like a revolving door, there is a management and leadership problem, not an operational or analytical problem.

4. **Organization and Operating Processes:** This challenge is actually another result of poor leadership and management cited above. Every intelligence center has some sort of organization, but it may not be effective. Does it change every six months in some manner according to someone else's "vision"? Are the subdivisions

a hindrance to operations or do they enhance interaction? If there are problems in an organization, it may be based off of personality rather than requirements and capabilities. Similarly, processes also must work consistently. Too often, SOPs are the reflection of someone's personality or ego rather than focused on getting the mission done. If an operation has stated processes, but analysts are going around them as a rule rather than an exception, then the processes are broken. It's time to reassess why they were put in place.

5. **Training and Professional Development:** Training is often perceived as an afterthought, but is critically important. It's also a victim of budget constraints. General training topics can include threats, supported operations, technology, tools, databases, analytical techniques, and oversight regulations. Other topics of discussion could be, how well does an organization's analyst know these subject areas? Do they have an in-depth understanding of all the tools and databases at their disposal? How does an operation incorporate new technologies, new operating procedures or changes to analytical methods? What resources or programs are in place to meet the training needs of personnel?

6. **Understanding Who Is the Customer:** Who is the customer after all? Here's a big surprise to many of the heads of intelligence centers—it's not them. One of the common misconceptions of intelligence centers is that the centers are an entity in themselves and therefore the primary customers of their own intelligence. As important as these centers can be, when they are organizations in their own right, they have a tendency to operate in their own self-interest. Here lies the inherent danger of a center that self-identifies. Just as intelligence is for the customer first and foremost, an intelligence center works for those customers— not itself. Conducting analysis to support itself is an outgrowth of the political aspects of a self-identifying center. If the term "self-licking ice-cream cone" is thrown around in the daily discussion of the analysts in an intelligence center, there is a problem.

7. **Analytical Culture:** In most intelligence centers, analysts face a daunting challenge between their immediate threats and those over the horizon. Demands of customers for analysis on individual targets and the next 72 hours have pushed priorities away from longer term analysis. Understanding the historical, political, and cultural environment takes time and doesn't directly translate into a definable product or show results. Analysts are exceptional at tracking individual events and people and placing them in context of a network or group. As a trade-off, intelligence is losing the ability to grow analysts who can delve deep into a subject to some of the core motivations or rooted causes, hatreds, ideologies, or long-term trends.

8. **Budget:** Every intelligence operation requires money to operate. Funding goes into an operation in order to support a consumer. Poor levels of funding and/or mismanagement are some of the easiest ways to kill effective intelligence operations. Some funding restraints are obvious. Going cheap on experienced personnel, automation equipment, or data access gives exactly the same poor result, i.e.,

worthless or faulty products. Other funding challenges are harder to see. Training and professional development of personnel are some of the first things that are cut when budgets are constrained.

9. **Parochialism and Stagnation:** Because intelligence deals primarily with information, and information is power, intelligence professionals have a strong tendency to protect their information as a means of protecting their jobs. To these folks, freely sharing information without attribution is simply giving away the keys to their kingdoms. Resistance to sharing information is epidemic in some intelligence organizations. Rules that would normally look like security or oversight protection are habitually perverted to become bureaucratic barriers to sharing information for the protection of the analysts. If it sounds antithetical to the purpose of intelligence, it is—but it exists anyways.

10. **Current Ops Versus Long-Range Planning:** For intelligence support to a customer, it has to be relevant. Getting overwhelmed by the day-to-day flow of world events causes an intelligence customer and its supporting intelligence to concentrate on current intelligence or simply on reporting what happened while only looking forward between 36 and 72 hours. Long-range and in-depth analysis can quickly take a back seat to an intelligence center trying to compete with mainstream news outlets. As a result, an intelligence center becomes nothing more than "CNN with secrets" providing little that a customer can get themselves at no cost. This is way too much money for someone to regurgitate the news.

While there are definitely more challenges than those listed here, the above list covers a vast majority of troubles that can pop-up in every operation. They pose a direct threat to an intelligence center's ability to perform the crucial functions of a successful operation, and therefore a threat to their ability to support someone else.

One of the first tasks in looking at an intelligence operation is to take a hard look to see where (not if) these challenges exist and to what degree are they affecting the way the owner and the supported customer want to do business.

Assessing the Mission and Purpose of an Intelligence Operation

Whether it's a small section within an organization or an entirely stand-alone unit with multiple divisions of labor and authorities, creating a new intelligence capability or refining an existing one requires an understanding of many areas above and beyond the general nature and purpose of collecting and analyzing information about the threat. In designing and developing intelligence operations, it is easy to lose the original mission and purpose of the organization. Staying focused on the general intent and direction of the organization, when an operation's personnel are in the obscuring weeds of details and minutiae, must be a guiding principle along every step of the way.

The key to success in assessing the mission and purpose of an intelligence operation is in understanding that each must include the right levels of some critical components, coupled with effective management and the guiding hands of leadership.

As hit upon earlier, the foundational principle of having an intelligence capability is to support a customer. Again, they are the pivot point and the fulcrum for the balance of the entire operation. The design, development, and creation of an intelligence operation must be done in the context of what the customer needs, not what the analyst needs or would like. Every part of the mission, purpose, functions, and operational processes, should be created or redefined so that the support to a consumer of intelligence is always the driving factor. When considering what an intelligence operation needs to do, look to the customer's requirements. Within their requirements are the implied requirements of what the supporting intelligence operation also has to have.

Consider the following nine questions:

CHART 4.2   Nine Questions to Help Shape Intelligence Operations

1. Who drives the operation?
2. What is the mission/purpose of the customer(s) or their organization(s)?
3. What are the threats they are concerned with?
4. What are their organizational challenges?
5. What are the intelligence products they need to make decisions about their threats?
6. When and how often do they need these products?
7. What are their restrictions or limitations in using intelligence?
8. Does the customer already have an intelligence capability in support or does it need a new one?
9. What is the customer's knowledge/appreciation level for intelligence?

These questions seem pretty basic, but they are a critical first step toward improving or building a new intelligence capability. Sidestepping them is a way to certain failure. Just as with any other start-up business, intelligence organization must have a reason for existing other than because there are bad guys out there. Each of these questions is centered on the need to provide support to the customer among other drivers.

Intelligence Drivers

The way to start answering these questions is to understand the answer to the first question—what and who drives the operation. When building a new home, the person who is paying for its construction, i.e., the person with the money is the driver. Same goes for any project, be it making a movie, building a new website, or writing a competitive proposal.

While the primary driver for any intelligence operation is its mission and purpose, intelligence is a service-centered business like any others and is therefore driven by the people who sponsor or pay for it. This is true for both the people who provide as well as those who receive it.

As far as *who* drives a specific intelligence operation, the two primary drivers of that organization are the customer and the owner. This may or may not be the same person or organization. It's important to understand the distinction between the two. While the entire purpose of intelligence is the customer, it's the owner that makes things happen for them. If it's the same person or organization, it will be harder yet less important to make this distinction.

The owner may be the primary customer of intelligence produced by that center, or it may be one of the several organizations that benefit from it. An owner may also be a parent organization or a single person that runs the facility, but does so for an external customer.

Customers of intelligence drive the what, when, and why of intelligence operations. If they are outside of the organization they are seeking support from, they don't usually dictate a center's processes or resource allocation. In some cases, their priorities will also have to be balanced with the capabilities of the center in context with everyone else that center is simultaneously supporting.

What distinguishes the owner from everyone else is that the owner pays the bills. With that responsibility is the rule that he who controls the money controls the operating processes and the business rhythm even if they don't drive requirements. Owners are the primary drivers in how intelligence operations are conducted. If they don't drive this for themselves then they do it for someone else—the customer or consumer of intelligence.

The owner also drives the priorities of an intelligence center, as they are the ones that should be best poised to understand what the current capabilities and limitations of the center are. They should know what kinds of products are possible, how long it will generally take, and how much workload an analyst can handle in a given time frame. They should know how many resources it takes to create a given product both in terms of people, infrastructure, and other direct costs. They should also know what their center can't do, what their restraints are, and other limitations based on technical or human factors.

Intelligence follows most of the same principles that drives any other market-based industry. Just because a large part of it involves government doesn't mean market influences aren't there. The primary interaction between a customer and the owner of an intelligence center is similar to any other service-oriented business.

For example, following the project management triangle, an intelligence customer can have intelligence support fast, cheap, and in high quality, they just have to pick which two of the three they want. That is to say, if a customer needs a detailed intelligence product tomorrow, the costs are going to be a lot higher than if they need it in a couple of weeks. If they want something quickly without assigning or spending a lot of resources to get it, the quality of support will be very basic. This principle has a lot of different names associated with it in the business world, but it is basically the same in every type of customer-oriented business. Intelligence is not unique or different in this respect.

Need more proof of the importance of a customer for an intelligence center? Imagine one without a definable and dedicated customer or customer base and predict how long it will last. Intelligence operations are a continual drain on resources both in terms of technology and people. Like any business, if there isn't a customer there is no point of spending resources. Business—so to speak—dries up, people go find other work, and the intelligence operation goes out of business.

Spending resources on intelligence is even more difficult to justify because of the lack of any immediate tangible benefit. Tailored intelligence products do not have much of a persistent or intrinsic market value to someone other than the original customer. This is especially true when budgets get tight as they so often are.

So, while the customer drives the requirements of intelligence, i.e., what, where, when, and why, it's the owner that drives the how. The owners do this by building and operating a center that uses critical components to balance the cost, schedule, and quality of their product in order to meet the requirements of the customer.

Physical Layout

While not a driver, one of the unavoidable influences on an intelligence operation is the physical center or centers it occupies. As stated earlier, every operation takes up some sort of physical space to conduct business; this is the intelligence center. The virtual space is part of this, but it is considered here only in terms of how information enters and moves within the physical space.

Just like building any facility—no matter the size—creating the physical space for an intelligence center is quite a complex operation. Whether building a new facility or converting an old facility into an intelligence center, there are a myriad of considerations, requirements, and necessities that must be taken into account. Some are human driven, physically driven, or legally driven. The physical structure, the hardware and storage space requirements, electricity and power requirements, lighting and noise, sanitation, physical security and other related issues must be taken into account. Once people enter into the mix, issues will also include the safety and access requirements, air flow, lavatories, water, personal storage, aesthetics, and so many other considerations that require the expertise of an entire team of planners.

In the midst of physically creating a center, intelligence operators are also trying to make sure it will handle their operations. While some centers were built specifically for intelligence operations, most were designed for something else and repurposed or occupied by intelligence types years or decades later. Rare is the building designed and built exclusively for intelligence. For example, anyone working at or visiting the U.S. Army in Germany in the past decades may have noticed that several of the older buildings in the various Kasernes have large metal rings attached at uniform intervals along the length of some of their exteriors. These rings are signs of the original purpose of the building as they were used to tie up horses for the German Army during an era long gone.

Intelligence centers come in a wide variety of layouts from some of the nicest and aesthetically pleasing to some of the worst places for anyone to work. An intelligence analyst may work in a state-of-the-art modern facility adorned with polished metal railings and glass walls in one job or end up in a basement with no sunlight and exposed plumbing and IT wiring in the next. Analysts may fill a position that requires hours sitting at the same desk in a climate-controlled building and then switch to conducting analysis in a tent or on the front hood of a vehicle.

The layout and organization of each intelligence center tackles a fundamental task—managing something nonphysical (information) within the physical constraints of the facility itself. In addition, each floor plan or design has to provide the right balance of analysis, collaboration, and presentation by manipulating the physical entry, flow, and display of information. This may seem overly simplified, but in reality this is the primary purpose of an intelligence center. All other factors contribute to the effectiveness of a physical center's ability to satisfy this task.

There's very little that can be done to change the physical environment of the center without enormous expenditures of money, time, and other resources. The task, therefore, is to make the most effective use of the space provided; rooms with no windows, leaky pipes, etc. To determine how effective a center works for what the occupants need it to do, they must study their environment and look for ways to improve the efficiency of intelligence operations within its parameters.

Another key component of any intelligence center is the physical security measures required. As part of the overall security program within an intelligence operation, physical security includes considerations involving the actual structure the center is located in along with physical access of intelligence personnel to enter it. It also includes the physical measures taken to securely store protected and/or classified information. Each intelligence center will need to adhere to the requirements of both the owner and the customer as the primary drivers. This may mean shoring up a wall that is thin enough to hear conversations through it, it may also mean hard wiring data streams and networks to reduce their emanations to the outside. It can also mean several barriers to access that must be installed or, in some cases, the 24 × 7 presence of personnel to guard access.

While many organizations have specific requirements for the physical security of their intelligence operations and the centers they work in, there is no real commonly accepted standard across the intelligence industry. What's important to know is which standard is followed within the given organization.

Personal Perspectives:
Security Is in the Eye of the Beholder

As a portfolio manager for intelligence training with Lockheed Martin, I managed a training facility used by several of my programs in Northern Virginia with priority going to the U.S. Army Intelligence and Security Command (INSCOM). One of the most costly and frustrating tasks was our attempt to build up one of the classrooms in the facility so that our students could learn data mining tools using classified data sets from the Army. After having a review conducted by a government security expert, we spent tens of thousands of dollars reconstructing the room and installing several upgrades to meet the necessary security requirements. Contractors rebuilt the walls with a wire mesh inside, air vents were grated to prevent entry, doors were outfitted with advanced digital locks, and network connections were piped separately into our server room for the eventual hookup to a classified network.

After months of disruption and rising costs, everything seemed okay until a different security expert from within our company came into our facility to inspect the work that was done. They came out with a vastly different list of things that needed to be fixed because they were using a wholly different set of standards. To make things worse, they invited another expert from a different part of the company to take a look at what we had done, and that person had their own list of additional improvements that should be made. All of these were costly and would have put us way over our original budget estimate.

To remedy the situation, I invited all three experts to the facility to meet face to face, bought them pizza, and put them in the classroom together to come up with a consolidated list that they could agree upon. To my frustration, they came out after a few hours sticking to their own lists without an agreement. The government in the meantime, changed their strategic training plan and the facility was never finished nor cleared for secure training. I realized at that point that physical security is more of a subjective art than a science—and security itself is in the eye of the beholder.

FIGURE 4.2   Lockheed Martin classroom

This is a tough environment for intelligence operations and analysis to function in. The physical environment is usually more austere, and each different section is most likely operating in a space too small for what they need to have to function effectively. Intelligence professionals in these centers have to rely on scant pieces of information for their analysis because they are simply not allotted time to develop comprehensive or quality-reviewed products. Intelligence professionals who are used to working in strategic level, dedicated intelligence centers will have a harder time adjusting to this type of environment.

Three Main Functions of an Intelligence Center: Analysis–Collaboration–Presentation

An effective approach is to look at an intelligence center in terms of three basic functions to be performed there: analysis, collaboration, and presentation. Each of these three functions helps to delineate the overall purpose of a center, the functions it performs, and how the physical environment is currently laid out to support these functions. Almost every kind of analysis and work processes performed in an intelligence center fall into one of these three categories. While analysis is primarily a solitary function, collaboration and presentation are small- and large-group functions, respectively. Consider the following questions:

1. How suitable is this center to conduct *analysis?*

   a. How does information flow into the center?
   b. Where does information end up?
   c. Does this center provide the analysts a reasonable amount of privacy?
   d. What are the distractions/disruptions to conducting analysis?

2. How well can analysts *collaborate* with each other?

   a. Are there areas for small-group discussions?
   b. Are analysts able to work in groups for extended periods?
   c. Are analysts able to work in reasonable proximity within their team?
   d. Can analysts easily shift between analysis and collaboration?

3. Can I conduct effective *presentations* in this center?

   a. How important is presentation to the analytical mission?
   b. Is there an area to address large numbers of people without disrupting day-to-day work activities?
   c. Can the center display information that is required?
   d. How does the center properly display products for larger audiences?

Not all intelligence centers need to strike a perfect balance of these three. While these questions may push the thinking that the best intelligence center is one that strikes a balance between analysis, collaboration, and presentation, it doesn't always need to.

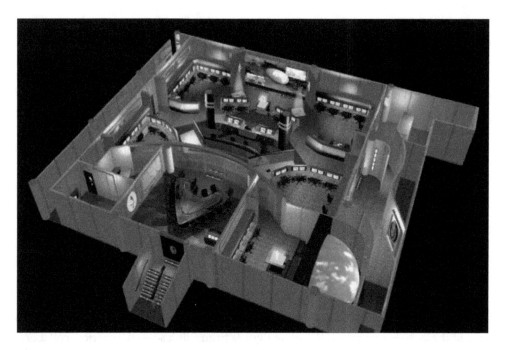

FIGURE 4.3   Concept design of the U.S. Army INSCOM's Information Dominance Center

Intelligence operations need to be able to simply function in the center—if the mission rarely requires the conduct of presentations for groups larger than a handful of people, the owner of the center doesn't need to sink millions of dollars into a huge presentation system. Likewise, collaboration may not be important either, if a center is primarily focused on providing products that are relatively simple and can be handled by individuals.

Balance Between Analysis, Collaboration, and Presentation

An intelligence center has to support the type of analysis required of the intelligence organization and the customers they support. As varied as intelligence operations can be, the physical and organizational layouts have to be suited so that the type of intelligence work conducted there can be conducted there. For this, a center has to have the right balance of three major functions of work: analysis, collaboration, and presentation.

Analysis is primarily an individual task and the key part of the Intelligence Cycle. Groups don't conduct analysis as a collective act outside of the science fiction like the Borg Collective from *Star Trek*. Analysts may work in groups, but they think by themselves, and for this task they need to be by themselves, if not physically then mentally.

Collaboration is the act of working in small- to medium-size groups for the purpose of bringing together different levels of experience, areas of expertise, and perspectives for projects that one analyst cannot plausibly conduct on their own. It requires a group of members who have conducted analysis (on their own) to bring together their information and ideas in order to the members to see a different and more complete picture. Group collaboration is most effective when their size ranges from two to eight people; the more members the richer the picture and more challenging the task of analysis gets.

Presentation is a form of dissemination that physical centers are suited to provide. Sending information out to remote and individual customers is pretty straightforward given the advancement of information technology, but the act of presenting information and analysis to an audience requires a means to display the work. Presentation requires space large enough to display and conduct oral presentations. While a center may have a virtual environment, the effectiveness of actual face-to-face contact is superior to the presentation as it (almost) completely cuts down on distractions that a virtual presentation is saddled with such as e-mail, web-surfing, or actions an audience can get away with.

The Office Versus the Tactical Operations Center

To incorporate the functions of analysis, collaboration, and presentation, every intelligence center takes the form of either an office-like or tactical operations atmosphere. These two types of centers are on the opposite ends of a linear spectrum. Most intelligence centers fall somewhere in between the two, leaning to one side or the other. Taking a look at the characteristics of each, we see that while an office space lends itself to more permanent operations, the life of a tactical center is limited but more flexible and responsive to a particular type of intelligence requirement.

Office Operations

A standard office is pretty self-explanatory. Any work environment that consists primarily of several rooms for one to three people falls into this category. Most offices contain some common areas, i.e., lobby, hallways, and break rooms, and most likely one or more conference rooms. All are not conducive for analytical work except the conference rooms that have to be shared, meaning they are not dedicated for one purpose for any extended length of time.

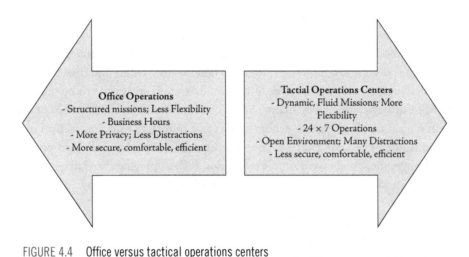

FIGURE 4.4   Office versus tactical operations centers

Offices are the most traditional and best areas for analysis because they offer the greatest amount of privacy for the individual to work without the common distractions of the workplace. They are a bit more difficult for any long-term collaboration or small-group projects and not at all adequate for conducting presentations outside of reserving a conference room. It would be a stretch to call a standard office building or suite a "center" without a way to add in the collaboration and presentation factors.

To use wide-open space many offices have, we have to consider an additional feature affectionately (meaning derisively) known as a cube farm. These partitioned workspaces provide a more cost-efficient way to put more workers into a given square footage, taking advantage of large and open office areas or bays. Privacy is somewhat sacrificed for the more efficient use of space, even more removed if the cube walls are only half-high. Some would argue that the entire term "wall" has been taken for granted in cube farms.

Want to know how popular cube farms are? Try walking through one without seeing a Dilbert cartoon posted somewhere amidst the grey and/or beige fabric walls. Cubicles are iconic symbols for rote, mundane, boring, and repetitive work environments. They are featured as such in movies like *Office Space* or the *Matrix* as the enemy of imagination, creativity, and individualism.

The ability to conduct analysis in a cube farm drops off here for the individual as the opportunity for distractions is much harder to avoid. Some overcome this challenge by mentally isolating themselves within their work area as best they can. Using headphones or trying to extend the height of their cube walls with plants and other items has varied success and can look downright tacky in the case of "that guy" with the Star Wars bobble heads on the top of his cube.

With that, some cubicle workspaces can be cleverly arranged into pairs and foursomes so that teams can work together more efficiently. Arranging them so that a group of folks can work together with established rules of behavior is a priority in these situations. The key here is to use the office space available to improve collaboration and presentation aspects of the center while retaining an environment also suited for analysis.

Work schedule for an office-type intelligence center is primarily daytime business hours with a nominal shift during the night, swing, or off-hour shifts. The permanence of an established building along with the longer-term cycle of requirements dictate the intelligence operational tempo (OPTEMPO) here, as does traffic and time zone among other unchanging factors. Therefore, office intelligence centers tend to be much more attuned to strategic, long-term analysis often conducted only in small groups or solo.

If an office-based intelligence center needs to be more dynamic and tactical in their operations, it can be changed to a more Tac Ops feel—operationally and physically. These changes must go beyond simple cosmetics, such as putting camouflage netting in the hallways and pretending that it is now tactically oriented.

Tactical Operations Centers

On the other end of the scale, Tactical Operations Centers or TOCs are almost always associated with military or emergency response operations and have some unique aspects not found in any of the other types of intelligence centers. TOCs are most often found in a remote and other austere environment, and in support of and ad hoc or otherwise temporary operation. Several aspects of this type of facility are obvious.

First a building is not required, nor are any of the amenities normally associated or taken for granted within a building like running water and plumbing or a total shielding from the elements. It's either too damn hot or freezing with intermittent rain and wind. Even rarer is when the weather is actually pleasant.

TOCscan be in repurposed buildings, tents, vehicles, or a makeshift combination of them all. Working conditions can also range from austere to luxurious, relatively speaking. The newest large tent-based operations in the military can be nicer than some buildings especially in underdeveloped areas or places that have recently met with a natural disaster. Then again, conditions can be as exposed as a tarp or a couple of ponchos stretched between two parked vehicles. Analysis here is done while sitting on boxes, camping stools, or coolers and can be as austere as using antiquated paper maps with acrylic overlays and markers.

Second, these types of centers are all about collaboration. That's why people work in them. As named, a tactical center is just that—tactical, immediate, and specifically focused. They are designed to be close to the action where people from different specialties need to work in a coordinated manner toward a clearly defined purpose including combat operations, disaster relief, terrorist attack, or a major crime.

Third and as a result of the first two aspects, distractions, i.e., noise, elements, movement of people, other work being conducted, briefing a presentation amidst everyone et al., are numerous and unavoidable in a tactical environment. Analysts working in a tactical environment will find that conducting analysis of current and near-term operations is possible, but longer term deep-thinking analysis requires a certain degree of solitude. In a TOC this is almost impossible outside 0200–0500 hours when it's not freezing cold or raining.

Intelligence Within Tactical Operations Centers

Keep in mind that many intelligence operations or functions reside in operations centers that are not exclusively designed or designated for intelligence alone. In many cases, analysts will find themselves as part of a larger staff or operational planning team. Intelligence is just one of the many functions or sections operating within the same building, tent, or some other physical facility. The other sections within the center could include operations, logistics, administrative, or personnel dedicated to other coordinating functions.

Example of these types of center include tactical and operational military headquarters, joint or ad hoc task forces, incident response centers, tiger teams, or fusion centers.

In these centers the main driver, owner, and consumer of intelligence is collocated with the intelligence analysts and supervisors. As a result, OPTEMPO has to keep up with the rest of the center. Analysis is quick, extremely time sensitive, and short term, with fluid changes to requirements. There is little time for deep-dive analysis or creation of intricate or detailed intelligence products. A large majority of deliverables are either presentations, formatted updates, or very short oral presentations.

It's All About Entry, Flow, and Display

An effective layout for an intelligence center must be the combination of two things: a physical environment designed to manage a nonphysical commodity (e.g., data and information) and the data and information themselves. More specifically, an intelligence center must help the people (analysts) working in it to transform data and information into intelligence, another nonphysical commodity.

To manage a nonphysical entity like data and information, the natural tendency is to treat it as if it has physical properties. Like electricity or other forms of energy, if data and information is viewed this way, it becomes much easier to figure out how to work with it.

The physical property assigned to data has commonly been water or liquid. Widely accepted data and IT words are proof of this. Terms like dataflow (software architecture), data stream (transmission of data in packets) data pipes (conduits for data movement), leaks (of classified or otherwise confidential or private information), spillage (leaks from a highly classified system or network to a lower or unclassified system or network), bit buckets (data repository), etc. all refer to vessels, conduits, and properties for water. Intelligence personnel swim in data and get drowned by too much of it. They even measure data by how much volume it takes up using kilo-, mega-, giga-, and tera- for prefixes to the number of bytes they're dealing with even though the physical mass of data is irrelevant.

In this sense, an intelligence center must be regarded as a center designed to handle the flow, storage, and distribution of water, almost as if it is akin to a water treatment facility. Raw data enters the facility through established data pipes, it is processed, parse, and categorized through the various data filters, and is then displayed for consumption by the users at the back end of the processing through the use of data mining and visualization tools. How information enters, flows through, is stored, and distributed is what is truly important to its end user, i.e., the analyst and the customer.

Drawing out or mapping the flow of data and information into and through a center is an effective way to help understand the types of data intelligence personnel are working with and how their available tools interact with it. One key feature is the understanding that data, like water, tends to flow where gravity pulls it. Every center has one or more centers of gravity where information pools, ends up, or is otherwise used and/or displayed.

Besides ending up in front of the analyst, some centers of gravity of information and analytical products are the large displays within the center. Information is pulled

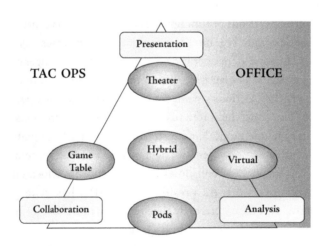

FIGURE 4.5 Types of intelligence centers

here for a variety of reasons; live news feeds, running displays, Situational Reports (or SITREPs), active planning sessions, Battle Update Briefs (BUBs), or other similar briefings are all examples. Intelligence assessments are also sent out as products either in physical (printed) or some form of electronic transfer (e.g., e-mail attachment).

While not an all-inclusive list, below are some of the more common configurations of intelligence centers along with their effectiveness in helping to perform the three main functions of analysis, collaboration, and presentation. These are subjective ratings as each offers significant capabilities to the people working there. In addition, each configuration has some significant drawbacks for a particular type of work.

The Theater

In this configuration, information may enter through a variety of points, but the center of gravity for the flow of information is one primary display. This display is usually a single large screen or set of screens showing the current situation, live feeds, or one or more final products made or imported into the center. Examples include the main screen of the Starship Enterprise, although it is more of a hybrid in its entirety. A layout could include any number of workspace arrangements, to include arranging personnel into rows of workstations facing the primary display wall. The primary customer or shift supervisor can also be set up in front of the main display able to make his decisions, while the display either presents him with a live feed or is continuously updated for him.

Theater-type centers are the best for conducting a presentation to a fairly large audience on a regular basis. It is also suited for conducting analysis and planning toward a primary ongoing operation. They are not well suited for conducting detailed analysis or for working in separate groups. As stated earlier, the flow of information flows to a primary wall as a display, meaning there is only one operation that can go on at a time collaboratively. For anyone working on something other than the current topic being displayed, this type of environment can be a huge distraction. Cross-coordination among the different types of people working in this type of environment can also be difficult as it goes against the flow of information that this type of center is designed for.

To compensate for the drawback, many analysts will opt to do their individual work somewhere else and bring their analysis for presentation and/or discussion to the center once they have something to show.

Personal Perspectives:
Layouts Reflect Command Climate

As the Intelligence Officer, or S2, of the 3rd (Phantom) Brigade, 3rd (Rock of the Marne) Infantry Division in 1995 and 1996, I've seen several different examples of Tactical Operations Centers (TOCs) in our and in other U.S. Army units. While in garrison, Army units worked in a standard office environment for each unit with allocations for the various staff sections and the command group. TOCs were either occupied buildings in the host country or within large modular tent complexes with tracked vehicles that were backed up and had their back ramps dropped to open up right into the main tent. Unlike in a garrison environment where members of each unit worked out of their own respective buildings, in a tactical environment every attached and supporting unit also had people who needed a place to work.

Each layout, style, and operational tempo was an indicator of the leadership and command climate in the unit. The presence of amenities and creature comforts, like wooden floors, heat, coffee, or food signaled an effective command sergeant Major (CSM) or senior Operations Non-Commissioned Officer (NCOs). The effectiveness of the physical center toward operations was highly dependent on the personalities of the unit commander (CO) or executive officer (XO).

One of the worst TOC layouts I encountered during my time as an S2 was a theater-style layout in another brigade headquarters where I briefly worked. Instead of a screen, there was a large battle map of the area standing along one side of the tent. Immediately facing the map were a couple of chairs for the commander, a senior officer. Behind this row of chairs were several rows of thin and long tables (known in Germany as Fest Tables) for each of the staff officers to sit. The more important your position was, the closer you were to the map. This layout directly reflected the personality of the commander as he was known to be somewhat egotistical, and at times loud or even boorish. His setup allowed for information to easily flow to the map directly in front of him, but made it much more difficult for information to flow in the other direction without his presence or for direct coordination between each staff section. In addition, cross-coordination between the different staff sections was much more difficult in this layout.

I was glad not to be permanently assigned to that unit simply by the indicators the physical layout signaled to me. Subsequently, I was able to observe that the fatigue and poor morale among the staff officers and soldiers within that Brigade's staff was much more prominent than in my own brigade.

The Game Table

A center in a game table configuration is similar to the theater, except that the center of gravity of information is a centrally placed table. This table can be a large map or provide for several key personnel to work collaboratively. Examples that the reader can visualize is the British RAF tracking centers from the Battle of Britain or long lacquer table surrounded by high-ranking officers in such movies as *Dr. Strangelove* or *Under Siege*. One limitation is that a single table of workstations can only fit so many participants.

Game table configurations also work well for conducting presentations, but to a much smaller audience than the theater can. The primary strength in using a table like this is during an ongoing operation where the collaboration between the different sections and lead personnel in the center is critical. A game table is much more efficient than a theater in this area because it allows the key players to situate themselves right next to the center of gravity where face-to-face discussions can take place. In a theater, everyone is looking at the wall instead of each other. The one key decision-maker in the center, be it the commander, etc., either has to face the wall like everyone else, or has to act like the headmaster of a class with various presenters forced to go up to the front to present. No one likes to listen to someone talking to them from behind while also trying to understanding what's on the wall.

A game table configuration allows for immediate and more candid discussion, albeit within a smaller circle of decision makers. The table itself is also much more dynamic and depending on the technology used can range from a map with markers or "game pieces" to some of the more expensive light and video displays. Once scientists invent a practical hologram display, these tables will be best suited for them.

Personal Perspectives: Gaming the Enemy

My brigade headquarters had an extremely effective Tactical Operations Center (TOC) using a game table layout. In the center of our modular tent structure was a large, custom-made wooden table with folding legs roughly around four by six feet. The top of the table was composed of two clear acrylic surfaces laid on top of each other with the top one attached by hinges. This allowed a paper map to be inserted between the two and held stationary as we used acrylic markers to show the operations graphics (phase lines, objectives, etc.) and moveable stickers to track enemy and friendly units. The surrounding walls contained different charts and documents each updated by the responsible staff section. This table acted as a center of gravity for information flowing into the TOC and allowed all staff members to take part in creating an integrated picture of what was happening on the battlefield. As the intelligence officer, either I or one of my lieutenants had to sit or stand opposite the executive officer in order to update the table with the latest information about the enemy, usually giving the rest of the staff our analysis of what we thought the enemy would do in the near future.

During operations our unit executive officer would be positioned directly below the map while each different staff element could report new information either by orally briefing everyone around the table or by updating one of the graphics on the map. As a habit, I and my officers had to learn how to write upside down so that all wording on the map could be easily read by everyone else. This was a relatively simple way to share information, keeping everyone aware at all times and was indicative of the climate of teamwork we had on our staff.

FIGURE 4.6   Author posing inside the 3rd Bde, 3rd Infantry Division TOC at Hohenfels, Germany, Summer 1995

Pods

In a pod configuration, planning and analysis is divided into two or more subsections, or pods. Pods can actually be separate rooms, or physical divisions within larger rooms. Such a distinct physical separation between areas is best suited for a center that supports many different types of customers without much need for collaboration or mutual support. For example, one part of an intelligence center may be devoted to counter-drug trafficking while another is working a cyber or financial operation with a distinctly separate purpose. Separation can be done through the use of different rooms, groups of cubicles that are opened enough to incorporate more smaller groups. It can also be within separated offices, or even an imaginative array of workstations in a large open area or bay.

Pod configurations allow for effective collaboration within small groups of analysts, but are very limited in terms of presentation. They also afford some protections from the distractions of a much larger open area, but the analyst can still suffer from smaller distractions within the group. Working in a pod-type configuration does not offer privacy, except from the other groups. Finally, this configuration allows a center to conduct multiple smaller efforts simultaneously, but limits the abilities of these groups to either collaborate with each other or if there is a need for more physical space for additional persons to support one of the groups.

Virtual

In this configuration, an intelligence center becomes less of a center and more of a virtual connection between all personnel and data repositories on a given problem set. This configuration is used when physically working together is impossible. A virtual configuration is almost limitless in the number of participants, and can bring together any set of people from a variety of organizations around the world.

Key to a virtual configuration is technology. Without the proper telecom connections, bandwidth for sharing information, or other supporting automation, real-time virtual collaboration would be impossible. Despite the growing ease of collaboration technology, having the right tools in place is critical to this function. A 24 × 7 persistent collaboration is more difficult, given the time zones and human factors such as sleep and time off.

What virtual configurations need in technology can be saved for the lack of need of any physical center. The only physical requirement is dedicated servers to run the operation, allowing everyone to work from wherever they are located.

Virtual configurations are best for ad hoc, temporary, or physically constrained groups that need to come together to work on a specific analytic problem. Analysts spending a majority of their time working alone only need to come together to review the group's work, gain an understanding of what everyone is doing, and set new directions and objectives. Once these are achieved, the group members go off and continue their work on their own.

Obviously, a virtual configuration has its limitations. Besides the limitations of technology already discussed, virtual collaboration cannot match the quality of having people in the same physical space working together, nor is it as effective at presentations in terms of maintaining the dedicated time of all participants. There are too many distractors like e-mail and lol cats that keep people from paying complete attention to a virtual meeting.

Hybrid

Hybrid configurations are a mix of the other configurations. They, therefore, can vary greatly depending on the particular center. One example could be a group of pods working within a large open bay with a large presentation screen at the front of the room. Each pod could be specialized, but not too separated from the work being done within the rest of the room. Another could be a large main work area with several offices adjoining it. For every trait built into a center that enhances analysis, collaboration, or presentation, the other two will generally suffer. To guarantee that a center can accommodate all three functions requires two things: Lots of money (to throw at it) and space (to provide both privacy and interaction for each individual).

The key to hybrids, and all the centers overall, is the ability to match an operation within the context of the physical environment. While there may be a desire to alter or tailor the physical environment of a center to what is needed operationally, intelligence professionals are generally forced into altering their operations to take the best advantage of the physical environment they're stuck with.

As with each type of center, making minor changes to the physical layout is always an option. It's also necessary every few years. Adapting the physical environment to changes in the mission and organization structure is an often overlooked but important aspect to maintaining the efficiency of intelligence operationss.

Having an optimal layout and physical organization won't guarantee success or failure of an intelligence operation, but it will be hard to achieve success with a poor one. As the information or virtual environment has overtaken physical workspace in importance, there are other critical aspects that must be considered.

The Four Pillars of Intelligence Operations

U.S. history is beset with numerous examples of the failures of intelligence. Indeed, several books have cataloged and studied these failures placing blame on a wide variety of reasons. Several major ones easily come to mind: Pearl Harbor, Chinese entry into the Korean War, Soviet invasion of Afghanistan, WMD in Iraq, and of course 9/11.

While not every failure of intelligence is the fault of the people working in intelligence (e.g., the decision-maker made the wrong decision despite an accurate intelligence picture), virtually every failure can be attributed to a breakdown somewhere in the Intelligence Cycle, usually involving a critical piece of information that was needed to form the correct picture and prediction. There may have been a problem where the missing piece of information was out there, but no one collected it. The critical piece may have been collected, but the organization responsible for working it didn't understand its importance or simply lost it downstream in the wash of the rest of the data coming into the organization. In some cases, the analyst may have had all the pertinent information to make an assessment, but simply made the wrong one—much in the same way a decision-maker can as described earlier.

Intelligence operations are designed to take requirements and turn around intelligence support as their service to the customer. This support can be in the form of a delivered product, a verbal answer, or some other kind of support. In order to do this effectively, there must be a combination, integration, and synchronization of four critical components.

Building an Intelligence Center from Core Components

As touched on earlier, creating a physical intelligence center is quite a complex operation. It would also make sense that creating an intelligence operation requires the same amount of complexity. While this is true for the details of almost every operation, sticking to the baseline critical components are the keys to success.

The pillars of data, tools, people, and processes are always present in every intelligence operation, and no operation can function without all of them working properly and in concert with each other. Data represents the raw material coming into the center, tools are the machines that process and transform data into useable information, and people conduct the analysis to create intelligence as a product. All of the actions required to do this work are performed through processes and procedures.

As a starting point to designing or improving an existing intelligence operation, these four component areas will help to organize a workable plan. By understanding each along with the working relationships between them is important in both designing a new intelligence operation and improving current operations. Working together, these four components make up the production line of providing a service to a customer. A critical weakness or breakdown in only one area is enough to render a center useless.

For example, intelligence analysts may find themselves working in a relatively brand-new, state-of-the-art technology intelligence center where there is ample data sets and tools to work with. They may also find themselves working alongside some highly qualified colleagues with tons of experience. The center is physically able to handle a variety of intelligence requirements and yet after working there for a while analysts begin to see and feel a level of frustration, negativity, and mistakes made on a regular basis. In these cases, further investigation could reveal that there is little in the way of a standard operating procedures (SOP) handbook or structured analytic methods being used. As a result, products are created that look unprofessional, amateurish, or are frequently late getting published. The problem with this center lies in its processes as they are either broken or missing entirely. These procedures may have worked in the past, but now have gotten stale, redundant, or overcome by a new set of data or technology.

Unfortunately, two of these components are routinely either taken for granted or overlooked in terms of importance: people and processes. One of the perennial problems in intelligence is the priority placed on data and tools at the expense of having quality personnel working on the operation through standardized and efficient processes. This problem is often perpetuated by those who look at intelligence strictly as a science. While common culprits are IT folks, software and network engineers, and SIGINT types, they do not hold exclusive rights to this phenomenon. Quotes that I have actually heard such as "the last human intelligence analyst has already been born," and "teach them (the analysts) the tools and plug them into the machine" only serve to highlight an attitude toward technology at the expense of people and sound processes. With the recent rush to conduct data mining as part of intelligence collection and analysis, the problem of the underappreciated human factors can be found in many places across the world of intelligence.

Taking a look at each of the four pillars in detail will help in understanding the challenges and risks associated with each along with considerations that can mitigate these risks with actions, and help in building or refining an intelligence operation that is best suited for the customers, the drivers, and the owners alike. As the reader goes through each component in more detail they will find that differing levels of priority on each of these areas are highly dependent on the types of missions their center routinely performs.

Summary

Every intelligence operation consists of four pillars that must be working effectively in order to ensure success: data, tools, people, and processes. In addition, each operation is conducted by some sort of intelligence organization, be it a small team or an entire federal agency. It mostly takes place within a virtual or a physical center, or a combination of both. As such, intelligence operations operate with a constant set of challenges that if not managed or mitigated will result in failure. To assist the intelligence professionals, there are several aspects to their operations, which if understood and planned for correctly will help in both scoping out and identifying key drivers behind their overall success.

Key Summary Points

+ While every intelligence operation has some unique aspects to their mission and organization, all share common fundamental characteristics.
+ The four pillars to effective intelligence operations are data, tools, people, and processes.
+ There are distinct differences between an intelligence operation and an intelligence center
  ○ An intelligence operation occupies one of more centers
  ○ An intelligence center is a combination of both physical and virtual spaces where the intelligence operations are actually conducted.
+ All intelligence operations occupy both a physical and a virtual space. These may be unique though they also share common characteristics. Each type of intelligence center will offer a differing balance of analysis, presentation, and collaboration for operations.

Discussion Questions

+ Besides the nine questions listed in this chapter, what other questions should planners ask that would help shape intelligence operations?
+ Of the listed challenges to effective operations, which should be deemed as the most important or least important?
+ In portraying intelligence centers in popular culture (e.g., movies, TV, books, games, etc.), which of the three main functions are emphasized the most or the least and why?
+ Besides the four stated pillars to every intelligence operation, are there any additional pillars that must be considered?
+ How do each of the pillars of intelligence operations related to supporting the customer?

Chapter 5

Data and Information

Learning Objectives

After completing this chapter, you will be able to:

- ▸ Understand the differences and purposes of data, information, and knowledge.
- ▸ Be familiar with the issues that must be considered in order to have the right data and information coming into an intelligence center or operation.
- ▸ Be able to evaluate applied uses of data and information using several methods.
- ▸ Be familiar with the issues surrounding the human limits of working with data and information.

The Commodity of Intelligence

Intelligence is a business that deals in two main commodities—data and information. Intelligence centers perform a service by taking in these "raw materials," processing and analyzing them, and creating intelligence in the form of a product or some form of support to a customer. As intelligence products are delivered to a customer, they are still in the form of information, but with added insight and emphasis. There can be an innumerate number of steps and subprocesses, but this is the basic method of intelligence and a center is simply a physical location created for it to happen more effectively.

Data and software tools represent two of the four critical components of an effective intelligence operation. As they are the technical components, they have to be acquired through either purchasing or gaining permission to their access. They do not have to be trained, fed, given time off, or praised for doing a good job. They are also fairly rigid compared to people and processes,

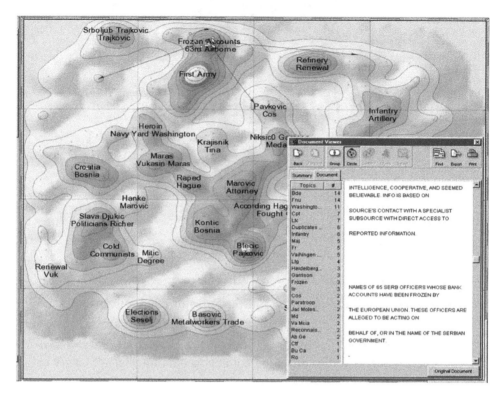

FIGURE 5.1   Information mapping chart of reporting related to the Serbian Military during the Kosovo Air Campaign of 1999. Created using a visualization tool called Themescape that was then owned by Cartia Labs

meaning they cannot be readily changed or adapted without some significant and costly technical work done.

Changing or evolving these tools can require so much work that it's easier to simply eventually replace them with more advance technology, especially when it comes to tools. Concepts like Moore's law, "Plug and Play," and "Bandwidth Is Cheap" come to mind when thinking of software and data sets in this context.

Data and software tools are similar in that they exist in the cyber realm and are therefore both made up of 1s and 0s. Taking a look at each reveals some stark differences between two and why they are listed as separate components of an intel center. Data and information alone involve many areas of consideration and planning when it comes to the best sources for your intelligence operation.

Data and Information–Raw and Refined Materials

Information itself relies on one raw material—data. Data is simply pieces of information and facts in raw form. Information is data that has been processed and organized in a way that it can be used in a given context. The process of converting data into information is through data mining or identifying patterns, associations, or relationships among the various pieces of data available.

Data alone is of very little use to an analyst. Data that has been organized, i.e., parsed, structured, collated, and formatted into something that makes sense, e.g., information, is what analysts need to work with in order to produce intelligence. Data mining tools simply help analysts work and manipulate data in order to create information. This distinction between information and data may be minor, but it is important to understand the difference in terms of their source, properties, contributions, and costs among other considerations.

The process of converting this information into useable knowledge is called analysis. If a given set of information pertains to threats or adversaries, it is intelligence or threat analysis. Knowledge about your threats allows customers to make informed decision about their operations in light of the threats and challenges facing them.

The main function of an intelligence center is to convert data into information and information into knowledge, knowledge pertaining to threats. As an analogy, data flowing into an intelligence center can be viewed as a process similar to metalworking. In this analogy, data is the raw ore harvested from the earth. The metal is then smelted into bars of information. This metal is then used to make all sorts of products. There are many versions of the chart below out in the public domain, but the basics of each are similar in that data must be transformed into information before intelligence can be derived from it.

Every technical function of an intelligence center concerning data boils down into this simple process of handling data and information. It's one of the key building blocks in the process of how an intelligence center interacts with their customer. This is one of the main reasons why throwing data and tools into a room without adequate processes or capable people to work it and calling it an intelligence center is a recipe for disaster.

Processes that transform data into information is now largely done through automated tools and is called data mining. Transformation of information into knowledge, while aided by automated tools, is primarily conducted by the human analyst. This will remain so for the foreseeable future despite the futuristic prognosticators who confuse computing power with actionable intelligence.[1]

FIGURE 5.2   Data, information, and knowledge

---

1   In a 1999 conversation with one of the lead software engineers assigned to the US Army's Information Dominance Center, I was told that the last intelligence analyst had already been born. If that was the case, they would have graduated high school already and readying themselves for a workplace that was by and large already phasing out human analysts. Obviously this is not the case.

Intelligence operations and the centers they occupy exist by their ability to collect both data and information. If it's data—processing it into usable information will have to be done in house. If it's information, someone else has already created that information from other forms of data or information.

Finding the Right Data and Information for Your Center

Shopping for the right data and/or information source is like shopping for a car. There are hundreds of makes and models, colors, and options to choose from. Looking for a car involves a number of criteria including style, budget, reliability, and functionality. Just as the average car buyer doesn't need to be a mechanic or a "gear head" to know what they want in a car, intelligence professionals also don't need to be an IT specialist or network engineer to know what kind of data they need for their operation. Instead, they need to have an understanding of data and information in the context of whether or not it's useful to them.

Building off the nine questions outlined in Chapter 4 that help to shape an intelligence operation, there are several additional questions that help shape an understanding of the right data and information feeds and sources for an operation. These questions are both functional and technical in nature. Also similar to Chapter 4, identifying the specific questions regarding data and information requires the perspective that an intelligence operation and the center that houses it work like a business. In this manner, an intelligence center serves as a physical center that takes in "raw materials" and turns them into product for your consumers, aka customers. Looking at it in this way will allow the identification of the most important questions and considerations that must be made. By following the chart, each question can be in the context of the overall function of your center—that is taking in data, information, and finished intel products and using those resources to create intel products for one or more customers.

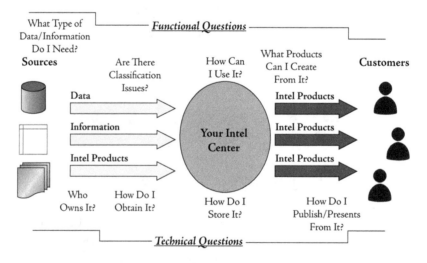

FIGURE 5.3   Intelligence data information considerations

All these basic questions must eventually be further supported by additional and more detailed questions and considerations. There are several evaluation methods that are available. While these are not inclusive or required to be followed to the letter, they are a way to assist in searching for new data sources or to help evaluate the current sources of an ongoing operation. *Each method attempts address the four primary aspects of data and information that you need to consider: security, reliability, discipline, and functionality.* Of all these, functionality is most important as discussed within that section.

Evaluating Data: Information Security

Data and information is commonly classified in terms of its storage and protection requirements. It can be classified as mission critical, sensitive, restricted, etc. depending on the nomenclature used. The U.S. government classifies data based upon the common security categories such as Confidential, Secret, and Top Secret levels, each with more complicated handling requirements and even more severe punitive measures for violating these requirements. For the security of an intelligence center and the operations within it, a center most likely already has a structure in place for classifying data and information according to security requirements. If not, personnel within that center must find and use some systems of data classification and associated security measures.

The vast majority of classified caveats, protocols, and restrictions are to protect either the way the information was obtained or to ensure the success of a current or ongoing operation. Protecting sources includes protection of the either the technical aspects of an advance collection system or the people working in dangerous environments either covertly or through clandestine means. Ensuring success of an operation is pretty straight forward—secrecy is required for success and either further required for the safety of the people involved.

Understand the Risks of Secure Information

One of the perils of working with classified information for intelligence is the sheer size and complexity of the many classification systems. Top of the list is the U.S. government. Even though there are only three basic levels, there are many further subdivisions of classified information called caveats that have further instructions and restrictions that further compartment a given category. This is especially so at the Top Secret level.

Personal Perspectives:
Black Is a Lonely Color

One of my jobs working in intelligence as a senior military intelligence captain placed me in very sensitive and highly classified operation and facility. It was a small, discreet operation where only a handful of us knew the entire breadth and depth of the entire program. To make things simple to the rest of the Army, we were simply known as a Black Program and that's about all that needed to be said for folks to understand that's all that could be said. Working in this environment required a lot of patience and deliberate face-to-face coordination since our work wasn't even permitted to be placed on regular *Top Secret* networks. Many times this required me to travel to the location of organization I was supporting, and even then I could only talk to the people who were also read into my specific program.

In one case, I was required to travel to a strategy session that involved dozens of Army planners, but only one person knew the specifics as to why I was there. To my frustration, I found out moments before the kickoff meeting that my contact was away on emergency leave due to a death in his family. As the meeting started, everyone there had to stand up and introduce themselves and why they were there. When they got to me, I stood up and said, "I am Captain Kleinsmith from LIWA and I am leaving apparently." When the colonel running the meeting asked why I stated "If you know what the guy who is on emergency does here, you know there is no one else for me to talk to here." The colonel understood, shook his head, and I was on a plane returning home within a few hours. Classifications may be completely annoying and dysfunctional at times, but they are deadly important.

One of the difficulties of working with classified information is that information may be classified without the user even knowing that it is. For example, a given piece of information that has been classified within a government program may also be available from either open or public sources. It may be listed in a different context, but when combined with other readily available information, it may become classified or protected in some other manner. Analysts working with sensitive information may not be privy to the classification criteria. For intelligence working purely within the commercial sector, this won't really be a problem since there is no expectation that they knew about it. But for analysts dealing with open sources such as WikiLeaks or some other hacked source, there is a serious risk of running afoul of security protocols along with the agencies responsible for protecting those secrets.

The key rule to understand here is: Just because classified information has been leaked into the public domain does *not* mean it is automatically de-classified. It doesn't matter if it was talked about on a news network or put out on a webpage. If unauthorized personnel decide to store, transmit, or use that information in an intelligence product, they are taking a significant risk. For this reason, it is critically important for every intelligence operation to have a security expert or manager either on hand or as an on-call consultant.

From a data and information security perspective, the primary purpose for classifying data and information is for the protection of the confidentiality, integrity, and availability of information from attackers and thieves. When the confidentiality of the data is attacked, the threat is attempting to extract data for their own uses. When its availability is attacked, the attacker is attempting to deny you access. When the integrity is attacked, the attacker is attempting to manipulate or change the data.[2] All these threats require active, robust, and adaptive defensive mechanisms and personnel to protect from intrusion, theft, and manipulation of data as well as denial of access to it by the people who should have access.

In this way data is perishable, not from time but from an erosion of the trust and confidence analysts must have in it. If an information source is known to have been compromised or has a poor reputation for its own security, it is less likely to be used in an intelligence product with confidence.

From a more cynical standpoint, information security also involves looking at it in terms of trustworthiness. In the age of WikiLeaks, private servers, unsecured e-mails, credit and identity theft, and other massive breaches of what is supposed to be highly protected, data is a plague on the world of intelligence. While a protected data source may come into an intelligence unhindered, if it's also available to the rest of the world, it may be somewhat useless or even detrimental to an operation.

Decades ago this wasn't much of a problem to consider, but it now leads into some other reliability issues involving security such as the possibility that this data has not only been compromised by someone, it has also been manipulated or changed by them whether through incompetence or malicious intent.

Consider some of the security-related questions involving data and information sources:

- **What Is the Classification of the Data or Information?** Depending on the level of classification, intelligence personnel may not even be authorized to see it, much less receive it, or store it within a facility. Virtually every form of classification comes with security requirements for transmitting, storing, and handling it. Some of these require official inspections approvals and extremely costly physical and network security measures. The physical location of the servers and databases within an intelligence center will most likely need extensive hardening and additional barriers to access.

- **Who Classified It and Under What Authority?** While the U.S. government has the common—Confidential, Secret, and Top Secret levels, there are other U.S. government protections over data and information that involve the personal privacy of U.S. persons. For example, the 1996 Health Insurance Portability and Accountability Act (HIPAA) establishes a privacy rule protecting medical records and other health-related information.[3] Similarly, the 1974 Family Education Rights and Privacy Act (FERPA) protects the privacy of student educational records.[4]

---

2   Singer, P. W., & Freidman, A. (2014). *Cybersecurity and cyberwar: What everyone needs to know* (pp. 69–70). New York, NY: Oxford University Press.

3   U.S. Department of Health & Human Services. *Health information privacy.* Retrieved from https://www.hhs.gov/hipaa/for-professionals/privacy/laws-regulations/index.html

4   U.S. Department of Education, Laws & Guidance/General. Retrieved from https://www2.ed.gov/policy/gen/guid/fpco/ferpa/index.html

These along with foreign government classifications and numerous proprietary protections combine to require significant amount of checks and similar due diligence prior to receiving different types of data and information.

+ **Has the Source Been Compromised in the Past?** Trust in a particular source of data or information is paramount—whether they are a single person or an enormous streaming/data feed. A little red-teaming and playing Devil's advocacy of sources would be helpful here. From conducting simple news searches to talking to physical and network security managers within the source's organization directly, researching the past history in order to find any compromises, thefts, or hacks in the past are important to establishing the trustworthiness of a data source. While there are simple ways to factor in the reliability of a single source (discussed later in this chapter), quite often there is very little research done on an entire set of data. Analysts like to trust that data from a news source or the U.S. government is trustworthy, but too often and embarrassingly, they've found that they are not.

Being able to completely answer these questions is rare. The fact that these problems exist should be a strong reminder to check the security of a data source regularly. Intelligence professionals should also make sure they aren't relying too much on data in an operation that is also available to their threats or easily accessed directly by hackers, crackers, and internet trolls.

Evaluating Data: Reliability

Besides trustworthiness, data and information coming into an intelligence center must also be evaluated in terms of how reliable it is. In order to have confidence in the intelligence products and assessments you're creating, you must have a level of trust in both the source and the data itself. Even information associated with a trusted and reliable source can be faulty or completely wrong at times while a dubious source may just have the most accurate piece of information. There are several widely used methods to evaluate the reliability of both a source and the content of the information they provide. A few methods are worth understanding in detail.

The Military Option

The U.S. military method of evaluating sources and content for reliability is spelled out in the doctrinal manuals, primarily from Field Manual or FM 2–22.3, Human Intelligence Collector Operations. Formerly known as FM 34–52, Intelligence Interrogation, it's fairly obvious why the Army decided to update the manual's title to something broader and less controversial.[5]

These manuals contain a source and information reliability matrix method that analysts can use to evaluate information and a source together, using an alphanumeric rating. To do

---

5 HQ Department of the Army, FM 2–22.3 Human Intelligence Collector Operations, September 2006, page B-1 to B-2.

this, each item of information is used in an alphabetic grade for the source (A through F) combined with a numeric grade for the content itself (1–6). So as an example, confirmable and consistent information from a reliable source would be assigned an A-1 rating. At the opposite end of the scale, a completely improbable or illogical piece of information from an unreliable source would be given a rating of E-5. Source and information content that simply cannot be judged would be rated F and 6, respectively.[6]

While this is a structured methodology, it is designed to evaluate the source in general terms while each item from that source is rated individually. It is best suited for information derived from human contact and sources (HUMINT) versus evaluating all the entities in a data base or any sort of streaming data feed. Using an alphanumeric rating also has its problems in that it can be confusing to anyone who doesn't know the rating system used. Customers who don't know the rating method would then ask questions about why the analysts determined, for example, that the source was a B (usually reliable) and yet the content was rated as a 4 (doubtfully true). It would appear to common sense that these ratings should be somewhat exclusive of each other. Without showing the scale for the rating or using it consistently and repeatedly throughout an entire unit or organization, this rating system is often misunderstood.

Because of this reason, virtually all military intelligence reports rarely contain this rating system in favor of just simply including a narrative like "source has displayed a pattern of reliable information in the past, but report contains conflicting information" or words to the same effect. Like many things in the U.S. military, this technique for evaluating information sources and content is taught—just not followed. Using a rating system like this or creating for either a source or the content of the data and information coming into an intelligence center requires a well-publish set of criteria and definitions for each grade.

This rating system can also be used for finished analytic products. To do so requires an awareness of the politics or sensitivities involved in grading someone or some organization externally without damaging a working relationship that may exist between both organizations. While most people and organizations will accept constructive criticism, few analysts appreciate being graded by someone they are supposed to be supporting. Risks include additional problems for future coordination and cooperation.

A More Academic Approach to Reliability

Several more comprehensive and categorically structured approaches to evaluating the reliability of information can be found within the academic community. Used as a way to critically think about and improve one's own line of thought on a particular problem set or issue, some colleges and universities have adopted a set of intellectual standards laid out by Drs. Linda Elder and Richard Paul in their 2008 book, *The Thinker's Guide*

---

6   Ibid.

to Intellectual Standards.[7] While both Elder and Paul explain that these nine standards can be bolstered by additional standards depending on the issue, they provide a great set of baseline criteria from a simple mental check to a formal rating process for information coming into your center.

While each of these standards can be used to evaluate a single piece of data, they can also be used to evaluate a source of data, i.e., an entire database, streaming data, a human source, or what's delivered by a collection system. Unlike college students and academic researchers, intelligence analysts often rely upon sources of information that are knowingly fraught with inaccuracies and deception. This is especially true for all-source analysts whose job is to fuse these different data sources together.

While it's relatively simple to understand the basic standards listed out by Elder and Paul, understanding them within the specific context of evaluating the data coming into an intelligence center requires bit more application. Listed below are the intellectual standards according to Elder and Paul, but with the addition of questions to ask about the data that intelligence tools and analysts rely upon. These questions should be applied to both the dataset and the source providing it from an intelligence point of view.

CHART 5.1   Descriptive Source Questions for Intelligence Purposes

Standard	Descriptive source questions for intelligence purposes
CLARITY	Is the information the source is providing clear? Does the source have the means to clearly convey the data? Is the dataset available in a clear, user-friendly format?
ACCURACY	Is the source conveying the truth or something that makes logical sense? Does the source or similar data display a pattern of being accurate in the past? Can the data be corroborated or validated by another source?
PRECISION	Could the source or data be more specific? Does the source have more details available? Does the source answer all the variables related to the issue?
SIGNIFICANCE	Just how important is the data this source is conveying? Is the source set up or directed to elevate the critical elements of information?
RELEVANCE	Is the information related to the problem set? Is it perishable by time or events? How much irrelevant or noise does the source have?
DEPTH	Does the source convey enough detail on the collection target or is more data needed? Can you drive down into the data to answer follow-on questions?
BREADTH	Does the source look at all possible meaning of a data point? Does it cover the issue in its entirety or only a specific aspect?
LOGIC	Does the source really make sense? Is it mutually supportive of other sources? Does it require leaps of logic on the part of the analyst?
FAIRNESS	Does the source have a vested interest in the issue? Does it take into account other perspectives or sources of information? Does the data have a cognitive, political, technical, or some other bias in it?

---

7   Elder, Linda, & Paul, Richard. (2008). *The thinker's guide to intellectual standards.* Tomales, CA: Foundation for Critical Thinking Press.

The adoption of intellectual standards within academia has become increasingly important over the past few decades with the growth of the Internet and its inherent lack of the same standards for source information that goes into more formerly published works like books, periodicals, and other peer-reviewed material.

Evaluating Data: Mapping Open Sources

For some time now, digitally based information has far surpassed data available in print as it is much more readily available from an ever-growing list of sources. Intelligence personnel pull information from media sites, social networks, and information brokers just as frequently as from classified sources. Unclassified information is easier to search for, obtain, and store than classified information, and while it may not be the best information to help with analysis on very specific or detailed target sets, it has long been the first type of information turned to for situational awareness and discovery analysis.

As new potential sources are coming into existence at a rapid pace, it is becoming increasingly difficult for intelligence analysts to keep track of the validity of their sources of information. Just as IT that has drastically changed what the intelligence community of practice looks like over the past 20 years, it has similarly changed the media landscape. The ease of availability of information has allowed smaller and more interest-driven outlets to dramatically alter the previous landscape where media was ruled by a few large media outlets. The previous landscape was more theocratic in nature where a small group of television and print news were the only sources that had the people, resources, and funding to publish or broadcast the most accurate and timely sources of news.

The costs and resources that are required to perform the basic functions of gathering information and repackaging it for consumers have been reduced to the point that small, start-up websites can now compete in the same media market. Search engines and algorithms are replacing reporters and investigators, and internet websites are replacing the need to broadcast systems.

While the analyst can use several techniques to evaluate open-source media, it is important to understand the dynamics of the entire media environment and how it's continually evolving. By laying out media sources in a similar way as today's intelligence community was done in Chapter 3, intelligence analysts can get a perspective of the different categories of media in the context of the all the others. In mapping the media this way, the analyst can create a landscape of the sources that come into their center and more specifically—which ones are being used within a specific operation.

Placing the old guard of the mainstream media in the center, with concentric rings of the newest types of media source, helps to draw groupings and add some sanity to what otherwise seems to be a chaotic landscape of established sources, new niche providers, and the fly-by-night rumor mills. Similar to the intelligence community of practice landscape, the center has an incredible amount of resources for collecting and presenting news that the outer rings simply don't have. They also operate in a much more restricted and constrained environment as publicly traded media companies. The further you get from the center ring, the more unrestrained the environment gets.

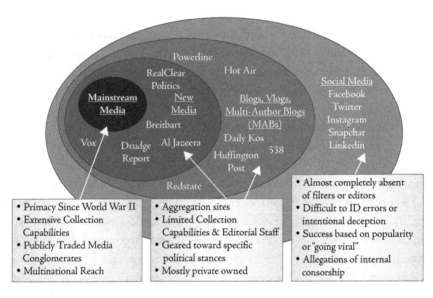

Powerline

RealClear
Politics

New
Media

Hot Air

Social Media
Facebook
Twitter
Instagram
Snapchat
Linkedin

Blogs, Vlogs,
Multi-Author Blogs
(MABs)

Mainstream
Media

Breitbart

Vox

Drudge
Report

Al Jazeera

Daily Kos

538

Huffington
Post

Redstate

- Primacy Since World War II
- Extensive Collection
  Capabilities
- Publicly Traded Media
  Conglomerates
- Multinational Reach

- Aggregation sites
- Limited Collection
  Capabilities & Editorial Staff
- Geared toward specific
  political stances
- Mostly private owned

- Almost completely absent
  of filters or editors
- Difficult to ID errors or
  intentional deception
- Success based on popularity
  or "going viral"
- Allegations of internal
  consorship

FIGURE 5.4   Mapping today's media

For example, major news organizations rely not only on a bevy of reporters and their camera operators but also on an army of producers, editors, graphics, and web designers. On top of this, they have their midlevel managers and corporate leadership. These personnel largely disappear or are consolidated into one multitasked person when you're looking at sources in the outer rings. The collection capability is there, but an outer ring source may tend to rely on speed of publication over quality checks in order to be first with a story.

Mainstream media stories will look more polished, professional, and vetted, but that doesn't mean they are any more accurate than the newer and less resourced sources from the outer rings. Accusations that the mainstream media are propaganda outlets for certain political factions or fake news has grown over the years, largely because the alternative news sources have been able to show their inaccuracies and inherent bias. The loss of trust in many of these venerable sources has also fueled the rise of alternative media as consumers of information no longer accept just one news source as their go to place for information. Intelligence centers are no different and should not be.

One of the more popular sites of alternative media sources are aggregate sites. These sites are news sources that take in media publications from a variety of other sources including the mainstream media, and then reorganize, prioritize, and present these reports according to the needs of their targeted market. Editing has already been done for each individual story or article, but the editors of aggregate sites perform a second level of editing that places the stories they think are more important more prominently on their page. In this way they are replacing the original editor-in-chief of the organization they drew the story from. While aggregate sites may replace the placement bias of the original source, it will in turn replace it with the bias of their own people.

The key to remember about open sources and the constant accusations of bias is that every source has bias. None are exempt. Bias may be politically, professionally, technically, or financially driven, but there are no open source sites that do not contain it in some form. For example, a technical journal is going to be naturally biased toward the niche audience they've been set up to cater to—aircraft, cars, military equipment, etc. Same goes for sources for health care professionals. While a fishing publication may contain some great information about the waterways of a given region, you would not expect it to have information about the latest stealth designs technology—although you shouldn't rule it out.

The last ring includes social media sites. These sites will provide you with good intelligence information, but it will be raw, unfiltered, and unedited for the most part. Success in this realm is determined by how many times a particular story, tweet, or set of comments are shared; not whether it's accurate or not. Intelligence can still take advantage of the outer ring. As one example and with the aid of data mining tools, intelligence analysts can study patterns, themes, and comparative weights of one conversation subject over another. Tools can also be used to identify legitimate stories over clickbait, but as history has proven, the perception and effect of a particular story are sometime more important that what actually happened.

Evaluating Data: Media Bias and Accuracy

A complementary method to evaluate data and information is through a comparison of the journalistic integrity of the source against its political bias. One method of doing this was developed in late 2016 by Vanessa Otero who, as a patent attorney in Colorado, could be considered an outsider to the intelligence profession.

Out of frustration that consumers of news weren't taking the time to understand the reliability and accuracy of their favored sources, Ms. Otero created a comparison method of analyzing news sources and then published it on social media where it has since been shared several times over.

The chart Ms. Otero created evaluates the integrity and bias of a data source and plots each source on a simply x–y axis chart. As the various media sources are individually evaluated plotted, they naturally form groupings that share some commonalities with other similar sources. Otero's original chart includes the names of various media sources according to her subjective evaluation of them, but a blank version of this chart is presented here so that the reader can concentrate on the analytical method that can be employed in a chart like this instead of getting hung up where she placed the various media sources:

For intelligence purposes, this type of chart gives the analyst a structured method to plot, track, and present the various sources used in their intelligence products. Use of it requires a caveat when publishing that the location of each source is based on the analyst's perception of that source and subsequently placed according a subjective set of criteria.

This chart is simple enough to be adapted to virtually any problem set where the final analytical problem set includes information from open media sources. Instead of classifying the bias of a source as Liberal or Conservative, the analyst can redefine the

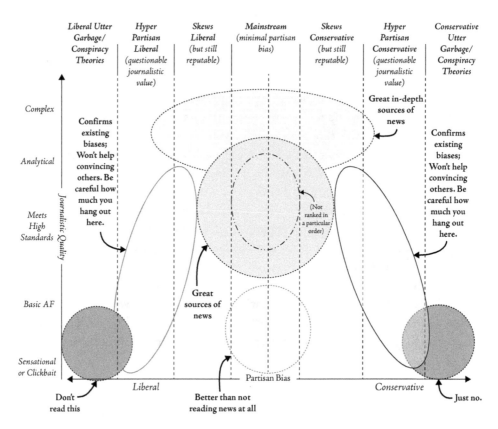

FIGURE 5.5   Otero method of evaluating open sources. Reprinted by permission, with original chart found here

x-axis, using other criteria that more accurately fit the sources they're using. For example, analysis of media in a foreign country or region can use other criteria such as State Run v. Independent or Opposition media.

Sources can also be defined by the bias toward or against a given scenario like Pro-Secession v. Pro-Central Government or alignment toward on or another faction such as Pro-Israel v Pro-Hamas or Hezbollah. As long as the bias evaluation along the x-axis is linear—meaning a dichotomy between two polar opposites—this chart gives the analysts an ability to understand, track, and explain their use of different sources in their products.

While Otero's chart includes bold type that seeks to steer readers away from what are deemed the least reputable sources, for intelligence analysts, sources that would be considered extremely bias and/or poor in journalistic quality are just as valuable as those that would be considered more mainstream or higher quality sources. Every source provides value, especially to those seeking to identify bias or inaccuracies as part of their analysis. This would include any analysis to identify deceptive practices or find areas where friendly information operations could exploit or otherwise deny or degrade an adversary's efforts to use propaganda.

Evaluating Data: Intelligence Disciplines

From an operations standpoint, the next way to classify data and information is through its discipline or, more simply, how it is derived or collected. Technical data has a distinctly different structure and purpose than information open-source news reports or imagery. Information from human sources differs significantly from information generated by technical collection platforms in a variety of ways. Besides the different ways that it is collected, it is also different in terms of how it gets into your center and what tools are needed to process, store, and visualize it. Different sources of data and information also have a best fit, i.e., where they are most likely to help in analysis.

Evaluating data and information sources in terms of the type of intelligence discipline, it contains is more of a practical method. Consider the following chart that evaluates the best fit of different sources of information based on some very broad levels of analytical detail:

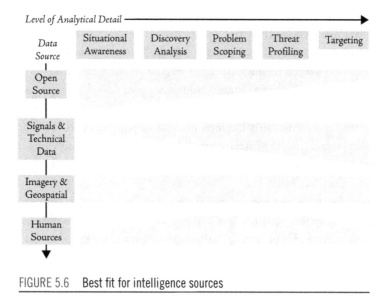

FIGURE 5.6   Best fit for intelligence sources

Levels of Detail Definitions

+ Situational Awareness: Entry-level analysis where a baseline understanding or situational awareness about a general topic is needed. Sometimes this level of detail is called the "one over the world" perspective or where you need information that is a "mile-wide and inch-deep" covering a lot of topic areas, but only with basic or surface-level information.

+ Discovery Analysis: A more specific look at a topic area to gain insights beyond a simple understanding of what it is. Analysis centers on identifying trends, patterns, anomalies, key players, and events. Most preliminary levels of analysis are forms of discovery analysis.

- Problem Scoping: Analysis that looks at specific information about a topic as it relates to your operations including critical requirements for success and failure, key actions, and events that must be achieved or avoided and the integrated connections between groups and individuals.
- Threat Profiling: Specific analysis of the key components of an organization including motivations, goals and objectives, organization, targets, and methods of operations. Also analysis of key individuals including biographical and psychological profiles.
- Targeting: Real-time, near–real-time, or live intelligence about a specific target for immediate and direct action. Includes intelligence needed to target lethal weapons or other direct disruptive or supporting action.

Open Sources

The vast majority of information needed for most analysis comes from open-source information. Also called OSINT, it is relatively easy to find, collect, and get into your center. It is also mostly free and compatible with common commercial software. Examples include news feeds, blogs, video and audio, twitter, books, and virtually any source of information that can be easily obtained through the internet, library, or mass media (TV and radio).

Open-source information is a fantastic source for entry-level analysis, i.e., for gaining an understanding situation, discovering key pieces of information, and scoping out the overall problem set. No matter what level of analysis you begin with, a single person, a group, or global trend (like the international drug trade), open-source information is an easy way for you to conduct preliminary levels of analysis to identify where more detailed analysis must take place later.

As the need for more and more detail is required for a given analytical problem set, open-source information becomes less and less valuable to the analysts. Because most open-source information is primarily available through a third party as the "source," it is not as timely as raw data feeds. Information that requires publishing, posting, editing, or formal presentation usually entails a time buffer. A couple of notable exceptions are social networks that do not have an editor or approval authority such as Twitter or Instagram. Other near–real-time sources will gain and wane in popularity on an almost constant basis.

Signals and Technical Data

This includes capturing any kind of technical or electronic data such as e-mails, radio signals, cell-phone calls, telemetry data, electronic and ultraviolet signatures, and even electromagnetic radiation. Collection of this kind of data usual involves a much higher level of technical sophistication than for any other kind of data or information, and because of this, this data is primarily collected by those who have ample resources. Signals and technical data also carry legal restrictions in terms of rights to privacy and the associated infringement of our liberties.

Technical data is generally not useful for broad-based situational awareness or discovery analysis. Because of its more abstract nature, data from signals and technical sources tends to be more useful for specific intelligence operations, especially when the need for information has to be specific and timely enough for actions to directly affect the target. This is especially true for military targeting—both lethal and nonlethal. Real or near–real-time information is critically important for a target to be at the right place at the right time.

Because of the overwhelming amount of technical data that can stream into a center, information from technical sources are usually preceded by other kinds of analysis and tipped or queued by indicators in other sources of information or data. This way, technical data can be specifically queried within a limiting set of parameters. This status has been challenged in recent years by the ever-increasing capability of automated tools. Supercomputers designed with voracious appetites pulling in what was thought to be unimaginable amounts of technical information have led many to believe that technical data can actually find patterns and anomalies themselves. One major problem with this view is the amount of information and computing power required to do this has the potential to run in direct violation of expectations and rights to privacy.

Imagery and Geospatial Intelligence

Imagery-based and geospatial related intelligence (IMINT and GEOINT respectively) is different from other sources in that its data has already been translated into a *visual* format prior to conversion into information. In this way the analyst can simply look at raw imagery as part of their process, thereby making it useful at each level of analytical detail.

For an analyst, it's the type of imagery and geospatial information that is important to understand in terms of when it's useful. For simple situational awareness and problem scoping, commercially and publicly available imagery is most prominent. This is mainly because of the ease of obtaining it. From internet photos to online mapping programs and GPS (Global Positioning System) data to video, commercially available imagery is readily available, and while it requires more memory and bandwidth than simple textual or raw technical data, it's one of the most proliferate sources of information for any analyst who knows how to search for it on the Internet.

While rapid advances in IT is continuously improving the levels of detail in commercially available imagery and geospatial information, the most detailed and operationally oriented imagery is obtained through more sophisticated and therefore not publicly available sources. This includes imagery from overhead platforms such as military aircraft (air breathers) and satellites (non-air breathers) as well as from human sources, be they open, covert, or clandestine in their collection. High-technology sources of GEOINT can also provide imagery and geospatial data fused with other types of information such as heat, infrared and reflective signatures, electronic emanations, or facial recognition technologies.

Obviously the costs both in resources and risks associated with the most advanced imagery often make it exclusive to the largest customer, i.e., the government. Getting imagery and geospatial data for Threat Profiling and targeting requires a connection to a government/military database or collection platform. As described above, analysis in support of targeting requires near–real-time data to ensure whatever is being delivered actually hits the intended target. Just "Googling" it isn't going to work here, at least for the time being.

Human-Based Intelligence

Human-based intelligence (HUMINT) is a strange outlier from the other sources of information for analysis in that it is useful for middle-range levels of analytical detail but less useful at the ends of the spectrum, namely situational awareness and targeting. This is because human-based intelligence sources are neither timely nor broadly based.

Information from human sources is fairly self-explanatory as collecting involves methods that are centuries older than other type of intelligence information. Whispers, conversations, interrogations, rumors, letters, diaries, photos, diagrams, schematics—virtually anything that is collected by passing information from the human source to the human collector can fall into this category. Even data classified into the other disciplines but derived from human-to-human contact falls into HUMINT for collection purposes at least from an operational point of view.

Because of the way it's collected, HUMINT has some unique aspects to how it is useful to the analyst. Setting up a human-based information network is measured in days, weeks, and even months; you can't just move into a region, flip a switch, and have this kind of information flowing into your intel center. Everything about HUMINT collection takes time. It takes time to identify potential sources, cultivate them, recruit them, and collect information from them about a particular subject. It also takes time to collect and process this type of information primarily because it involves humans versus technical platforms. Because of the time it takes to get setup and to collect once it is set up, HUMINT is rarely effective for situational awareness or real-time targeting.

HUMINT is also fraught with other challenges. It is resource intensive in terms of workforce requirements. Sources have to be judged for their reliability. It is also potentially fraught with some of the darker aspects of intelligence, i.e., payment, bribes, extortion, blackmail, theft, false flags, covers, lies, and a host of other acts that can be deemed illegal, immoral, or both. Risks to the sources and collectors is significantly higher than any other type of collection, especially when dealing with covert collection efforts where exposure of any part of the effort could lead to retribution of some sort.

Even with these inherent risks and detractors, HUMINT provides detailed information about a subject that simply can't be collected from a remote or nonhuman platform. Getting into the mindset of a person, their thoughts, observations, perspectives, motivations, and decision-making processes are best suited for HUMINT, which is why it rates so highly in problem scoping and Threat Profiling. It may be messy and untimely, but in many cases, it's the only way to gain this level of understanding. Much of what HUMINT provides can't be derived from an overhead image, phone call statistics, or from a media outlet.

While rapid advances in IT are blurring the divisions between these sources of information and intelligence, there are still and will always be specific and exclusive functions of each type of information relevant to an intelligence operation.

Evaluating Data: Functionality

A final way to look at data and information sources is in terms of how it fits into a particular operation. This is more of list of things to consider when shopping for data sources to collect for a specific operation than evaluating a single message or item.

The functionality of data and information is paramount to all other considerations. These questions concern the Who-What-Where-When-Why of the data and information that is needed and desired for analytic work. One thing to keep in mind despite any disagreements from software or network engineers is that all related technical questions are subordinate to the functionality of the data. Evaluating data from a functional standpoint uses several basic questions as an iterative process.

CHART 5.2   Functional Considerations for Intelligence Data and Information

Area to consider	Pertinent questions to ask
NEED	What products do you need to create?
	What kind of data is needed for your analysis?
SOURCE	Who owns the data?
	Why was this data set or stream created in the first place?
	Who or what source contributes to it?
	Who else uses the data and for what purpose?
TYPE	What kind of data/information is it?
	What are its technical parameters for use?
	What classification is it?
	Does it contain any U.S. persons or nonpublicly available information?
	Which applications work well with it?
	Which applications do not work well with it?
	How does this data set rate against the intellectual standards?
ACQUISITION AND STORAGE	How do I gain permissions to get the data?
	How do I physically get it into my center?
	How do I ingest, parse, and get it into my current tools?
	Do I need additional applications in order to work with it?
USE	How can I use the data?
	How can I see/visualize it?
	What kinds of analysis does this data support best?
	What new analytical methods can I perform with this data?
	Does this data lend itself to easy dissemination in products or as a source?
COST	How much does it cost?
	Is there a cheaper alternative that gives me similar capabilities?
	Are there any lingering or hidden costs?

These questions do not address the quality, bias, or security as much as it addresses how to handle the data, i.e., how to obtain, pay, store, work, present, and transfer it.

Water, Water, Everywhere and Not a Drop to Drink

One final question an intelligence operation must address when looking for data is how much is too much? The U.S. Intelligence Community, much like many other countries, has invested an enormous amount of resources to build up the capability to collect massive amounts of information and yet intelligence analysts are getting overwhelmed by amount of data they must work with.

As intelligence operations emerged from the Cold War, our ability to collect information has dramatically increased. We've gone from kilobytes to megabytes to gigabytes, and terabytes within a little more than a single generation of analysts as several dozens of messages received has turned into several million messages streaming in every month. With an adult average reading speed of 300 words per minute and no foreseeable way to increase or evolve ourselves, the human part of the intelligence center machine has been unable to effective read, comprehend, or use a large percentage of information available to them from any given database or data stream.[8]

After many recent intelligence failures, it's been relatively easy to point the finger of blame at the intelligence analyst or organization. After any sort of violent terrorist or extremist attack, there will inevitably be critics that will say that the U.S. Intelligence Community had information that could have prevented it but didn't act on it. This type of criticism is well founded, but not in the right areas. Sure, an intelligence agency or organization could have collected that critical piece of information, but it sat hidden in plain sight among millions of other similar bits of information or was washed downstream into some bit bucket, so room in the queue could be made for the next day's data dump. Intelligence people are not to blame; they simply lack the capabilities as human beings to handle all the information available to them.

Instead, the blame for this lies in our ability to set up an intelligence operation with the right data mining and visualization tools and technologies. Having data come into an intelligence center unabated may cost a lot of resources in terms of bandwidth and storage but being able to do anything worthwhile with that information is another more complex and resource-intensive challenge.

While each of the methods outlined in this chapter works well for evaluating handful of articles or data files, working in an environment where data is coming in by the giga-bytes and terabytes makes it impossible to evaluate each message manually. Instead, each source has to be evaluated with a general rating for the expected veracity of the content.

Any set of data needs automated tools to help the analyst work with it and sift through it. Just as any deep-sea fishing expedition requires a boat, any decent level of analysis using stored or streaming information requires tools. If data is the technical lifeblood or flowing water of an intelligence center, software tools are its heart and eyes. It's through these tools that data is pushed, pulled, and stored within the center. It's also the way we can visualize the data and information available.

---

8   Nelson, Brett. (2012, June 4). *Do you read fast enough to be successful? Forbes Magazine.* Retrieved from https://www.forbes.com/sites/brettnelson/2012/06/04/do-you-read-fast-enough-to-be-successful/#5f354d08462e

Summary

Intelligence is a business that deals in two main commodities—data and information. In order to turn data into relevant information and information into useful knowledge, intelligence professionals must constantly ensure that the right information is available for their analysis. To assist them, there are many methods and tools to evaluate their available data and information sources. The key here is start with a series of questions to help define the data and information requirements of the specific operation in question. From there, data and information can be evaluated for security, reliability, bias, accuracy, discipline, and function.

Key Summary Points

- Data, information, and knowledge are each required within an intelligence center or operation, but each differs from the other in terms of how it's derived and used.
- The variety of data, information, and finished intelligence used for intelligence analysis requires different methods to evaluate and determine which are the best fit for operations.
- Effective evaluation methods include information security, reliability, mapping open sources, bias and accuracy, intelligence discipline, and functionality

Discussion Questions

- What are the advantages and risks of data, information, or knowledge (in the form of finished intelligence) when applied to analysis?
- Other than those cited in this chapter, what are the other methods of evaluating data, information, or knowledge for intelligence operations?
- Which method of evaluating data, information, and knowledge can be expected to change the most in the near future?
- In using open-sourced information, particularly from media sources, what are the advantages of using information that has been evaluated as having poor reliability, quality, or is untrustworthy?

Figure Credits

Fig. 5.1: Terri Stephens, "Themescape Picture." Copyright © 1999 by Cartia, Inc.
Fig. 5.5: Source: https://twitter.com/vlotero.

Chapter 6

Data Mining and Visualization Tools

Learning Objectives

After completing this chapter, you will be able to:

▸ Understand the operational purposes and capabilities of data mining in support of intelligence analysis.

▸ Be familiar with the arguments against data mining along with the importance of oversight.

▸ Be familiar with the pertinent questions to ask in evaluating data mining tools.

▸ Understand the methods of data mining footprinting and water flow charting in planning where data mining tools will best support intelligence operations.

Data Mining Is Inquiry

As noted in the previous chapter, the base materials that analysts use to create intelligence products are data and information. In this sense, data is the raw material that is refined into information in order to create analytic products. To effectively use data and information, whether it's stored or streaming, intelligence centers must have the capability to organize, categorize, tag, and parse data in order to convert into information. They must also have the capability for analysts to visualize, absorb, and discover new information in order to create a product pertinent to their problem set. While the human mind can do this to a limited extent, having the capability of working with massive amounts of data and information requires software tools.

To tackle the vast amounts of data and information available to a given intelligence operation or center, analysts take advantage of software tools to identify patterns in large data sets, and extract them for their analysis. The most popular term for this is data mining: The act of using automated software and algorithms to examine, investigate, and exploit large data sets to identify new and usable information. Other terms somewhat synonymous to Data Mining include information discovery, knowledge discovery and knowledge extraction. Data mining as a term can be somewhat confusing or misleading to new analysts. When we are gold mining, we are extracting gold as the product from the earth. When we mine data, we are extracting and creating usable information from data—not simply creating more data.[1]

The objective of data mining using software and other automated tools is for analysts to spend less time sifting through the data and more time doing what they're supposed to do—conducting analysis. Data mining aids in this effort, tackling large data and information sets and stream separating the important information from all the noise, chaff, and unrelated data that flows into our world at a constantly growing rate. For an intelligence community of practice that spent vast amounts of treasure over several decades on spy planes, ground sensors, satellites, multispectral radar arrays, and even unmanned collection platforms, e.g., drones, intelligence analysts became overwhelmed with the amount of information available. It was only until very end of the 20th century were we able to come up with ways of managing and making sense of the rising tide of data. Even so, many analysts would argue the success of these tools.

The essence of data mining is inquiry, or the act of posing a question. Directed or focused inquiry allows analysts to frame what they need to know from the data and information available to them. If not available, it then allows collectors, whether they're human or machine, to search for the right information and bring it into the center.

Intelligence analysts are constantly working off specified, implied, or identified requirements that are created by their supported customers. These can be formal, such as priority intelligence requirements, PIRs for short, or informal, such as questions that form in the process of analytic work.

Data mining simply doesn't work without that question or inquiry. Without getting into the technical aspects of data mining, every data mining tool has to be taught—i.e., programmed to identify patterns, commonalities, relationships, and anomalies within a given data set. Programmers write these instructions in the form of algorithms that are sets of tasks or steps a computer program is directed to take to fulfill a task. Data mining algorithms are instructions specifically written to find certain patterns or anomalies in a given data set or actively streaming data feed. The number of types of algorithms is as limitless as the limits of spoken or written language.

Even further, analysts cannot expect a data set to reveal what's important by itself as it needs some sort of inquiry that is framed in a way that is compatible with the type of data it holds. For example, a financial analyst working for a credit card company can't just ask a database of customer records and say "show me everyone who is going to be a problem paying their credit cards off." Instead their question must be framed in a way so that software can search the database looking for patterns that have already been

---

1   Han, Jiawei, & Kamber, Micheline. (2001). *Data mining: concepts and techniques* (p. 5). Burlington, MA: Morgan Kaufmann. ISBN: 978-1-55860-489-6.

identified as credit risks. In this way, data mining tools must be programmed to take the analyst's query in the spoken language and turn it into one of more sets of instructions in the appropriate machine language.

Going back to the credit card scenario, an analyst may want to know who is going to have a problem paying their credit card, but in machine language terms, a software engineer would need to create queries, association rules, and predictive and descriptive models using algorithms that will allow a data mining tool to find sets of data associated with payment problems. These could include identifying accounts that have previously had late or missed payments, accounts that are never paid fully, or credit debts that have been paid from another source of credit.

In addition, the software engineer could create a query that looks for social/human indicators, and search for indicators that may signal an account holder is most likely going through a divorce, sudden lawyer expenses, purchase of legal document or notary services, marriage counselor payments, etc. There are many more things they could look for as an indicator associated with a missed payment, but again each of these must be programmed into some sort of query in the machine language of that particular tool and the data source it's searching.

As the science and engineering of data mining develops, analysts may find themselves overwhelmed by its technical aspects. They may even come to believe that they must learn all the technical aspects of data mining such as algorithms, coding, association rules, or classification clustering in order to be an effective intelligence analyst. While studying data mining from a scientific perspective is helpful, understanding it from the perspective of its operational applications is more immediately and directly related to what they need to do.

A parallel metaphor would be that a rifle marksman doesn't necessarily need to know about metallurgy in order to effectively engage targets with his weapon, but he does need to know why it's important for the ballistics of his round.

Arguments Against Data Mining

Data mining is not without its detractors. Indeed at the turn of the 21st century when data mining was somewhat nascent, many people were apprehensive, fearful, or simply ignorant in the ways that information technology could support their efforts. These arguments revolved around a general angst of relying on machines to do some of the heavy lifting for analysts. Below are some of the top arguments against data mining that took root at the beginning of the information and yet are still prevalent today:

1. **Data Mining Is an Invasion of Privacy:** Vacuuming up massive amounts of data and information or using web crawlers and other automated methods inevitably leads to personal information about innocent people to be consumed as part of it. Data mining automated search tools and harvesters collect it all without regard to privacy laws or oversight regulations required for government collection.

As a society, we've slowly surrendered our expectation of privacy for security; some may argue we no longer have either.

2. **Data Mining Is a Waste of Time and Resources:** Collecting and searching through massive amounts of data and information requires enormous amounts of computing power for both the search/mining capabilities as well as processing and storage capabilities. Likewise, this means spending massive amounts of money to have the latest technology that can do it more effectively. Given the estimated rate of return for the investment, resources spent trying to mine data could be better spent elsewhere.

3. **Data Mining Can Lead to Abuses:** With all that data and information available to the intelligence analysts, in some cases the weak point can be the intelligence analyst themselves. By adding to old adages that "information is power" and "power corrupts," one can logically conclude that information corrupts and massive amounts of information corrupt absolutely. Data mining allows even relatively small intelligence operations the ability to tap into personal or derogatory information far beyond the purview of their purpose as analysts. Trusting humans to not to abuse this power is illogical.

4. **Data Mining Is Inaccurate and Leads to False Positives (proximity algorithm example):** Not all analysts trust data mining tools, either in the way their algorithms were programmed to search for information or in the way they display data returns. For example, an analyst looking for information related to Secretary Hillary Clinton and an unspecified threat to her security at an upcoming event. They query a search tool to find all instances where the words "Clinton" + "Attack" are mentioned in the same data record. The returns will come back with information about Secretary Clinton, President Bill Clinton, prominent Clinton family members, the town of Clinton, Maryland, or even British General Henry Clinton who fought in American Revolution. This overly simplified scenario highlights the perils of false positives in data mining. Now imagine doing similar searched using names in foreign cultures that analysts are not inherently familiar with.

Personal Perspectives:
Get Its and Don't Get Its

As the Chief of Intelligence for a relatively new U.S. Army unit called the Land Information Warfare Activity (LIWA), much of the work of my roughly two dozen intelligence analysts was conducted with the U.S. Army Intelligence and Security Command's (USAINSCOM or just INSCOM for short) Information Dominance Center or IDC. Newly opened at the beginning of 1999, the IDC was futuristic looking and employed some of the most power data mining and visualization tools in the U.S. government. As such, the IDC also drew a lot of visitors requiring periodic briefings and presentations depending on their VIP levels.

The audience for these presentations, more affectionately known as Dog and Pony Shows within certain circles of the military, could range from a couple of VIPs to a large audience of 30 visitors. We demonstrated the IDC's data mining and visualization software and their operational applications to fellow military officers, high-ranking government civilians, the media, and even members of the US Congress.

Providing the intelligence analysis portion of the presentation was one of my primary responsibilities. For nearly two years as the Intel Chief, I gave an estimated 80–100 of these presentations. During my portion of the presentation, I made it a habit to scan my audience and assess whether or not they understood the concepts of data mining and the predictive analytic capabilities of our tools. Those who would genuinely look interested in what I had to say would slowly nod their head as I spoke or ask pointed and specifically relevant questions, which would be evaluated as a "Get It" by either myself or one of my senior folks in attendance. Those that looked confused, lost interest, or asked argumentative or trick questions were labeled as a "Don't Get It." The relations we were trying to build to the rest of the military and U.S. government were based on identifying and strengthening relationships with the "Get Its" while minimizing the fallout or reaction from our detractors.

While the reader may feel that these arguments have been made as straw men to be knocked down by data mining advocates, the fact is they are all true to an extent. Data mining, if conducted poorly or capriciously will most certainly fail. If conducted without moral or ethical restraint will most certainly lead to abuses and potentially illegal privacy violations. These arguments can be easily validated by a cursory search of data mining abuses and failures with a simple search of recent news stories (ironically using current internet search engines).

As a caveat to these arguments is that collection of massive amounts of publicly available information is leading our society blindly toward an Orwellian future. Governments, through intelligence and other agencies and using data mining tools, is evolving into "Big Brother" eroding our sense of privacy with each passing year.

The truth is that while abuses of data mining by government into the private lives of its citizens will forever be a legitimate concern, what is more concerning are potential abuses in the commercial sector. Internet providers, search engines, and social media sites routinely mine information coming in from its users. Even further, a myriad of other types of companies that rely on consumer information to predict purchasing patterns, assess credit risks, investigate financial and insurance-related fraud among other topics, and have the potential to know virtually everything about an individual that was once deemed private. In an Orwellian sense, it's not the one big brother that should be of concern as much as it's the thousand little brothers that are invading every part of our private lives.

Mining massive amounts of data can be an incredibly powerful tool for intelligence analysis, and intelligence operation must have proper policies and procedures for both collecting and handling data and information. These policies must include oversight, internal reviews, and clearly defined rules for data mining within an organization. They must also include specific rules to both analytic and operational processes for the operation that gives both collectors and analysts to tools to mitigate any risks of either failure or abuse.

Intelligence Oversight and Data Mining

One of the chief problems with collecting or "harvesting" massive amount data and information is the potential—rather almost certainty of picking up information related to U.S. persons by an intelligence organization. While this may not seem to be a serious issue in the commercial sector, for intelligence operations within the U.S. government it is a very serious issue.

U.S. persons, by definition, are not just citizens of the United States. They are "any United States citizen or alien admitted for permanent residence in the United States, and any corporation, partnership, or other organization organized under the laws of the United States."[2] These persons and corporate entities have certain rights to privacy as outlined by the U.S. Constitution and more specifically by Presidential Executive Order 12333 originally signed by President Ronald Reagan and validated by every administration since. Depending on where an intelligence operation is located within the U.S. government hierarchy, additional regulations are also in effect.

For the U.S. Department of Defense, regulation or (DoD Reg)5240.01 and 5240.1-R establishes oversight policy and rules for conducting intelligence activities, respectively, that further protect a U.S. person's right to privacy. Further regulations are included within each of the DoD service components. These regulations cover various procedures that must be followed by intelligence professionals including who the restrictions apply to within the U.S. government and in what specific manner information about U.S. persons can be collected, retained, and disseminated.[3]

Data mining tools that have massive collection capabilities are generally programmed to cull out information regarding U.S. persons. They will collect everything in an unbiased unemotional manner. This automatic collection poses several dilemmas to intelligence personnel operating under the restraints of intelligence oversight rules. Based on the four areas covered by oversight regulations, there are several issues to consider:

+ **Applicability:** Now that data mining has allowed the practice of intelligence to slip beyond the U.S. Intelligence Community, should other parts of

---

2   U.S. person as defined by Title 22 of U.S. Code. Retrieved from https://www.gpo.gov/fdsys/pkg/USCODE-2010-title22/pdf/USCODE-2010-title22-chap69-sec6010.pdf

3   The Department of Defense Intelligence Oversight Program. Retrieved from http://dodsioo.defense.gov/Portals/46/Documents/DoD%20Basic%20Intelligence%20Oversight%20Course.pdf

government and society also be applicable to intelligence oversight? Government and contracted personnel employed at various intelligence agencies are certainly subject to intelligence oversight, but what about those working elsewhere but still conducting analysis against threats? There are several organizations that don't consider themselves part of the U.S. Intelligence Community and are not funded by an intelligence budget and yet conduct their own analysis under the auspices of "information analysis." Should intelligence oversight of some form also apply to other parts of our society such as state, local, or tribal government, commercial, and academic sectors?

- **Collection:** Intelligence oversight regulations have fairly specific procedures regarding information that is collected incidentally. Is information about a U.S. person collected using data mining tools based on a search query considered incidental collection or a directed effort on the part of the intelligence operation? What if the collection was conducted without the knowledge of the authorized person, e.g., with a web crawler or spider-bot program?

- **Retention:** Since information about U.S. persons is allowed to be retained by a specified number of days (currently 90 days), does the retention clock start when this information was initially harvested by data mining software or when human analyst actually discover they have it or see it? How can the human analyst effectively identify and delete information about U.S. persons from massive data sets? How has cloud computing made this more difficult? Once the retention period is up, is it practical to expect analysts to be able to selectively cull U.S. person related information without deleting the entire data set that it resides in or does it all have to be destroyed?

- **Dissemination:** Can a massive data set that may have information about US persons be shared if the center sharing it is unable to determine if there is? What about streaming data? Is an entire massive data set restricted from dissemination if there are only a few or a single known instance of U.S. person related information? Can we expect analysts to selectively edit this information prior to it being shared?

Each of these questions helps to highlight the potential conflicts between data mining and intelligence oversight regulations at the U.S. federal government level. Owing to the fact that several of these regulations are decades old, many of these questions are left up to legal interpretations and as such can vary from organization to organization, and from time to time within the same organization.

Since the use of data mining tools increases the risks of violating intelligence oversight regulations, it's critically important for procedures of handling information about U.S. persons or other privacy-/proprietary-related information be well-thought out, legally vetted, and widely disseminated within and intelligence center and operation. Disregarding this risk will most certainly guarantee a violation of these regulations at some point.

Personal Perspectives:
Bureaucratic Restrictions on Data

Able Danger and hunt for Al Qaida terrorists prior to 9/11 certainly ran into intelligence oversight issues for my analysts while working in the IN-SCOM IDC. Working what was arguably the first successful use of data mining and visualization tools in support of intelligence analysis, our team quickly ran afoul of both Army and DoD legal counsel who were both unfamiliar with data mining technologies as well as the enormous

FIGURE 6.1   UA Flight 175 hits South Tower—9/11

potential we had to identify and map out the terrorist network perhaps better than any other intelligence agency could without the need to put massive amounts of resources, i.e., agents and collection systems in the field to find them.

One of the first problems we ran into was the question of incidental versus directed collection on U.S. persons. Since we ran queries on Al Qaida based on some very general search terms, there was a 100% probability that information about U.S. persons would be found among all the data, especially when we harvested directly from internet search tools. We just had no idea whose information we pulled in or if it was relevant to our analysis. Once we were ordered to cease our operations, we were forbidden from even accessing what we had already collected. Because of this, we had no way of either sorting through or culling out irrelevant information from what we collected. Once the 90-day clock came up, it all had to be deleted. I now believe that we had information related to the 9/11 attacks prior to 9/11 and yet the strict interpretations of intelligence oversight restrictions kept us from conducting this critical analysis.

After several long months on hiatus, my analysts were able to continue our analysis on Al Qaida. A second issue involving intelligence oversight arose when we were attempting to gain access to the U.S. State Department's Student VISA database. Even though this database was specifically created to catalog foreign students within the United States, we were denied access for two reasons. First, as our liaison explained, the State Department was months behind in updating this database and second, the owners could not guarantee that any foreign student who had a record in the database did not become a U.S. person (either through citizenship or other legal residence) in the time they've been in the United States as students. We therefore couldn't see any of it. We continued our analytical work in disbelief that we couldn't access one of the most critical sources of information due to antiquated technology and bureaucratic incompetence.

The Purpose of Data Mining for Intelligence Analysis

While all the arguments listed above are valid, there is one argument that belies a misunderstanding of how data mining supports intelligence. It is encapsulated in the proverbial statement that "you don't find the needle in the haystack by adding more hay." While the statement is true on its face, that's not the reason or intent of effective data mining.

Intelligence analysts don't use data mining and visualization tools to simply dive into a massive amount of data in order to find that one lynch pin piece of evidence puts the entire intelligence picture together. They also don't use data mining to find and extract a single piece of information to use outside of the context of what the rest of the data indicates. For intelligence operations, the amount of data or "hay" is irrelevant beyond having enough to conduct effective analysis.

Indeed, the purpose of data mining for intelligence is to provide analysts with the ability to identify trends, patterns, and anomalies within a massive amount of data, sometimes referred to as Big Data. Data mining tools must also allow analysts to visualize and display the findings in a way that the analyst can understand the results and apply them within the context of the supported operation. Their results must be in turn, presented or produced in a product so that the data is not lost in the process, but clearly able to reinforce an assessment or provide proof to confirm or deny a preliminary read. In summary, data mining allows analysts to conduct their jobs in an environment where the amount of data available has now overwhelmed the ability of the human mind to process and extract new knowledge using manual methods.

Operational Capabilities of Data Mining for Intelligence

Even further, effective data mining provides several capabilities to intelligence that previous generations of analysis simply could not do. While there are many minor or even anecdotal benefits to data mining, the top eight are listed here. Keep in mind these are not *technical* capabilities of some of the tools themselves, but *operational* capabilities that help intelligence analysts conduct their work more effectively and allow intelligence center using these tools to do new things with the same data and information feeds:

+ **Faster Learning:** Because analysts can sift through data and information more quickly, they can identify the key issues, people, events, or relationships faster than manual analytic methods. Instead of reading through everything line by line, they can switch to visual learning within their data and jump from pertinent point to point slowing down to read and evaluate what's been identified as important. Data mining tools won't tell the analyst why something it identified is important, just that it is important based on what was asked. In this way they can more quickly and efficiently understand the background of a new subject or area of an existing one and more efficiently ask second-tiered sets of questions while delving into the more pertinent parts of data sets.

- **Priorities of Work:** Most data mining tools were created to work on the front end of the Intelligence Cycle rather than the back end. More specifically they were created to collect, process, organize, and store incoming data and information so that the analyst doesn't have to spend all their time doing those tasks. Instead, data mining allows analysts to spend more time understanding, learning, analyzing, and creating products; one of the reasons many people chose to become analysts in the first place. There are some drawbacks with doing less of the front-end housework that analysts must mitigate as they are more detached from understanding the data they need to work with. In some cases analysts can become solely reliant upon a software engineer to help them run some of the basic collection and processing functions within their center.

- **Knowledge Discovery:** Analysts are limited to the number of linkages and relationships they can identify by manually working on a set of data. Therefore, their ability to discover items of interest and the knowledge gained from as well. Trying to discover new relevant items and knowledge across multiple and sometime incompatible data sets is virtually prohibitive. Data mining tools that can handle much larger and cross-correlated data sets will yield many times more items of interest for the analyst to consider. And while the analyst will require more time to consider and evaluate these items for relevance, data mining tools can help to organize these items for quicker work.

- **Patterns and Trends:** Poor analysis can sometimes be attributed to a tendency for analysts to get "lost in the weeds" of a particular problem or within a given data set. Moving slowly through data or query returns with limited time available can push analysts into creating products with a limited set of data points or with only a surface-level assessment in the rush to get send something to the customer. Data mining allows the analyst to step back and approach their analysis at a different level. Being able to visualize and work with larger sets of data (again, more "hay") allows the analyst to identify several more points of interest and therefore look for any patterns or trends across a given data set that they wouldn't normally notice while buried in an individual record or piece. Seeing the forest for the trees is a critical part of being able to answer the proverbial "so what" questions from their customers. With data mining tools, analyst can more effectively do that.

- **New Analytic Techniques:** As new tools with new algorithms designed to query, collect, organize, and visualize data are created, analysts using data mining tools will find they can either improve existing or create new analytic techniques to tackle their workload. For example, seeing a series of related events that have taken place is one thing while seeing them on a timeline is another. Seeing these same events geo-located or correlated with some other data set such as the names of who took part in each, a correlation with the days of the week, the weather, holiday schedule, or even friendly events/operations gives an entirely new perspective to intelligence analysis. Detailed analysis can be long, painstaking, and even mundane or sometimes frustrating work. Having data mining tools can help analysts with new ways to work the problems they encounter such as a gap in information a particular relationship that didn't make sense.

+ **Checks and Balances:** Several contrarian analytic techniques such as Team A/Team B and Devil's Advocacy are effective, but fairly time consuming and require resources, i.e., manpower that an intelligence operation simply may not have available. With the almost constant requirement of having to churn out analytic products day after day, many centers place a priority on conducting quality assurance checks or reviews of analytic work. Data mining allows for analysts to streamline these techniques, whether it's a detailed step prior to disseminating a product or a simple set of checks on an analysts source material.**Change Directions:** Analysts working on a problem set for days, weeks, and months tend to be protective over their work. Realizing a fundamental flaw in their work after spending a lot of time and resources is a dilemma no analyst wants to face. Missing a key data set that contains information refuting their original analysis or discovering that they've been using data in violation of intelligence oversight regulations can be monumentally frustrating for intelligence professionals. While traditional methods of analysis requires an almost restart of a project, data mining allows an analyst to more quickly and effectively retool their queries and display the correct data and relationships in the even more limited time they have available.

+ **Presentation:** Data mining tools with robust visualization aspects allow analysts to show their math. Using tools to visualize data sets instead of mundane lists of tables, data entries or text is a powerful feature for presenting information to intelligence customer, especially those who like to see for themselves or dive into the details of a given intelligence product. An analyst's ability to earn their support and customer/decision-maker's trust on their read is of prime importance. Many customers, once they understand the capabilities of some of the tools actually will require analysts to show how they came to a certain conclusion or prediction. There are uncounted ways through which tools can display data and information, it's up to the analyst to use the ones that help to explain their analysis more effectively.

A caveat to this list is that all of these capabilities are the results of an *effective* data mining operation and not every intelligence center functions well enough to enable some of these capabilities. As discussed in Chapter 4, effective intelligence center and the operations it hosts require the right combination and synchronization of people, tools, data, and processes in order for them to support their customers, including the use of data mining tools as part of this support. Dysfunction is one or more of these four components and will result in an ineffective operation or overall poor quality of support to the customer. This is especially true of intelligence operations that rely on data mining tools.

Data Mining Considerations

Besides the requirement for a successful integration of people, tools, data, and processes, several other planning considerations are needed to effectively use data mining tools in support of intelligence operations. First is an understanding that these tools don't eliminate bias, deception, or propaganda—aka lies, mistakes, and errors. They don't reveal them to the analyst, but they do help an analyst identify indicators of bias and other falsehoods through both quantitative and qualitative analytic techniques.

For example, propaganda, fake news, or just spin can be identified by collection information from several sources and comparing key words and adjectives in association with them. Propaganda just doesn't happen on its own and therefore starts with a single source. It then must propagate through several willing or ignorant accomplices who use it, incorporate it into their own reporting, or simply share it without checking its accuracy or truthfulness. Propaganda works because human being wants it to; within those who knowingly want to spread it or those who want to believe because they're already predisposed toward one side or another on a topic or issue. As a propaganda theme proliferates among several sources, the searchable phrases stay relatively constant.

Data mining tools can search for the terms associated with a particular theme, measure that sources are picking up on it, and through time stamping of incoming data, narrow down the relative start point and the organization that started it. This is difficult to do as a manual process, but working effective search techniques with tools can help to find bias and deception as either outlying data points or part of a growing theme albeit with a limited shelf life.

As tools don't eliminate bias or deception, they are also unbiased themselves in how they process information. If the source of collected data or information has some sort of bias to being with, e.g., technical or political, the tool won't weed that information out or asterisk it for you—it will work with it as the given truth. It will also not eliminate bias on the part of the analyst. If a given query or set of instructions used by the tool is the result of a skewed or prejudicial viewpoint, data mining tools will run based on the skewed instructions it receives.

Data mining is about more than just data and tools. As stated in Chapter 4, data mining is just a method in itself for people to use data and tools more effectively against the volumes of data and information available to them. If an intelligence center cannot take advantage of data mining tools effectively in support of a customer, there is something wrong, not just within the tools, but also with the data, analytic and operational processes, or mindset of the people working within that center.

Personal Perspectives:
Faster Learning thru Data Mining

After being approached by military planners at U.S. Special Operations Command (SOCOM) for the possible involvement in their operations against Al Qaeda, I was invited represent LIWA in an interagency working group hosted by the Naval Surface Warfare Center in Dahlgren, Virginia. Numerous intelligence agencies had also sent representatives each gave a summary of what they knew of Al Qaeda or its leaders. During the brain storming session that followed, my SOCOM point of contact approached me and asked what LIWA analysts could bring to the effort using our data mining tools. I called back one of my senior analysts and asked her to run a quick preliminary analysis of different data sets, sending me the results in a few slides that included screen captures of the some of our visualizations.

After receiving the results, my SOCOM point of contact pulled me into a separate conference away from the larger session and asked me to present what we found. Several of the group members who had already shown their hostility to LIWA and our data mining tools came with us to listen in. As I proceeded through my impromptu presentation, these skeptics quickly became vocal, attacking our analysis.

"Nothing you're briefing us here is new information, our agency (to remain nameless) has been working on this for months and knows all of this already," said a senior officer from another agency. My reply was simple as I had run into this type of hostility before.

"Yes, but my analysts figured all this out in 90 minutes."

We had caught up with them in less than a day, using independent sources, mined and analyzed by my best people using tools no one else had at the time. SOCOM representatives requested our support to the program known as Able Danger shortly afterwards.

COTS, GOTS, and Custom Tools

Each data mining tool has a different purpose behind its creation—whether it's to conduct link analysis, geospatial analysis, parsing, collection, tagging, etc. As such tools are primarily created within three different environments. They can be commercial off-the-shelf, or COTS tools, government off-the-shelf or GOTS tools, or they can be custom tools: Each has differences in their creators, why they were created, and associated consideration in their employment given their origin.

+ **COTS Tools:** Both commercial and government off-the-shelf tools are designated as such because they were originally developed for some other purpose, but identified and obtained for other operations as mostly finished products that are ready to plug in. The person who obtained these tools for their operation, in essence, pulled them off the shelf as an already viable product. COTS tools were created within the commercial market for sale to a variety of operations. They may be very effective for the specific marketspace they were created for (e.g., law enforcement, fire and emergency services, financial sector, etc.), they will most likely require additional technical integration into an intelligence center so that they can link with other tools and correct data sources.

- **GOTs Tools:** These are similar to COTS except that they were developed within a government agency. For tools with direct intelligence application, their source will most likely be another member of the U.S. Intelligence Community. Also like COTS tools, they will require technical integration within a given intelligence center, but depending on their original organization they will not have the same security hurdles to overcome prior to employment on another government site. They also will most likely not have additional costs to purchase since one part of the government already owns it. In this case, the major hurdles to obtaining them are gaining permissions to use and overcoming inherent parochialism and resistances within the originating organization.
- **Custom Tools:** Custom or Internal Tools are those developed specifically within a given the technical staff, i.e., engineers, assigned to that center. They can be created by organic or contracted personnel but their purpose is usually going to be the same and distinctly different from COTS and GOTS tools. While some COTS and GOTS tools may have redundant capabilities to each other, custom tools will most likely have a specific, refined, and unique purpose within a center. They can be created as a stop-gap measure, as a front-end tools working transparently to the analyst, or simply a method to allow one COTS of GOTS tools to talk to each other.

Additionally, some centers may obtain and use a Tool Suite. These are combinations of both COTS and GOTS tools that have already been technically integrated to work together. Analysts can use a Tool Suite that actually has the same or most of the same capabilities as each stand-alone tools present within it. Some data mining tools already have multiple capabilities, but by integrating these tools together in a laboratory, program office, or other technical section may allow the analyst to use these tools more effectively, in a different manner, or with additional capabilities that were not present when each tools stood alone.

Evaluating Data Mining Tools

Every data mining and visualization tool was developed with a purpose—to provide automated assistance through one or more phases of the analytic process to the human analyst. The tools don't replace human analysis but allow them to conduct analytic techniques using more data and information than can be handled manually.

Similar to evaluating data and information, data mining tools can also be evaluated against a variety of criteria. Whether these tools developed a government agency, purchased commercially, or is home-made/customer software, each has given strengths and weaknesses as it applies to a specific mission or given set of data/information.

CHART 6.1   How to Evaluate Data Mining Tools

Evaluation criteria	Pertinent questions to ask
SOURCE	• Who originally developed the tool? • What are the legal or proprietary restrictions in obtaining it? • Is it a product or a service? • Will it reside with a center's firewalls or is it cloud-based?
TECHNICAL CAPABILITIES AND LIMITATIONS	• What does the tool actually do? • What does it not do? • Does it do what it is being advertised to do? • Does it have additional capabilities that are not advertised? • Is it a "plug and play" tool or does it require extensive software integration in order to work in a center? • Is it a stand-alone tool or is it part of a suite of tools already optimized to work together? • Will it require a work around in order to make it function in a center? • Is it suited for a standing database or streaming data? • What's the minimum–maximum amount of data this tool requires to work as intended?
OPERATIONAL FUNCTIONS	• How does this tool let me do things better, faster, or more accurately? • What analytic techniques can I now use with this tool? • Are there new analytic techniques that I can create using this tool? • Where would this tool fit in analytic and operational processes?
INPUT/OUTPUT AND USER INTERFACE	• What are the mechanisms for inputting data/information? • How do I get data into the tool? • How does the tool export for analyst use or directly into another tool? • What kinds of data are best suited for this tool? • What does the end product or visualization look like? • Can I brief or disseminate information straight from this tool? • Do I have to translate the results into another tool or product?
COST	• How much does the tool cost? • Are there reoccurring costs? • Are there additional costs required for certain data/functions? • Does the base cost include the entire tool or are there add-ons, patches, or downloadable
SECURITY	• Has it passed inspection by network security managers? • Does it have a history of privacy issues? • Who makes it and where was it made? • What was its original purpose/customer?

Those looking to obtain software for their center or operation will need to answer most if not all of these questions prior to committing what could be an enormous amount of funds toward their purchase. In order to do this, there needs to be input from several different members of the intelligence organization to include personnel who work in operations, analysis, technical, management, and administrative (i.e., finance) sections.

Unfortunately, most software procurement is done almost solely by technical personnel within an intelligence center, leaving out operational or other requirements. What may sound like a great idea for a group of software or network engineers may not be workable, usable, affordable, or secure. To combat this, many organizations resort to a process of official procurement that includes a validation of the need for a purchase along with a deliberate process to identify the operational requirements of a tool.

Within the U.S. military, these two requirements take the form of a Mission Needs Statement or MNS (pronounced "Minz") and an Operational Requirements Document or ORD (pronounced "ord" as in Lord). An intelligence center destined for problems is one that has neither took the mission or operational requirements into account either at its creation, or in the search for the latest data mining tools. The documents mentioned may seem archaic or cumbersome to an organization that thinks itself to be too agile to go through such a long-drawn out process, but the foundational purpose of them are critical to ensuring the right resources are spent on the right tools and equipment. Even a streamlined, abbreviated, or otherwise tailored version of an acquisition process is critical to ensuring the right tools are obtained within an intelligence center. After all, if a formal acquisition process is required for a combat weapon system, it should be required for data mining tools which can be just as critical to an operation—or worthless.

Besides asking these questions for new purchases, they can also be asked of current tools within a center or in support of a given operation. Periodic review of current data mining tools can be conducted for a leadership or management turnover, as part of an organizational efficiency review, or to troubleshoot the root cause of a problem that may occur in a center's ability to support a customer/decision-maker.

Where the Tools Fit Part I– Data Mining Foot Printing

Once tools are decided upon—whatever the method, it's up to the analyst as the end user to figure out what to do with them. Expanding upon questions asked about operational functions, intelligence analyst must understand the tools well enough to be able to either apply them to their operation or analytical problem set.

This can often be a confusing and frustrating process for the first timers or for those not trained in a specific data mining tool, or tools may end up feeling a victim of technology rather than a beneficiary of it. Once trained, a good analyst will be able to apply tools toward current analytic techniques and methodologies used within a center. A great analyst will be able to develop new analytic techniques and resulting products based on the introduction of a new data mining function. In every case, understanding tools well enough to apply them toward analysis takes time and requires training and applying tools toward a given problem set, whether it is in a classroom or on-the-job or mentored learning environment.

The intelligence analyst understands the practical applications of data mining tools much more easily than a tool's academic or technical aspects. This is similar to a sniper or a marksman who don't need to know the metallurgy of the barrel of a rifle or the specific tooling process to create a weapon as much as they need an understanding of how the weapon works in different environments and in different weather against a varied type of targets.

Analysts need to understand the application of a data mining tool and certain databases that have some inherent analytic capabilities according to the center they are working in, their analytic requirements, the data and information they have access to, and the types of products they need to produce. This fusing of tools with analytical and operational processes is important to the success of intelligence operations as it involves the integration of two of its four critical components. It also helps to demonstrate overall processes to supported customers and will help to explain what would otherwise be somewhat overwhelming to new analysts unfamiliar with the tools.

An effective technique in helping an analyst understand the application of the data mining tools used in a center or for their operation is to classifying them according to analytic processes. While the analytic process used here is explained in more detail in Chapter 8, there are several other analytic processes that can be used. The key is that each cover the same fundamental steps, albeit with different emphasis or with varied sub-steps. Next is discussed an analytic process first developed to more effectively handle asymmetric threats, but can be used with any type of threat from conventional to complex.

Using this process as a baseline, the analyst can then classify and plot each data mining tool they have available or are planning to obtain based upon the functions they actually perform. For example, if a particular tool is designed to automatically collect either structured or unstructured data and then has the capability to display their initial relationships based on one or more algorithms, it should be plotted as both a "Collect Information" and a "Preliminary Analysis" tool.

Once all the tools available or required are plotted, the analyst can take a more holistic and comprehensive look at the overall capabilities of the entire intelligence center or the operation it is supporting.

As an example, below is a set of tools used by the U.S. Army INSCOM's IDC during the turn of the century. This is the first use of this type of chart created using this technique. It was created to assist both the intelligence analysts and leadership in understanding all the leading (bleeding) edge data mining technology that had been put into the center by the chief scientists, software, and network engineers. Almost every one of the listed tools has been superseded by several generations of technology since.

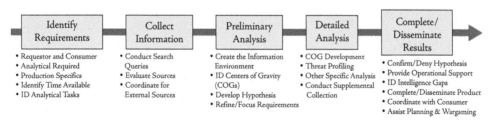

FIGURE 6.2   Intelligence analysis steps

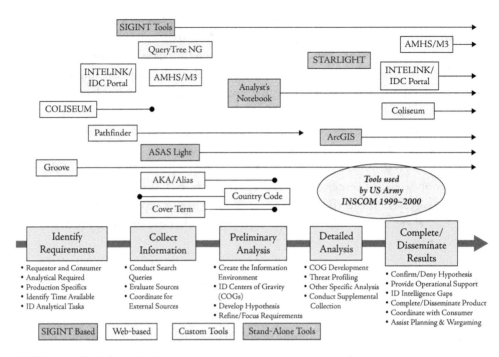

FIGURE 6.3   IDC data mining footprint

This data mining foot print will help the analyst and other intelligence personnel in several ways. Intelligence personnel in a center or its supported operation will be able to:

1. Gain a better understanding of which analytic functions robustly support versus which are only lightly or unsupported by data mining tools.
2. Show the interconnectivity or lack of connectivity between different tools.
3. Identify areas work arounds that must be developed in order to bypass certain gaps or weak areas of support.
4. Identify what types of overall products and methods of disseminating these products are currently available to the center or operation.
5. Identify areas of need for future plans to purchase, upgrade, or conduct life-cycle replacement of older tools.
6. Develop a workflow of automation to help plan analysis through each analytic phase from receipt of requirements to creating and disseminating a final product.

This list is not all inclusive since intelligence personnel can also add in different factors or classifications to further refine their function chart of data mining tools.

Plotting the data mining and visualization tools in this manner reveals that there are some tools the analyst needs to turn to for data and information collection that cannot be used for analysis or in creating a final product. As well, many of the tools that are best suited for creating a final product cannot collect information. In fact some of the best analytic tools required some way to get information into it, which in turns forces the center's operators to ask what are the methods that are needed for certain tools to ingest certain types of data or information. Even if it is a structured data, it must be in a format that the tool can recognize.

Personal Perspectives:
Finding More Than Just Footprints

Soon after leaving the military, I used the data mining footprint technique as a consultant to a few intelligence organizations that were just turning to data mining tools after 9/11. In one particularly embarrassing case, I created a data mining footprint for a government organization that used intelligence analysis in support of their primary mission of conducting criminal investigations. Since I already had working knowledge of several of their tools, I only had to conduct a few interviews and study those tools that I was not familiar with to create the following chart

I presented this chart as part of my findings to several members of the organization's analytic staff. As the chart came up and I continued presenting my findings, I noticed many of the analysts in the room growing more and more agitated. When I finally paused to asked the room if there was anything wrong with my assessment thus far, one of the analysts blurted out,

This is the reason why it sucks being an intel analyst here. We have all these tools that collect information but very little to help us do analysis. The truth is we don't so any analysis here, the lawyers do.

Other analysts immediately jumped in agreeing with their colleague. They were very frustrated with the perception they were being treated like glorified

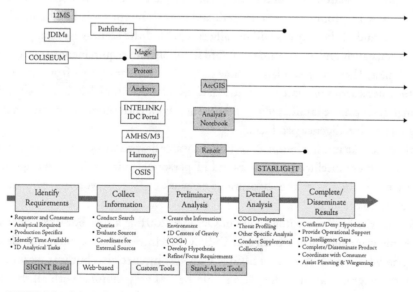

FIGURE 6.4   Criminal investigations footprint

law clerks for the attorneys. I stood in silence as they began to air several other problems related to tool ingestion, connectivity, and the menial tasks they performed instead of doing the jobs they were paid to do. The leadership of the center may not have been happy with how the meeting degenerated, but several changes were almost immediately implemented that empowered analysts making the entire effort run more effectively. All triggered by one chart that revealed their frustrations.

Where the Tools Fit Part II–Water Flow Charting

Another way to understand the same tools is by fusing them with data and information sources. While data mining footprinting helps intelligence professionals understand their tools according to analytic processes, water flow charting portrays data and information using the analogy of water flowing into a center as discuss previously in this book.

Water flow charting is conducted by creating a map or network of an intelligence center's tools concentrating on how data moves from the original source, to and through various tools, toward the final product. It includes the external source or sources of data and information as it enters the center, the search engines, or web crawlers that may be required to pull the data in. It also includes tools that process, parse, tag, organize, format, and conduct entity extraction, and store data and information before they even get to the first visualization tool used by the intelligence analyst. Going beyond just data mining tools, water flow charting includes external data sources as well as internal databases.

In this way, intelligence center personnel can get a better idea of the interconnectivity of all things IT related in a center. They can analyze the different steps that data goes through, how its properties are changed, and how different tools handle it. The tools at the front end of the process will usually run behind the scenes, especially if they are running constantly and are running standard functions as a requirement to receive certain types of data. They can also identify how data and information gets from the front end tools to either a series of databases or to a data visualization tool. It's these back end tools that analysts are more familiar with because they work with them to conduct analysis or create various intelligence products.

Unlike the data mining footprint technique, water flow charting requires collaboration between a center's intelligence analysts and IT personnel as it entails knowledge of many tools that are inherent to the software or network engineer's work but almost totally transparent to the analyst.

I created the first water flow chart in October 2001 as a collaborative effort with a U.S. Army warrant officer working at INSCOM's Information Operations Center or IOC. The Warrant Officer was a SIGINT analyst by specialty, but was working more as system integrator at the time. As a result, he was very familiar with all the custom and in-house tools and automated ingestion, processing and meta-tagging tools, and had gained the trust of the local engineers to work within their space.

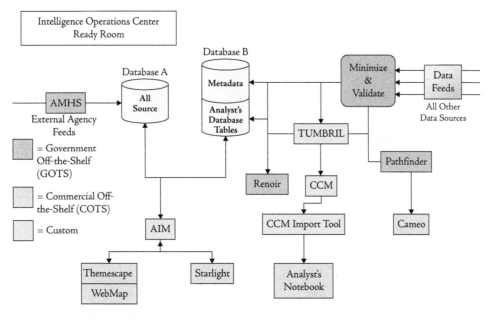

FIGURE 6.5   Data mining–Water flow charting example

While there is an inherent cultural divide between software and network engineers who develop data mining tools and algorithms, developing a water chart showing how data and information enter an intelligence center, and how the various tools and processes and data repositories are interlinked in a functional way will help to bridge that divide.

For the analyst, it will help to shed light on what engineers are working on or more aptly put—what goes on in the kitchen in order to get their meal to them. For the engineers, it gives them both structure and requirement to articulate their world for the analyst as the end user of the data and tools. For both, it provides a common structure or map to help communicate to each other on technology being used in their intelligence center.

Using this technique, analysts can also discover how their various tools may be disconnected with each other. Getting data from a database or from another tool to the one the analyst needs is not guaranteed. Indeed many custom tools that are unique to a particular center are created by software engineers so that the disparate tools and forms of data can talk to each other.

This is more than likely when tools are purchased commercially and simply plugged into the center without going through what could be a pretty significant integration process by software engineers. Not all data talks to each other, and allowing analysts or managers to run out and bring in their own tools will most likely be ineffective.

Water flow charting of tools can reveal these gaps and disconnects along the flow of data in a center. In addition, they may also identify makeshift or ad hoc methods to work around them. These methods can be put into place by both engineers and analysts. As an example, a term used by analysts to manually transfer one set of data into another tool or system is called "sneaker gap," meaning they have to physically walk from one system to the next with the data on a storage device, provided these devices are allowed in the center in the first place.

Summary

Information technology related to intelligence analysis is a rapidly changing environment. The most important factor in getting the most effective results from these tools is in understanding their functions, i.e., what they actually do and don't do along with the where they fit in both the analytical and technical processes within a given center. While analysts are not usually the ones who decide which data mining and visualization tools are available to assist in their work, there are several considerations and methods to evaluate them to ensure the right tool provides the needed capability.

Key Summary Points

+ Data mining is about inquiry. Implicit to this is that analysts supported by engineers must direct their tools through queries and associated algorithms.
+ There are many arguments against data mining, all of which are valid when applied to ineffective, wasteful, or even illicit use of the tools.
+ The purpose and capabilities of data mining tools are numerous, each is focused on aiding the human analyst to collect, process, and analyze data and information faster and more effectively than if done manually.
+ To make the most effective use of data mining tools, analyst must be able to evaluate and understand the operational capabilities of the tools available for their operation.
+ Analysts must also understand how their data mining tools can be applied to their analytic processes as well how they can be applied to the various data and information sources their center relies upon.

Discussion Questions

+ Besides the capabilities listed in this chapter, what are additional capabilities that data mining tools can offer in support of intelligence analysis?
+ What are some of the major differences in the perspectives of analysts, engineers, or tools vendors themselves toward data mining capabilities?
+ Are there additional criteria that should be used in evaluating data mining tools?
+ By combining the three different types of tools into a Tool Suite, what additional benefits could this provide to an intelligence center or operation?

Figure Credits

Chapter 7

Intelligence People

Learning Objectives

After completing this chapter, you will be able to:

- Recognize the primary sources for intelligence personnel.
- Understand the four planning factors associated with building an effective intelligence team.
- List methods to create an intelligence manning plan and organizational structure.
- Identify the needs of intelligence personnel in the creation and maintenance of an intelligence work environment.

The Last Intelligence Analyst

There is a debate taking place within science, technology, and military circles that the evolution of unmanned aerial vehicles (UAVs), drones, and their related technologies has either caught up or has overtaken the capabilities of aircraft flown by pilots. The popular catchphrase that encapsulates this debate is that the last fighter pilot has already been born. What required a human operator to navigate an aircraft to a given area, conduct reconnaissance, or deliver a weapon's payload toward a target can now be conducted remotely and safely from a computer screen using instrumentation and controllers to a video game. One of the primary reasons for the last pilot arguments is that unmanned aircraft do not have to take into account the requirements needed for a human pilot such as oxygen, physical weight, and enormous expenses related to training.[1]

---

1   Grey, Kevin. (2015, December 22). The last fighter pilot. *Popular Science*. Retrieved from https://www.popsci.com/last-fighter-pilot

FIGURE 7.1   The MQ-1 Predator, unmanned aerial vehicle takes off from Tallil Airbase, Iraq, 2004

Technology related to intelligence collection, processing, and analysis has developed along a similar trajectory as the UAV and drone technology. With the increasingly available amounts of data and tools that can collect, organize, and visualize them is it safe to say that the last intelligence analyst has already been born as well? There are some who could argue this point today, especially those who have a more technically oriented mind or are working within technical fields. These people could include signals or technical intelligence professionals or software and network engineers.

The counter to this argument is simple, there is and never will be a replacement for the human beings' ability to analyze and make decisions—however flawed they may be. Human beings make decisions based upon a combination of logic and emotions and rational and irrational mind-sets using conscious, subconscious, and unconscious levels of thought processes. In regard to recent and ongoing advances in information technology, the human mind has never been more important to intelligence analysis. The human component in intelligence operations is therefore now more critical than ever.

The Most Critical Component

Of the four components required for successful intelligence operations, people are the most important and yet they are often overlooked in terms of designing, planning, building, and operating an intelligence center in support of operations. Intelligence chiefs spend millions of dollars building or repurposing a facility for analysis, they spend additional capital on the right tools and data feeds for the center that in itself requires extensive resources to integrate the tools and data together and conduct the various processes they are required to perform. These are not onetime costs, but rather continual as the capabilities of the center must be perpetually maintained.

Burying ourselves within the technology that supports intelligence risks the perception that people are simply there as a given and will work within any intelligence environment without much further consideration. So while it's obvious that an effective intelligence operation requires intelligence people, the requirements in bringing effective intelligence people into an operation are not so obvious. Indeed, even the most experienced director, chief, or supervisor can overlook some of the critical aspects that pertain to building or managing an effective team of intelligence personnel.

Lessons in Intelligence:
Plug Them into the Machine

One of my first programs as a defense contractor in the U.S. Intelligence Community was to create a foundational course for intelligence analysts in the United States Army Intelligence and Security Command (INSCOM) Intelligence Operations Center (IOC). The course was to be designed to teach analysts to conduct basic analytic functions and applications using the center's data mining and visualization tools. As part of my development process, I sat down individually with several of the center's leadership and supervisors so that I could ensure this course's training objectives fit with their expectations as well as gauge their requirements. Since the IOC was a relatively fluid and fast-paced environment for these leaders, I found it was smarter for me to give them a draft to look at first rather than just solicit their opinions from out of the blue.

As I met with one of the managers of the IOC, I was amazed that they were not happy that I had included several hours of analytical methods to start the 40-hour course. I thought it was important to establish a baseline set of analytical skills in the course prior to teaching the students the applications of each tool for much of the remainder of the course. The manager I was briefing clearly disagreed.

"I don't want you to waste time teaching analysis. They (the analysts) should already know this stuff. Just teach them the tools and plug them into the machine." I was actually taken aback as his comment revealed to me what he thought of his own people who worked in the center. They only wanted us to teach the tool's "buttonology," not the applications of the tools as part of the intelligence process. I replied that I felt these were the most important blocks of instruction in the course and I would not remove them. After a short back and forth, I finally had to tell him that while he was one of the leaders in the IOC, as a contractor I did not work for him, and he would have to take it up with the INSCOM civilian who managed my contract if he had a problem with it.

That course became known as the Basic Analyst/Managers or BAM course. Over the next 10 years I had several instructors teach it to several thousand students, and it became the foundational course for a training program that is still in operation today for the U.S. Army intelligence analysts.

Where the Intelligence People Come From

For an often-asked question, "How do I get into intelligence as a career?," the best and most simple response is, "Go do something else first." Judging by the background of a majority of people who work in it today, intelligence is largely an accession career. It relies on a constant feed of personnel who have experience in other areas that can be brought to bear within its ranks.

Unlike many other professions, there is no one clear path for getting into intelligence—either for the outsider looking toward intelligence as a career or for the people responsible for filling intelligence positions, be they project/program managers, first-line supervisors, or hiring managers for either government or commercial organizations.

In comparison, the military relies upon well-established programs such as Reserve Officers' Training Corps (ROTC) for its officers. Law enforcement relies upon the various academies and law enforcement training centers for its police men and women. Law firms rely on higher education as successful bar exams for their attorneys. For intelligence, there are a variety of paths toward a career.

The Military Option

With recent overall estimate of roughly 850,000 people who work in the U.S. Intelligence Community where the U.S. Department of Defense makes up about two-thirds of IC programs, the U.S. military is arguably the largest intelligence trainer in the world.[2] This is one of the few paths to intelligence that involves training its personnel from the ground up. The screen for getting into military intelligence is inherent in the various recruitment processes for enlisted personnel or competitive accessions boards for warrant and commissioned officers.

As mentioned, the first thing a new member of one of the military branches goes through is training. The intelligence training within the Department of Defense is extensive, with several entry-level schoolhouses for every branch of service. This training continues with various specialty courses and programs both in the schoolhouses for servicemen who are in the workforce. As intelligence personnel within the military advance through their careers, additional training that becomes available include some options for postgraduate education. There are training courses for analysis, data mining tools, languages, and operational tradecraft depending on the intelligence specialty.

All of these courses and years of experience make intelligence personnel within the military highly desirable within the rest of the intelligence community of practice and commercial marketspace. Hiring managers and supervisors in the rest of the intelligence marketspace aggressively recruit intelligence personnel from the military because of the training and experience they know, these individuals will bring to the

---

2   Arkin, William M. & Priest, Dana. (2010, September). A hidden world, growing beyond control. *Washington Post.* Retrieved from http://projects.washingtonpost.com/top-secret-america/articles/a-hidden-world-growing-beyond-control/

job without having to pay for the training. To lure this kind of quality, hiring managers know they will cost more. The candidates themselves similarly know they can easily convert their knowledge, skills, and experience into a higher salary. In the long run, the lure of a higher paying job without the demands and sacrifices required of military duty is strong and constant.

The Life of (Fighting) Crime

Law enforcement personnel are an additional source of intelligence personnel, as many of the skills in analytic tradecraft picked up while investigating crimes or active policing are very close to skills required of intelligence analysts. While there is still a significant cultural barrier between badge-carrying agents of officers of the law and supporting analysts, intelligence, i.e., the difference between conducting an investigation as to what events happened in the past and predictive analysis to determine what is going to happen in the future is very small.

Indeed, there are many skills shared by both law enforcement investigations and intelligence analysis. For example, understanding the organization of a crime family or a gang including their leadership, hierarchy, and necessary connections can all be working with a link or a social network analysis diagram. These same diagrams are used by intelligence analysts to understand conventional military, paramilitaries, guerrillas, and terrorist groups. The over purpose for doing may be different, but the baseline functions in creating a link diagram of a particular group are the same.

As law enforcement organizations become more accustomed to working with their supporting intelligence analysts, it is only natural that cross-training occurs along with many law enforcement personnel turning to intelligence as a new but similar line of work. While law enforcement personnel do not have as strong infrastructure for intelligence training available to them as the military does, they do have numerous skills and sets of experiences that are highly desired in most sectors of the intelligence marketspace.

The Way of Technology

A career in information technology is a third and lesser known way into a second career in intelligence. This is primarily because it is limited to IT personnel who have already worked with intelligence in their capacity as either a software or network engineer. Those who develop software tools to mine and visualize data and information for intelligence or investigative purposes not only have skills and experience related to intelligence analysis, but they also bring a deeper knowledge of the inner workings of either the tools themselves or the networks where they reside.

Many of the best IT persons who can bring these skills to an intelligence operation can be used to help integrate tools, develop patches, algorithms, and technical work-arounds within a center. There is also the possibility these people will take on additional roles as super users, those user who develop a specific expertise for a given set of data or more complex data mining tool. In this way, they can more efficiently work a specific aspect of data mining for an intelligence center that other intelligence analysts could turn to for a variety of problem sets.

An IT specialist can also take on roles as on-site tools mentors, providing desk-side training and expertise to other intelligence analysts who work with data mining tools on a regular basis. In this capacity, they are able to provide pre-quality control checks before analysts spend time working on a project with flawed data sets or incorrect queries. These "Super Users" of technology can provide an informal liaison between intelligence and IT personnel by articulating user requirements to other engineers and translating tech-speak into operational language that users can understand.

The Learner's Path

This path brings in the youngest and least experienced personnel into an intelligence center or operation, and also brings in those who have a foundational education in a wide variety of areas well beyond what the intelligence marketspace provides in training. A college graduate's actual applied knowledge and skills directly related to the mission of a given operation or center may be limited, but they've already demonstrated their ability to learn, and don't carry many of the parochial stubbornness of more seasoned analysts.

There are only a handful of colleges and universities that provide intelligence as a bachelor's or master's degrees in the United States, but this should not be a limiting factor. Intelligence requires and also benefits from personnel who've been educated in a wide variety of degrees. For example, conducting analysis into the financial structure of a terrorist organization can certainly benefit from someone with a degree in finance, business, law, international relations, political science, criminology, accounting, or even sociology.

A sampling of the degrees carried by the personnel in any given intelligence center would reveal many different degrees that would be seemingly unrelated but in the aggregate provide a diverse set of knowledge needed for many discovery-based analytic techniques. Recent college graduates provide a relatively inexpensive population of analysts, usually that are already in tune with technology or possessing the ability to more easily learn data mining tools than more senior analysts who've become set in their ways at a higher cost.

None of the Above

While the military, law enforcement, IT, and college are the four most common paths, there are other less well-defined ways people can get into the world of intelligence. As discussed in Chapter 3, the need for intelligence is slowly being recognized in almost every part of our society. It is, therefore, only logical to deduce that intelligence needs experts in almost every field from agriculture to zoology. The ability of people who have other types of expertise to obtain an intelligence position is highly dependent on the specific needs of a given center or operation. Those needs are defined by the missions,

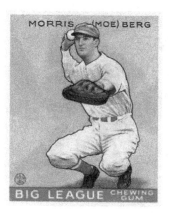

FIGURE 7.2   Josephine Baker, taken in 1949

FIGURE 7.3   Moe Berg's 1933 baseball card

FIGURE 7.4   Sterling Hayden as an actor in 1953

requirements, and problems that a given intelligence operation or center will tackle. The timing of these missions and requirements is also critical. While gaining personnel from professions seemingly unrelated to intelligence is rare, the intelligence marketspace still needs members from diverse backgrounds from time to time. Some notable examples of this path are as follows:

+   Josephine Baker—Legendary African American dancer and entertainer, spied for the French Resistance during World War II. Used invisible ink on sheet music to transport vital information.[3]
+   Morris "Moe" Berg—Major League baseball player for 15 seasons as a shortstop, catcher, and coach. Got into intelligence through his prewar baseball trips to Japan. Served in the Office of Strategic Services OSS during World War II.[4]
+   Sterling Hayden—Actor who played in such films as *Dr. Strangelove* and *The Godfather*. Parachuted into Yugoslavia during World War II to provide weapons to partisan elements there.[5]
+   Jeff "Skunk" Baxter—Musician and bass guitarist for the Doobie Brothers and one of the founding members of the band Steely Dan. Baxter's interest in music

---

3   Von Reynold, Shola. (2016, October 5). Dancer, singer, activist, spy: The legacy of Josephine Baker. Retrieved from http://www.anothermag.com/fashion-beauty/9133/dancer-singer-activist-spy-the-legacy-of-josephine-baker

4   Central Intelligence Agency News & Information. (2017, January 17). "Moe" Berg: Sportsman, scholar, spy. Retrieved from https://www.cia.gov/news-information/featured-story-archive/2013-featured-story-archive/moe-berg.html

5   Feeney, Mark. (2016, March 18). Sterling Hayden brought large presence to the screen. *The Boston Globe*. Retrieved from https://www.bostonglobe.com/arts/movies/2016/03/17/once-you-seen-his-face-you-never-forget/YkFWATfMGqwhA9I0ZDK1eK/story.html

FIGURE 7.5   Jeff "Skunk" Baxter

technology led him into research-ing and consulting on defense and intelligence-related technology.[6]

Building an Effective Intelligence Team

Almost every intelligence team exists within a larger organization that does not conduct intelligence as its primary mission. The intelligence team can be referred to as a team, unit, section, branch, division, or some other organizational name that shows its subordination to the larger organization. Alongside personnel, security, logistics, resource manager or finance, and other sections they are a supportive function of the larger organization's mission and purpose.

In this light, building an intelligence team is usually intelligence pure—meaning there is rarely a requirement to include the other supportive functions within the team as the larger organization provides this already. With the exception of tactical and operational level intelligence units or entire intelligence agencies with a few hundred personnel, intelligence teams are not meant to operate independently or autonomous of another organization. Even if it is owned by one organization but attached to another, its parasitic nature requires that it is supported by a larger organization. They require a steady supply of support from that organization from logistics, security, administrative, and in some cases they need the basic human requirements such as food, water, and shelter.

Planning for an effective team requires several areas of consideration including the mission, tasks, processes, and skills, among several other factors. Just as in planning for the right data and tools, the goal isn't to just simply fill an intelligence organization or center with people and "plug them into the machine." Leaders and managers have internal and external, specified and implied, and simply and complex requirements that must be satisfied by competent people. To have any chance of success, an intelligence operation must have the right people with the right skills and in the right numbers to be effective.

Planning Factor 1: The Intelligence Process
Every intelligence team or section has many unique characteristics in regard to the customers they support, the intelligence requirements they routinely satisfy, the data and

---

6   Bonderud, Doug. (2017, May 24). From music to missile defense: The very interesting life of Jeff Baxter. Retrieved from http://now.northropgrumman.com/from-music-to-missile-defense-the-very-interesting-life-of-jeff-baxter/

information they collect, their analytic methods, and the products they provide to a supported decision-maker. While each operation is different from all the others, this regard they are not different in that they all provide intelligence.

All intelligence operations perform the same basic processes, no matter what type of intelligence they are providing or customer they are supporting. All intelligence operations receive requirements, they all collect and process information, they all conduct analysis, and they all provide a product of some sort back to a supported customer. These tasks are all

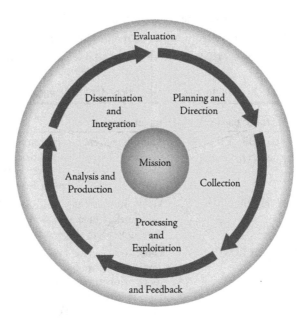

FIGURE 7.6   The joint intelligence process as shown in U.S. Department of Defense Joint Publication 2.0, Joint Intelligence

contained in what is commonly known as the intelligence process and are fairly inescapable as a common paradigm for all intelligence organizations.

The intelligence process is covered in much more detail in Chapter 8, but for purposes here it can be defined as a cyclical process that includes the following steps: planning and direction, collection, processing and exploitation, analysis and production, dissemination and integration, evaluation and feedback.[7] Each of these tasks is performed by intelligence personnel as a standard way of providing intelligence support to a customer no matter the scenario or circumstances.

Planning for building a team of intelligence personnel is therefore based on identifying and placing the right people to accomplish the tasks of the intelligence process. These tasks can be performed by one of more personnel assigned to the organization, and they can also be performed as a part-time or full-time job. The assignment, separation, and workload required for these tasks are estimated against available personnel as affected by the other considerations and planning factors.

Planning Factor 2: Operational Considerations

Taking the tasks outlined in the intelligence process is a start, but planning for personnel involves considering several additional factors. They may seemingly be unrelated, but while the intelligence process helps to identify standardized tasks to be performed, other

---

7   Joint Publication 2.0, Joint Intelligence, US Department of Defense, October 22, 2013. Retrieved October 24, 2017, from www.dtic.mil/doctrine/new_pubs/jp2_0.pdf

factors help to define the environment in which intelligence operations take place. Each of these can have from minor to major effect on both the skill set and quality and quantity of personnel that are needed or available to fulfill mission requirements.

CHART 7.1   Factors of Considerations for Intelligence Personnel

Factor of consideration	Description
AUTHORIZED NUMBERS	Many intelligence organizations can be restricted on the number of personnel based on authorization. Within the government this can be dictated by law such as Defense Authorization Act, while in the commercial environment it can be dictated by contract.
PHYSICAL SPACE	While physical intelligence centers can only seat a limited number of personnel, remote operations still require dedicated workspace even if it is geographically dispersed.
LABOR COSTS	Labor costs include total salary requirements and associated benefits for employing personnel depending on numbers, experience levels, and levels of required expertise. These costs have to be weighed against the return on investment (ROI) expected, which may be a tangible number or intangible evaluation of success.
CUSTOMER REQUIREMENTS	Includes not only the specific intelligence requirements of a single customer but also the total number and timeliness of multiple requirements. This helps to understand the expected workload and level of overall details required of products during a given time period.
TECHNICAL FACTORS	Includes the degree of expertise required to perform the functions using data mining tools and other software. Also includes management of organic collection assets and platforms if owned by the center or organization conducting collection operations concurrent to analysis.
HUMAN FACTORS	Includes the environment conditions of the center including tactical versus office conditions, business hours versus 24 × 7 requirements, and level of human resources required as overage to support larger organizations.

Effective planning for personnel within an intelligence center or operation can be accomplished by considering the mission-related tasks of the intelligence process alongside the personnel considerations listed in Chart 7.1. In this way, leadership and management can develop a plan for personnel within a center or operation that includes the number and types of intelligence personnel required. Once this is accomplished, the development of a workable, efficient organizational structure can then start to take shape.

In the context of a newly created organization or supported operation, deliberate planning for personnel against both tasks and the listed factors for consideration will help to identify the required positions, the numbers of people in these positions, and skill sets needed to accomplish the missions. In the context of an already ongoing operation or working center, this method of planning can be used to evaluate the current manning plan as well as reveal gaps, redundancies, and mismatches of personnel both in terms of expertise and numbers assigned.

Planning Factor 3: Labor Calculations

Building off the planning considerations and armed with the identified key positions that every intelligence operation holds, a baseline organizational structure can begin to emerge. Again, planners must account for each of these tasks, as performed by key positions with the their available . While the time required for tasks of the intelligence process must be estimated based on the mission and factors listed in Chart 7.1, the amount of people and the number of labor hours they can be expected to perform are finite and therefore tangible numbers.

These numbers are not a secret as they are used for personnel planning across both the government and private sectors. Labor planners regularly use the following labor calculation numbers to plan for hourly labor rates, part-time versus full-time employment, and associated benefits.

CHART 7.2   Labor Hours per Person

Labor time	Number of hours
AVERAGE WORK WEEK (8 HOURS A DAY, 5 DAYS A WEEK)	40
AVERAGE WORK YEAR (AVERAGE WORK WEEK TIMES 52 WEEKS A YEAR)	2,080
AVERAGE WORK YEAR MINUS HOLIDAYS, VACATION (20 DAYS TOTAL)	1,920
AVERAGE WORK YEAR ADJUSTED FOR ADDITIONAL DISTRACTIONS (10 DAYS)	1,840

A full year of labor from a single individual is known as a full-time equivalent (FTE) and expressed in total number of hours. Adjusting for additional distractions includes illnesses, family emergencies, or internal organizational requirements not intelligence related (compliance training, organizational picnic, etc.). While the work week and work year are relatively constant numbers, factoring in vacation and additional distractions are more flexible and are regularly adjusted by other considerations included in planning factor 2.

It is especially important to know all of these numbers and how they were calculated since all these numbers are used for different planning purposes. For example, a financial planner or comptroller within an organization could use 1,920 as a number since a certain number of vacation and sick days are usually included for pay and salary calculations, while a contract manager could use a lower number for government reporting since the government usually doesn't pay for time away from work for any reason. Many contractor personnel work against a defined number of hours specified in their statement of work (SOW) and therefore do not have the ability to work more than hours listed since they are not technically getting paid for it. While this may seem absurd for something as important as the business of intelligence, but working beyond specified hours can be deemed as a gift and therefore in violation of federal law.

For planning purposes then, a single individual can reasonably be expected to perform for approximately 1,840 hours per year. These hours are then calculated against the estimated time requirements of tasks performed on an intelligence operation, or within an organization or center.

As an added caveat, these planning numbers can also be adjusted to take into account differing work environments such as any intelligence operation that doesn't follow the standard work week. For example, intelligence personnel in military or deployed operation don't have weekends or holidays to consider. In some extreme cases, the only time not devoted to intelligence labor is when an individual is sleeping and that may be restricted during combat operations. 24 × 7 staffing and periods of personnel surge must be factored and planned for in a different manner as they entail a different set of work and environmental conditions and considerations. These operational planning factors are addressed in more detail in Chapter 11.

Planning Factor 4: Key Positions Within Intelligence Centers

As already stated, planning for personnel requires defining and assigning key positions, their duties and responsibilities in terms of the number of people necessary to perform tasks along with any specified or implied limitations on the total positions that can be filled with quality people. Since the tasks required of an intelligence operation are constant and dictated by the intelligence process, intelligence operations of all size must perform all tasks effectively whether the operation has a small crew of personnel available or a large multi-facility operation where there are several hundreds of personnel available or assigned.

In very general terms, there are several positions that along with their associated responsibilities need to be filled in any intelligence manning plan:

> **Intelligence Chief:** The intelligence chief is overall responsible for everything that happens in an intelligence operation or within an intelligence center. As stated before, an operation and a center are not synonymous, but both require an intelligence boss to manage the mission, requirements, personnel, and operations during every step of the intelligence process. While other positions can scale to add more of the same type of person for larger operations, there will only ever be one intelligence chief or boss no matter what size the operation. Some intelligence chiefs can be in charge of only a handful of other personnel with a very limited scope of duties. Other intelligence chiefs can run entire intelligence agencies such as the Defense Intelligence Agency or the National Security Agency where their personnel number in the tens of thousands. In a very general sense, and effective intelligence chief must be proficient leaders, managers, and a subject matter expert in a relevant area of intelligence.
>
> **Collection Manager:** Collection managers are responsible for both collection planning and execution. As collection is both continuous and concurrent to other intelligence operations, it requires separate planning and considerations. An intelligence operation relies upon data and information from both queried

returns as well as continuously streaming sources. A majority of collection assets are not owned by the intelligence center themselves as even in the tactical environment, intelligence relies on other sources besides its own. A dedicated collection manager as a full-time position is generally not needed for intelligence sections of less than 20 overall persons. Besides owning the collection step of the intelligence process, they may also find themselves carrying out other duties such as processing, exploitation, dissemination and integration.

Production Manager: Production managers are primarily found working in the latter part of the intelligence process—i.e., the back end where analyzed intelligence products are created, delivered to a customer or customers, and disseminated to the rest of the community. Like collection managers, a dedicated full-time production manager is not necessary for an intelligence operation with less than 20 people. Production managers perform quality assurance and control checks on all outgoing finished intelligence and therefore help to ensure that the various intelligence products that are created by different analysts within an intelligence operation are in agreement with each or are of one voice. They also ensure products are free of errors from sourcing to grammatical.

Technical Integrator: Technical Integrators are relatively new positons and often not considered as key positions. They can be either those with an intelligence or engineering background, but the most critical skill they all must possess is the ability to speak in both intelligence and engineering languages. These persons are most active working with intelligence analysts as well as software and network engineers as they are required to bridge the cultural and operational gaps between the two. At the front end of the intelligence process, they are important in helping intelligence analysts in understanding the capabilities and limitations of the data sources and associated mining and visualization tools. They are also important in helping to articulate intelligence analyst's requirement to the engineers. They've been called super users, embedded mentors, or simply intelligence analysts who have been identified as technically savvy.

Human Support: Almost all intelligence organizations exist as a section within a larger operational organization, complete with its own human resources or personnel sections to assist the people working there in regard to salaries, promotion, interpersonal conflicts, and accountability among other tasks. With that, there is still a need for a basic level of human support within that section. The overall purpose of this position is to ensure that people are doing their jobs well with minimal distractions. These persons can be dual hatted as analysts or other positions, but they carry the additional responsibility of taking care of minor issues the rest of the personnel may have during work. The military again has this position down by designating a senior noncommissioned officer (NCO) who not only works their positions, but also manages schedules, tracks the overall status of training, and provides counseling among their other duties. The human support person will only be required as a dedicated position in the largest of intelligence organizations.

Team Chief: As soon as an intelligence operation grows to over a handful of people, there is a need for a first-line supervisor. Larger intelligence organizations have specialized teams of analysts and operators usually divided by intelligence disciplines or type of intelligence products. Team chiefs will have experience and skills that correspond with the team they lead. Within the military, these could be NCOs, warrant officers, or junior officers depending on the mission or area of technical sophistication, but each team lead could be responsible for around two to eight personnel. Team chiefs not only perform the same tasks as their personnel, but they must also display small unit leadership for their team and in carrying out directives or the overall intelligence chief. Often they will also be responsible for tracking accountability items within their team to include managing priorities of work, ensuring any training is conducted, or which systems are in need of technical support. They are the first face of leadership and management for the analysts during day-to-day operations.

Intelligence Analyst: The majority of the positions within an intelligence operation or center that supports multiple operations are that of the analysts. They are the worker bees of the colony as the success or failure of a center hinges on their performance. Not all intelligence analysts are the same as many are specialized according to intelligence disciplines or types of intelligence products they create, similar to their team chiefs. All intelligence analysts have to start somewhere so many of them will mostly likely be relatively junior. While an intelligence analyst will have very little intelligence-specific education, they can be reasonably expected to possess either (a) some level of intelligence training or (b) experience from a previous line of work that can be brought to bear within their assigned center or supported operation. There will also be several senior analysts who can not only conduct their work but can also handle more complex intelligence requirements. Senior analysts are also looked as a pool of candidates for technical support positions, team chiefs, or collection or production managers given the need and their corresponding levels of experience.

Intelligence Personnel Manning Plans

Creating an intelligence personnel management plan involves integrating all four of the planning factors into a workable plan: the intelligence process, operational considerations, labor calculations, and key named personnel. While many of these factors allow for flexibility on the part of the planner, there are a few are relatively inflexible factors such as the limits of physical space and restrictions on number of personnel authorized within the organization. Both of these represent limits to the number of personnel and the overall size of the operation. Because of this, the number of personnel available is a key start point for any manning and organizational plan.

With a number of personnel available or authorized, personnel planning can then scale or adjust the tasks performed by within an intelligence organization according

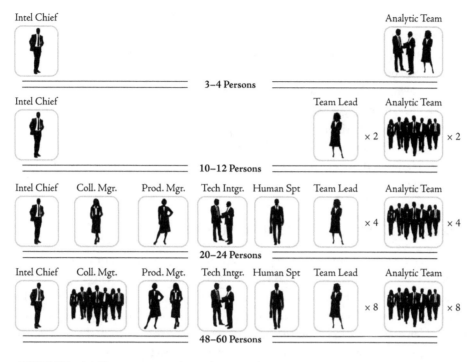

FIGURE 7.7   Intelligence personnel manning examples

to other requirements identified by the other planning factors. This scaling of effort based on the number of personnel by position is important as it helps to delineate separate sections, teams, or entire divisions of intelligence personnel according to common duties and responsibilities. Whereas a small intelligence section must have each person assigned to perform several tasks within the intelligence process, larger organizations can devote persons and even entire sections or divisions of personnel toward one specific task. For example, a single intelligence analyst working on a remote tactical team must perform every step of the intelligence process themselves, understanding the limits of what one person can do. A larger team of over two dozen analysts can divide these tasks among the personnel available and can assign a single person or even an entire section who only handles the tasks associated with a single part of the intelligence process.

This analysis of intelligence process tasks along with the number of people available among other considerations then requires identifying the key named positions that are present in almost every intelligence center or required for the operations they support. While there may not always be a need for every position to be filled by a full-time dedicated person, there is always a need for someone with the appropriate skills to perform the tasks these positions cover. For larger operations, there could a requirement to fill a key position with several people.

Figure 7.7 shows several examples of the numbers of key positions present within different sizes of intelligence organizations. While the chart shows sample breakdowns of personnel up to an organization of 60 personnel, it can easily be extrapolated to larger sized organizations. There are many organizations that are much larger than what is shown. The larger they are, the more the need will be to subdivide labor and positions into mission-specific areas as well as a more complex hierarchy.

The larger organization also increases the need for self-sustainability—meaning the organization can no longer rely on the feeding and care of a larger organization and must provide for itself. Functions that are left out of smaller intelligence-pure organizations will have to be factored into planning such as human resources, logistical and facility support, finance and budgeting, legal and contracting offices, network and IT support, and even physical security measures and personnel.

Creating an Organizational Structure

Each of the sections delineated in Figure 7.7 can be seen as teams or even subsections within an intelligence organization. As such, they can be used as the building blocks of an organizational structure that is normally portrayed by a traditional line-and-block chart.

Going to the next step in creating such an organizational chart requires placing the already identified positions and teams into a structure that defines the relationships between them. The standard organizational chart method places key individuals and teams in either a supervisory or a subordinate position to another part of the organization. Organizational charts will normally include the intelligence chief as the person who is overall responsible for everything that happens within the organization. It will then include the various identified teams arranged in subsections along one or more levels of hierarchy.

The composition and position of each person and team within an organization require revisiting many of the planning factors already discussed in this chapter. For example, while a planner may have identified the need for a team of approximately four personnel to work in collection management or on an analytic team, the physical layout of the center they work may not allow for that many people unless they work in shifts or physically split up with the same facility or among multiple facilities. Lack of workstations could also preclude the size of an analytic team that requires access to a limited number of analytic or data mining workstations.

Some intelligence organizations are dictated according to a standard design. For military organizations, where the baseline requirements to support a given unit at the tactical or operational level are the same for each unit, intelligence sections are structured as a standard makeup according to the parent operational unit's organization. Using military lingo, the standard authorized structure is called an MTOE (Modified Table of Organization and Equipment). In this system, every intelligence section for every U.S. Army mechanized infantry or armor battalion, known both as the S-2 section or shop, is going to look relatively the same with a military intelligence captain, a lieutenant, a senior NCO, and a number of senior and junior analysts. Other types of units will similarly have a standard structure for their S-2 section including support, combat support, or special operations units.

Outside of the military, standardization of intelligence is neither possible nor desired as each must be tailored according to the outlined planning factors. Figure 7.8 presents an example of organizational chart that includes several levels of hierarchy for mission and leadership purposes as well as the number of people included within each section. In the example, the nonanalytic teams are placed together under a support operations section (support ops). The larger number of all-source analysts require two teams under a section leader, while technical analysis section that tackles SIGINT, MASINT, and TECHINT requirements is under a single team lead. Finally, a current operations analysis section tackles many of the standard product requirements that don't change from week to week. These requirements include a daily/weekly briefing or read-file along with a synopsis of external intelligence reports.

Both an intelligence personnel manning plan and organizational structure have to incorporate two seemingly conflicted principles: stability and flexibility. For stability, personnel manning and organizational plans need to show a degree of permanence in the positions so that standard operating procedures and working relationships can be established. This allows personnel also establish and streamline workflow to fulfill more complex requirements within shorter timelines. For flexibility, they need to give an intelligence organization the ability to surge and adjust to unseen problems or issues such as unexpected or catastrophic events or changing requirements. Without this quality, an intelligence organization will quickly find itself locked into a certain paradigm with an inability to support customers with usually demanding or radically changed requirements.

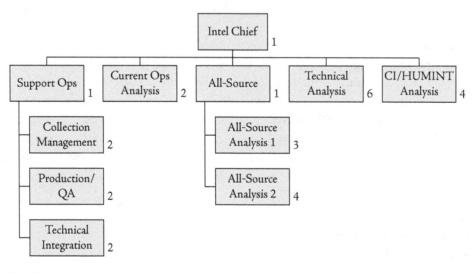

FIGURE 7.8   Intelligence organizational chart—example

Bold Colors of Diversity in Personnel Manning

In 1975, while speaking in a political context of whether or not Americans needed a third party, President Ronald Reagan stated that the Republican Party needed to raise *"a banner of no pale pastels, but bold colors which make it unmistakably clear where we stand …."*[8] This is the same approach that is needed for diversity of thought among intelligence personnel. Instead of trying to reduce the differences between intelligence people, diversity in the context of intelligence seeks to bring out the positive aspects of our differences in bold colors.

While diversity has become a buzzword in the workplace associated with inclusiveness, nondiscrimination, and as an antidote for racism, there are several studies that have confirmed the benefits of diversity within a workforce, even if for purely business and profit-motivated reasons.[9] As a distinction from politically correct perspectives on diversity, diversity in the context of intelligence is more of diversity of thought rather than diversity of skin or ethnicity. Instead of using required training as a onetime annual injection of diversity into a workforce, intelligence planners should include diversity within their personnel manning decisions every day in order to create a welcoming climate for different perspectives and associated ideas.

To do this requires staffing an intelligence organization with a diverse set of people from different backgrounds, generations, sexes, religions, cultures, and even political leanings. It does not mean establishing quotas or deliberately hiring or moving people around just because of their race or sex. Instead, diversity means understanding that people from different background will more likely than not have different mechanisms for receiving and digesting information, perceiving and analyzing a given subject, and making decisions as a result.

Diversity of thought brings about differences in perspectives, experiential thought processes, and even misperceptions and biases. Building an intelligence team with many different perspectives will foster new ideas, new approaches to problem solving, and more imaginative analysis within each type of intelligence team or section.

Diversity of thought requires identifying and including as many different types of personnel toward a given problem set. This may translate into placing a female on an all-male analytic team, or bringing in a counterintelligence analyst to look at a technical set of data or draft product. It can also include having an analyst with only a high school degree, matched with a PhD or getting the perspective from both a baby boomer and Gen-Xer on analysis involving financial transactions. These may seem like ludicrous and even politically incorrect actions, but they are crucial to grow and foster a working climate for intelligence operations that is better able to conduct diagnostic, imaginative, and even contrarian analytic techniques.

---

8   "Bold Colors - No Pale Pastels." (2010, September 15). *Excerpt of Ronald Reagan's video address to members of the Young Americans for Freedom.* Nth2AK. Retrieved from https://www.youtube.com/watch?v=2OznoFCZdS8

9   Rock, David & Grant, Heidi. *Why diverse teams are smarter. Harvard Business Review.* Retrieved from November 4, 2016, from https://hbr.org/2016/11/why-diverse-teams-are-smarter

Diversity of thought opens up the possible solutions to a given problem set that a more homogeneous group would be less likely to identify, but just moving people around or bringing in new analysts without building a culture of inclusiveness along with it poses some significant risks of disagreements or even hostility to new or different ideas. Opinions and assessments that are new or not in sync with the majority of a group should not be discounted out of hand. In some cases this requires deliberate acknowledgment and practice within an intel center, especially if it has many personnel who have been in positions for quite a while and therefore set in their ways of doing business. Accompanying moves and assembling working groups with a deliberate policy of diversity and inclusiveness are important for the success of these groups.

Lesson in Intelligence:
Leadership Through Diversity

In the Spring of 1999 when I became the first active duty military officer as the Chief of Intelligence for the Land Information Warfare Activity (LIWA), I found the intelligence branch to be in disarray. Several of some two dozen personnel were subjected to an investigation (both affectionately and derisively known as a 15–6 investigation named after the corresponding army regulation). Communications were poor among the two dozen branch members and there was an underlying conflict brewing between several of the Army civilians and the warrant officers with the NCOs and soldiers caught in the middle.

One of the immediate problems I discovered is that there was no official organization for the branch; at least not one that anyone could show me. As a default, the analysts spent most of their time working with their own kind— warrant officers secluded in one office, and civilians in their own area. My first task as the new intelligence boss was clear. I needed to fix this environment.

Within a few weeks I put together a new organizational structure for the entire branch. In it, I created two all-source analytic teams, a Transnational Threat Assessment Team (TTAT) that would tackle cyber threats, and a current intel team that worked directly on the main floor of the Information Dominance Center handling urgent priority and quick turnaround requests and presentations. Each team would be led by a warrant officer, and include one civilian, one NCO, and one or two enlisted personnel.

In this way, I would be pushing the warrant officers to lead, the civilians to support, and foster a mix of different perspectives toward analysis and problem-solving. While not without its bumps, the new way of working within the branch took hold quickly and many of the interpersonal problems seemed to rapidly dissipate. Morale improved and the quality of work in products began to receive accolades from support combatant commands in Europe, the Pacific, and perhaps most importantly from the special operations community.

The Intelligence Work Environment

Once a personnel plan has been developed and executed and an intelligence organization is working with a full staff of quality qualified personnel, the next critical task is the care and feeding of these people. Taking care of people is an ongoing challenge for any intelligence organization as it can't be solved by a onetime event. Instead, an environment has to be created that is healthy and inclusive. In this way, it must give to its personnel challenges, rewards, and overall job satisfaction.

While the challenge of taking care of people is similar for any organization, intelligence organizations present some unique facets. First, the intelligence marketspace is highly competitive. As discussed in Chapter 4, it is a growing desegregating community that is no longer confined to the government or military. As a result, intelligence positions for qualified, experienced personnel are in high demand with a relatively low supply of new intelligence personnel.

There is also a cultural problem in the intelligence workplace. Intelligence organizations that are either in support or an organic part of a non-intelligence organization can have a tendency to look upon intelligence personnel as second-class members of that organization. Since they are in a supporting role, they may be seen as subordinates rather than critical partners working toward a common goal.

Finally, intelligence technology has grown in importance to shape a work culture where training and education of people is sometimes seen as a lesser priority. One of the proverbial sayings in intelligence is that as soon as budget cutting takes place, training is the first thing to go.

Because, in part, of these facets an admittedly subjective assessment about intelligence organizations is that many of them do a fairly poor job at taking care of people. There are many reasons for this as each organization is unique in terms of personality, leadership, and management styles. Gaining and maintaining high-quality intelligence people is a constant challenge, and poor leadership and management will always exacerbate these challenges.

Root Cause Analysis of Intelligence Personnel Issues and Problems

Given this environment, every intelligence organization will encounter personnel issues and problems from time to time that are serious enough to require a manager's or first-line supervisor's attention and corrective actions. These problems will present themselves with one or more observables or events, or through reports, data, or any other statistic. There may be personality conflicts, numerous and frequent absences, an increase in the number of grammatical and factual errors in intelligence products, harassment, unwillingness to work with others, or a myriad of other problems.

Every intelligence supervisor eventually has to deal with many of the most common personnel problems, often concurrently. Failure to properly address, fix, or mitigate personnel problems can often be traced to an incorrect diagnosis of the root cause of a problem as opposed to surface indicators or symptoms. There are several known ways of conducting root cause analysis for this type of problem. They all focus on identifying the problem and then seeking out the underlying causes that may not be so apparent at first glance.

One of the most common personnel problems frustrating many intelligence managers is a high attrition rate among their intelligence workforce. Intelligence personnel coming and going from an organization on a perpetual basis isn't out of the ordinary, but when it's done frequently and at a persistent rate, the disruption and risk to successful operations increases dramatically.

All new personnel to an intelligence organization need time to familiarize themselves with the tools, the data sets, the requirements, and the operational procedures of any position, and it may be weeks to months before someone can work at peak efficiency depending on the mission and environment. Frequent and continual changes to the personnel roster of an organization guarantee that a high percentage of the workforce's performance will not be totally effective.

Persistently high attrition within an intelligence workforce is a significant problem, but it is not the root cause of the problem. In fact there may be several factors or "roots" that can be identified as contributing to the problem. An obvious contributing reason of high attrition rate is that people leave the organization in order to work somewhere else. When people were asked why they were leaving the organization, some root causes appeared; four to be precise.

The following four primary conditions that contribute to the work satisfaction of any given employee were identified.[10]

1. **Location:** Includes remoteness, permissiveness, safety and security, commuting distance, and distance from friends and family.
2. **The Job:** Includes the organization and customer missions, requirements, duties and responsibilities, day-to-day tasks and functions, and operating procedures.
3. **Compensation:** Includes salary, benefits, and opportunities for advancement.
4. **The Work Environment:** Includes leadership, personal relationships, management, perks, professional development, and physical conditions.

A person who is satisfied in all the four work conditions will most likely not leave an organization or a particular position within it unless rare extenuating circumstances force them to. Even if three of the four conditions are being met, it is a good bet that a particular individual will not look for another job. Once the satisfaction falls to only one or two of the four, they can be expected to leave as soon as is feasible. For example, personnel who have to commute a long distance or are even away from home for a certain period of time will be happy with their jobs as long as the work is satisfying, they are happy with their pay, and have no issue with the environment they are working in. As soon as one of the

---

10   These four conditions were related to me while working with Ray Bernhagen for a mid-size defense contracting company called SYTEX in September 2001. While the conditions are more clearly defined for the use as an analytic tool in this book, the basic discussion centered around investigating why so many well-trained intelligence officers were leaving the military mid-career, including myself.

other conditions is deemed unacceptable for any reason, the intelligence supervisor can expect to have to hire to back-fill vacancies soon.

While the decision to leave an intelligence organization is an individual one, the attrition rate indicates a pattern or a common set of problems affecting many people within an organization. As they investigate the observable problem and determine associated reasons, managers will almost always find the cause in one of these four broadly categorized areas. Understanding they may not be able to address certain aspects such as the location, or employee salaries, there are several aspects of the job and work environment that are well within the power of the manager to correct or improve.

The Work Environment–A Reflection of Leadership

One of the most challenging aspects in leading an intelligence organization is the creation and maintenance of a healthy work environment for the personnel assigned to it. Just as there are a myriad of customer, mission sets, data sets, and tools that make up an intelligence operation, there are also widely varying degrees of successful work environments for an organization's personnel. Well-led organizations have environments that foster peak performance and help to maintain high morale for its personnel. Others can be unhealthy, oppressive, or in extreme cases completely dysfunctional.

The quality of any work environment is the responsibility of the intelligence leader or manager. Leadership within an intelligence organization can be one of the most difficult aspects of an intelligence career. Not only does it require expertise in many of the intelligence specific missions, technologies, and operations, it also requires both management and leadership skills. Mastering all three is very difficult as some people are simply not suited for it. Intelligence as a profession tends to attract people who possess intellectual or technical skills over people skills. It is not a surprise therefore that many

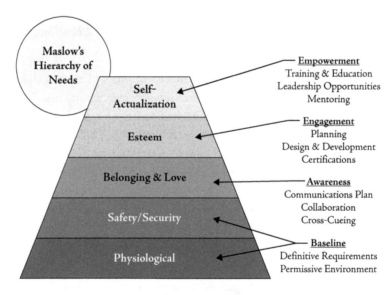

FIGURE 7.9   Hierarchy of intelligence personnel needs

intelligence organizations that suffer from low morale of employees and high attrition rates are in reality suffering from poor leadership that has not created or maintained a healthy work environment. In effect, lack of quality leadership removes one of the four conditions for work satisfaction.

The study of leadership, especially national or military leadership, is itself an enormous subject that has been studied throughout history. While there are many sources available for the student to become familiar with the principles of leadership, the specific aspects of leadership required for the here and now of intelligence operations must focus on applying various leadership attributes and competencies in order to build a cohesive team and foster an effective work environment for that team to work in.

Effective leadership within an intelligence center must result in three applied aspects; all three of which involve taking care of people according their needs. All of these entail taking care of personnel through communications, engagement, and empowerment.

One method to help identify the specific aspects of taking care of personnel is by placing the needs of the individual within the context of Maslow's hierarchy of needs. Abraham Maslow was an American psychologist most well known for developing a model of individual human needs according to their priority over each other. Individual needs, placed in general categories such as physiological or safety and security, were deemed more important, and therefore they were placed near the bottom of the pyramid. If an individual was in a situation where their physiological needs such as eating, breathing, and sleep were threatened or deprived, the other needs in their life simply did not matter at that point. Higher needs such as those categorized by esteem (achievements, respect) or self-actualization (morality, creativity, overcoming prejudice) can only be attained once the lower level needs are already satisfied.[11]

While Maslow's hierarchy has its critics, it is very useful for identifying the personnel needs within an intelligence operation. Using the different levels of needs as displayed in the following chart, intelligence managers can gain an understanding of where the aspects of awareness, engagement, and empowerment align with the needs of the individual as well as in relation to each other.

Baseline Requirements

Every intelligence operation has features that are required to be in place in order for it to be defined as an operation. Before anything else can be considered, it actually has to have a reason for existence in the first place. There needs to be a job, a mission, a customer, and a physical environment established. There have to be people, data, tools, and both operational and analytic processes. All of these features make up the baseline requirements for intelligence personnel needs. Without any of these, it would be difficult to say that an operation even exists in the first place.

---

11   Boeree, C. George. *Abraham Maslow 1908–1970. Personality Theories.* Retrieved November 18, 2017, from http://webspace.ship.edu/cgboer/maslow.html

In addition, all intelligence managers also need to provide a certain degree of safety and security for its personnel. It's fairly obvious that any intelligence operation must take place within a permissive environment as its personnel need to be able to focus on intelligence, not perimeter security, or natural and man-made disasters.

Once both physiological and safety/security needs are met, intelligence operations can take place—albeit at different levels of effectiveness given leadership ability to address the next three areas.

Awareness

Conducting intelligence analysis is a relatively solitary task. The act of collecting, reading, visualizing, and analyzing information about our threats is largely an individual thought process. Conducting analysis as part of a group is possible and often helpful in the creation of intelligence products, but group analysis is an action conducted by individuals which is then shared and integrated with other analysis. While intelligence analysts are relatively independent workers, they are always working in support of someone else and must have an understanding of things beyond their own organization and mission.

Intelligence managers must, therefore, place a priority on ensuring that their personnel maintain situational awareness of operations within their own organization as well as within their customer's operations. This includes understanding the customer's mission and objectives, their capabilities and limitations, and challenges on an almost continual basis. Maintaining situational awareness of intelligence personnel allows them to better understand not only the context of their assigned work, but also the overall intent of why they are doing a certain task or creating a specific intelligence product.

The benefits of personnel taking pride in belonging to an organization start with keeping them informed and situationally aware. Intelligence managers must constantly look for effective ways to ensure their personnel are kept informed of both day-to-day and long-term tasks, as well as initiatives, problem sets, and issues that are associated with each. In this way, intelligence personnel don't simply work in an intelligence organization or its center, they are kept informed and treated as if they are part of the organization.

Communication models for intelligence operations and the organizations that work them can include both face-to-face and electronic communications, each with its own benefits and limitations. Creating an effective plan helps to create a tempo of operations, a standard schedule, and structure of operations. These plans can include daily stand-up meetings, sometimes known as battlefield update briefs (BUBs) in tactical military environments. They can also include periodic staff meetings, summary e-mails, or reporting processes for scheduled events and prominently displayed priority missions and requirements for ongoing events requiring awareness.

Effective communications techniques are covered in Chapter 11 with a focus on creating an environment where situational awareness is ever present.

Engagement

Once an environment of awareness and belonging is created and maintained, the next part of a healthy work environment for intelligence personnel is one where they are included and engaged in many of the decisions that arise both on a day-to-day as well as on a long-term basis. Engagement means ensuring that personnel not only know what's going on but also take an active part in providing input, feedback, and opinions on the direction of the center and its operational procedures.

To do this, an effective communications model must include plans and channels for keeping personnel informed and situationally aware, and yet it should not be unidirectional. Not only should communications within an intelligence operation flow top-down and bottom-up, lateral communications is also important. Analytic teams that can keep each other up to speed on their current priorities of work can benefit from corroboration and cross-cueing each other's capabilities.

Engagement activities can include the following items, events, and activities:

+ **Periodic Staff Meetings:** Scheduled to take place weekly or semiweekly with only key players and following a structured agenda.
+ **Consolidated Weekly Reports:** Following a simple reporting format with assigned input from various key players within your organization. Also requires dissemination plan, and a clear set of criteria for what is deemed reportable and what is not.
+ **Skip Level Meeting Attendance:** Having personnel observe meetings that are attended by the leader on a regular basis. Meant to accompany, not replace the leader required to attend.
+ **Right Seat Analysis:** Assigning new analysts to work with an experienced analyst on a given problem set in order to learn their specific analytic techniques and understand the application of certain analytic techniques.
+ **Cross-Level Training and Work Sessions:** Assigning both new and experienced analysts to work within another group to learn their operational processes, business rhythms, and provide feedback.
+ **Stand-Up Meetings:** Daily or semi-daily meetings of all personnel within an organization to quickly understand the priority items for the day along with any other operational or administrative announcements.
+ **In-Progress Reviews:** Regularly scheduled reviews with a limited scope toward the review of the progress, issues, and challenges of a specific program or problem set.
+ **Sensing Sessions:** Either periodically held meetings or review of written feedback to analyze performance or work environment issues related to any part of the organization.

Empowerment

Education and Training Opportunities–Leadership Mentoring

Perhaps one of the most difficult work environments to create and maintain for an intelligence organization (or for any other industry) is one that not only fosters awareness and engagement of its personnel but also empowers them. Empowerment involves taking direct measures and actions to instill experience, confidence, and a degree of autonomy and self-fulfillment within an organization. For intelligence organizations, empowering work environments are those that place the growth and strengthening of personnel as a top priority once they've ensured that an acceptable level of awareness and engagement has been met.

Empowerment includes training and education opportunities and associated development of skills, experience, and leadership of personnel through on-the-job learning and mentoring programs. Encouraging personnel to constantly learn through structure curricula, applied training, and on-the-job experiences is an act of investing in personnel and establishes a culture of people over technology within an intelligence organization.

Unfortunately, leadership and professional development as empowering activities are often seen as detractors from the immediate missions and customer priorities. Indeed they can be. Those who recognize their importance and work to integrate empowering measures into an organization understand the long-term gains made by turning personnel from mere employees into team members and future leaders and managers.

Leadership and Professional Development

Empowering personnel through leadership positions can include creating first-line supervisor positions as well as project leads. Whereas the former is primarily responsible for a defined set of people over several problem sets, the latter involves leadership over several different personnel assigned to completing a specific project or task. Leadership development requires additional considerations. First, these leadership positions can be permanent or temporary, but they must be within the skill level of the person filling it. Placing someone into a developing supervisory analyst position or giving them additional responsibilities in collection or production management without the confidence that they will succeed and grow within that position will return the expected results of poor performance.

In addition, leadership opportunities within an intelligence center that aims to empower its personnel must also allow for learning through mistakes. Leadership is learned primarily through experience, and mistakes and setbacks are all part of that experience. An environment where either the senior leadership or mission parameters has zero tolerance for mistakes, errors, or missteps would risk mission fulfillment and drop support of a customer to an unacceptable level. Allowing new leaders to experience setbacks while maintaining top-level customer support is an ideal and often difficult environment to establish.

Training and Education

While education for intelligence personnel focuses on the foundational level knowledge sets, training focuses on knowledge and skills applied specifically to a certain aspect of the job. Many large organizations in both the government and commercial sectors already have education and training programs that help employees cover their costs. Some also have their own internal training programs or the ability of their personnel to attend training externally. For an intelligence organization that seeks to empower it's personnel, both training and education opportunities are critical for personnel growth.

- **Education:** Currently there are only a handful of higher learning institutions that offer intelligence as a bachelor's, master's, or doctoral degree. For such a large industry in terms of both government and commercial funding for intelligence, it seems strange that intelligence is not a larger area of academic study. This is because, as explained earlier in this chapter, intelligence takes in people from many different parts of society. As an accession profession, intelligence hires people based upon skills needed to understand these different parts—from economics to sociology and from military to politics. As long as there is an association between an employee's education plan and their role within an organization, education should be enthusiastically supported.
- **Training:** Training should include learning skills in data mining tools, analytical methods, and operational processes as these skills are directly applicable to duty requirements within intelligence centers. They should help prepare employees for both their current and higher level positions as well as a certification that they should obtain to continue their professional growth. Training can be conducted internally or externally and can be both individual or group and classroom or online based. Unlike education, training will have direct, tangible, and measurable results for personnel within an organization provided it is adequately supported by current leadership. Planning considerations for effective training within an intelligence organization will be covered in Chapter 11.

Identifying measures and actions associated with empowering personnel also requires understanding why it stands at the top of Maslow's hierarchy. As an added consideration, leaders and managers of intelligence organizations must also understand that effective engagement requires an environment that already creates and maintains situational awareness. Empowering employees without either awareness or engagement carries significant risks for an organization. Employees achieving personal growth without an attachment to an organization will only stay with that organization long enough to achieve enough growth necessary to leave it for a better position elsewhere. Instead of solving any specific personnel problems or creating a work environment that fosters growth and professional development, it will only exacerbate problems of morale and attrition due to employee dissatisfaction.

Lessons in Intelligence:
Addressing Symptoms Instead of the Problems

As the program manager and creator of an intelligence analyst training program for INSCOM, my instructors were training thousands of intelligence analysts from INSCOM and around the DC area annually. Our most popular courses such as the counterterrorism analysis and applied critical thinking courses had six-month waiting lists for both locally held and mobile training team (MTT) courses around the world. The popularity of our courses allowed our training team to grow from an initial 7 personnel to 14 and later to over 30 instructors and support personnel team.

Suddenly and inexplicably, student registrations for our locally held courses dropped significantly. My instructors were reporting less than capacity classes, with a significant drop in students from INSCOM headquarters itself. We knew there were hundreds of analysts working within INSCOM IOC with a constant rotation of new personnel. Investigating further, my instructors told me that there was a new policy within the IOC that new employees were allowed to take our BAM course when they first arrived, but were then only allowed to take an additional course every six months. This meant that analysts would be largely untrained in both tools and analytic process used by the IOC until many months into their employment.

Both the on-site manager in charge of IOC analysts and his supervisor happened to come from my company on a separate contract. During a discussion about this issue between the three of us, the on-site manager blamed my training program for the constant loss of personnel. In his view, his new analysts would start work in the IOC, take three of four of our training courses back-to-back, and then quit for a higher paying job elsewhere; adding our courses to their resumes. The attrition rate for analysts on their contract was an astonishing 83% annually. To remedy this they had decided to change the training allowance policy for their IOC analysts so they would wait longer to get our training before leaving.

My rebuttal was straightforward—knowing that this particular manager treated his people poorly, and rarely held any meetings, stand-ups, or face-to-face discussions with his people, we were disregarding his responsibility to establish a successful work environment through awareness or engagement. Our training program was only a symptom of a more persistent morale problem resulting in high employee turnover, many of them asking to become an instructor on my team. I informed my government contract representative, but we were powerless to do anything else. It wasn't long that contract was lost to another company and the on-site manager had conveniently moved to a government position somewhere else near DC.

Summary

In considering the effective use and application of the four components of intelligence operations—i.e., data, tools, people, and processes—people are the most important. Intelligence leaders and managers must consider the primary sources intelligence relies on for personnel along with the various planning factors to properly man an organization. The goal is to bring in the right people with the right skills and experience in the right positions in order to ensure intelligence operations and processes are performed successfully. An added challenge for intelligence managers is to create an inclusive work environment that allows for awareness, engagement, and empowerment of personnel with policies, measures, and specific actions as part of their operating procedures. Personnel are the lifeblood of the organization. Without an effective manning of intelligence personnel, all other functions of the organization become difficult, dysfunctional, and ultimately ineffective in support customers.

Key Summary Points

+ The intelligence profession relies upon four main sources for its personnel: the military, law enforcement, students, and information technology industries, as intelligence is primarily an accessions profession.
+ Planning factors for intelligence personnel include the intelligence process, operational considerations, labor calculations, and key positions within intelligence centers.
+ Creating a manning plan and organizational structure for an intelligence organization requires an understanding of all planning factors along with the number for personnel authorized for sustaining customer support.
+ Maintaining effective intelligence operations requires taking care of personnel as a top priority. This includes an effective work environment for personnel that maintains awareness, and engages and empowers its personnel in a hierarchical manner.

Discussion Questions

+ Besides the four primary sources mentioned, what are other potential areas that intelligence could draw from for its personnel? What are the benefits and drawbacks from each?
+ Besides the planning factors described, what other considerations must intelligence leaders and managers take into account for an effectively manned organization?

- In what ways would the creation of an effective work environment that maintains awareness, engages, and empowers personnel differ between a consolidated and a desegregated organization? What about between a permanent and an ad hoc organization that draws its personnel from other well-established organizations?
- What are the risks and additional issues that should be considered in creating an organization that includes a wide array of diversity? What mitigation measures could be taken to reduce these risks?

Figure Credits

Chapter 8

Intelligence Processes–The Intelligence Operations Process

Learning Objectives

After completing this chapter, you will be able to:

▸ Understand the importance of processes as one of the four components of effective intelligence operations.

▸ Identify the criticisms of the intelligence process used predominantly within the U.S. military and U.S. government.

▸ Understand the steps and actions of the Intelligence Operations Process as outgrowth of the basic communications model.

▸ Understand the steps and actions of the Intelligence Analysis Process as a distinct subprocess of the Intelligence Operations Process.

Every Operation Requires Processes

Understanding that any intelligence operation requires the combination of data, tools, and people is fairly obvious. This is primarily because these components are tangible, meaning they must be physically acquired, housed, and maintained, albeit in different ways. They must also be tracked and accounted for once they are part of the operation. By definition, an intelligence operation can't really be considered an operation without the effective integration of all three.

Conversely, intelligence processes are the only one of the four components covered in this book that are intangible and therefore more difficult to recognize as a critical requirement. They have the highest tendency to be disregarded, overlooked, or neglected from a planning and management perspective. As a result, intelligence centers and their supported operations may have all the right tangible components, but are still ineffective at supporting a customer.

175

Processes include actions, methodologies, and procedures that must be taken, followed, adhered to, and completed in order for intelligence to be produced to satisfy customer requirements. They can be operational, analytical, mechanical, automated, or a combination of all of them. Everything in intelligence involves processes. While analytical processes involve the use of inquiry and methods of thinking about a given problem set, operational processes are associated with conducting the business of intelligence. In short, analytical processes are about thinking and operational processes are about doing.

Another distinction should also be made between a methodology and a process. A methodology is defined as an application of one or more methods, usually associated with a given field of study or similar activity.[1] Alternately, a process is a series of actions conducted to achieve an end or a result.[2] For intelligence planning purposes, methodologies are more frequently associated with analytical steps and actions and can involve one or more thought processes. Processes are perceived in intelligence as more operational, even though some of their steps can include sub-steps or subprocesses that are analytic methods.

Care in creating, evaluating, and improving both methodologies and processes are critical to the success of intelligence analysis and operations. Use of sound analytic methods are important because they help to articulate the thought processes used by analysts, i.e., it helps them to "show their math" when creating products or developing a predictive read on a threat or problem set. Workable processes are just as important because they provide the structure, rules, parameters, operational tempo, and work flow of the entire operation.

Intelligence operations that neglect deliberate planning and use of either sound methodologies or processes are set up for failure from the outset of a new problem set. Often, organizations that have bad or ineffective processes have some tell-tale indicators. Analysts who neglect them often end up encountering unnecessary challenges with collaboration, have trouble articulating how they came up with a particular assessment, and also find difficulty in recreating a given analytic methodology for a similar and comparable result. As a result, intelligence products lack standardization and often have a higher degree of either mistakes or conflict with previous or parallel assessments. Gut feelings, winging it, and doing analysis on the fly and similar terms are those frequently used within organizations that needs improvement to their processes.

In order for processes and methodologies to work within an intelligence operation, there are certain aspects they must possess. These requirements are fairly straight forward but worth articulating.

---

1   Definition of methodology according to Merriam-Webster's online dictionary Retrieved from https://www.merriam-webster.com/dictionary/methodology

2   Ibid. Retrieved from https://www.merriam-webster.com/dictionary/process

CHART 8.1   Rules for Intelligence Processes

Processes must ...	Notes
BE POSSIBLE	It must be carried out within the capabilities of the available data, tools, and people involved. Must also be logical and within time constraints.
BE REPEATABLE	People and data systems must be able to recreate the process several times over with expectation of consistency of results.
HAVE A PURPOSE	It must support either another internal process/operation or a customer. If internal, the supported process must eventually be traced to supporting a customer.
PRODUCE A RESULT	It must have both an entry as well as an end-point. If cyclical, it must have somewhere to start or join in. End-point can be a tangible product or a resulting action.

Applying, Adapting, and Creating Processes for Intelligence

Not every process within every intelligence center or supported operation need to be created from scratch. The study of intelligence analysis is largely the study of various processes that have been proven to work consistently over time. Many have shown themselves to be so successful that they've been named as industry standards to a certain degree.

With that, there three ways to integrate new processes into intelligence operations:

Applying: Applying a current process is the act of simply taking a current process used somewhere else and using it to the letter within another operation. This is most frequent and easiest to do within very large organizations such as the federal government or the military. Processes in this category could include the Intelligence Cycle, intelligence preparation of the battlefield or IPB (also known as intelligence preparation of the battlespace and intelligence preparation of the operating environment). Good analysts can apply various processes that are considered industry standard.

Adapting: A vast majority of processes used in a particular intelligence operation were created for another purpose. Of these, almost all of them must be adapted to the specific data, tools, requirements, and desired products that need to be created by the operation. Adapting these processes is the act of modifying or tailoring them in a way that best fits the current environment. Examples of intelligence processes that are routinely modified include the threat assessment process, Threat Profiling, and almost every type of structured analytic technique. Great analysts find ways to adapt a variety of analytic methods and techniques to their problem set.

Creating: Perhaps the most difficult aspect of working with processes in intelligence is when the need to create a new one from scratch has been identified. This could be because of an entirely new requirement has been levied by a customer, a new set of data, data mining tool, or capability has become available, or an entirely different school of thought, strategy, or method of operation has taken place. In unlike applying or adapting, there are no current processes that have complied with the four rules for intelligence processes listed previously. Creating a new process from scratch requires the aid of another process, the scientific method, that include developing theories on how a particular analytic process should work, formulating a hypothesis on which would be the best or most preferred process, and then testing that process within the work environment. Truly outstanding analysts are able to create their own analytic processes that allow an intelligence center to produce new and unique products and results for customers.

Lessons in Intelligence:
Propaganda Templating–The Foreign Propaganda Problem

In 1999, one of my first tasks after being assigned as Chief of Intelligence for the Army's Land Information Warfare Activity (LIWA) was to understand the functions and applications of the various data mining tools within the newly created U.S. Army Intelligence and Security Command's (INSCOM) Information Dominance Center (IDC). One of these tools was a visualization tool that would ingest a queried pull of up to several thousand related documents or web pages, read them, and then arrange each of them on the analyst's screen according to common words or phrases they shared with each other. The more the common phrases shared between the documents, the closer together the documents would be plotted.

For example, if a queried data pull of several news web pages was conducted using the term Serbian Military + Kosovo, the collected web pages which would then be arranged in groups or clusters in accordance with other common phrases they shared or did not share between each other. The resulting visualization would look like a landscape or overhead view of a map with hills representing each of the several clusters that the tool had determined shared a common phrase for each. Phrases like specific "1st Army" or "63rd Airborne" would come up in close proximity to each other as they were units that took part in the late 1990s conflict. The visualization capability of the tool even colored the different elevations of the map using dark green for low points and light green and white for the highest peaks of common web pages clusters.

In the middle of discovering how best to use this and other tools, my section received a request for support by the U.S. Pacific Command or PACOM to support their efforts in understanding the propaganda surrounding an upcoming election held by a U.S. ally in the Pacific region. More specifically, PACOM needed a better understanding of the various domestic and foreign propaganda efforts designed to sway the election one way or the other. Using our tools, I worked with the assigned analysts to create a process that would identify the most commonly used themes or talking points in the media, knowing that the most successful ones would be picked up by other news outlets and reverberate more strongly and persistently over time.

The developed process would allow my analysts to identify the most common themes that could then be queried to identify when they started, in which news source the phrase first appeared, and then create a timeline graph to show how strong it grew over time as well as when it later weakened or died out completely. The process also included patterning sets of themes and phrases depending on the source or country of origin.

Not only was this extremely helpful to PACOM analysts about an upcoming election, our products also gave them a template on how propaganda efforts from a given adversarial country would work in the future. Since many propaganda efforts followed their own regimented plans, certain themes, political spin, and outright lies could be predicted and acted upon prior to them being published and disseminated. This was an entirely new way of conducting intelligence analysis and it was only made possible by the new capabilities provided by data mining tools.

The Intelligence Process

One of the most commonly accepted processes in intelligence is the aptly named intelligence process, also known as the Intelligence Cycle or the analytic cycle. It is one of the first processes taught to new intelligence personnel in both government and commercial sectors as it is a foundational part of intelligence operations with the U.S. military. This is primarily because the Intelligence Cycle is both simplistic and comprehensive at the same time. Working through the steps of the Intelligence Cycle encapsulates or touches upon every other intelligence process from collection to analysis to production and dissemination.

As shown in Chapter 7, the intelligence process is a never-ending process that in general captures all of the steps that intelligence operations must follow in order to support a customer. This process is the essence of what intelligence is all the about, the act of supporting a customer and their decisions by collecting and processing relevant information about threats to their mission and operations, analyzing that information in order to generate new insight or knowledge, and then providing that analysis to the supported customer while they are making decisions that could be impacted by those threats. Every action undertaking by the intelligence professionals must be tied to a portion or the entirety of the intelligence process.

As far as academic research is concerned, there is no one author to the intelligence process. It's the product of evolution of the business with the first noted mention and

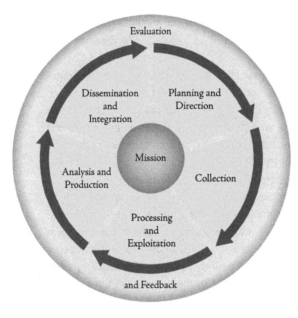

description arising out of the post World War II intelligence instruction.[3] While there are several versions of this process available in the public domain, they are all similar to each other as they all share common and undeniable steps or subprocesses that must be performed.

One of the most standard representations for the intelligence process is one that is part of current the U.S. military doctrine.[4] As the customer/commander's mission is the primary reason for intelligence support and therefore the center of this process, each step is conducted in subsequent but frequently overlapping succession.

FIGURE 8.1   The joint intelligence process as shown in the U.S. Department of Defense Joint Publication 2.0, Joint Intelligence

Planning and Direction: Developing, receiving, and validating requirements; understanding customer intent and priorities for intelligence; continually managing intelligence operations.

Collection: The act of obtaining relevant data, information, and finished intelligence in relation to current and probable future requirements; an ongoing subprocess involving the tasking of internal or owned assets, or requesting support from external assets or sources.

Processing and Exploitation: Managing data, information, and intelligence that has been or is being collected; converting data and information into forms or formats that can be used by data mining tools and subsequently by the human analyst.

Analysis and Production: The creation of usable intelligence analysis and conveyed through various types of products or services for the customer.

---

3   Wheaton, Kristen J., PhD. (2011, January 4). *RFI: Who Invented the Intelligence Cycle? Sources and Methods Blog.* Retrieved from http://sourcesandmethods.blogspot.com/2011/01/rfi-who-invented-intelligence-cycle.html

4   Joint Publication 2.0, Joint Intelligence, U.S. Department of Defense, October 22, 2013. Retrieved from www.dtic.mil/doctrine/new_pubs/jp2_0.pdf

Dissemination and Integration: The delivery of intelligence products or services to a customer along with subsequent integration of intelligence into customer operations.

Evaluation and Feedback: Measuring effectiveness of intelligence products, services, and subprocesses in order to improve future operations and methods employed to support a customer with intelligence. This is a concurrent subprocess that is continually in play.

While the Intelligence Cycle as a process does not have a start or an endpoint (one of the requirements of a cyclical process), the standard way to enter the cycle is to start with planning and direction. In this way, all subsequent work starts with the customer and their intelligence requirements as the priority driver for all other actions.

Criticisms of the Intelligence Process

The intelligence process is THE foundational process that all other intelligence processes align with, compliment, or are embedded within it. It is also probably the one most frequently cited, taught, or used in planning operations.

Perhaps the greatest flaw of this process is that it is not accurate. Intelligence as an operational process along with its numerous and varied subprocesses generally follows the path of the Intelligence Cycle, but the cyclical model used contains several flaws and inaccuracies when compared to the actual conduct of the process in real-world operations.

For these reasons, there are several criticisms of the U.S. military and other similar portrayals of the intelligence process in various intelligence writings. Perhaps the most comprehensive and detailed coverage can be found in Robert Clark's 2004 book, *Intelligence Analysis: A Target Centric Approach*. The most common of these criticisms are as follows[5]:

Criticism 1: The process is not up to date with the current changes to customers and their requirements: As explained in Chapter 3, intelligence customers have grown to appreciate (and overestimate) the capabilities of information age technology and its impact on their operations. They are also increasing their demands on the capabilities of intelligence operations, especially those that have effectively employed data mining and visualization tools. As a result, decision-making processes are more streamlined, compressed, and subject to frequent change. Demands on intelligence are therefore increased in both quantity and quality. Customers are looking for immediate returns, initial reads, and ongoing involvement of intelligence personnel throughout their decision-making processes.

As is, the intelligence process, once completing the planning and direction phase, does not involve the supported customer until dissemination and integration. Collection, analysis, and production steps are largely conducted independently or in an environment

---

5   Clark, Robert M. (2016). *Intelligence analysis: A target centric approach* (5th ed.). Washington, DC: CQ Press.

isolated from the customer. Following the steps to the letter this way would not provide the comprehensive support that intelligence customers and decision-makers need.

Criticism 2: Intelligence in practice is a dynamic, not cyclic process: Included in the diagrams for various intelligence processes are arrows showing the direction of progression, usually clockwise. These arrows denote a requirement for a given step to be dependent on the completion of the previous step on the chart. The only exception is the evaluation and feedback step that is ongoing throughout the process, but still dependent on the other steps. According to the model for this process, intelligence professionals must go through each step in turn prior to delivering or disseminating a product.

In practice, intelligence actions do not take place as a strict sequence of events. It is nonlinear, fluid, and personnel working on an intelligence operation frequently find themselves moving back and forth between the steps listed. For example, during the analysis and production step, analysts may discover an anomaly in the collected data that spurs an entirely new line of thinking for their given problem set. In order to develop the best analytic product possible, they find that they must go back to the collection and processing step to bring in additional relevant data. The intelligence process as a cyclical process doesn't allow for this.

Criticism 3: The steps are isolated from each other: The intelligence process of receiving a requirement in the planning and direction phase, and then running collection thru analysis to dissemination lists several steps that are separate and distinct from each other. As touched upon in Chapter 7, personnel are even specialized in terms of skill sets for each of these steps; more so for the largest intelligence agencies and organizations. While necessary for analysis to determine the right personnel for an intelligence organization or operation, an additional resulting challenge are the gaps between each step.

In many cases, different people need to perform specialized subprocesses within each step of the intelligence process. There is an inherent risk of failure if either personnel who specialize in a given step or the step's subprocesses are not properly aligned with the rest of the cycle. For example, personnel working in production can end up focusing on their own tasks without regard the happenings in the rest of the cycle.

Criticism 4: Following the process "lock-step" exposes vulnerabilities: The intelligence process, as a doctrinal concept, is well known among the entire U.S. Intelligence Community. It is reasonable to assume that it is also well known by U.S. threats and adversaries. Following the intelligence process as doctrine without diversion, omission, or short-cuts requires the intelligence professional to complete the requirements of each step before proceeding with the next. Adversarial planning can exploit this adherence through deception efforts or through more disruptive means. For example, a false message successfully planted in the collection phase would not be discovered until proper analysis was conducted to reveal it. If all analysis was restricted to the analysis and production phase, the deception would be allowed to survive and fester for some time, influencing friendly operations.

Perhaps it is a mixed blessing that the U.S. military doesn't spend enough time reading their own doctrine and therefore not as compelled to follow it.[6] Analysis is conducted continuously, not just in the analysis and production phase. Similarly, collection is not just conducted in the collection and processing phase, but as a separate concurrent operation and usually independent of a particular analytic problem set. Understanding the Intelligence Cycle helps our adversaries template the decision-making processes tied to the cycle and could work to the disadvantage of those who follow it to the letter.

Criticism 5: Data mining for intelligence supersedes the process: As the Intelligence Cycle is many years old, it was designed around the manual collection, processing, and analysis functions. In the age of Big Data and the ability to automate many different steps, analysts have the ability to jump around the Intelligence Cycle. Information Age technology also allows decision-makers to conduct their own collection and analysis of information albeit in a rudimentary and ad hoc fashion.

Data mining tools allow analysts to backtrack and conduct additional collection with ease, they can also rely on an unending stream of relevant information thereby never completing or closing out the collection and processing phases. Product deliverables can be updated as simple as updating a web page as the formalities of creating, peer reviewing, and publishing a product seem archaic compared to streaming and cloud-based data sets.

Patterning the Intelligence Process off Communication Models

These criticisms of the intelligence process may beg the question, "why should the Intelligence Process be taught if it's so irreparably broken or never followed?" The answer is that the intelligence process isn't broken; it is just incomplete and doesn't completely reflect the reality of how it is actually conducted during operations.

As the primary purpose of intelligence is to support a customer, the intelligence process should model the interactive process between a customer and their supporting intelligence organization. It includes passing requirements from the customer to their intelligence point of contact, any additional information regarding the supported mission, and the purpose and intent of the request. It also includes implied responses and additional interactions throughout the entire process.

An accurate model of how intelligence works as a process must include the customer and supporting intelligence asset as active participants along with their interaction and working relationship. Communication, therefore, is the essence of what an intelligence process must model.

---

6   Leonard, Steve. (2017, May 18). Broken and unreadable: Our unbearable aversion to doctrine. *Real-ClearDefense*. Retrieved from https://www.realcleardefense.com/articles/2017/05/18/our_unbearable_aversion_to_doctrine_111407.html

Given this, the most straight forward way to accurately model the intelligence process operations is to start with how communication works at its foundational level. A basic communications model works with at least two entities, one of which is the sender who sends a message to the receiver using sort of medium or method of delivery to transmit it. The medium could be verbal or written language, and could include e-mail, video, landline or cell phone, text or instant messaging, or even the visual mediums such as video, sign language, or smoke signals. The message is converted or encoded into the appropriate medium and then decoded or translated once it is accepted by the receiver. One-way communications can stop here, but effective communications requires the receiver to send feedback to the sender using similar methods. This feedback could be acknowledgment that the message was received, understood, or a response to the message content.

While there are several publicly available models of communication that can be easily researched, virtually every form of communications requires both a sender and receiver along with the message, feedback, and appropriate means to deliver, transmit, or convey both the message and feedback. These common elements are shown in Figure 8.2.

Using the basic communications model, it is easy to see that the relationship between an intelligence customer and their supporting intelligence asset is very similar. By replacing the sender and receiver with the customer and the intelligence analyst, respectively, the rest of the model falls into place with other intelligence process components.

The customer can be anyone that needs intelligence support: a decision-maker, commander, director, or even another analyst. The receiver can be anyone within an intelligence organization that has been designated as the point of contact with the customer: an analyst, manager, or liaison. Intelligence requirements are the message, while the resulting intelligence products are feedback. Incidental communications such as "I need support" and "I understand what you need" also occur frequently between the customer and intelligence asset but can be accounted for as an implied part of the interaction.

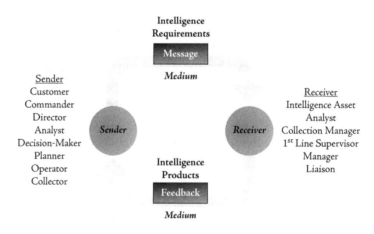

FIGURE 8.2   Basic communications model for intelligence

The Intelligence Operations Process

While the communications model is inherently simplistic, it serves as the foundation of the intelligence process. Adding steps included in the intelligence process shown in Figure 8.1 gives an operational picture of how the intelligence process emerges (see Figure 8.3).

While the Intelligence Operations Process is also a cyclical process, the engine, impetuous of it is the customer. The customer is therefore the logical start and end point in understanding the various components and movement between steps. It also includes the customer's supporting intelligence asset, known for ease of discussion as the analyst. The following steps and entities are summarized with a more detailed explanation of some of them later in the chapter:

1. **Customer:** The customer can include anyone that requires intelligence support, be they decision-maker or another intelligence asset. A customer can also include other intelligence analysts or organizations as they need intelligence to support the decisions they make in their own analysis. For the purposes of the intelligence process, it is the customer that starts it, and their requirements drive the rest of the steps. More information about intelligence customers can be found in Chapter 12.

2. **Customer Generates Requirements:** Customer requirements are the what, when, and why that a customer needs from intelligence. Requirements can be a one-time request or they can happen on regular basis for the same customer. They can also be an independent request or part of an ongoing operation with periodic scheduled deliveries of the same updated, product. Finally, requirements can be specified or implied and formal or informal and the distinction between these will dictate what form or format the requirement will take during transmission.

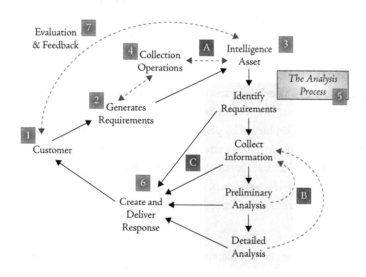

FIGURE 8.3   The intelligence process in practice

3. **Intelligence Asset:** Intelligence in support of a customer can be a single individual, a small team or personnel, or an entire organization up to the size of the largest intelligence agencies at the national level. Transmission of requirements can be a personal interaction between two people or a formalized and bureaucratic process in itself. The analyst, upon receiving requirements from a customer will conduct their own process of ingesting, understanding, evaluating, and analyzing the requirement in order to plan their approach to satisfy it.

4. **Collection Operations:** While collection is part of the analysis process that is specific to the requirement, there are collection operations that are concurrent and ongoing for all intelligence operations. These operations run both specific to the problem set at hand or can be ongoing collections totally independent of the current requirement that happens to have information that could be of use. Collection of vast and varied amounts of information can't just wait until a requirement is levied, they must be established beforehand and be actively running in the expectation that a decision-maker is going to need information about a particular subject area. Collection operation is covered in more detail in Chapter 11.

5. **The Analysis Process:** Similar to collection operations, analysis is a process itself and therefore a subprocess of intelligence operations. These steps include identifying the specified and implied analytic requirements, collecting information, and conducting both preliminary and detailed analysis according to the details needed in the requirement.

6. **Create and Deliver Response :** The intelligence asset, acting off the requirements of their customer, conducts the steps of the Intelligence Cycle in order to create a sufficient response that could include a verbal answer, a briefing or presentation, or the creation of a product that is delivered physically or electronically. Their results are then sent to the original customer, often requiring the creation of a product to include some form of report, chart, or presentation. These results are also made available for other customers within the organization or community that need to know or have asked a similar question. During and after this dissemination, the intelligence asset remains available for coordination, clarification, or follow-through.

7. **Evaluation and Feedback:** Evaluation of the effectiveness of a particular process step, product, or other results happens throughout this process. Since evaluation and feedback is conducted by people and entities, this step is positioned to connect the customer, the collector, and the intelligence assets. It is a form of communication itself and as such is conducted as a subprocess at various points during the overall process. Methods of effectively evaluating and providing feedback for intelligence operations, primarily by the customers, are discussed in more detail in Chapter 12.

Besides understanding the seven steps and entities within the Intelligence Operations Process, it is important to understand the actions and relationships within the process. These are noted as arrows in Figure 8.3. The solid arrows identify the main process thread, which is both cyclical and unidirectional, similar to the standard intelligence process as outlined in Figure 8.1. The dashed arrows identify interactions and two-way communications that every intelligence operation requires to operate effectively. Some highlighted areas are noted in letters on the chart:

A. **Collection Requirements:** The interactions between personnel involved in collection operations and the rest of intelligence operations are constant and multidirectional. Customers who own their own collection assets will task or levy collection requirements on them directly. Intelligence assets will translate customer requirements into collection requirements in the form of tasks and requests. Feedback and results are transmitted to both the customers and the intelligence asset depending on the types of requests or tasking authority.

B. **Analysis Backtracking:** While the analysis process included virtually every depicted intelligence process, the reality of operations means that there is also an ability for intelligence to go back and collect further information while they are in the midst of either preliminary or detailed analysis. Collection is not a one-time singular event as depicted in many cyclical models of the intelligence process. Analysts who have conducted their initial collection of data, information, or finished intelligence will often discover a new person, event, or area of interest that requires them to conduct subsequent collection.

C. **Leaving the Analysis Process Early:** Similar to backtracking within the analysis process, following the entire process step-by-step without any deviation is not necessary. Often times a question or requirement posed by a customer for intelligence has already been asked by someone else or can be easily answered with a preliminary run-through of collected information. There is no need to go through every step of the analysis process if an adequate answer is already in hand. The operational intelligence process includes various exits to the analysis process to more accurately capture how intelligence supports the commander during operations.

In comparison with the different models of the intelligence process, the Intelligence Operations Process differs in that it is built around the interactions and communications between the customer and their supporting intelligence assets. As stated at the start of this book and so often throughout, intelligence's primary purpose is to support the customer. Therefore, this relationship between intelligence and the customer is the heart and foundation of all other intelligence processes. As such, the portrayal of this process has to be rooted in the reality of how this relationship is actually supposed to work during operations.

To help explain this process further, several areas and subprocesses are worth going into further detail. These areas include understanding intelligence requirements, collection operations, the Intelligence Analysis Process, and issues related to delivering the response.

Understanding Intelligence Requirements

During operations, customer requirements drive more than just analysis; they drive analytic techniques, production schedules, collection efforts, and in the longer term as an aggregate drive the mission, structure, and budget of intelligence organizations. A single requirement is a task, the mass of requirements intelligence organizations handle are their reason for existing. Some requirements are converted in one-time requests for intelligence support, while other can be longer-term standing requirements that persist throughout an operation.

Intelligence customers who make decisions for their organization or in carrying out an operation base their decisions on relevant information. This information could be about anything that must be considered, from the weather to status of their people, equipment, or technical capabilities. For intelligence, the information they need pertains to the threats to their success. These pieces of information are requirements for intelligence personnel to handle and satisfy

Intelligence requirements come in different forms and formats. Some are standardized while others are ad hoc or levied in the midst of fluid and ever-changing operations. Intelligence organizations and the operating centers must be able to handle each of the different types of requests they were established to support. As requests come in from different customers and in many different ways, this may seem like an impossible task to organize and manage an intelligence operation for every type of requirement that is expected.

To help in planning for requirements, there is a relatively simple way of classifying them: They are either specified or implied and either formal or informal. This gives the intelligence planner only four major types of intelligence requirement their organization must be prepared to handle.

CHART 8.2   Types of Intelligence Requirements

Type of requirement		Examples
SPECIFIED	Formal	Requests for information (RFIs), high value target lists (HVTLs), Priority intelligence requirements (PIRs), SIGINT amplifications
	Informal	"The Commander wants to know…", "What's your initial read on the fallout from the death of _____?"
IMPLIED	Formal	Person, location, event, or subject is within the analyst's area of analytic responsibility
	Informal	Requirement identified as a priority through other analysis

Specified–Formal

Specified requirements are those that are directly assigned or requested by a customer to their intelligence asset or assets. They are usually fairly direct in their submission with the

Specified and formal requirements will usually follow a standard format and can either be submitted using a request form or posted/displayed as a running requirement. One of the most common types of submitted request is the request for information or RFI. These requests are submitted using a format that includes key items of the request such as the question itself along with the time an answer or product is required, and any specific instructions on the creation of the product. Much of the work with large organizations such as an intelligence agency operates off of formal RFIs and some budgets are even tied to the amount of formal requirements are satisfied in a given period of time.

Standing requirements such as priority intelligence requirements are created or approved by the support of the decision-maker and will stay relatively constant throughout all or a portion of an operation. They are usually found in a tactical environment and are meant to give intelligence personnel an idea of what's important for the commander to know without specifically asking over and over again. They are usually in the form of a posted top 10 list of items that are important for both the decision and their entire organization to know. Displaying this list within an Ops Center helps to keep all personnel keyed into what's important as they work on their own individual tasks.

Specified–Informal

Specified and informal requirements are more of an on-the-spot requirement that comes up periodically in the middle of an operation. They are in general ad hoc and usually require an immediate response. They are usually verbal questions or requests from a decision-maker such as "I need to know which route this enemy unit is going to take as they travel towards this location," or "how much time do I have before I can expect subject A to leave their current location." While these requirements are the stuff of Hollywood movies and are portrayed as the only type of requirement intelligence personnel work on, they do in fact happen often in the midst of operations especially at the tactical level. For specified-informal requirements, there is little time or expectation of a formal product or presentation.

Different types of intelligence operations will handle each of these four requests in different ratios to each other. While the majority of requirements coming into a tactical intelligence team in either a law enforcement or combat environment will be informal, formal requests are more often satisfied by larger organizations with more robust collection assets and production capabilities.

Implied–Formal

All implied requirements are classified as such because they are not specifically requested by a customer, but in order to satisfy their current and expected future requirements, the intelligence asset must collect information and conduct analysis on it.

Implied and formal requirements are those that are understood by an intelligence analyst to be necessary because it falls within their area of expertise or assigned subject area. Many intelligence analysts work within assigned areas separating their priorities of work by geographic region or by subject areas such as military forces, organized crime, terrorism, or more specific areas such as a particular rival company, a named gang or terrorist group, or even a single high-value target or person of interest.

For example, there may be a standing requirement to provide biographies about the leadership within a certain gang. Because the intelligence analyst already knows they have illicit gang activity in their geographic area of responsibility, they also understand that they will need to look at person X or person Y who appear to be leaders of this gang in their area. While no one asked for information specific to those individuals, the implied requirement for the analyst was that these people met the criteria of the larger and somewhat vague requirement. They would need to create a biography for both persons.

Implied–Informal

Implied informal requirements are those that are discovered through analysis and are generated almost exclusively within the intelligence asset. While working within a particular subject area, an analyst often discovers a new aspect, wrinkle or complication that requires a deeper understanding before they are able to proceed further with the original requirement.

An example of a legitimate implied and informal requirement is when an analyst is tasked with creating an intelligence product that will predict bombing activity in the near future within a given geographic area. In order to more fully understand the threats he is working with, the analyst may find that they need to do more detailed analysis about which threat groups have already demonstrated their penchant for bombings. Even further, the analyst may also need to learn about the different types of bombs that have been used most frequently as well as their physical and chemical compositions.

While these types of requirements pop-up frequently within the intelligence analytic process, there is an inherent risk to follow one after another and distract analytic efforts away from the original requirement. This risk is more commonly known as "going down the rabbit hole" and can ruin the ability of intelligence to support a customer given the limited time and resources available.

Common Elements of Requirements

Whether a customer conveys or an analyst identifies a requirement, there are specific pieces of information that these requirements must contain in order for their supporting intelligence organization to have any chance of success in satisfying it. Formally submitted requirements such as a RFI usually follow a form or format that must be filled out as part of the request. These formats contain required elements that help the intelligence manager and assigned analyst understand more than just the subject or question posed.

CHART 8.3   Essential Elements of a Request for Information (RFI)

Element	Notes
NAME OF REQUESTOR	This may be different from the actual customer or decision-maker. If so, it will most likely be another analyst working in support of their own customer.
CONTACT INFORMATION	Include redundant means for questions and coordination throughout the rest of the intelligence operational process.
SUSPENSE DATE	When they need it. Can also include a date/time of when the information is no longer useful; also known as the latest time of intelligence value or LTOIV.
REQUIREMENT	The heart of what the requestor wants to know. Must include specific details what is needed in clear and concise language.
JUSTIFICATION	Includes the intent or why the request is needed. Almost as important as the request itself. Understanding why helps the analyst immensely.
SOURCES ALREADY CONSULTED	Listing which sources of data or information has already been used if any can help to reduce redundancy and wasted time.
PRODUCT SPECIFICA-TIONS	Include the format (oral, written, or graphic) as well as the method of transmission (e-mail, presentation, instant message, phone call, etc.).
CLASSIFICATION	Both the request itself and the product can be at different classifications to each other. Include classification levels for both and handle appropriately.

Putting these elements into a request help the intelligence asset more effectively start work in satisfying it. Every requirement received undergoes an evaluation by the receiver so that the intelligence asset can best analyze and plan how to tackle it.

Requests for support that are poorly articulated, whether in writing or verbally, are almost guaranteed to be returned as an unsatisfactory response. Analysts responding to garbled, unclear, or vague request often end up guessing what the customer wants and can also end up doing too much work in order to cover all the possibilities of their request. This happens at every level from the battlefield to the national-level agencies.

Lessons in Intelligence: Resisting Change

Spending the first years of my intelligence career in a mechanized infantry battalion and armor brigade taught me how to handle requirements at the tactical level. Intelligence in support of combat units primarily meant handling formal (both specified and implied) requirements during the planning stages of a mission, and then quickly changing to handling specific and informal "What about___?" requirements during operations.

Moving from this environment to a strategic one was challenging in several areas. Upon becoming the Chief of Intelligence for LIWA, I quickly learned how dysfunctional the handling of intelligence requirements could be without a proper management system. Formal and specific requirements were supposed to be handled by my branch of roughly two dozen analysts, but since each division within the organization had a single analyst assigned directly to them, there was no centralized control over requirement either coming in or going out to other intelligence agencies. As a result, each division only relied on a single person for analysis while the capabilities of my branch were left idle. Compounding this problem was a series of personal conflicts between intelligence personnel across the entire organization.

Among the many things I changed when I started as Chief of the Intel Branch of LIWA, one of my first actions to remedy the requirements management issue was to direct that all requests for intelligence going out from LIWA had to go through my collection manager no matter whom the intelligence analyst worked for directly. In this way, we could more properly manage all LIWA requirements to avoid duplication of effort. We could also determine if Intel Branch personnel could answer the requirement in-house using data mining tools available. We also fixed the RFI process so that all formal requests would be in writing using a standard format.

While these changes were well-received by most of the other analysts in direct support of their respective divisions, not all of them agreed with what I had done. In one response, my branch received an RFI from one of the other analysts, which printed out to over 25 pages in length—the longest I had ever seen in my career. In a most passive–aggressive way, the analyst who submitted it was setting my branch analysts up for failure and in the process demonstrate that only they themselves working solo could handle the requirement.

Despite the resistance, the changes to the requirements process had several positive effects. First, it fostered closer ties within the entire organization. The independent analysis started to work more closely with the analysts in my branch, and the division chiefs within LIWA could see a marked improvement in the support they received from both their own analysts as well as from my branch.

Within my branch, the collection manager became more empowered to do their job, and became much more effective as a team player. Analysts in turn were happy that they were actually supporting customers as opposed to left in the dark while operations took place around them. As a secondary result, this one simple act helped to improve morale and make analysts happier to come to work.

The Intelligence Analysis Process

Intelligence analysis is an action, not an entity. It is a process of converting data and information into knowledge as a basic function of intelligence operations, but doing it requires several logical steps and subprocesses that make the art and science of analysis the heart of why intelligence exists as a profession.

Like many other areas in intelligence, there is no one who agreed upon definition of intelligence analysis. Depending on the source, there will be slight variations in perspective and purpose for conducting analysis. In a manner similar to understanding other concepts in this book, looking at the common elements of what defines intelligence analysis among the different definitions leads to discovering what intelligence analysis is at a foundational level.

One of the key and most common elements of intelligence analysis is the act of thinking about a particular subject. The subject could be anything for simple analysis, but since intelligence is about threats, a definition for intelligence analysis must include the act of thinking about threats.

A second key element is the purpose for that thinking. This is where the customer once again drives the process. Analysis is conducted against threats in support of a customer—actually their threats, not necessarily threats to the one doing the analysis.

With these two key elements identified, consider the following definition:

> Intelligence analysis is the act of critically thinking about information related to a threat, enemy, adversary, or competitor in order to answer questions and create products that support decision-making.

This definition attempts to capture these key elements such as thinking about information, relating that information to a threat, and the ultimate purpose for doing so, i.e., in support of decision-making that ties everything back to support a customer. Whether it's the analyst themselves, their customer, or someone else, it's done to answer their questions, provide some sort of assessment, and help make decisions based upon what the other side has been and is going to be doing.

Intelligence analysis is an important part of Intelligence Operations Process, the diagram shown in Figure 8.4 prominently shows several of the key steps of analysis instead of a single step. The four steps involved in intelligence analysis are in themselves subprocesses requiring further explanation and study, especially in understanding and mastering the two levels of analysis, preliminary and detailed analyses. So much so that they are covered in much more detail in Chapters 9 and 10, respectively.

At first look, it appears that the steps included in the analysis process can be found elsewhere in the Intelligence Operations Process and are therefore redundant, especially when considering the first two steps of identifying the requirement and collecting information. While this may seem true, the distinction here is that these steps are primarily for the individual analyst instead of the entire organization. So, while intelligence collection is an ongoing operation conducted across every available asset, the individual still needs to collect that information themselves from wherever it was held or stored once collected.

Intelligence analysis is primarily conducted by the individual analyst, not the entire group or organization. Problem sets can be tackled as a group, and there can be a great amount of collaboration on analytic tasks, but act of thinking in analysis must be done in the mind of the individual. Even in a group brainstorming, discussions, or analytic exercises, the individual analyst still takes in information shared within the group and

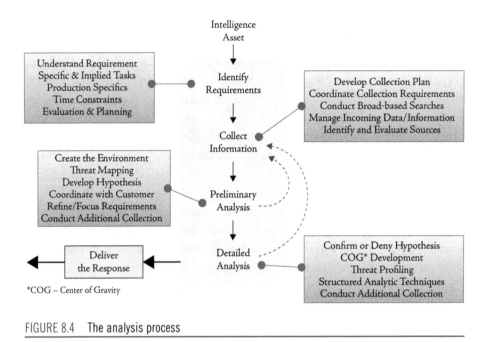

Intelligence
Asset

Understand Requirement
Specific & Implied Tasks
Production Specifics
Time Constraints
Evaluation & Planning

Identify
Requirements

Develop Collection Plan
Coordinate Collection Requirements
Conduct Broad-based Searches
Manage Incoming Data/Information
Identify and Evaluate Sources

Collect
Information

Create the Environment
Threat Mapping
Develop Hypothesis
Coordinate with Customer
Refine/Focus Requirements
Conduct Additional Collection

Preliminary
Analysis

Deliver
the Response

Detailed
Analysis

Confirm or Deny Hypothesis
COG* Development
Threat Profiling
Structured Analytic Techniques
Conduct Additional Collection

*COG – Center of Gravity

FIGURE 8.4   The analysis process

conducts their own thought processes with it. Going through the steps of the analysis process will help to draw the distinction of these individual tasks more clearly.

Identify Requirements

Intelligence analysis starts with the identification of a requirement. While this process usually starts with the receipt of a requirement from a customer, this is not always the case. Often, intelligence analysts can realize the need for analysis and identify requirements independently. They may have a great working relationship with their primary customer or may understand their customer's mission and operations to the point that they can reasonably predict what they will want to know before it is articulated in a request.

For example, a law enforcement intelligence analyst working in support of a task force on gangs may come across a link between a known gang and the first indications of a splinter group. It would be fairly obvious that there will be a need to understand this splinter group as soon as they are significant enough to gain the attention of police investigators or task force leadership. The analyst could start collecting and running through some or all of the preliminary analysis steps in preparation for what would most likely be a request to do so in the near future.

In identifying implied requirements, there is a temptation for analysis to divert from the current specified mission and "follow their nose" on something they think is important at the time but in reality is just tangential to where the focus should be. This phenomenon is often called "going down the rabbit hole." Management of requirements within an Intel organization includes keeping tabs on the work analysts are conducting. While a vast majority of the analysts are working toward the current priority requirements, there is always this risk of veering off course with the potential to waste time and resources in the process.

Identifying requirements is coupled with an individual evaluation and planning process. Whatever the source or way the requirement is received, analyst must evaluate the requirement in order to identify all the tasks that must be completed in order to fulfill it. Analysts must ensure that they understand what they are specifically tasked to do or derive their own tasks based on what is known about the requirement, filling in the gaps with their own analysis and estimates of the work required as well as a prioritization of tasks.

Developing specified and implied tasks allow analysts to plan for their approach to collection and analysis. A well-written RFI will contain a great amount of detail to help the analyst in this regard, but they must be prepared for vague, ad hoc, or poor articulate requests. Even the most clearly articulated requirements won't tell analysts everything they need to do; they must be derived by the analyst themselves. Standard operating procedures (SOPs) and experience will help them weigh tasks against time constraints and product specifications as well as other capabilities and limitations.

Collect Information

As the analysis process is largely an individual effort, so is collecting information. This step may mirror the collection operations process to a certain degree but only in as much as the analyst needs information for their own problem set. In this way, collection actually happens twice in the Intelligence Operations Process: Dedicated personnel and systems collect it for the entire operation and the analyst pulls information into their own workspace.

Collection planning occurs in this step, similar to collection operations, but in the case of intelligence analysis, it's done by the individual to identify what can be collected by the analyst and what cannot.

While an analyst does collect information, it is generally limited to cyber-based—technical—periodic systems otherwise known as search engines. These searches and a subsequent mining of information can be done within a data repository owned by the intelligence organization itself, sent out to other data sources, or into the wilds of the World Wide Web. Collection of constant or streaming data and information can be of use to the analyst as well, but is very short lived because of human factors. This type of collection is usually conducted through technical means and is processed and stored for subsequent searches.

What cannot be collected with relative ease by the analyst must be articulated in collection requirements as previously discussed. In larger organizations, collection require-ments are sent by the analyst to the collection manager who handles the process for the analyst from there. For smaller organizations, the analyst coordinates for the collection themselves through various avenues and formats. Some requests may be as simple as a phone call or face-to-face coordination; others may involve a formal request that is sent across organizational boundaries and bureaucratic layers.

Once data and information are received, there must be a method to organize, ingest, parse, categorize, tag, extract, and store it. The different ways to do this depend on both the size, and relative resources of the organization as well as its operating environment. Tactical and street-level intelligence can be received by a phone or radio call, pertinent details are copied and then plotted or manually entered in a database or operating system. Larger data mining pulls or streaming data is run through data mining tools that handle the information according to algorithms that are designed to tag entities, events, or other significant data points before storing it in a data repository. That information can then be queried and pulled over and over for specific search engines and visualizations.

While much of this is discussed in Chapter 5, a key reminder for the intelligence analysts is to continually evaluate the sources of data and information they are relying on for the different stages of their analysis. Intelligence operations that rely on Big Data and data mining tools and visualizations will have such massive amounts of information on-hand or readily available, but it will still be the analyst's job to understand, manage, and evaluate the items that are needed for a particular product or assessment.

Conduct Preliminary Analysis

Analysis occurs throughout the Intelligence Operations Process to understand the mission or problem set, to support collection activities, and to support planning for the intelligence analysis. *Preliminary analysis is the act of identifying, defining, understanding, and mapping threats within the context of the given requirement and operating environment.* As a subprocess to intelligence analysis, it is the initial phases of learning what is known and not known about the threat, identifying the areas of interest, and determining the subsequent analytic methods that must be employed to develop an intelligence response of product that satisfies the requirement.

Preliminary analysis involves imaginative and creative thinking methods as the intelligence analyst must create the environment from a conceptual perspective, and within that environment place the known threats, mapping them by their people, assets, associations, and events. They must identify potential capabilities and associated focal points of the threat organization known as Centers of Gravity or COGs.

From these initial analytic methods, the analyst develops an unrefined picture of the known threats related to the requirement or problem set. This then can better prepare them to develop a plan for more detailed collection and analysis along with an initial hypothesis of the threat's intentions and future actions. These findings can then be coordinated with the customer who can help them refine the requirement and response specifications if necessary.

Preliminary analysis is the most critical part of the Intelligence Analysis Process because it is here where the analyst determines what needs to happen during the rest of the process. The actions and steps conducted during preliminary analysis set the tone and pace for the rest of the Intelligence Cycle whether they are conducted effectively or not.

As important as preliminary analysis is to intelligence operations, it is also the weakest link in terms of analytic performance. Relative to other detailed and structured analytic techniques, it is often poorly understood or disregarded as an effective and critical part of intelligence analysis. Junior analysts tend to not understand its importance while the more senior analyst tend to disregard in favor of relying on their previous experience.

As discussed in detail in Chapter 9, preliminary analysis is underused, underappreciated, and underresourced in terms of time and intellectual capital, and yet is pivotal to developing a clear, common understanding of the problem, the environment, and threats within that environment. Many of the analytic processes that are conducted in the detailed analysis step of the Intelligence Analysis Process start in or rely heavily upon the steps and result of preliminary analysis.

Conduct Detailed Analysis

Following preliminary analysis, the next steps within the Intelligence Analysis Process could go in any number of directions. Further analysis, which techniques are used, and additional information required for it is highly dependent on the customer's requirement and their response or product specifications, i.e., what they want to see from the analyst handling their requirement. *Detailed analysis is the use of one or more analytic methods or techniques to specifically satisfy a requirement about an already identified threat or threat-associated event.*

Detailed analysis involves the conduct of specific and structured analytic methods as this is the phase that results in the most refined and finished product. While preliminary analysis is meant to initially define the environment and threats and identify what is known and not known, detailed analysis builds off these initial thought processes and drives deeper into the subject matter, using specific methods and techniques to build a refined, polished, and defendable response to the requirement.

As such, detailed analysis can require a deeper understanding of specific aspects of the threat. If the threat is a group, analysis at this stage can develop a profile of the group, its organization, methods of operations, and most importantly, its intentions that are in agreement with its goals and objectives. Analytic techniques in the phase also help to identify the group's targets, strengths, capabilities, vulnerabilities, and weaknesses. By profiling a threat group in this manner, intelligence analysis can more easily, efficiently, and accurately contribute to operational planning, and countermeasures designed to affect the threat adversely from disrupting their operations to defeating them in totality.

Besides Threat Profiling, the number of structured analytic techniques conducted during the detailed analysis phase is limitless. There are several well-known techniques such as analysis of competing hypothesis or ACH, high impact–low probability analysis, link and social network analysis, or time-event analysis that could be employed by the analyst. While several of these are covered in other intelligence-related publications, the key to their use is in the analyst's ability to know which ones can be used, but more importantly can be applied to their unique problem set. As discussed in Chapter 10, the effectiveness of detailed analytic techniques is in the analyst's ability to either adapt known techniques or create new analytic processes from scratch.

Exiting the Analysis Process Early

As discussed earlier, the commonly accepted model of the intelligence process or cycle involves unidirectional progress through the steps with evaluation and feedback taking place throughout the process as necessary. The Intelligence Operations Process was designed to reflect the reality of how intelligence is actually conducted effectively instead of imposing a new way of doing business that intelligence personnel must adhere to. The Intelligence Analysis Process, as a subprocess of intelligence operations shows this recognition by allowing analysts to backtrack and collect additional information during both the preliminary and detailed analysis steps. This feature is included as an understanding that collection happens several times and analyst are never beholden to a one-time only collection step.

Another way, the Intelligence Analysis Process reflects reality of operations is in the way the collection of information, and preliminary and detailed analysis steps can be skipped altogether. Skipping steps can reduce redundancy, more efficiently expend collection and analysis resources, and ultimately provide a more flexible and responsive intelligence operation, especially in a more face-paced and fluid environment where time is critical and resources are limited.

In order to do this without sacrificing quality or risking inadequate customer support, an analytic effort must meet and satisfy specific criteria. This criterion is different depending on where the analyst determines there is no need for continuing through the process. Consider the following table with criteria for exiting the analysis process early:

CHART 8.4   Criteria for Exiting the Analysis Process

Analysis step completed	Criteria for exiting the process
IDENTIFY REQUIREMENTS	*Answer to question is already known* or is on hand and in a presentable format. Most likely for simple requests or requirements such as an oral question that can be immediately answered and does not require collection and analysis of additional information.
COLLECTION OF INFORMATION	*Requirement has already been recently satisfied* by someone else in a similar fashion. The answer or product created has been stored within a system that the analysis can easy access and retrieve.
PRELIMINARY ANALYSIS	*Requirement can be answered rather easily*, but still requires a certain degree of collection and cursory analysis. Detailed analytic steps are not required and would not enhance or improve the response delivered to the customer
DETAILED ANALYSIS	*Analysis process complete*

Leaving the analysis process early without satisfying the appropriate criteria, even in a most general sense, will most likely produce incomplete, sloppy, or inaccurate results. It is also an indicator of an intelligence analyst who is cutting corners prematurely. The primary reasons for this are the pressures of time, analyst fatigue, poor or inadequate collection results, or a poorly written communicated requirement—whether it is written or oral. If this type of cutting corners is found to be the case for a single analyst as a pattern, training or retraining is in order. If it is systemic throughout the organization, a much larger problem exists and a root cause analysis process is in order to determine the overall cause or causes.

Creating and Delivering the Response: Production, Dissemination, and Coordination

Creating and producing an intelligence product requires a certain degree of planning, thinking, and even analysis, but it is not part of the Intelligence Analysis Process. Analysis related directly to thinking about a threat ends at the end of the detailed analysis steps.

Delivering a response is about taking the analysis and then creating and delivering a response to the customer. The response must effectively answer the requirement, it must do so in the time required and in a format that is usable by the customer usually outlined in their original request. Optionally but preferably, the response can also be delivered in a way that it can be shared, thereby benefitting other organizations that are either aligned or share the same or similar problem set.

Creating and delivering the response to an intelligence requirement involves quality control or QC checks, production of a presentable, deliverable, and shareable product, and then delivery of the response whether it is done verbally or in a tangible document, presentation, data set, annotated image, map, or software visualization. Delivery itself can be a single customer or posted to a location that can be seen by others. It also involves coordinating with the customer, following through with the results and actively participating in planning, war-gaming, and assistance in generating new intelligence requirement as a part of ongoing operations.

Similar to the other steps of the Intelligence Operations Process, success in delivering the response affects the success of the entire operation. As delivering the response is a part of the constant and ongoing relationship between intelligence assets and their customers, aspects related to it are discussed in more detail in Chapter 12.

Summary

One of the reasons why intelligence as a process is presented in the context of operations is because intelligence itself is a collection of analytical and operations processes and subprocesses. As such, intelligence operations are part of much larger operations conducted by customers or parent organizations. It is only one part of several intertwined operations that share the same goals and objectives while reducing or eliminating any threats in the process. While the most common representations of intelligence as a process show it as a unidirectional cycle that is conducted in its own world. The process presented here shows intelligence in practice and as such includes the realities of how it is practiced as an operation.

Key Summary Points

+ Intelligence is conducted as an operational process. As such, it must be articulated and practiced in a manner that is possible, repeatable, have a purpose, and produces a result.
+ While common representations of the intelligence process contain the basic and fundamental steps of what must be conducted, a more accurate way to understand intelligence as a process is to understand it as an operational process in the context of larger operations.
+ The Intelligence Operations Process includes both the customer and their associated intelligence asset since the focus of the steps center around this relationship.
+ Embedded within the Intelligence Operations Process are several other subprocesses, most notably the Intelligence Analysis Process that includes its own critical steps that must be conducted in order to develop and deliver an effective response to the customer.

Discussion Questions

+ Besides the criticisms listed, what are other problems with the commonly accepted intelligence process presented in Figure 8.1?
+ What are the risks of poor performance of the various steps of Intelligence Operations Process to the subsequent steps? Are there any actions and intelligence manager can take to control or minimize these risks?
+ Besides the preliminary and detailed analysis steps, where else in the Intelligence Operations Process is analysis conducted? What type of analysis is it and what is the intended result?
+ Without referring back within this chapter, what are your definitions for the intelligence process and intelligence analysis? How can your definitions support each other so that intelligence analysis is shown as an integrated part of intelligence operations?

Figure Credits

Fig. 8.1: Source: https://www.jcs.mil/Portals/36/Documents/Doctrine/pubs/jp2_0.pdf.

Chapter 9

Intelligence Processes–Preliminary Analysis

Learning Objectives

After completing this chapter, you will be able to:

- Understand the definition and the five primary objectives of preliminary analysis.

- Walk through the steps in conducting preliminary analysis explaining each step in more detail.

- Understand the definition and steps of threat mapping in the context of various problem sets.

- Understand the importance of threat course of action development as well as determine the area of interest.

Analysis Has Already Started

It is crucial to understand that analysis is actually an ongoing process. Even while identifying the requirement and collecting information, the analyst considers the scope of the mission, the problem set, and the initial methods needed to satisfy the requirement. In other words, as soon as the analyst is first introduced to the topic or problem set, they immediately start to envision the subject along with what they can expect to be dealing with.

Whether their requirement is to analyze a person, organization, event, mission, trend, or geographic region, the analyst will picture the setting, the key personnel, and groups of people that are most likely involved, as well as a tentative idea of who is or should be considered a threat. For example, when a requirement is received with the header "Russian White Collar Cyber Crime," it immediately prompts the analyst to think of Russian government and business entities, known and suspected crimes, financial transactions, organized crime syndicates, foreign links, or potential cyber tradecraft or methods of operation.

Once they've sketched out in their mind the subject or problem set, the analyst then starts to think about their initial steps in terms of collection sources and search terms, keeping in mind the specifics of the requirement along with the desired format of the answer or intelligence product. In this way, the analyst attempts to get and understanding of what they know at the start and more importantly, what they don't know and where they think they will find relevant information to fill in the gaps in their knowledge.

Analysis during the steps prior to preliminary analysis is centered on forming a plan of action using the scant bits of information either received in the requirement or already known by the analyst. Once the initial returns of collected data and information are received, the analyst starts conducting the preliminary analysis as a deliberate series of actions.

Defining Preliminary Analysis

Preliminary analysis is the process of thinking, creating, understanding, and articulating the environment related to a given subject or threat for which more detailed analysis is to be conducted. It is a continuous learning process where the analyst takes their first look at the initial set of information collected and begins to develop an idea of what they think they are dealing with in terms of the identified entities that are relevant within the context of the given problem set. These initial impressions may well determine the direction and priorities of further analysis. Depending on the requirement specifics, an effective analyst can virtually eliminate the need to spend time and resources on more detailed analysis.

Preliminary analysis is not a newly created method of understanding a problem set for the information age. Preliminary analysis is just a common name for similar analysis conducted in many professional fields, and it has occurred all throughout history. To take an example from military history, good generals and commanders would often conduct a thorough analysis of their situation prior to battle. Military battles up until the industrial age were often set-piece affairs, meaning the armies would confront each other and then prepare for battle in a deliberate fashion sometimes taking hours or days prior to the start.

During this time, commanders would ride out with their staff to survey the terrain taking notice of both natural and man-made features such as hills, rivers, wooded areas, or roads, houses, walls and fences, or other built up areas. In some cases, they would be able to see the enemy army arrayed before them: where their heavy infantry and skirmishers stood, where their cavalry and artillery were concentrated, and how large was the overall force. They, then, would analyze their situation to determine their plan for battle, which included how they would deploy their army and how they would like to fight the upcoming battle. As the evolution of technology expanded and stretched the battlefield to the point that the commanders could no longer see it in its entirety, they began to rely on maps, scouts, and ultimately surveillance technology and intelligence officers to assist in their analysis.

In U.S. military intelligence, the term used for the conduct of preliminary analysis has changed over the years. One of the first terms to enter into doctrine was called Intelligence Preparation of the Battlefield or its more well-known acronym of IPB. As more modern warfighting concepts considered the three-dimensional battlefield to include the airspace over the battlefield, IPB became known as Intelligence Preparation of the Battlespace. This term did not last long as these concepts changed again to incorporate all the entities and factors that affected both battle and nonbattle operations such as peacekeeping, crowd control, humanitarian assistance, or evacuation operations. In 2007, Battlespace was thereby changed in joint military doctrine to Operating Environment.[1]

The U.S. Military Intelligence doctrine today uses the term Joint Intelligence Preparation of the Operational Environment along with its related acronym, JIPOE.[2] While JIPOE is perhaps a more accurate term for U.S. military operations, many defense intelligence personnel still use the persistent term of IPB out of habit and simplicity.

While IPB is predominantly a military term, other professions have their own terms and methods for conducting preliminary analysis. Medical doctors conduct triage to determine the urgency of patient's illness or injury. Computer or auto repair technicians conduct diagnostics to determine the most likely cause to a problem. Police conduct preliminary investigations to determine if there is enough initial evidence to charge suspects.

While each of these terms for preliminary analysis is conducted for a purpose specific to their own fields, they share some commonalities in that they are all conducted as the first look at a problem set to determine the most important aspects of the problem. These aspects are then prioritized for further study and analysis. As the steps to conduct IPB within the U.S. military are the closest to the preliminary analysis method presenting in this book, a direct comparison between the two will be included later in this chapter.

Lessons in Intelligence:
Creating and Evolving Preliminary Analysis

The steps to preliminary analysis presented in this book, like other intelligence processes and methodologies, have evolved over the years. I first used the term while creating a block of instruction on asymmetric threat analysis for a Joint Counterintelligence/Human Intelligence Management Course (also known as the J2X course) taught at the Defense Intelligence Agency in late 2001. Preliminary analysis was part of an intelligence process I taught, but it was not covered in detail.

As I started another intelligence training program for U.S. Army Intelligence and Security Command (INSCOM) in 2002, I naturally transported my analysis instruction into the first course created for that program, the Basic

---

1   Joint Publication 2.0, Joint Intelligence, June 22, 2007, p. iii.

2   Ibid., p. GL-13.

Analyst/Manager's or (BAM) Course. Unfortunately, changing leadership within the command would place a higher priority on tool-centric versus analysis-centric training, and data mining tools would take precedence over instructing analysts on preliminary analysis or other more detailed-oriented analytic methods.

It wasn't until 2005 that I began development on an analysis-specific course for the U.S. Army. In creating the Counterterrorist Analysis Course or CTAC, I spend a lot of time flushing out the specific steps to preliminary analysis after finding that the military's IPB process did not reflect the change in capabilities that analysts had in the form of data mining and visualization tools.

This course was part of a shift toward analysis; another set of new leaders at INSCOM expressed to me that intelligence analysts were learning the "buttonology," i.e., the basic functions of data mining tools, but needed more help in applying them in their day-to-day problem sets. Almost immediately following the creation of the CTAC course, my instructors created a sister course on applied critical thinking along with several other applied versions of tool-based courses. For years, these courses were so popular with Army intelligence soldiers that my instructors were operating off a six-month waiting list for the courses.

Unfortunately, the Army intelligence leadership eventually swung back toward wanting tool training over analysis—especially in the light of the political battle that took place between the government-developed tool suite called Distributed Common Ground Station or DCGS (pronounced Dee-Sigs) and a tool called Palantir, which was developed commercially by a California company of the same name. All analysis-based courses were eventually canceled at the high of their popularity as my instructors were reflagged as DCGS instructors. As a result, preliminary analysis was no longer taught as part of the training curriculum to Army intelligence analysts.

Objectives of Preliminary Analysis

While all analysis is about learning, preliminary analysis is about learning the scope, definition, and parameters of the problem set. Whether approaching an entirely new area, issue, scenario, or problem set, delving into a new aspect within it, or following a sequel, follow-up, or next phase of an operation, preliminary analysis provides a structured method for the intelligence analyst to learn about a subject more efficiently and in a timelier manner. It also allows them to be better able to articulate and apply their learning in other analysis or product creation.

Preliminary analysis is different from more detailed analytic techniques in that the analyst spends a majority of their time learning, identifying, and prioritizing the most important aspects of the environment as opposed to diving deep into one or more particular aspects. Metaphorically, while detailed analysis is intended to dig deep into the available data and information, preliminary analysis tells where to start digging.

The five primary objectives of preliminary analysis are as follows:

1. *To gain an immediate, albeit initial and unvetted picture* of the environment they are or will be dealing with.
2. *To identify the most significant issues,* entities, and factors that are most likely to affect or influence operations.
3. *To identify the threats related to the problem set,* to include their composition, disposition, and intentions.
4. *To display these issues,* entities, and factors *in the context of each other,* thereby building an initial knowledge base for subsequent and more specific analysis.
5. *To identify persistent gaps in knowledge* where additional collection is needed.

In many ways, the most essential—and most difficult—objective in conducting preliminary analysis is filling in the gaps in an analyst's or customer's knowledge base related to the given problem set. If this is the first time the analyst, decision-maker, or their parent organization is encountering a particular problem set, these gaps will be significant. These gaps should be considered essential information that must be known and can be articulated in the form of questions. Some of the most common questions include the following:

+ What is the requirement and who is the customer?
+ What are the major subject areas or topics that I will need to understand in order to effectively conduct this analysis?
+ Is the problem centered on a geographic area, cyberspace, or within a particular aspect of society?
+ What does the geographic and information environment related to this problem set look like?
+ What are the significant features of the environment?
+ Who are the threats already identified in the requirement?
+ Are there any additional threats that need to be considered?
+ What do I already know about these threats?
+ What do I *not* know about these threats?
+ If I am required and able, can I make an initial read (hypothesis) about the threat's future activities?
+ What should be my approach to conducting further collection and analysis?

If the analyst is required and able, they should also be developing their initial hypothesis related to the primary's threat-predicted actions. Understanding that intelligence is an analysis related to a threat and by its nature is focused on predicted future actions of that threat.

Steps to Conducting Preliminary Analysis

While each intelligence organization will design or tailor their own method for conducting preliminary analysis, to effectively accomplish the five objectives previously stated, the analyst must follow a series of steps in a sequential and systematic manner. The steps used for all analysts across an entire organization should also be standardized so that analysts can work as teams, allow for quality checks from other analysts or supervisors, and most importantly be able to explain their results to a customer or anyone who was not involved in the analysis themselves.

1. Analyze the Requirement
2. Crzeate the Environment
3. Identify Confirmed and Potential Threats
4. Conduct Priority Threat Mapping
5. Identify Threat Goals, Objectives, COAs
6. Define the Area of Interest
7. Provide Initial Feedback to the Customer
8. Adjust the Analytic Strategy

FIGURE 9.1   Preliminary analysis steps

Given this, the baseline steps for conducting preliminary analysis are as follows:

In order to understand what happens within each step and why they are in the order they are, a more detailed explanation for each step is required.

1. Analyze the Requirement

Analyzing a requirement for intelligence work may seem redundant, since the step of identifying and analyzing the requirement was conducted in the first step of the Intelligence Analysis Process, but it's important to touch upon it again at the start of preliminary analysis. In this step, the requirement is analyzed to help frame the problem set and set parameters for each of the subsequent steps.

As customer requirements drive the intelligence operations and intelligence analysis processes, there are specific aspects of the requirement and the supported customer that the analyst needs to understand at the start of preliminary analysis. Most of these aspects can either be pulled directly from the specific language of the customer's requirements or through coordination with the customer. If not, the analyst can estimate them, although this is not the best approach. Aspects that must be understood up front include the following:

Area of Operations

For intelligence purposes, an area of operations (AO) is defined as the area where the supported customer is currently conducting or will be conducting their operations in the near future. This area will either be specified by the customer themselves or broadly defined by the customer's mission or purpose. A well-defined AO should not limit where intelligence needs to look. Rather, it helps define parameters with respect to where the customer operates and what they can influence. An AO will always be defined in terms of a physical environment but will also include aspects within information and sociopolitical environments. An AO is also not defined by the supporting intelligence asset unless that asset is a part of, or temporarily assigned or attached to the customer.

An AO is also not defined by where the threat is operating. While both have physical, informational, and social features, the customer's AO is defined up front, usually in specific terms. Conversely, determining where the threat is operating is one of the primary objectives of preliminary analysis. As such, defining the threat is conducted during steps 3 and 4 of the process.

Area of Influence

In addition to understanding the supported customer's AO, the analyst must also consider the reach and influence of their customer. An area of influence is directly tied to the AO. As a supported organization will have parameters and limits to where they can operate, the area where their actions influence the environment, events, or other entities is quite different. This is likely a larger area in terms of geography, information, and society footprints.

For example, if a tactical or operational military unit is considered, they will have a specified physical footprint often limiting their actions to a given geographic area such as an assigned zone, sector, or theater of operations. The influence of that unit's actions, such as control of a vital city or port, or destruction of a portion of the area's infrastructure (i.e., electricity or transportation hub) could impact a much larger portion of the battlefield. The influence of the supported customer, for better or for worse, must also be understood by the intelligence analyst.

Specified and Implied Analytic Focus and Tasks

Analyzing the requirement will help the analyst to identify the focus and tasks of their impending work. Written requirements such as requests for intelligence will specify the primary focus but the analyst will also have to estimate other areas that must be looked into in order to satisfy the requirement. Determining implied tasks should not require in-depth analysis. As an analyst becomes more experienced in a particular subject area, implied tasks will become obvious.

For example, the specific requirement may ask for an organizational breakdown and projected targets of a given paramilitary or gang operating along the United States–Mexico border. The primary focus of analysis is specified as the gang, but in order to understand their organization, the analyst would determine that they would also need to understand associated or similar gangs operating in the same area, the status and capabilities of local law enforcement on both sides of the border, the way the physical terrain and weather can be expected to affect operations, and other criminal aspects such as the drug trade, human trafficking, and latest patterns of violence along with their effects within the AO.

Determining specified and implied focus and tasks helps to solidify the parameters of the analytic effort and therefore combat a tendency for some analysts to get into something called analysis paralysis. This phenomenon occurs when the analysts follow their instincts in research, continually jumping from one subject to the next until they found themselves analyzing subjects that are completely outside of what was asked in the initial requirement. By following their noses "down the rabbit hole," they end up wasting a lot of time and effort doing analysis on something that may seem important at the time, but ultimately of no use to the customer. Consciously identifying and sticking to the specified and implied requirements from the outside take a combination of experience and discipline.

Product Specifications and Time Required

After ensuring the analytic effort will be focused on what the customer wants, it is also important for the analyst to understand how and when they want it. Like planning navigation through a maze, the analyst has to keep in mind what the exit is supposed to look like. As well, spending a majority of their time collecting and processing information without leaving in time for analysis and product creation will result in a sloppy, incomplete, and often unvetted or checked result.

Primary to understanding product specifications is the format for the product. Simple oral responses are different than formal presentations just as a written product will be different than annotated imagery or a complex link chart. Each of the various types of products that intelligence assets provide requires different software, materials, expertise, and time to create.

Understanding these aspects of the intelligence requirement from the outset of analysis will help the analyst plan their next steps, while keeping them focused on the customer, the problem, and the product required.

2. Create the Environment

In conventional military operations, one of the primary tools used by commanders, planners, and intelligence analysts alike is the map. As a two-dimensional representation of a three-dimensional surface a map is normally thought of as an overhead view of the earth, drawn to scale on some sort of medium. In days past, a map would be portrayed on a paper and contain natural and man-made features such as hills, ridges, waterways, vegetation, cities, and roads. Operations and intelligence personnel would use these maps to analyze their surroundings, plot the locations of the enemy, and plan their own operations accordingly. Even with the evolution from the paper to digital maps, analysis and planning for military operations still centered around understanding the enemy dispositions in the physical environment.

Today's operations can no longer rely strictly on an analysis of the physical environment. An effective map of an operational environment must also illustrate the information environment as well as the sociopolitical environment. As analysts have to understand all three of these areas in relation to their requirement or problem set, they are no longer simply given a map—instead they create one.

Creating a map of the environment involves conducting surface level searches, collection, and analysis with the intent of identifying the key features, events, trends, organizations, structures, key individuals, and entities that directly affect or are expected to influence operations. Combining all of these features on a conceptual level can be quite daunting, tempting the analyst to spend a lot of time and resources to create an overly complex model. While there are other many more complex breakdowns of this environment, the simplest way to convey this is by using three basic categories or layers of the environment:

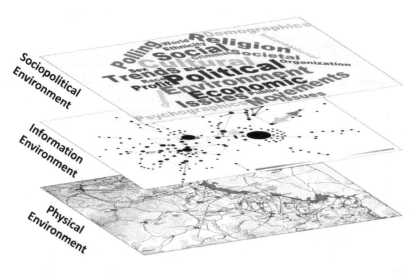

FIGURE 9.2   Concept of the environment[3]

Physical Environment: The physical environment is defined by geography using natural and/or man-made features. Natural features could include a continent, region, or natural waterway. Man-made boundaries could include a country, county, or municipality. Land-based military units are often restricted by zones or sectors of operations. Many supported organizations are specifically assigned to a specific geographic area, thereby setting limits to where they will and will not operate.

During preliminary analysis the analyst considers the physical features that can affect operations. They determine where mobility is best and worst, look for the key terrain that gives whoever controls it a decisive advantage, and the areas that are open and blocked to both visual observation and direct influence (such as military weapons). The U.S. military has excellent methods to analyze the physical environment for tactical operations, but there are other physical features that affect things such as the weather, economics, ecology, and demographics among others.

---

3   Map layers: Sociopolitical Environment created by author using www.wordclouds.com; Information Environment created by Siobhán Grayson. Retrieved from https://commons.wikimedia.org/wiki/File:Network_visualisation_incorporating_sentiment_analysis_of_the_subreddit_%27skeptic%27_from_Reddit.png; Physical Environment is a map of a portion of the Battle of Bulge in 1944 and found at https://commons.wikimedia.org/wiki/File:Battle_of_the_Bulge_7th.jpg

Lessons in Intelligence: Terrain Analysis in War-gaming

When my son turned 10, several years ago he, along with his friends, became interested in a tabletop miniature game called Warhammer and Warhammer 40k. These games are respectively set in a fantasy and science fiction setting and are usually played on a six- by four-foot surface using miniatures and terrain that you assemble and paint.

I've been a war gamer since I was first introduced to them at age eight, so I was happy to indulge in his interest. I already had a setup in my basement for historical war games so it was an easy shift for me to start assembling various armies and terrain features to play with him. We would go to the hobby stores and conventions together and talk about different games quite often.

After a while of playing this game with his friends and getting myself interested, he came to me and asked for my help in understanding how best to set up his Army of High Elves.

"I want to learn how to study terrain like you did in the Army," he stated. I immediately knew what I needed to teach him. I dropped whatever I was doing that night, grabbed a dry-erase board and we headed to the game tables.

While most of the world was spending New Year's Eve out celebrating, my son and I spent the evening going over the Army acronym used in analyzing

FIGURE 9.3   Miniature battle within games Workshop's Warhammer—Age of Sigmar Universe. Photo Taken by the author

terrain called OCOKA.[4] As he already knew his army was strong in ranged combat but weak in melee, he was concerned about how to keep his friend's army from forcing him into a close-in fight. I taught him how to look for the enemy's avenues of approach and where they would be covered from his bow and ballista fire as they maneuvered to get in close contact. I also showed him how to pick out the best areas for shooting and how position his units so that the enemies would have to go through them. We spent hours together trying different setup combinations that would protect his army while dealing damage to his enemies.

A few days later my son went to his friend's house to try out what he had learned. When he returned, I asked him how the game went.

"My friends want to learn terrain analysis." He responded.

---

4   OCOKA stands for Observation and Fields of Fire, Cover and Concealment, Obstacles, Key Terrain, and Avenues of Approach.

Information Environment: Operations in this environment are less tangible as they are defined by information and associations rather than physical features. Mapping the information environment includes identifying key organizations, events, and relevant actors that create, use, and make decisions based on information related to the overall problem set. It also includes portraying both information itself as well as the structures and infrastructure that carries, transmits, stores, and propagates it. This infrastructure includes the cyber realm as one of the fastest growing conduits for transmitting information. Often it is mapped as a link chart that includes key nodal points as well as the associations and relationships between nodes. It can also be linked directly to the physical environment placing people and events in specific locations at specific times.

A key aspect of the information environment is its sensitivity to time. Mapping the information environment involves capturing a moment in time, which can quickly become outdated. Critical events are overcome by other events, relationships change, communications networks wax and wane, and actors become more important, less important, or nonexistent.

Sociopolitical Environment: Simply put, the sociopolitical environment is the environment of ideas. It is defined by events, issues, trends, and facets of one or more segments of society. This includes social, political, economic, religious, or cultural issues that have an impact or potential impact on operations. It also includes the demographic breakdown of the population as well as relevant sentiment, opinions, and advocacy for or against the customer's organization and operations.

While the sociopolitical environment has many similar characteristics of the information environment, it is more esoteric and therefore more removed from the constraints of the physical environment. A critical task to mapping the sociopolitical environment is identify the most prevalent ideas and link them to the other environments by showing the tangible effects these ideas can have on the other relevant aspects of the supported operation.

Basic Versus Complex Analysis
While these three environments are presented in a general manner, each can be further categorized and subcategorized requiring a substantial amount of time and resources to fully analyze and portray them in the context of operations. Adding to their complexity is their interconnectivity. As the analyst begins to identify the key aspects within one environment, they will find it impossible to understand their importance without understanding their impact and influence within the other two environments. As a result, every supported customer's areas of operation will be defined as a combination of these environments.

The key for the analyst to remember in creating the environment at this point is that they only need to construct a surface-level look based on the information that is readily available. It does not require a detailed breakdown of every single detail they come across in the initial searches nor does it require an exhaustive pull of additional information. The intent of creating the environment during this phase is to simply draw the major features of the "map," understand their importance to the supported operation, and then to identify those features that should be earmarked and/or prioritized for more detailed analysis later in the analysis process.

3. Identify Confirmed and Potential Threats
A customer that understands how intelligence assets support their unit or organization will also understand that their primary purpose is to analyze threats to their operations. Therefore, many threat organizations will already be identified in the customer's requirements. Indeed, the most intelligence requirements, whether they are formal or informal, task intelligence assets to provide analysis of a named threat.

Threat individuals, groups, or networks of groups that are confirmed within an intelligence requirement are considered primary threats for analysis. As such, the analyst should expect a substantial amount of information and intelligence to be already available from either their supported customer or from other intelligence assets.

Confirmed threats are not the only threats that the customer needs to consider in their operations, however. As the intelligence analyst creates collects, organizes, and analyzes information to create the environment, they will identify other potential threats. Potential or secondary threats could be groups similar or associated with the threat or threats named in the requirement. They could also be groups that oppose the supported organization in a general sense and in the course of creating the environment, the analyst could have come across proof or indicators of their physical presence or ability to influence operations—usually in a negative manner relative to the customer.

For example, in the previously mentioned scenario in support of a customer operating along the United States–Mexican border, a law-enforcement organization operating along the border will have a priority need to have predictive analysis conducted on the notorious Los Zetas drug cartel on an ongoing basis. Los Zetas is the primary threat group. Intelligence personnel, conducting collection or preliminary analysis in either an initial or refresher context, will undoubtedly run into significant associations between the Zetas and the Gulf, Sinaloa, or other cartels operating in their areas, both physically and figuratively. These associations may be amicable or hostile, but they will certainly be significant enough to include these other groups as threats to law enforcement operations. In addition, other threats could include organizations whose majority footprint is within the United States.

As the analyst confirms the primary threat from the requirement and other threats from their own preliminary analysis, they will need to prioritize the groups into primary and secondary threat groups. As a primary threat, the analyst is identifying the group for further threat mapping and more detailed analysis as a priority. Secondary groups can be considered with time and resources available, or simply in the context of their association with the threat group.

By identifying and classifying threat group into primary and secondary categories, the analyst also must evaluate the threat based on some common elements such as the goals and objectives of the group, their capabilities, and organization, and possibly even their past targets. This is the beginning of building a profile of the threat, which is discuss in much more detail in Chapter 10.

4. Conduct Priority Threat Mapping

After identifying the primary and secondary threats groups operating within the environment relative to the operation, the next task of the analysts is to map out these primary and possibly secondary threats. *Threat mapping is an analytic process that portrays a threat group or groups based upon their capabilities, dispositions, functions, and relationships within the operating environment.* Conceptually, threat mapping is the analysts' way of taking the assembled knowledge about a group that is either on a paper or in a database format and displaying it within the context of the physical, informational, and sociopolitical environments.

The basic structure of the threat map is created using a technique called link or network analysis. These charts are created by plotting objects or nodes for various types of entities and then linking these nodes to each other through their associations, often depicted as connecting lines or borders around an entire grouping of nodes.

For a threat map, the people, places, things, and events associated with the chosen group are plotted as nodes, icons, or points on the map. These nodes represent a group's tangible elements or definitive events or actions. Associations, on the other hand, are represented as the links between the nodes or groupings of nodes along with the common relationship they share with each other. Events can be displayed as either a node (as in a meeting was held at a certain time and place) or it can be an association (showing how person A is related to person B by meeting with each other, etc.).

A threat map can include, but is not limited to, the following elements:

CHART 9.1   Threat Map Elements

Entities			Events	Associations
People	Places	Things		
Individuals	Safe houses	Vehicles	Arrests	Comradery
Leaders	Training sites	Property	Attacks	Romance
Groups	Base camps	Weapons	Meetings	Subordination
Organizations	Homes	Contraband	Communications	Transactional
Governments	Cities	Accounts	Transfers	Adversarial
Victims	Regions	Companies	Payments	Criminal
Families	Countries	Equipment	Movement	Financial
Cliques	Businesses	Websites	Deaths	Communicative
Units	Land features	Money	Intrusions	Religious
Nodes			Both	Links

The important associations, groupings, and other types of relationships will connect entities and events across each environment. A threat map is, therefore, portrayed as a hybrid map of these three environments tying various parts of the group with the others.

For a threat map to be effective, it must identify the key elements of a threat group in the context of the supported customer's operation. Simply put: Who is doing what and where are they doing it. As an analyst sifts through the available information about a group, they will have to identify and prioritize what they find, so that the map contains all and only those items of immediate importance that help portray the group accurately and concisely.

Threat mapping takes experience, as an analyst must be able to identify what is important and what is not. They must also be able to conduct analysis that is thorough enough to identify all of the key elements without getting bogged down into the details and minutiae of everything related to the group. While each node plotted on the threat map can have enough related information to tie up hours and hours of time and analytic resources. The analyst(s) creating or updating the threat map have need to be disciplined in their work so that they are focusing covering as many subject areas as possible within a limited amount of time. This is known as "mile-wide, inch-deep" analysis, noting that the object is to create as accurate a threat map as possible without spending time researching into one particular aspect of the subject area related to the threat group.

Threat mapping like creating the environment in step 2 is done with a surface-level look rather than a deep dive into the available information. All that is learned and identified about a threat group as important enough for inclusion must be easily portrayed,

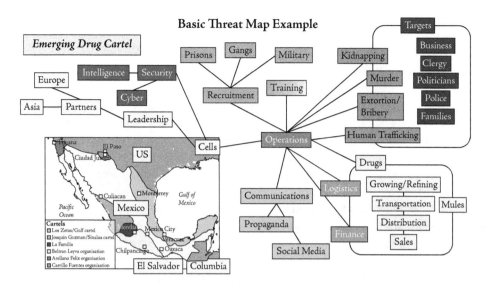

Basic Threat Map Example

FIGURE 9.4   Basic threat map example

presented, and explained to a customer. For example, a terrorist group will have several areas of importance to portray in order to understand their makeup, capabilities, and intentions quickly and concisely. If presenting a threat map takes more than a few minutes, it probably has too much detail for this level of analysis.

The threat map displayed in Figure 9.4 is a very simple and basic look at an emerging drug cartel. The different aspects, functions, and rudimentary organizations of the group are portrayed using individual nodes and grouped by operational functions. The relationships between nodes are depicted as a tree diagram, meaning the different nodes all branch out from a center point. In this case, the obvious center point for this group is their operations. Even though the analyst will find numerous links and associations between different nodes, using a tree diagram keeps the chart clean and presentable with as little clutter as possible. This is not a requirement as the analyst will find they have a lot of flexibility in creating threat maps for their problem sets.

Unlike geographic mapping that is tied to the reality of the earth's surface, the only hard requirements for threat mapping are that the group must be portrayed in the context with the customer or the problem set. Everything else is flexible and therefore can be tailored to what the analyst identifies and prioritizes, and what the customer and subsequent analysis will most likely need to see. A threat map can emphasize as many aspects of a group as possible, or it can center around a single yet important aspect of a threat group's operation. For example, a threat map just about the process a particular group undertakes in the growing, refining, packaging, moving, distributing, and ultimately selling drugs can be the primary focus of a threat map along with the any association elements that are critical for someone to learn about that part of a threat group.

Lessons in Intelligence:
Threat Mapping the USS Cole Bombing

On October 12, 2000, while the U.S. Navy destroyer, USS Cole, was refueling in Aden Harbor, a small boat with two Al Qaeda operatives laden with explosives pulled up to the ship's starboard side and detonated an explosion that tore a 60-foot-wide hole through the hull of the ship. Seventeen sailors were killed and another 39 were injured, many while eating or waiting in line for lunch in the ship's galley.

In the wake of the bombing, personnel from the U.S. Central Command J2, under the leadership of then Brigadier General Keith Alexander, came to Army's Land Information Warfare Activity (LIWA) for our analytic support, already aware of our capabilities in mapping the Al Qaeda network before we had been ordered to cease work earlier that year. Unfortunately, our previous customer, U.S. Special Operations Command had lost patience waiting for Army and DoD leadership to work through privacy and oversight issues related to our data mining and decided to try to recreate our capability elsewhere. U.S. CENTCOM had no such capability at the time, so their J2 personnel came to LIWA to work with my branch directly.

During our initial meetings with the team from CENTCOM, one of their analysts who was assigned full time to track terrorist threats in their theater

FIGURE 9.5   Damaged done to the hull of the USS Cole from terrorist bombing on October 12, 2000

presented us with a link analysis chart that he had created to map out the dispositions and associations between all known Islamic fundamentalist terror groups operating in the Middle East. The chart was created using a visualization tool called Analyst's Notebook, which we had not used before. The chart presented was massive and both the analyst and CENTCOM J2 leadership were proud to show it off. It showed several hundred members linked to Al Qaeda, its affiliate group Islamic Jihad of Yemen, and other associated groups. As the analyst presented it, he noted that it took him six months to create and it was probably the most comprehensive product that had mapped out these terrorists to date.

After the presentation, my analysts gained access to the chart and were able to study it in detail along with the data behind it. In doing, they quickly determined it to be almost worthless for our use in any capacity. In the time that it took to create the chart, about a quarter to a third of the members listed had been killed—most of which died fighting in Yemen or Afghanistan. In addition, while each node was annotated as a person by name and other supporting information, none of the links or associations drawn between the nodes had any data behind them. We had no idea why each link was created by the analyst and over the time he took to create the entire chart, he had forgotten why created many of the links.

This chart, taking approximately 1,000 hours of an analyst's time to create, was next to worthless to our team in mapping out the network. Our support to CENTCOM had to start from scratch.

5. Identify Threat Goals and Objectives, Potential Courses of Action

Threat mapping products, whether they are delivered to a customer as part of an ongoing dialog with their supporting intelligence asset, or used by analysts themselves for subsequently more detailed and specialized analysis later, are only static snapshots of a threat group. Without actively updating a threat map, it becomes a perishable product that will eventually become overcome by more recent events.

As intelligence is a predictive profession, preliminary analysis also requires the analyst to take time to identify the goals and objectives of the threat group or groups as well as make an initial read on what they expect the threat to do in the future. From an academic standpoint, this is akin to developing an initial hypothesis about a group. Subsequent analysis may present the analyst with the opportunity to confirm or deny their initial read. As a result, the analyst will be able to update their courses of action (COAs) and possibly even the known or assessed goals and objectives of the group depending on whether or not it will be necessary or required by the customer.

Goals and Objectives

Every group has goals. Yet not every group states their goals up front, so often they have to be derived through analysis. The obvious starting point for analysis of a threat group's goals is that their goals are in conflict with the supported customer's goals in some significant way. Without that conflict, they aren't really considered a threat. Objectives are subgoals or conditions, actions, or events that need to take place or be accomplished in order to a group to advance toward their overall goals. Understanding a threat group's goals and objectives is such an important part to understanding the overall group it, along with understanding the motivations of the group's member is one of the eight components of Threat Profiling. As such, these two aspects of a group will be covered must more extensively in Chapter 10.

Potential Courses of Action

In developing an initial set of potential COAs, the analyst takes into account the capabilities of the threat group (what they can do) and compares them to their goals and objectives (what they need or want to achieve). Added to this is a bit of complexity where the analyst must also take into account factors that are external to the threat group but could affect their operations. As threat groups do not operate in a vacuum, many aspects of the environment or even other actors can/will support or deter their efforts. The time frame covered in developing potential COAs is dependent upon three factors: the stated requirement, the best use to the customer, and how far in the future an analyst can reasonable predict the actions of a given group with confidence.

The most common external factors are the actions of the supported customer. This is an often-overlooked part of analysis as it requires an understanding of the customer or "friendly" forces/organizations. Intelligence concentrated on just what the threats are going do to without considering their interaction with all elements in a problem set is only going to come up with a partial and overall unrealistic picture.

While it may seem a bit artificial and oversimplistic, one of the most effective ways of presenting potential COAs to a customer is to present only three to the customer:

+ **Most Likely COA:** This COA is one which the analyst gives the highest probability of occurring within the given time frame and within what the analyst understands as the actions and reactions of their supported customer.
+ **Most Dangerous COA:** While less probable, this COA is one in which the analyst believes will have the most severe or damaging effect on the customer's mission and operations. It will most likely involve a higher amount of risk of failure for the threat but reap the largest amount of measured success for them as well. One of the primary reasons for presenting the most dangerous course of action is knowing with almost certainty that a capable threat has identified this COA or something similar and analyzing the feasibility of success in the same way the analyst is.
+ **Possible COA:** This COA should be assessed as the least probable of the three but important to include as a way to note the effects some actions would have on the entire operation. As an additionally templated COA, this one would need to be created to show some distinct differences from the other two—noting which

observable actions would have to change and in which way that would make this one more feasible for the threat to take.

Since conducting this type of predictive analysis is the heart of why intelligence exists to support a customer, there are many in-depth techniques available to the analyst. The key to determining goals, objectives, and potential COAs for a threat group during preliminary analysis is to understand that like threat mapping, there is limited time and resources available to do it. COAs, therefore, must be developed in a timely and resource-efficient manner. Conducting an immense amount of analysis and taking complex steps to develop every possible pathway, branch, sequel, or any other nuanced tangent will overwhelm both the analyst and their support customer, once they are present with such a complex set of possibilities.

Rules for Threat Course of Action Development

- **Keep It Simple:** Every COA is templated, based upon a large number of variables that the analyst consciously and subconsciously weighs in order to portray a predictive series of future events and actions. The analyst eventually must deliver and present their findings to someone else, most likely their customer. To explain their analysis effectively, they must be able to identify the three to five key variables that lead them to the particular COA. This is why three COAs along with a few potential minor variations are key for the customer.
- **Consider Potential Variations, Branches, and Sequels:** Similar to weighing the different variables in developing a COA, the analyst must also weigh the slight variations and sequencing of these variations. If the result of an initial phase of a predicted COA will determine which direction a threat group will go next, the analyst must take that result into account along with the possibilities. Again, the key here is to keep this simple: noting the potential variations, branches, and subsequent events and why, but in a way that won't develop into a complex set of options that overwhelm a supported customers' ability to make decisions from them.
- **Use an Adversarial Perspective:** Analysts must factor in what the threat is doing to achieve their own objectives and protect themselves in the process. The people within the threat group go through their own planning and decision-making processes, identify near and far objectives, prioritizing them for future actions, and weighing certain actions against each other along with the requirements and risks in making them happen. Thinking like the threat groups is an incredibly difficult task as it is fraught with several types of analytic bias on the part of the analyst.
- **Show Your Work:** The analyst who relies on a gut feeling as to why they think a threat group is going to take a particular COA is merely an analyst who can't articulate their thought process to someone else well enough. Effective analysts must back up the assessments with tangible evidence or note where the evidence

is lacking and why they've made an assumption or determination in lieu of it. The ability to clearly and concisely articulate and defend their position helps create credibility to the customer. Establishing credibility is especially important when additional information starts to come in that may lead to reassessing their initial read.

+ **Set the Conditions to Confirm or Deny:** One of the final parts of developing threat COAs is to define a set of criteria that can be used to determine which of the developed COAs the threat is going to take. It may be that their threat is taking an entirely different option that was never considered in the first place. Building a set of observable conditions to look for in subsequent searches or monitoring of the situation can be weighed against the initial read as well as with past patterns. As information pointing to one or another action is available, the analyst is always able to change their templated COAs, just as long as they have the ability to get these changes to the customer in a timely manner.

6. Define the Area of Interest

By creating the environment, the analyst builds the landscape needed to map priority threat groups. As a result, they also discover areas of concentration for the threat group's operations: what is their primary business, where they are doing it, and who they are doing it with and to. As the analyst digs through available information and plots the multiple data points related to a threat group, their threat map will reveal patterns, trends, and areas of concentration across the entire group. The more entities, events, and associations discovered the clearer pattern that will emerge. Once the threat map is developed to the level of detail and clarity that satisfies the analyst and customer, it becomes the defining parameters of the area of interest.

An area of interest is defined by the range of threat capabilities and operations that can affect the customer's operating environment. As such, it is also the area where the customer and their supporting intelligence assets should focus their attention, planning, and analysis. Identifying and marking out an area of interest can be done by posing a simple question: Where is the threat operating? Wherever that is, the customer and their supporting intelligence assets should be interested in it.

Similar to both the operating environment and the threat map, the area of interest is neither solely defined by the physical environment nor is it limited to a single threat group. It can include the aggregate of several similar group's operations and can also include particular aspects and areas of concentration identified across the information and sociopolitical spectrum. As an example, a very broad look at the area of interest of Islamic fundamentalist terror groups is presented in Figure 9.6.

Islamic fundamentalist terror groups are known to operate worldwide, but simply drawing a circle around the earth and stating that intelligence is interested in the entire globe is a worthless exercise. There are certain areas of concentration as well as patterns and trends as to the types of operations intelligence analysts are identifying that can be

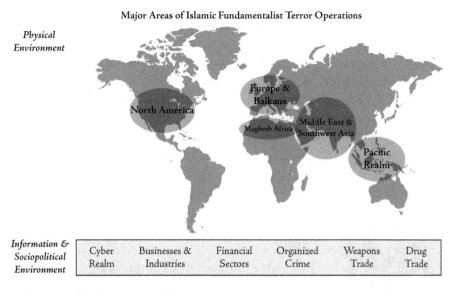

Major Areas of Islamic Fundamentalist Terror Operations

Physical Environment

Information & Sociopolitical Environment

Cyber Realm	Businesses & Industries	Financial Sectors	Organized Crime	Weapons Trade	Drug Trade

FIGURE 9.6   Defining the area of interest

attributed these threats. From a physical environment standpoint, the area of interest for the aggregate of these groups is noted in Figure 9.6 within the red shaded areas. Adding to this are several capabilities and demonstrated actions that are concentrated in a few primary areas that cannot be linked to a single geographic area such as cyber operations, and the financial dealings of these groups.

While the term area of interest is also a doctrinal term for a similar area used by our military, an area of interest for the use of preliminary analysis is focused on where the threat is within the context of a customer operations. If the intelligence customer is the leadership of a company or business in a given industry, the area that supporting intelligence assets should be focusing on still applies—wherever their competitors are operating that can affect the success of the company. More specifically, if the supported customer is a company or business within the energy sector, their area of interest will include the aggregate of capabilities and operations of competitor companies, hostile or potentially hostile governments, and even paramilitary forces, hackers, and organized crime ventures operating in their part of the world or within their area of business.

While an area of interest may seem like unimportant or complication of the obvious, deliberately spending the time to identify it and presenting it to the customer as one of the products of preliminary analysis will go far in assisting intelligence support to customer going forward in a number of ways. First, it helps to identify and prioritize the important areas of within both the created environment and threat operations. Second, it also serves to restrict and focus collection, analysis, and planning going forward toward those areas of importance. Third, it builds a common picture of understanding between the customer and their intelligence assets. Finally, it reduces the risk of wasting time and resources looking at unimportant areas.

7. Provide Initial Results to the Customer

After conducting the first steps of preliminary analysis, the analyst should have an understanding of the requirement in the context of the problem set and be able to articulate and present the environment, the threat groups, the disposition of those threats within the context of the environment, and their expected future COAs. It is at this point that customers need to be brought in as an active participant in the preliminary analysis process, even if they were already involved at different points previously.

Presenting initial findings of preliminary analysis to the customer during this step establishes a communications and common understanding of the work that intelligence assets have been doing up until this step of the process. The customer is given either a formal or informal presentation, of simply delivered with a message, file, or some other product that allows them to walk through the analysis that has already been conducted toward their problem set and requirements.

Providing initial feedback allows the customer to quickly gain a degree of awareness of the threat situation. As the customer learns what their intelligence assets have learned, they are then able to provide feedback and guidance before the heavy analytic work proceeds in the detailed analysis phase. Primary objectives for providing initial feedback to the customers include the following:

Initial feedback objectives:

+ Educate/familiarize the customer with the results of preliminary analysis
+ Confirm or deny analytic focus and direction
+ Get initial customer feedback, decisions, guidance
+ Reduce risk of miscommunication and product failure
+ Identify areas of adjustment in analytic strategy

In terms of familiarization, providing initial feedback to the customer arms them with enough key pieces of information to have a level of situational awareness that allows them to be on par with the supporting intelligence assets that conducted the preliminary analysis for them. This awareness is important to achieve agreement with their supporting intelligence assets on what the important elements of the problems set are: the critical aspects of the environment, what are the priority threats to the success of the customer's operation, where these threats are operating, and where the customer should have interest in understanding the course of their decision-making going forward.

As all customers undertake their own independent decision-making, giving them enough information to make informed decisions, even if it's based on a preliminary first look, is one of the most important reasons why intelligence exists in the first place. Decision-makers rely on intelligence throughout the planning and execution steps of their operations. It is, therefore, important to provide them with a preliminary read of the threat early on rather than a more complete or detailed set of analysis later, especially in the midst of tactical or otherwise fluid and fast-paced operations. A rough estimate provided in time makes all the difference in the early stages of an operation. Conversely, an excellent product that is late is next to worthless in supporting a customer.

Giving the customer preliminary analysis can be done in a very quick and informal setting, as a formal presentation or somewhere in between. Unlike the formats specified in a formal intelligence requirements, the customer will not usually require a specific format for preliminary analysis results. Analysts must therefore either rely on standard procedures or doctrine or create their own format for delivery. In the doctrinal world of U.S. military intelligence, a standard method of presenting the results of preliminary analysis is through a format called the intelligence estimate. This format and ones similar to it are useful guides to help the analyst keep in mind the require elements that are similar to every military mission: Analysis of the terrain, the doctrinal aspect of the adversary, and how they expect the adversary to function in that environment.

While the customer benefits from receiving preliminary analysis by gaining an overall awareness of the situation and initial findings of the analysts, the supporting intelligence asset also benefits from preliminary analysis by receiving initial feedback from the customer. This feedback can be in the form of acknowledgment or confirmation that they are on the right track and looking at the right things. It can also be subsequent and refined sets of guidance, direction, and preferences for the analytic work going forward. Unlike the formats usually required in a final intelligence product, the customer will not usually specify how they would like to see the preliminary analysis, or in what format.

Involving the customer near the end of preliminary analysis reduces the risk of miscommunication between the analyst, the supported intelligence organization, and the customer. It also reduces the risk of wasting time, and analytic resources of looking in the wrong areas, identifying the wrong priorities of work, and creating products that are ineffective in supporting the customer's decision-making. A strong communications link between the customer and their supporting intelligence assets are discussed in more detail in Chapter 12. Using preliminary analysis as a means to create and maintain these links will benefit analysis going in the other phases of the intelligence analysis and operations processes.

8. Adjust Analytic Strategy

After coordinating with and receiving feedback and guidance from the customer, the next logical and final step to preliminary analysis is to adjust the strategy and plan for analysis going forward. While working through the previous seven steps, the intelligence analyst will either receive specific guidance from their customer or identify several potential changes to their initial strategy through their own analysis. Additional actions and tasks that will need to be added to or removed from the overall plan or different approaches to solving problems and challenges will need to be implemented. All of these changes and adjustments will need to be included in order to fulfill the updated collection, analysis, and production requirements.

One technique in capturing potential and confirmed adjustments to the analytic strategy is to organize them into the steps of the analysis process. In this way, the analyst can place each identified change into one of four categories:

CHART 9.2. Categories of Analytic Adjustments

Category of adjustments	Examples
REQUIREMENT	Identification of a previously unknown threat; changes to the area of interest or time available; changes to the specific questions that must be answered.
COLLECTION PLAN	Additional information sources or queries from current sources; new tasks for collection assets; coordination for additional external support; reprioritization of current collection assets.
ANALYTIC APPROACH	Additions or elimination of analytic techniques; use of different data mining and visualization tools; adjustments to in use or planned analytic techniques.
PRODUCT SPECIFICATION	Changes to format, classification level, date/time required; changes to methods of product delivery or means to evaluate effectiveness; changes to coordination post-product delivery.

Adjustments to the requirement and collection plan means going back to previous steps in the intelligence analysis process and reworking them. How much revision can be done is entirely dependent on the time and resources available. While it may be important to fix a critical error or omission in the requirements or collection steps, spending the necessary time doesn't mean that every step in-between must also be repeated in detail. It also doesn't mean that the analytic effort must pause until adjustments take effect. Analysts can certainly move forward and begin the detailed analytic steps concurrently.

Summary

Preliminary analysis is about learning the scope, definition, and parameters of the problem set. It's the first time that analysis is specifically conducted toward answering the requirement and in that regard is more about defining and creating the environment to give the problem tangible context and attachments to the real world. In conducting effective preliminary analysis, the supporting intelligence asset is able to identify the key aspects to the environment, the priority threat groups, and in turn develop a baseline set of knowledge about their capabilities, dispositions, and potential future COAs. Preliminary analysis is not as much about presenting the customer with a complete and polished product as an interim step to supporting to their main requirements as it is about the analyst developing their own understanding of the situation and the important areas of concern before deciding upon and executing one or more detailed analytic techniques.

Key Summary Points

+ Preliminary analysis is the process of thinking, creating, understanding, and articulating the environment related to a given subject or threat for which more detailed analysis is to be conducted.

- One of the first aspects of preliminary analysis is to create the environment in which the problem set and threats can be portrayed. It involves an integrated look at aspects of the physical, informational, and sociopolitical environments.
- Threat mapping is an analytic process that portrays a threat group or groups based upon their capabilities, dispositions, functions, and relationships within the operating environment. Threat mapping requires understand the capabilities, dispositions, and intent of the threat.
- A critical part of preliminary analysis is the involvement of the supported customer, primarily near the end of the process. In this way, the customer is able to learn what the analyst has learned, and can provide feedback and guidance to ensure analysis going forward is on the right track to satisfy their requirements.

Discussion Questions

- What other professions or industries are known for conducting preliminary analysis as part of their business or operations? How does preliminary analysis in these sectors differ from intelligence?
- What are the major similarities and differences between preliminary analysis and the military doctrinal approach, which is known as intelligence preparation of the battlefield, battlespace, or operating environment?
- What current visualization tools or techniques would threat mapping benefit from? In what ways?
- Given different types of customers of intelligence, what is an optimal number of COAs that an analyst should develop? How many is required to capture all the potential branches and sequels of a COA and how many would be considered too many options to consider?

Figure Credits

Fig. 9.4b: Source: https://www.britannica.com/topic/Mexicos-Raging-Drug-Wars-1575131.

Fig. 9.5: Source: https://commons.wikimedia.org/wiki/File:INTEL-COGNITIVE-Cole.jpg.

Chapter 10

Detailed Analysis and Threat Profiling

Learning Objectives

After completing this chapter, you will be able to:

- Be familiar with the Detailed Analysis Phase of the Intelligence Analysis Process and how it differentiates from the conduct of Preliminary Analysis.

- Understand Threat Profiling as an analytic and organizational method along with each of its components.

- Identify the various features and benefits of Threat Profiling when applied to other areas of the Intelligence Operations Process.

Building Off the Foundations of Preliminary Analysis

Preliminary Analysis sets the stage for more detailed analysis. After completing the steps of Preliminary Analysis, Detailed Analysis can go in any number of directions using any number of processes or methods. For every type of intelligence problem set, there is no universal standard for what type of detailed analytic techniques must be used. Rather, the specific steps are dictated by the requirement or the product to be created. Because of this, learning about detailed analysis entails learning the purpose and function of many different analytic methods as well as understanding when and how to apply the most effective method for a given problem set or requirement.

Detailed Analysis is the step within the Intelligence Analysis Process where specific analytic methods and techniques are employed to directly answer or satisfy requirements issued by a supported customer. In many cases, satisfying requirements includes creating a product that effectively displays the results of the analysis. As discussed in Chapter 8, the intelligence requirements that start the Intelligence Analysis Process can be satisfied at several points prior to reaching detailed analysis; the answer may already be known, it may have been satisfied somewhere else and simply needs to be collected, or it may be satisfied by analysis conducted in the Preliminary Analysis steps. That said, if the Intelligence Analysis Process makes it all the way to the detailed analysis phase, it is most likely answering a fairly detailed and complex requirement in terms of the question being asked or in the expectations of the product/deliverable.

Effective detailed analysis is never conducted at the outset of a problem set. It is never conducted in a vacuum or just done on the fly. Detailed analysis relies on the success and completion of the previous steps of the Intelligence Analysis Process. As such, virtually every analytic technique conducted during detailed analysis relies on previous work—an understanding of the requirement, the collection of information, and the creation of the operating environment along with a threat mapped within that environment.

Leveling Up the Analytic Tool Kit

While the previous steps of the Intelligence Analysis Process are conducted in a relatively standardized fashion, Detailed Analysis has a wide range of analytic methods and processes available to the analyst. Depending upon the specific details of what the customer requires, analysts have to be prepared to conduct a myriad of different tasks, processes, and analytic methods.

Several of the most commonly used techniques are detailed in both government and commercial print and online sources. Intelligence literature relating to analysis often invokes the notion of an analyst's tool kit or toolbox. This is the idea that analytic techniques are like a carpenter's, repairman's, or mechanic's tools; after learning how to use them they are collected and kept in their kit ready for the right job.

As an intelligence professional begins their career, their initial training will most likely provide them with some basic or foundational analytic techniques such as link analysis or time-event analysis. No matter if they are destined to become collectors, operatives, or analysts, the initial set of analytic techniques are crucial for every type of intelligence professional as they give the analyst a basic ability to identify, evaluate, and produce an intelligence product based upon the associations of the entities they will study or encounter.

As the analyst becomes more experienced, the number of their tools grows and quality improves. Upon completion of initial training, intelligence personnel will learn additional techniques that are required or habitually conducted as part of their first job or position. These techniques will be added as new tools in their tool kit or as adaptations to the basic foundational techniques they've already learned. There could be over a dozen new techniques that they are required to learn, but for entry level positions, analyst will normally only end up using a handful of them as part of their daily routine.

After working in an intelligence position for an increasing amount of time, new analytic techniques and tools will most likely be acquired because a certain change has taken place. There will be a change in mission, threat groups, data, tools, or even the analyst's position within the organization. They could also run into a problem that needs a new approach. They could even change jobs, or move to another organization entirely. These operational or career changes will subsequently require the analyst to build off their current analytic tool set by adding or adapting even more techniques and methods to employ. Every change should be seen as an opportunity to conduct new analytic techniques or conduct known techniques in more effective ways. By the time an analyst reaches their mid-career, their analytic tool kit should be extensive with the ability to make adaptations to almost any new problem set.

Applying Detailed Analytic Methods

While different mechanical tools are meant for different types of jobs, each analytic technique is created and adapted toward specific types of analysis. As the analyst gains knowledge and practical experience in many types of analytic techniques, they will come to find that many share the same basic functions and steps or are based on similar analytic principles.

For example, a type of matrix analysis used by decision-makers to weigh courses of actions on a given problem set can be adapted by intelligence analysts to template similar decision-making by threat organizations. And while the matrix analysis can help in deciding which threat target is the most important to disrupt, using a similar matrix analysis technique can help in identify friendly assets that the threat would most likely attack.

Given the similarity and adaptability of many analytic techniques, creating an analytic tool box is more than just remembering more and more analytic techniques to use during preliminary and detailed analysis. More importantly, it requires the ability to adapt various analytic methods to a variety of problem sets. Chart 10.1 shows several of the most popular and adaptable analytic methods.

CHART 10.1   Frequently Used Analytic Methods for Detailed Analysis

Analytic method	Description
LINK ANALYSIS	Analysis of the links or associations between like and unlike entities. Also known as social, network, or nodal analysis. Often used to map out organizational structures along with its members but can also include linking places, things, or events along with their relationships to other desired entities.
ASSOCIATION MATRIX	Analysis of associations or relationships between like or unlike entities using a graphic matrix. Differs from link analysis in that intelligence is derived from patterns of associations rather than mapping out an organization through its individual links. Created by cross-referencing desired entities with each other by listing them along two sides of a graph or spreadsheet.
TIME-EVENT ANALYSIS	Analysis of significant events along a time line in order to identify patterns or aberrations within the operating environment or threat operation. Used to understand both the causes and effects of certain events by portraying them sequentially over a given period.
PROBABILITY ANALYSIS	The act of assigning words of estimative probability to a given unknown or predicted unknown instead of percentages. Ranges of highest to lowest probability are phrased as "almost certain," "probable," "chances about even," "probably not," and "almost certainly not" with assigned percentages of confidence.

(Continued)

Analytic method	Description
ANALYSIS OF COMPETING HYPOTHESIS (ACH)	Analysis of a given set of different hypotheses related to a single problem set. Conducted by comparing and weighing-related information in terms of which hypothesis the information supports or does not support. Hypotheses that are most supported by related information are kept, while least supported hypotheses are discounted.
CENTER OF GRAVITY ANALYSIS	Identification and analysis of a threat's primary source of power and strength, the critical capabilities that come from it, and the corresponding critical requirements that must be in place for each capability. Also includes analysis of the critical vulnerabilities that can be identified for each requirement. Helps to focus and prioritize operations against the threat.
INDICATIONS AND WARNINGS	Development of indications of possible future threat actions requiring a trigger for friendly protective or countermeasures. Usually conducted by the creation of a series of events or conditions related to the threat that can be observed or tracked.
THREAT PROFILING	An analytic technique that helps to organize, understand, and apply intelligence information related to threat groups for supported operations or further analysis. Helps to build the foundation of knowledge that other detailed analysis must draw upon in order to be conducted.

Threat Profiling

While the intelligence analyst builds their tool kit through experience, they will come to see that the common factor among the different analytic techniques is that every detailed or structured analytic technique requires some degree of understanding of the threat. Without this understanding or ability to pull in information about the threat, most analytic techniques simply cannot work for intelligence purposes. In other words, every single analytic method outlined in Chart 10.1 that is used for detailed analysis of a threat must draw from an available body of threat data, information, and knowledge.

In order to support these detailed analytic techniques more effectively, the analyst must be able to collect, organize, and draw information about the threat from this body or repository. The analytic technique that supports this effort is called Threat Profiling. Because this is such an important and universal method in supporting every other analytic technique, the preponderance of this chapter is devoted to Threat Profiling and its application.

Threat Profiling is an analytic technique to help analysts organize, understand, and apply intelligence information related to threat groups for supported operations or further analysis. It is a way for analysts to effectively capture all of the collected and known information about a threat group in a way that this information can more effectively be accessed according to a standardized set of components. They can then repeatedly use this information for a variety of analytic techniques depending on their needs or the specific requirement related to that group. Threat profiling therefore becomes a universal organizational and analytical requirement for every other type of analysis.

During the Preliminary Analysis phase of the Intelligence Analysis Process, analysts concentrated their study of the threat in terms of identifying and understanding a group's dispositions, capabilities, and intentions. In this phase it was important to look at the threat in a very broad but surface-level manner. Threat Profiling is an analytic technique that looks at an already identified threat in a much more in-depth and focused manner.

At its core, Threat Profiling is conducted by organizing all available information about a threat group based upon a set or standard number of components or categories. For ease of use, the total number of components of a threat profile should not be more than can be memorized and easily recalled, like the number of digits in a phone number including the area code. The Threat Profiling techniques presented in this book uses eight components. Using too many categories defeats the purpose of effectively organizing the available information for ease of retrieval and presentation.

Personal Perspectives:
The First Threat Profilers

Like many structured analytic techniques, there is currently no single or doctrinal method for conducting Threat Profiling. My first encounter was a rudimentary version of it while I was Chief of Intelligence for the Army's Land Information Warfare Activity (LIWA). At this time, from 1999 to 2001, my branch conducted analysis on a number of different threat groups to include foreign military and intelligence forces, hacker groups, and terrorist organizations. One of the LIWA's senior civilian analysts, Dr. Eileen Preisser, had introduced Threat Profiling to LIWA as a way to organize and present the information that our nascent data mining tools were able to pull on a given threat group.

While Dr. Preisser used a rather straightforward method of profiling threat groups using eight broad categories, my cyber analysts were independently developing more complex profiles of known foreign hacker groups. Their intent in profiling these groups would be to assist the Army Cyber Emergency Response Team (ACERT) in a combined attempt to identify and match known foreign hacker groups from the technical indicators and forensic evidence of intrusions during attacks on Army networks.

After leaving the military in 2001, I spent over a decade going through several versions of design for Threat Profiling as an analytic method. My 2005 version became the core of a counterterrorism analysis course as well as part of several other DoD intelligence courses.

Because of the ubiquitous nature of this method of Threat Profiling, it has been used by counterintelligence agents, cyber threat, criminal, and competitive (business analysts) against a wide variety of threats. One of my students from Interpol in Europe used this method to profile groups of Somali gangs, presenting his work at a conference near Washington DC. Afterward, he relayed to me that his presentation was such a great success that the Federal Bureau of Investigation (FBI) agents attending the conference asked him where he learned Threat Profiling as an analytic technique. He laughed as he told them he learned it from the intelligence course he took from me while at Lockheed Martin in Alexandria, Virginia—only a few miles from their academy in Quantico.

Comparisons with Racial and Serial Profiling

Threat Profiling is often associated with other types of profiling; most predominantly racial profiling and serial profiling that have achieved notoriety from social justice activists and criminal investigative shows and movies, respectively. While certain aspects of these methods may appear similar to Threat Profiling, their purpose, function, and effectiveness are very different.

Racial Profiling is the targeted analysis of a person or suspected person based upon their perceived race or ethnicity. Besides the fact that such a prejudicial technique is simply wrong on a morale level, racial profiling is also very ineffective as it assigns one or more characteristics, such as a suspicion of wrongdoing or a propensity to kill, to an individual or group based on single visual characteristic such as the color of their skin or facial features that are assigned to a given race. The faulty inductive reasoning of assigning a broad generalization for an entire group feeds into a type of deductive reasoning based on a false or unprovable premise that a certain individual is going to act or behave in a certain way because there is evidence that a few people from the same race or ethnicity has done so in the past.

Serial Profiling is a method primarily developed by law enforcement investigators to understand the psychological makeup of a serious criminal offender, such as a serial or mass murderer, by analysis of the physical and forensic evidence found in their crimes. It is also known as offender profiling or criminal profiling. This type of analysis primarily uses abductive reasoning to form a hypothesis about the identity of an individual based on the incomplete set of evidence uncovered in an investigation. It is frequently portrayed in many movies and TV shows related to criminal investigations because of the way it assembles seemingly unrelated pieces of evidence that leads to a conclusion and is therefore conducive to the unfolding of a gripping story.

Threat Profiling is distinctly different from racial or serial profiling because of its focus and intent. It is different from racial profiling because it takes into account a wide array of both social and psychographics of the individual members of the threat group and rejects the false premise that race or ethnicity is a sole indicator of future actions. It has more similarities with serial profiling, but where serial profiling analyzes the behavior and psychological makeup of an individual, Threat Profiling focuses on understanding an entire group of individuals as a single entity. While Threat Profiling can include individuals, it does so by looking at them as a group with a single member and then focuses on their actions and decision-making rather than indicators of why they think like they do.

Components of Threat Profiling

A standard method of organization for Threat Profiling would use the following components:

Each of these components captures every critical aspect of a threat group in terms of organizing and retrieving information for analysis. Virtually every piece of information that can be collected, discovered, or analyzed about a threat group can be categorized into one of these eight categories. While this book presents the following eight components, individuals and organizations can adopt their own versions of the threat profile as they see fit; the foundational principles, features, and benefits remain constant for different variations.

Motivations, Goals, & Objectives
Demographics & Psychographics
Organization & leadership
Targets
Methods of Operation
Sustainment & logistics
Strengths & Capabilities
Weaknesses & Vulnerabilities

FIGURE 10.1   Threat Profile Components

Conducting Threat Profiling is as much a synergistic type of analysis as it is an organizational one. The components shown here are inextricably related to each other. An in-depth understanding of one component will invariably lead to a better understanding of the other components. For example, if an analyst has conducted detailed analysis about the targets of a terrorist organization, they will also have an understanding of their methods of attack (methods of operation) as well as their reasons for attacking (goals/objectives).

This is because understanding one of the components requires the analyst to learn about it within the context of the others and the profile as a whole. Understanding the organization and leadership of an organization is extremely difficult without understand the people that make up the organization to include their demographics and psychographics as well as the motivations for persons to be a part of such groups.

Form this point, it is important to understand the definitions and complexities of each component in detail.

Threat Profiling Component: Motivations, Goals, and Objectives

Motivations, goals, and objectives are what creates a group and binds its members together. Without goals and objectives, the group has no purpose. Without motivations, the people that make up the group have no reason to be in the group. While all these three labels are grouped together for the sake of understanding this aspect of a group, they are actually quite different from each other in how they relate to the group's existence. Looking at motivations, goals, and objectives in turn.

An often-made mistake in analyzing a threat group is when the analyst assigns a single personality to an entire group. In doing so, they assign one or more motivations to the group assuming that everyone who has joined it has done so for the same reasons. The analyst can also fall into the trap of discounting individual goals and objectives and replacing them with a group's goals and objectives. This type of analysis may look sound in a presentation or product but will eventually run into errors in logic and predictions of future courses of action for the people within the group.

In reality, a group will never be motivated in itself. While base motivation is what drives the behavior and actions of everyone, it is an individual characteristic. Each individual within a group joins and operates within it under a variety of motivations. These

Motivations	Goals	Objectives
• Why we do what we do as individuals • An emotion, desire, or physiological need/requirement • Motivation is the reason the threat becomes the threat • Motivations is an individual characteristic, not a group characteristic	• A desired end-state • May be set for an individual or a group • Overarching purpose of a group's existence • A goal is established to be attainable or within the realm of the possible • Primary reason for people with different motivations come together as a group • Not necessarily based on current group capabilities	• Operational and tactical level conditions that must be met for group success • Must be tied to one or more goals • Each goal will have many objectives • Each objective will have many requirements • Sequential objectives must be achieved in order • Parallel objectives can be achieved concurrently

FIGURE 10.2   Threat group motivations, goals, and objectives

motivations are influenced by a person's environment, their psychological makeup, and any ideologies they either follow or subscribe to at some level.

Environmental factors vary widely as they depend on a complex and interconnected social and cultural set of conditions that affect both an individual and their community. For example, analyzing members of an extremist group would reveal indicators of environmental conditions that can be linked to their membership in the group. Many of these conditions are typically found to be negative; harsh or unacceptable to the point that joining an extremist group is seen to be the only or best solution to rectify or eradicate. These could include living in the shadow of any perceived form of systemic injustice, authoritarianism, hatred, failure, tragedy, failure, violence, or some other hardship. As a result, members of these groups who have experienced these conditions will more likely be driven to extremism as their solution to rectify the wrong or destroy the perceived perpetrator. While environmental factors are inextricably linked to social and psycho demographics, no one person will experience the exact same set of environmental conditions. For example, even within the same family, the birth order of children comes with their own patterns of psychological effects.

The psychological makeup of a person's mind is an area fraught with complexities and unknown. Driving into a person's psyche is such a wide and still unexplored arena, any requirement to do so for intelligence purposes necessitates the involvement or coordination with medical personnel or other psychology professionals. In lieu of this type of involvement, analysts should not attempt to construct or rather deconstruct a subject's intricate psyche themselves. Personnel with significant psychological issues or illness such as schizophrenia or acute narcissism don't follow the predictive patterns of what is considered a normal and therefore predictable decision-making process. Instead analysts should concentrate on any confirmed or suspected psychological patterns or abnormalities for the purposes of understanding their decision-making process and predictive behavior in the context operations.

Along with environmental and psychological factors there are also ideological factors. Ideology is a way of thinking that expresses values and beliefs and motivates one to behave according to an established set of rules. These rules are usually written by someone else such as a major religion, social stance, or a political party platform. Understanding a person's ideological adherence or leaning requires research into the one or more ideologies that they identify with, along with the degree to which they are assessed as adhering to that group's ideas or rules. Some ideologies are both political and religious; analysts should understand that the separation of religion from politics is primarily a western idea and not so clear cut in ideologies from different parts of the world.

Relations Between Motivations, Goals, and Objectives

Analyzing an individual's motivations may not be so readily apparent when there are clear indications that a person is being coerced or forced by a group to take certain actions. Why would a slave willingly place themselves in such a status? Why would someone allow themselves to commit a horrific or immoral act? Why would someone commit a suicide attack? Each answer requires a look at how motivations, goals, and objectives are related to each other as there are situations where group's identity, along with their goals and objectives, become more powerful than an individual's identity.

As stated earlier, motivations are an individual characteristic whereas both individuals and groups have goals and objectives. While each person has their own motivations for joining and extremist organization, a company, a nation's military, or a political group, they will join and stay with that group as long as they believe that share the same goals and objectives with the group. If not, group membership is tenuous at best, by very likely to be impossible to maintain.

Once the goals and objectives start to diverge within members of the same group, the future of the group as a whole is in jeopardy. An individual or faction within the main group that comes to believe either in a different goal or set of goals for the group, the status quo cannot be maintained. Those diverging from a group's goals or objectives will either persuade the group to their view, attempt to take over the group, or splinter off into their own group. They can even continue to believe in the same overall goal but disagree with which objectives need to be accomplished in order to achieve that goal. Since groups of people almost never will come to this realization simultaneously, these actions are usually instigated by a single member that possesses the trust and leadership to inspire other dissenters.

For extremist groups such as those involved in crime, terrorism, or piracy, the risk of death exacerbates diverging goals and objectives. In these groups, splintering will rarely take place by those seeking to be more moderate in their approach. Therefore, when analyzing the motivations, goals, and objectives of an extremist group that has recently splintered or is showing indications of a split, it is the more radical and potentially violent faction that will splinter off, not the other way around.

Understanding motivations, goals, and objectives of a group will help the analyst to make better sense of the other components within the threat profile: why the targets are selected, who is predisposed to support and become a member of the organization, among other subsequent analysis.

Threat Profile Component: Demographics and Psychographics

While motivations, goals, and objectives provide WHY a threat group does what it does, demographics and psychographics provide WHO are drawn to the group, and the patterns in determining the type of people a threat group tends to recruit and inspire.

The demographics of Threat Profiling involve analyzing the statistics of the people that join and actively support the organization. It involves identifying individual qualities such as age, sex, education, wealth, religion, marital status, family life, occupation, physical features, geographic origin, skills, experience, psychological makeup, and significant life changing events among a myriad of others across the entire group or each subgroup. These traits will tell the analyst a lot about the story and background of an individual, but when looking at the entire group, the trends and patterns of demographics will tell a completely different story in how the group operates and behaves.

Psychographics of Threat Profiling combines the study of demographics with thought processes of the members, their attitudes, and aspirations and even their motivations. While demographics will identify a pattern in terms of one or more traits listed above, psychographic analysis attempts to understand and predict how members within that pattern group think and make decisions. It is therefore inextricably linked to understanding motivations, but further refines it within a chosen subset of individuals that share other personal commonalities.

Using demographics and psychographics, analysts look for patterns within a group's members that would indicate something important about the other components in the threat profile. As a supported customer cannot directly target or affect a threat group's demographic makeup, analysis of demographics can reveal capabilities that must be countered, or vulnerabilities that can be targeted.

For example, Chart 10.3 was created using information from Rex A. Hudson's *Who Becomes a Terrorist and Why*, which was a 1999 study of the U.S. Government Federal Research Division to better understand the allure that terrorism had on the members of various group prior to the rise of Islamic fundamentalist groups.

By comparing the ages of various groups stated in Hudson's study, an analyst can quickly identify several areas of interest worth further collection and analysis. With such general and nonscientific information, the analyst cannot reach any definitive conclusions but can definitely make some analytic judgments and identify areas that merit further study.

For example, in just looking at the recruitment ages, an analyst can identify several patterns and areas of interest. It is fairly obvious that terrorist recruits are likely to be younger than operatives and leadership. There appears to be a significant difference between German and Japanese recruits and those from Muslim countries, i.e., Arabs, Iranians, Algerians, and Sri Lankans (LTTE aka Tamil Tigers). The differences in recruitment ages are a clear signal that there are probably differences in the recruitment sources, the recruits' motivations, and skill sets they bring in to the organization.

For the youngest recruits, there are probably only three ways they can be identified, groomed, and brought into an organization—through their schools, their families, or the streets. As well, an analyst can expect them to bring in almost no inherently useful skill set other than that of a basic soldier or suicide bomber, helping to validate the etymology of the word infantry.

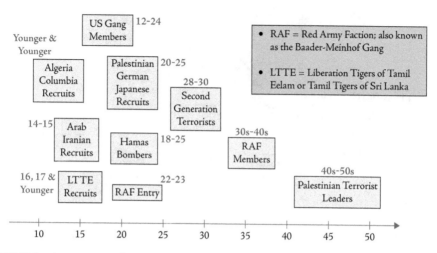

FIGURE 10.3   Average ages of pre-Islamic fundamentalist terror groups[1]

Besides looking at recruitment, there are several other areas of interest in this single chart that can help to paint a picture of an extremist/terrorist group. Analysis of the demographic/psychographic makeup of the people within an organization will help provide insight into patterns in terms of who tends to perform which roles or functions. Analysis can also be used reversely to provide insight into the required skill sets of the group, while also identifying where the required types of people are going to come from or receive training once they enter the group.

Using the extremist threat group as an example again, the analyst can identify basic skill sets and group them according to the overall goals and objectives of the group:

Basic combat, support, logistic, and management skills within a group are naturally going to pull people from different backgrounds, areas of expertise, ages, and education levels depending on the needs of the group. When a group fills their organization with people possessing certain skill sets, they can also be analyzed in terms of their recruitment and training operations as well as their organizational management.

Because a threat organization is nothing without people, understanding the demographics and psychographics of that organization will help to reveal where their personnel came from, how they got into the organization, and what their jobs are within it. In understanding the individuals, the analyst can make a more informed read and prediction on a group's future actions and behavior.

---

1   Hudson, Rex A. (1999, September). *The sociology and psychology of terrorism: Who becomes a terrorist and why?* (pp. 46–47). Washington DC: Federal Research Division, Library of Congress.

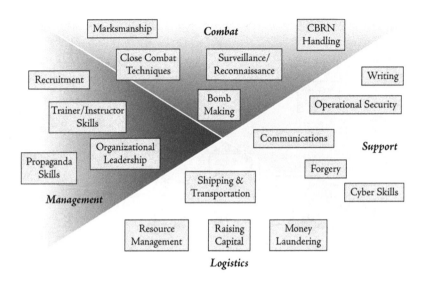

FIGURE 10.4   Extremist threat roles and responsibilities

Threat Profile Component: Organization and Leadership

Analyzing the previous two components reveals the WHY and WHO within the threat group. *Analyzing threat organization and leadership takes into account how a group arranges itself to perform functions, conducts, and coordinates their operations, and how they are led.*

The study of organizational structure is a major focus within the science of organizational management, usually for the purpose of better tailoring a commercial or business-related organization for increased efficiency and productivity. For intelligence, analyzing a threat's organization in terms of its structure, function, and leadership is primarily for offensive and defensive reasons; to identify strengths and weaknesses and with that knowledge, predicting and countering their operations.

Every threat group has a system for organizing its personnel. Discovering a group's organization along with its functions for intelligence often starts with the identification of the group's members and charting them using their position, interactions, and both formal and informal relationships to other members. Once enough members and their relationships or links are plotted, a larger picture begins to emerge of what the organization looks like as a whole.

As stated earlier in this chapter, the process of link analysis can involve a painstaking level of manual input depending on what tools or data sets are available to use. Gaining an effective understanding of a threat group's organization and leadership requires identifying the overall characteristics of the group from what is known about the individual members, their roles and responsibilities within the group, and their contextual relationships with the other members or more simply put—seeing the forest for the trees. This includes identifying the elements that determine or influence the overall characteristics of an organization as well as the overall type of the organization itself. From these two areas of analysis, an accurate picture of a group's functions, behaviors, and tendencies can be patterned and ultimately predicted.

Several organizational factors can be analyzed to identify a threat group's characteristics. Several of them can be gleaned by studying organizational management for business. The ones of most interest for intelligence analysis include, but are not limited to the following:

CHART 10.2   Organizational Factors in Analyzing Threat Group Characteristics

Organizational factor	Description
DUTIES AND RESPONSI-BILITIES	The functions that a threat organization must perform in order to achieve their goals and objectives and other requirements. These functions can be assigned to both individual positions and subdivisions within the group.
LEADERSHIP	The leadership structure along with the resultant environment within the organization. Can include both formal and informal leaders, emerging leaders along with the effects of differing leadership styles across the organization.
CHAIN OF COMMAND, AUTHORITY, AND INFLUENCE	The links between leadership and members of the threat organization. Includes upward and downward levels of subordination and communication, focusing on who makes required decisions and at which levels within the organization.
CENTRALIZATION AND DECENTRALIZATION INFLUENCES	The internal and external forces that result the collection of authority at a certain level or within a limited number of positions. Also includes forces that require decision-making to be dispersed or desegregated to lower levels within the group.
INTERNAL PROCESSES	The standard ways of conducting business along with ability to adjust or be flexible toward differing situations. Includes day-to-day administrative or bureaucratic operations as well as key decision-making processes.
HIERARCHY AND FLATNESS	The numbers of known levels with an organization. Can range from a single level to very bureaucratic organizations with several levels of authority. More layers dilute duties, authority, and autonomy, while less layers carry more vulnerabilities and limits to flexibility.
SECURITY	The external and internal factors that threaten the physical and information security of the organization and its members. Includes considerations of survivability and protection of operations from external competitors and adversaries.

In addition to identifying organizational elements of a group, analysts can also map a group's members and links between members to identifying the group type. The three primary types of organizational structures include the following:

While these three types of organizational structures are common in any type of group, analysts need to do more than simply attempt to plug what they know about a particular threat group into one of these models. Combining these types with other organizational dynamics such as hierarchical, flatness, tallness, pyramid, and others will allow analysts to gain a baseline of knowledge of how a group organizes itself and more importantly, why it is organized in such a way and how it functions within that structure.

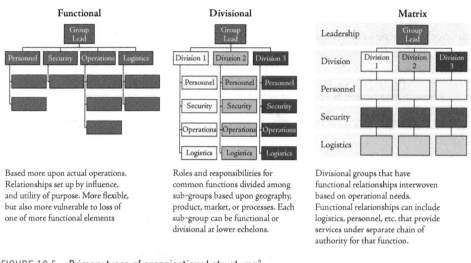

Functional	Divisional	Matrix
Based more upon actual operations. Relationships set up by influence, and utility of purpose. More flexible, but also more vulnerable to loss of one of more functional elements	Roles and responsibilities for common functions divided among sub-groups based upon geography, product, market, or processes. Each sub-group can be functional or divisional at lower echelons.	Divisional groups that have functional relationships interwoven based on operational needs. Functional relationships can include logistics, personnel, etc. that provide services under separate chain of authority for that function.

FIGURE 10.5   Primary types of organizational structures[2]

In analyzing organizational structures of threat groups, analysts will gain a better understanding of how to map the various known associations within the group and place those associations within the context of the organization rules that are assessed for the group as a whole. Concurrently, analysts should be looking for strengths, capabilities, weaknesses, and vulnerabilities depending on current situation as part of their overall analysis of the organizational structure.

Leadership

Perhaps the most critical factor in understanding the organization of a threat group is to understand its leadership along with the influence leaders have upon the organization. Just as with many other components of threat profiles, the study of leadership is an expansive field that has been studied for centuries.

Analysis of leaders within a threat group is important for two primary reasons. From a personal standpoint, understanding a leader as a key individual within a group is important in understanding their decision-making processes, and what external factors have molded their psychology, personality, and ideology. Analysis here should focus on the predictive aspects of individual leaders within an organization for the purpose of getting inside their decision-making cycle and understanding the external factors that affect their decisions such as their psychology, personality, or associated ideologies.

2   Partially derived from Alton, James. *4 Common types of organization structures.* All Business. Updated July 9, 2017, Retrieved from https://www.allbusiness.com/4-common-types-organizational-structures-103745-1.html

Understanding how key leaders within an organization as well as how their leadership styles affect operations requires a baseline understanding of some of the common leadership models that are currently used within other parts of society. These effects are also known as the command climate or leadership environment.

Identifying Key Leaders and Members

Perhaps the most difficult part of analyzing the leadership within a threat organization is in identifying where the leaders are. Not every organization has a clearly defined leadership node, and not every leader within an organization is officially titled.

Several methods can be used to identify certain leaders and other key members within an organization. Often a group's official leader is simply revealed or announced by the group itself. They may also be the group's spokesman, or carry a title designating their appropriate position or weight or responsibility. For many groups, various key positions will already have been identified in previous studies or analysis conducted on the group. In these cases, finding information about a leader is simply a matter of collecting from trusted sources.

Finding leaders in unknown organizations or finding secondary leaders in known or unknown organizations is much more difficult. Secondary leaders could include a group's named deputy, or the lead of any major subgroup or section within the main group. They could also include informal leaders such as up-and-coming stars or young guns within the organization. In these cases, analysts must spend time drilling into available data and known information to identify leaders using analysis of their positioning within the organization or activities in terms of their actual role. What would appear to be indicators of a leader will vary from organization to organization depending on the organizational factors previously discussed.

One method to identify leaders and key members is to first analyze a chart of the organization that includes individual members as nodes within and then identify those nodes that stand out from the others simply by their location or juxtaposition amidst the other nodes or members of the group. Tapping into link analysis as an analytic technique again, a key model to assist in this analysis is the Kite Model developed by David Krackhardt.[3] As outlined in Figure 10.6, the Kite Model portrays a simply social network in a way that allows a student to understand how a person's social position within a group is key to understanding their potential roles.

The beauty of Krackhardt's social network model is in how it shows analysts the different ways that key players can be identified: those with the most connections (degree centrality), those who have the shortest distance to reach every other member of the group (closeness centrality), those who are located as a hub connecting important subgroups (betweenness centrality). While Krackhardt doesn't include the key roles that

---

3   Rozental, David, & Helman, Tali. (2015, October). SNA-social network analysis. *2Know Magazine: Sharing KM Knowledge*, Magazine No. 193f. Retrieved from http://www.kmrom.com/Site-En/Articles/ViewArticle.aspx?ArticleID=144

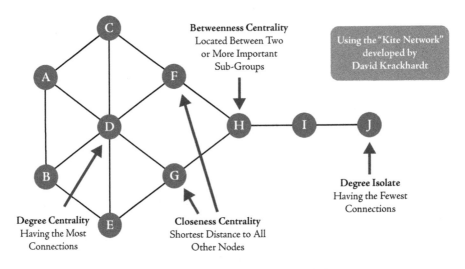

FIGURE 10.6   Identifying key leaders through social network analysis

isolated members can play within a threat group, they are just as important as the other key positions in the same way that each of these nodes provides distinct and unique advantages over the others. The people within an organization at any of these locations should therefore be considered as potential leaders, whether they are previously known or unknown as leaders or whether they are formal designated or informal/emerging leaders.

Understanding a threat group's organization and leaders will help the analyst understand how the members of the group interact with each other, how they are organized for operations or functionality, and where their critical and weak links exist.

Threat Profile Component: Targets

As every threat group has objectives, they all also have targets associated with those objectives. *Targets can be considered objects, people, places, or things that a threat group must affect to achieve their goals and objectives.* These targets are usually under the control of someone else, thereby requiring the threat group to act in a way that is not in the target owner's best interest. For intelligence purposes, the supported customer will often be that target owner, or rely upon a targeted asset for the success of their own operations.

The need to affect a target in a way that favors a threat group offers a near limitless number of options to be considered. Targets can be attacked, stolen, sold, held captive, hidden, copied, extorted, or any other number of options. Military planners involved in information operations use a definable set of lethal and nonlethal target effects to help categorize their own targets. These include effects such as destroy, deny, degrade, disrupt, delay, and deceive.[4]

---

4   U.S. Army. (2003). *Information operations: doctrine, tactics, techniques, and procedures, FM 3–13.* Washington, DC: Government Printing Office, pp. 1–16.

For analysis purposes, narrowing down potential and most probable targets along with the potential actions that can be taken against it requires application of some baseline rules.

The most important rule to remember is that all targets are linked to a group's goals and objectives. Except for targets developed and attacked by those who are mentally unstable, usually as lone actors, no threat group conducts operations against targets randomly or senselessly. The direct linkage between a group's targets and their goals and objectives also implies that every group conducts a deliberate target selection process, whether it be through the rationale of a single decision-maker or a more deliberate process involving several people within the group.

Following this rule of association, analysis can continue in two directions. First, if a threat group's goals and objectives are known, they can be used to predict future targets. Conversely, if a target or set of targets can be attributed to a group, analysis can then be conducted to postulate a group's goals and objectives. Essentially, analysis in either direction uses a known to determine the unknown. Because targets are inseparable from goals and objectives, this can only be accomplished with a high degree of certainty if the known factor is verified or not under question itself.

Targets that do not logically associate with a threat group's known goals or objectives require additional analysis to determine the reason. There may have been an error in determining the goals and/or objectives or the group could have metastasized therefore altering its initial goals and objectives. There could also be external factors influencing the goals and objectives of the group that must now be considered or relooked.

One such external factor could be a previous undiscovered or disregarded relationship with another group. This relationship could be so strong that the initial group in question has either replaced or subordinated their own goals and objectives with those of the other group. This can be for several reasons including some sort of subordinating themselves to the other group as part of larger network. As a result, the goals, objectives, and targets of the other group must be looked as well as why and how they have influence over the first group.

In each of the above cases, the more the target data or information about a group's goals and objectives, the more accurate and validated the linkages will be.

Analyzing Targets Using Planning Criteria

Besides understanding the inseparable linkage between a group's targets and their goals and objectives, effective target analysis also requires an understanding the criteria that a threat group uses to select their targets. This can be done by viewing the criticality or importance of potential targets using both friendly and threat perspectives. In doing so, several methods can be adapted for use of intelligence assets from friendly vulnerability assessments to conducting target analysis from the mind-set of the threat planners.

Vulnerability Assessments

Friendly owners of assets that can be targeted by threat groups regularly conduct vulnerability assessments. There are several different methodologies available to conduct vulnerability assessments, some of them supported with analytical software. Vulnerability Assessments can be conducted against the physical security of a single facility, the information network, the people, or the various technological operations that are conducted within a specific facility, especially those involving design and development.

The fundamental function of any vulnerability assessment is to integrate the various protection factors that are deemed important to the asset owner. These factors are usually evaluated separately and then weighed in relative importance to the other factor. Factors can include the critically of the asset, any known weaknesses that could be exploited, and the consequence of the either the loss or degradation of that asset. Often these evaluations are translated into some sort of comparison matrix, using numerical scores to determine which asset is deemed the most critical or most vulnerable.

One such vulnerability assessment model (VAM) used by the U.S. Coast Guard is the Maritime Security Risk Analysis Model (MSRAM), which "was designed to identify and prioritize critical infrastructure, key resources and high consequence scenario's across sectors using a common risk methodology, taxonomy and metrics to measure security risk from terrorism at the local, regional and national levels."[5] Another is the U.S. Army's Asymmetric Warfare Group (AWG) VAM, which identifies adversary and friendly vulnerabilities to assist in planning and allocation of resources.[6]

Target Analysis for Planning

Analyzing targets from an adversary's perspectives requires a different approach than vulnerability assessments. Often, what is deemed critical to protect from a friendly or owner's organization is not what is considered important to attack from the adversary's viewpoint. This is because the factors considered by the two can be quite different. Only looking at potential targets using friendly criteria is considered risky as it assumes the adversary thinks in the exact same way as the friendly organization. Looking at potential targets from an adversarial viewpoint requires a thorough understanding of the threat, including many of the aspects captured within other components of the threat profile. Doing this allows the analyst to develop a series of criteria for target selection that closely mirrors what is estimated to be important to that group. As

---

5   Gordon, G. A. (2014). *Maritime security risk analysis model*. USCG Presentation to Area Maritime Security Committee. Retrieved from http://faculty.uml.edu/gary_gordon/Teaching/documents/MSRAM-Presentation.pdf

6   Schnaubelt, Christopher M., Larson, Eric v. and Boyer, Matthew E. (2014). *Vulnerability assessment method pocket guide: A tool for center of gravity analysis*. Santa Monica, CA: Rand Arroyo Center. Retrieved from https://www.rand.org/content/dam/rand/pubs/tools/TL100/TL129/RAND_TL129.pdf

with vulnerability assessments, the U.S. military provides a few good examples of target analysis criteria:

CARVER: Criticality, Accessibility, Recognizability, Vulnerability, Effect, Recuperability[7]

MSHARPP: Mission, Symbolism, History, Accessibility, Recognizability, Population, Proximity[8]

Both of these methods can be considered Detailed Analysis techniques in that they use a definable structure and method to perform and present a comparison of different potential targets. While CARVER was developed for U.S. Special Forces during the Vietnam War to assist in planning combat missions against hard targets, MSHARPP was developed for softer target selection such as a regional population for influencing noncombat actions.[9]

Each of these acronyms contains several criteria used for planning friendly operations against selected targets. For intelligence purposes, using these same criteria will help the analyst logically understand the important targets for the enemy. This is done by creating a decision matrix; comparing several probable targets within a given area against each other, and rank ordering them according to each of the criteria.

For example, an analyst supporting the security of a foreign country during a presidential inauguration has received vetted intelligence that an extremist group opposed to the ceremony would be attempting to use a Vehicle Borne Improvised Explosive Device (VBIED, aka car bomb) to disrupt the event. They could use a CARVER to develop a list of what they assess are the targets of highest value to an extremist attack. Their target analysis matrix would look something like Chart 10.3.

CHART 10.3   CARVER Target Analysis Example

Target	Criticality	Accessibility	Recognizability	Vulnerability	Effect	Recuperability	Totals
National Plaza	2	1	3	1	2	5	14
City metro	4	5	5	5	5	3	27
Local airport	5	2	4	2	4	4	21
Governor's residence	3	3	2	4	3	1	16
Capitol Building	1	4	1	3	1	2	12

---

7   Department of the Army. (2014). *Special operations forces intelligence and electronic warfare operations (FM 34–36, Appendix D)*. Retrieved from https://fas.org/irp/doddir/army/fm34-36/appd.htm

8   Rovito, Sarah Maria. (2016). *An integrated framework for the vulnerability assessment of complex supply chain systems*. Cambridge, MA: Massachusetts Institute of Technology.

9   Ibid, p. 64.

Using a standard decision matrix, the analyst would rank each potential target with the lowest number in each category deemed either the most desirable or feasible for the threat group with this capability. Each of the criteria, noted in the columns, is first ranked against each other for each potential, with number 1 being the most desirable to the threat. Once each column has been assessed and filled in, the numbers for each potential target are then added up to create a total number at the end of each row. The lowest overall total number would determine the overall ranking of the most to least critical target. In the example shown in Chart 10.3, the easiest target would be an open area with a lot of people like a national plaza, followed closely by the Governor's residence.

Of course the criteria contained in CARVER and MSHARPP may not accurately reflect the particular threat group that is being analyzed. Other factors and criteria may be more important such as the need for symbolism, demonstration of capabilities, and the amount of risk or avoidance of failure. In addition, many friendly capabilities are targeted by threat groups because they are critical for the success of either friendly or threat operations. These are distinctly different aspects involved in targeting. While this type of analysis is a sound way of showing comparisons to a customer, it is most effective if it aligns with the target selection criteria of the threat.

Threat Profile Component: Methods of Operation

Performing Detailed Analysis of a threat group's methods of operation (MO, pronounced phonetically as Em-Oh), analysts concentrate on the actual steps, processes, methods, paradigms, and ways that a threat group conducts virtually any action of importance. Analysis of a group's MO can be general or very specific toward a certain action, such as the ways they like to conduct reconnaissance and surveillance before taking actions such as stealing corporate information, hacking a network, or one involving violence toward a particular target.

Analyzing methods of operation can therefore be seen analyzing the HOW of the organization. A threat group decides upon goals and objectives, they organize themselves in certain way, they select targets to attack or influence. Analyzing a group's MO looks at how they select or agree upon their goals and objectives, how they organize themselves, and how they conduct target selection among a myriad of other functions, tasks, and processes. Analyzing MO attempts to understand every step of a group's operations, how they move, execute a plan, communicate, and everything else in between that has to do with the conduct of operations.

The overall goal of analyzing a group's methods is to predict, template, and, perhaps, interdict, mitigate, defeat, or affect their operations prior to their execution. In order to do this, analysts must be able to identify patterns, methods, and processes that have been conducted in the past and extrapolate these processes into future scenarios.

Like individuals, a group's preferred method for doing anything is based on knowledge and experience of what works best. As such, those operations or methods that have proven to be the most successful or involve the least amount of unmitigated risk are those that will be used over and over by the group—that is until something goes wrong with that method or their adversary develops an effective countermeasure against it.

Tactics, Techniques, and Procedures (TTP) that are common or routine within an organization are often known as Standard Operating Procedures (SOPs). They are practiced in the same way so often that the members of the organization know or are familiar enough with the procedure as to not require instructions, guidance, or rehearsals every time they are conducted.

While each threat group follows a particular set of TTP, many group functions are also beholden to doctrine, dogma, or ideologies that pervade all operations to a certain extent. This can include political, religious, or simply a set of standardized rules that are pervasive throughout an organization. Doctrine, dogma, or ideologies may influence decision-making and other operations toward a certain way of performing them. Understanding the motivations of group members along with the goals and objectives will help to establish parameters of behavior and therefore what are acceptable and unacceptable actions.

Personal Perspectives:
Partnership for Peace in Ukraine

As the intelligence officer or S2 for the 3rd "Phantom" Brigade of the 3rd "Rock of the Marne" Infantry Division in 1995, our unit took part in NATO's Partnership for Peace programs, which were aimed at building trust and comradery between the military units of the North Atlantic Treaty Organization (NATO) and former Warsaw Pact countries. Our Brigade's partnership unit was a motorized rifle regiment (MRR) the Ukrainian 24th Motorized Rifle Division (MRD).

One of our first joint exercises was at the 24th MRD's training area near L'viv, Ukraine in June of that year. During the exercise, my Brigade Commander and I were going over the map of the operation, studying the lay of the land and how several decades of training had left their imprints on the terrain. As we analyzed the terrain together, Colonel Douglas Tystad turned to me with an inquisitive look.

"Okay, Deuce, tell me what you see when you look at this map," he asked. He looked as if he wanted to see if I noticed the same thing he had. We were looking at a huge open area in the middle of the training area deliberately cut into the surrounding forest to enable an MRR to practice the maneuvering according to their strict Soviet-era doctrine. Each step in their doctrinal pattern of attack had been followed so closely over the years that their routes of travel had become pronounced enough to be recorded by mapmakers as permanent paths. From the east, it was easy to identify the three main roads heading west along with each split at doctrinal intervals further on. When I responded to my commander, I didn't want to tell him that I could simply tell what he would tell, I wanted to give him an assessment that went one step further.

FIGURE 10.7. Map of Ukrainian training area, 1995

"Well sir, you know how our Army adapts our tactics to fit the terrain? These guys adapt their terrain to fit their tactics," I responded.

My assessment had already been validated Russian forces using the same doctrine during the first and second battles of Grozny that had taken place in 1994–1995 and 1999–2000, respectively. After their lead elements took massive casualties from lightly armed rebels using the Chechen city for their defense in late 1994, the Russian solution was to hold additional maneuver forces back and then unleash a massive barrage by artillery and air attacks. By adapting the terrain to fit their tactics, i.e., reducing the city to rubble, Grozny was named by the United Nations in 2003 as the most destroyed city. My commander was impressed by answer; this was one of the ways I could show my competence and gain his trust in my intelligence assessments going forward.

There are two broad approaches to understanding a threat group's MO. The first is to gain a specific understanding of the internal processes used or followed by the group. This requires collecting specific and verifiable evidence of these processes either through observation of past occurrences or obtaining codified processes used by the group.

Many groups would like their internal workings kept a secret and therefore place a high priority on securing them from prying eyes and keyboards. For one reason, being able to obtain specific information regarding a threat group (who is protecting this information by the way) is very rare without using expensive, intrusive, or risky methods of collection.

Without this type of fairly detailed and specific information, the analyst must then rely upon a second approach, which is to construct models of what they assess their operational processes to be. A vast majority of Detailed Analysis about a group's methods of operations is done through this approach in lieu of concrete intelligence about a group's MO. A primary analytic model used in this approach is predictive modeling.

To do this, the analyst must have a general understanding of the specific operation or process that needs to be modeled. They then start with a generic model and then modify or tailor it to the specific threat group using available information combined with further analysis.

For example, if the analyst needs to understand the planning and execution phases that a terrorist group would take, they would begin with a general model that can be more easily obtained than specific information about the attack planning process within the group itself. A common terrorist attack planning cycle could include the following steps[10]:

1. Target selection
2. Surveillance
3. Planning
4. Weapons acquisition
5. Deployment
6. Attack
7. Escape
8. Exploitation

Each of these steps involves processes and subprocesses that as creatures of habit will generally be conducted in a similar manner, usually following a previous successful. Intelligence collection should center on validating these steps in order or look for aberrations and why the particular threat group would deviate from the standard or expected model. Answers to these questions will most likely be found in the other components of the threat profile. For example, the involvement of females in a group may alter the target selection process from that of an all-male terror group. Changes in the sustainment and logistics of a group such as the sudden influx of financial capital could change the type of attack and weapon systems used.

Every group conducts operations and therefore has patterns and preferred methods they use. While terrorist attack cycles are easy to model, other groups such as competitive businesses, foreign government, organized crime, and hacker groups will have

---

10   Unknown. (2012, February 23). *Defining the terrorist attack cycle*. Stratfor Worldview. Retrieved from https://worldview.stratfor.com/article/defining-terrorist-attack-cycle

operations that are unique to their type of group, but similar to other business, foreign governments, etc.

Understanding the sheer number of different methods employed by a threat group for every aspect of its operation is a daunting task. For larger organizations, knowing how everything happens within it is simply unknowable by one person, even by a member of the organization itself. Analysts must focus their efforts on the requirement they are trying to answer or support. The requirement combined with the available time and resources will also dictate how deep analysis of a group's different methods can dive into a given area.

Threat Profile Component: Sustainment and Logistics

Analysis of the sustainment and logistics of a threat group is the study of those things that fuel, drive, and allow a threat group to survive for continued operations. Sustainment and logistics are similar to methods of operation in terms of the analytic approaches commonly used, but they are different in that MO covers the details of a group's primary functions where sustainment and logistics are the capabilities required for the sustainment, security, and survivability of a group along with the various threats against those areas.

Perhaps the best way of looking at the sustainment and logistics of a group is that while these aspects of a threat group are not directly related or directly contribute to group's success or advancement toward its goals and objectives, they are critically required to prevent failure and live to fight another day. Successful logistic operations won't win the battle, but the failure of providing them will certainly lead to failure.

The following operations are included in the sustainment and logistics of an organization:

CHART 10.4   Threat Group Support Operations

Support operation	Description
PERSONNEL AND RECRUITING	Includes providing support, security, training and development, advancement, pay and compensation within the organization. Also includes prospecting, grooming, and recruiting new personnel to the organization.
FINANCIAL AND BUDGETARY	Includes raising, securing, laundering, transferring, and hiding capital resources as well as accounts, transactions, business contracts, revenue, and cost structures.
SUPPLIES AND EQUIPMENT	Physical assets including weapons, explosives, vehicles, buildings and facilities, and any important items required for mission success.
COMMUNICATIONS AND MESSAGING	Person-to-person as well as mass communications capabilities including secure communications, virtual private networks, social networking, and physical messaging (couriers, postal service, etc.).
FREEDOM OF MOVEMENT	Includes movement of people, equipment, and other assets worldwide. The ability to penetrate borders, facilities, and both physical and information security measures.

An interesting aspect to each sustainment and logistic operation is the dependency on capabilities and resources that are external to the organization. A threat group may operate in relative isolation from the rest of the world during their most decisive operations such as attacks, espionage, extortion, etc., but no group can sustain itself without external associations or relationships. Often the threat group with the most secure operations will have its greatest vulnerabilities outside of their organization.

Every relationship, linkage, association, partnership, agreement, and alliance external to an organization takes place within the support base of the organization. *A support base and sympathetic base are the entirety of groups and individuals that both actively and passively support a threat group's operations.* As such, every group has a support base that comprises a unique footprint of groups and individuals that do not take a direct part in a group's operations but support the group's goals and objectives in other ways.

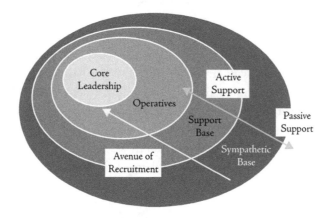

FIGURE 10.8   Levels of threat group involvement[11]

A support and sympathy from external sources can be direct or indirect, willing or unwilling, legal or illegal, and witting or unwitting. In some cases, they can also be welcome or unwelcome, e.g., the case of being unwelcome, a political movement may not want the support or sympathy from a radical or fringe group that shares the goals of the movement but does so in a more extreme or violent manner.

Supporters and sympathizers of a threat group can be individuals, groups, networks, political factions, government agencies, commercial businesses, military, paramilitary, or even extremist groups in themselves. The key to understanding a support and sympathetic base is that the people and associated groups will mirror many of the aspects of the threat group itself. The closer individuals align with the goals and objectives of the group, the more active their support can be expected.

---

11   Partially derived from US Army TRADOC. (2008, March 15). *A military guide to terrorism in the twenty-first century.* TSP 159-T-0001. Retrieved from http://slideplayer.com/slide/9262807/

Recruitment of new blood into a threat organization must also rely almost exclusively on the support and sympathetic bases. Especially pertaining to extremist groups, it is extremely rare for a recruit to come from anywhere outside of these rings with the exception of brainwashing or some other psychological coercion. Tomorrow's group members are already either sympathetic to the group's struggle or are actively supporting it in some form. Because of this, the demographics and psychographics of the threat group members will closely resemble the members of their support and sympathetic bases.

Strengths, Capabilities, Weaknesses, and Vulnerabilities

The final two components of the threat profile can be discussed together since the approach to understanding them are similar. Both components are really composed of two related attributes: a group's strengths are related to its capabilities and its weaknesses are related to its vulnerabilities.

All these four attributes of a threat group are based off of assessments rather than hard data or stand-alone information. Detailed Analysis into a threat group's strengths, capabilities, weaknesses, and vulnerabilities requires either basing them off their analysis of the other threat profile components or drawing from other previous assessments that they've collected. Often, information about capabilities and limitations will be discovered or derived from threat mapping during both the preliminary and detailed analysis phases.

As a way to understanding the importance of these attributes as well as their relationships to their prospective counterparts, some basic definitions are in order:

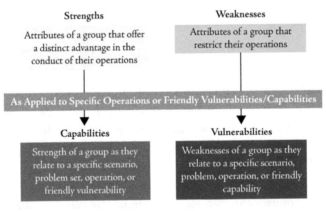

FIGURE 10.9   Defining strengths and capabilities, vulnerabilities and limitations

While every group has innumerable strengths and weaknesses, what matters for the intelligence analyst is which ones can be applied to the given scenario or circumstance of the group. Identifying capabilities and vulnerabilities in this way requires an understanding of not only the other components of a threat group's profile but also the customer, friendly or blue force, or whoever the threat group is against.

For example, a street gang may have a robust recruitment operation within a given city or region, but it can't be considered a relevant capability unless there is a sizeable and supportive recruitment base or populations within that city. Conversely, a business competitor may have poor or lackadaisical security protecting their research on their next product, but that weakness can only be considered a vulnerability to those who have the capability and intent to illegally obtain, i.e., steal, it.

There are *four primary rules for analyzing a threat group's strengths and capabilities, weaknesses and vulnerabilities:*

1. **Prioritize Analysis:** Every terrorist organization has hundreds of strengths and weaknesses—don't try to analyze everything. Instead, focus your assessments based on the specific and implied analytic requirements. Those that fall outside of the parameters of the requirement should be noted, but not pursued or developed in further detail.

2. **Identify Threat Profiles:** The key to identifying capabilities and vulnerabilities is to understand the other components of the threat profile. Capabilities and vulnerabilities are the result of the application of these other components to the current situation. If there is an aspect of a group within another threat profile component that has little or no bearing on the current operation, it should not be considered a capability or vulnerability.

3. **Define the Threat Profile:** Conversely, having a good understanding of a group's capabilities and vulnerabilities will help the analyst understand and validate other components of the threat profile. A group's capabilities are the only way to achieve success in meeting their goals and objectives. Understanding a capability will help to narrow down possible goals and objectives to those that they actually are capable of achieving.

4. **Identify Associated Analytic Tools and Methods:** There are many detailed analytical tools and processes that will aide assessments. Use the ones that will help assess a required component such as Center of Gravity Analysis, Vulnerability Assessments, development of High Value and High Payoff Target Lists (HVTLs and HPTLs) among other techniques. Each of these involves different analytic methods and steps to conduct, but they all rely on or seek to understand a group's capabilities and vulnerabilities.

Threat Profiling Applications

In using Threat Profiling, intelligence analysts are able to give structure to an unstructured threat and give organization to the mass of unorganized information that is available and sought after by intelligence personnel. Because the foundational aspects of Threat Profiling, defining, and analyzing a threat group using Threat Profiling provide several applications, features, and benefits:

1. **Threat Profiling Breaks Down a Threat Group into Malleable Analytic Elements:** Threat Profiling allows the analyst to both understand the threat in terms of each individual profile component and in terms of the relationships, affects, and symbiosis between the each of these components. As stated throughout this chapter, understanding one component assists in the learning and understanding of the other components as all are related to each other in some form. A well-developed threat profile provides the analyst an understanding of both the specific functions of the group and how these functions are related and affect each other.

2. **Threat Profiling Helps to Organize Collection Efforts:** Even before populating a database or file of relevant information about the threat, threat profile components can assist in tailoring and prioritizing collection plans and data queries. Rather than blanket analytic searches that pull information about a group as a whole, using the structure of the threat profile allows analysts to tailor their collections toward those components that are aligned to specific requirements or customer needs. As more focused data and information returns come in, analysts can more easily arranged, organized, or in some cases program automated processors to identify and label different pieces of information into the profile component categories. In addition to using the threat profile to collect toward the requirements, it can also more easily identify those areas that are unknown—aka gaps in knowledge about the threat.

3. **Threat Profiling Assists in Structuring and Prioritizing Analytic Workload:** In breaking the important aspects of a group into smaller and more manageable elements, Threat Profiling allows analysts to concentrate on those components that are directly related to requirements. For example, analysts who work within a financial analyst center or team will routinely be fulfilling intelligence requirements related to a threat group's ability to raise, secure, store, and transfer valuable capital and marketable assets. Analysis will take place in both physical and information/cyber environments. While their analysts will need a preliminary level of understanding of each threat profile component, their requirements toward financial analysis will naturally focus Detailed Analysis toward methods of operation and sustainment and logistics.

4. **Threat Profiling Creates a Common Framework of Understanding of the Threat:** Just as Threat Profiling supports the individual analyst, it is also very useful in small group analytic work as well as in production and presentation of the threat to customers. By collecting, processing, storing, and analyzing threat information using the standardized structure that Threat Profiling offers, an analyst can more easily enter someone else thought processes or even re-enter their own previous work. For group work, the analytic workload can be split among several analysts using the accepted profile structure. This allows planning for human factors such as eating, sleeping, and taking time off during longer projects. Using a common framework also benefits the creation of products or presentations for the customer, again, by providing or explaining the threat in a

way that more easily recreates the analytic work conducted and organizing the results within the context of their mission or problem set.

5. **Provides the Basis for Other Detailed Analytic Techniques:** As stated earlier, Threat Profiling serves as baseline of knowledge required for almost every detailed or structured analytic technique. Whether they are diagnostic, contrarian, or imaginative techniques,[12] every analytic technique that seeks to dissect, template, predict, or portray something about a threat group will inevitably pull information from different profile components. Simply having collected information dumped into a database or folder without any structure or organization is a waste of time or in some cases creates an overreliance that data mining tools will be able to recall the pertinent information later. Using Threat Profiling creates a working structure for future analytic work without the need to know exactly what type of work will be required.

Summary

Detailed Analysis is the step within the Intelligence Analysis Process where specific analytic methods and techniques are employed to directly answer or satisfy requirements issued by a supported customer. Building from preliminary analysis, detailed analysis can involve any number of techniques only limited by available information, tools, and the analyst's imagination. As a foundation for understanding threat groups, Threat Profiling is an analytic technique to help analysts organize, understand, and apply intelligence information related to threat groups for supported operations or further analysis. Among other benefits, Threat Profiling helps the analyst to organize and prioritize their work and provides a basis for any other detailed analytic technique.

Key Summary Points

- Detailed Analysis is the step within the Intelligence Analysis Process where specific analytic methods and techniques are employed to directly answer or satisfy requirements issued by a supported customer.
- Threat Profiling is a universal detailed analytic technique to help analysts organize and understand intelligence information related to threat groups.
- There are several applications for Threat Profiling throughout the Intelligence Analysis Process including the ability to understand a threat group by individual components as well as the relationships and synergies between these components.

---

12 Unknown. (2009, March). *A tradecraft primer: Structured analytic techniques for improving intelligence analysis.* US Government. Retrieved from https://www.cia.gov/library/center-for-the-study-of-intelligence/csi-publications/books-and-monographs/Tradecraft%20Primer-apr09.pdf

Discussion Questions

- What are common analytic techniques or methods can analysts expect to conduct during the detailed analysis phase?
- How would you tailor the threat profile components toward different threat groups and missions? Which components would you add or subtract from the eight presented?
- Besides the features and benefits of Threat Profiling presented, what other applications would benefit from Threat Profiling?

Chapter 11

Delivering Intelligence

Learning Objectives

After completing this chapter, you will be able to:

▸ Be familiar with the three areas of an intelligence customer that must be understood in order to deliver effective intelligence.

▸ Be able to ask the right initial questions in order to begin building a working relationship with a customer.

▸ Understand the most common methods of delivering intelligence to a customer along with the major differences between the various types of products and presentations.

▸ Be familiar with the common elements of intelligence products and presentations.

▸ Be familiar with the concepts of Quality Control (QC), Quality Assurance (QA), and evaluation and feedback.

Creating and Delivering the Response to the Customer

The end result of every analytic process is ultimately the creation of a tangible response to the customer. The intelligence asset, acting on the requirements of their customer, conducts the steps of the intelligence process in order to create a sufficient response. The form of this response can include a verbal answer, a briefing or presentation, or the creation of a software or hardcopy product that is delivered physically or electronically.

Besides the primary customer, the results of the intelligence process are usually meant for other customers, either within the organization or community. Many products or presentations that are requested by one customer are also needed by others. During and after this dissemination, the intelligence asset remains available for coordination, clarification, or follow-through. As the primary purpose for intelligence is to support a customer, the overall measure of success for any intelligence organization is a successful customer along with the success of their mission or operation.

Similar to the other steps of the Intelligence Operations Process, delivering the response is critical to the success of the entire operation. Often overlooked aspects of the Intelligence Operations Process are the actions involved in creating and delivering the response along with coordination or working to integrate intelligence into the customer's plans and operations. The best intelligence in the world is useless to the customer if it cannot be delivered in a timely or effective manner, or if the supporting intelligence asset simply doesn't understand the mission, requirements, or leadership style of the support decision-maker.

Coordination and open communications between the intelligence asset and the customer is critical during this phase of the Intelligence Operations Process. A typical result of poor coordination is simply taking the results of intelligence gathering and proverbially "throwing it over the fence." Proper coordination involves spending additional time and resources to properly follow through with the customer.

Production, dissemination, and coordination are usually displayed as part of every common adaptation of The Intelligence Cycle. During the Intelligence Operation Process presented in this book, the actions taken to create and deliver products are distinctly positioned outside of the Intelligence Analysis Process. Much like collection operations, creating, producing, presenting, or delivering a response to the customer is not an analytical function. While both collection and production/ dissemination require careful thought and task-oriented analysis, both are primarily operational functions.

Also similar to collection and requirements management, larger organizations will have the functions and steps of producing intelligence organized into a separate standalone section or division. Management of intelligence production, much like management of collection operations, is considered an operational rather than an analytical function. It should, therefore, be clearly assigned to an individual, section, or an entire division as either a full- or part-time job within the intelligence organization. Likewise, a production manager should also be designated, even if working within a small group.

In delivering the requirement, the supporting intelligence asset has to accomplish four tasks—no matter the customer or problem set. They must:

+ Answer/satisfy the original requirement
+ Accomplish their tasks in the time required
+ Be in a format that is usable
+ Be in a format that can be shared with others

Whether an intelligence team is creating a read-file, providing an updated organizational chart of a criminal organization, or delivering an intelligence estimate to a combat commander, failure in any one of these four areas equates to an overall failure to support the customer. While it's important to understand intelligence processes, analysis, and associated tradecraft, being able to accomplish each of these areas requires an understanding of both the types of intelligence products and presentations available and the customer themselves.

Understanding the Customer

As is stated throughout this book, primary purpose of intelligence is to support a customer. In this respect there are several parts of the customer that intelligence professionals must understand. Dr. Kristan Wheaton, in an article published on his own blogsite, Sources and Methods, talks of three areas an intelligence professional must know before discussing requirements with the decision-maker. To paraphrase, these three areas are the supported organization, their current situation, and the decision-maker themselves.[1]

Upon closer look, these things are actually categories, each containing several additional areas that the analyst must understand. The analyst must also understand how these categories are related to each other as well as how they define and refine both the intelligence requirements as well as the delivery of the response.

Understanding the Customer

The Supported Organization	The Current Situation	The Decision-Makers

- Mission & Purpose
- Primary & Secondary Functions
- Organization & Personnel
- Rhythms & Paradigms
- Capabilities & Limitations

- Problem Set or Objective
- Threat
- Obstacles & Challenges
- Avenues & Courses of Action
- People
- Time
- Influences

- Leadership Style(s)
- Experience & Expertise
- Knowledge
- Personality

FIGURE 11.1   Understanding the customer

The Supported Organization

While much of intelligence focuses on supporting a customer as a decision-maker or single person, intelligence assets must spend the time understanding their customer as an entire organization that relies on their analysis and products. The primary decision-maker of any organization is that organization's leader but decisions are made at every level of

---

1   Wheaton, Kristan J. (2018, July 2). 3 things you must know before you discuss intelligence requirements with a decision maker. *Sources and Methods*. Retrieved from http://sourcesandmethods.blogspot.com/2018/07/3-things-you-must-know-before-you.html

an organization, including primary and secondary staff, analysts, logistics, finance and support personnel, and the subdivisions and subordinate organizations.

For intelligence assets that are either organic or otherwise found within a supported organization, their understanding of the different aspects related to that organization is intrinsic and an obvious requirement for even day-to-day functions. Those organizations or centers that provide intelligence to a variety of external customers must spend extra time and effort understanding each supported organization. This task becomes more difficult if different supported organizations have wholly different missions or are found at different levels of operating environment.

Much like Threat Profiling, there are some standard aspects that each supported organization shares. Understanding each of these aspects as well as the features that are unique to each supported organization is crucial in creating, delivering, presenting, and coordinating effective intelligence for them.

CHART 11.1   Understanding the Aspects of the Supported Organization

Organization Aspects	Description
MISSION AND PURPOSE	Why the organization exists; the stated mission and vision of the organization often includes the background or history.
PRIMARY AND SECONDARY FUNCTIONS	Tasks that the organization performs as part of their overall mission. Include both specified and implied tasks the organization must successfully perform with resulting effect.
ORGANIZATION AND PERSONNEL	How an organization divides and connects its tasks and requirements among its member. Includes areas of personnel specialization and subordinate organizations.
RHYTHMS AND PARADIGMS	Operational processes during both day-to-day and crisis or surge periods. Includes both specific and implied processes as well as requirements and responsibilities.
CAPABILITIES AND LIMITATIONS	Specified, observed, and assessed abilities of the organization as well as limits to their abilities as it relates to their mission and required functions.

The Current Situation

Intelligence assets that come to understand the organizations they are supporting must do so knowing that the organization constantly changes. A detailed understanding of an organization as well as its leaders and decision-makers is only a static snapshot. The problems the organizations face will change. Old hands leave and new people will join it. External factors that threaten or enhance the organization will grow and recede. In order to provide effective intelligence to a customer, intelligence assets have to identify, predict, and adjust the priorities and resources for both current and future operations.

Here again, there are distinctly different challenges for intelligence assets that are inside an organization than for assets that are external and in either a direct or general support role. Internal assets will more easily understand the current situation because they are experiencing it along with the organization. External assets have to make more of a concerted and ongoing effort to keep abreast of the happenings with one or many organizations.

No matter the relationship with their customers, intelligence assets must gain and maintain awareness of the current situation as well as integrate themselves with the organization. Operationally, this requires intelligence assets to become part of a supported organization's planning, rehearsal, wargaming, and execution of operations. This can be done passively or actively, virtually or by assigning personnel to conduct physical liaison within the organization. For large intelligence organizations, providing a single person or team of personnel to physically relocate within a working proximity of a supported organization allows for more responsive intelligence. Once integrated, intelligence assets will find themselves dealing with the same problems and issues as the supported organization and therefore part of the current situation themselves.

Other aspects of the current situation will include, but are not limited to, the following:

CHART 11.2   Understanding the Aspects of the Current Situation

Situational Aspects	Description
PROBLEM SET AND CURRENT OBJECTIVE	Primary problem, crisis, or situation that the organization is trying to solve as well as current objectives they are attempting to accomplish.
POSSIBLE COURSES OF ACTION (COA)	Current avenues that the organization is considering in their approach to either solve primary problems or achieve their objectives. Directly ties to the current problem set.
THREAT SITUATION AND CAPABILITIES	Current threat map including primary dispositions and capabilities as it relates to the supported organization.
INTERNAL CHALLENGES AND OBSTACLES	Includes current problems, distractions, or dysfunctions within the organization including personnel, logistics, financial, or administrative issues.
TIME AND ENVIRONMEN-TAL INFLUENCES	Issues and problems that affect the organization in their mission and operations but are primarily outside of the control. Includes weather, natural disasters, or events in an outside of the organization's operating environment.

The Decision-Makers

As discussed in Chapter 4, decision-makers are intelligence's primary customers. While there are several other types of intelligence customers such as planners, primary and supporting staff, and other intelligence analysts, providing intelligence to help someone in authority make decisions is the most vital role intelligence can play. Often, the supported decision-maker is the commander, director, chief, or in some other sort of leadership position. For this reason, it is important for intelligence professionals to understand those customers who rely on their analysis and products for their decisions.

Leadership Style(s)

Every organization's mission, their people, and everyone external to their organization who supports the operation is affected by the decisions of a leader. Understanding the leadership style of the decision-maker helps to understand their unique approach to accomplishing the mission along with how they value and treat their people in context of it. Understanding leadership styles includes both the decision-maker's personality and their decision-making processes.

The ultimate purpose in understanding the leadership style of the supported decision-maker is to understand how intelligence can best support that style. Depending on the source, the number of broadly categorized leadership styles listed in academia range from a handful to a dozen or so. Styles include the coercive, authoritarian, laissez-faire, democratic, paternalistic, and team leaders among others. Whichever method is used to determine the leadership style of a supported decision-maker, effective intelligence, as a support asset, must take advantage of the positive aspects of leadership that are conducive to open communications and open decision-making processes.

Conversely, intelligence assets must also minimize the negative aspects of certain leadership styles, finding ways to continually provide accurate and effective intelligence despite any perceived dysfunctional aspects of who they are supporting. For example, an autocratic leader may tend to micromanage intelligence operations, becoming the de facto collection manager or getting into the minutiae of the analysis instead of leading their organization as a whole. A laissez-faire leadership style may leave intelligence assets too little guidance, leaving them to guess or assume the amount or type of support that is needed.

There is no magic answer for overcoming these challenges, and much of how intelligence can best support a given decision-maker is done through trial and error. Support leaders who are not completely versed in the capabilities and limitations of their intelligence assets may not be able to directly or succinctly articulate what type of intelligence they want to see. Often this is called the "I will like it when I see it" challenge, where the supported decision-maker needs to see an example of what intelligence can do for them before being able to provide specific or helpful guidance going forward. While intelligence assets continually strive to be effective, it often requires telling a difficult customer some hard truths about what intelligence can and cannot do for them.

Experience and Expertise

Every decision-maker relies upon what they observe or understand in order to assess the best courses of action available to them. These inputs into their decision-making are translated through the filter of experience and expertise that every decision-maker builds upon over time. Often, the experience and expertise of a leader have such a powerful presence within their decision-making that it can override incoming information and observations. In this way, strength has the possibility of becoming a blind spot.

Intelligence professionals in support of a decision-maker should take the time to get to know the personality and leadership style of their supported decision-maker but also understand their background, what their customer has seen and done, and what trials or lessons learned they may have picked up along the way. Military veterans, police officers, educators, politicians, bureaucrats, scientists, IT specialists, pro-athletes, medical personnel, all have unique sets of experiences that shape the way they look at the world and make decisions.

Even within each of the previously mentioned examples, there are significant variations that supporting intelligence personnel must learn and understand. The experience of a military veteran can vary widely depending on their nationality, branch of service, rank, tours of duty, or relevant combat, or other traumatic experience. Police officers can come from rural, urban, or suburban backgrounds, or spend their time in specific departments from vice to missing and exploited children to organized crime. Just as the intelligence analyst will obtain more and more analytic tools and methods with each passing year and position, decision-makers will have a sizeable decision-making toolkit based upon trial and error and the results of other decisions made in the past.

Besides identifying areas of their experience, analysts will also want to identify or assess those areas in the supported leader's experience where they do not have an adequate background. If they've spent their entire career up to that point in a strategic environment, they are going to be fairly ignorant of operations and capabilities at the tactical or street level. Conversely, if they've spent most of their time on the street, conducting murder investigations or similar cases, they will not be as versed about the more holistic or strategic aspects of complex threat groups.

Often, a supported decision-maker's background can be researched with relative ease, usually by coordinating directly with them or their office. Many high-profile decision-makers will have their biographies online in some form or within literature related to their position. Besides this, the supporting intelligence lead should then get to know the decision-maker personally in order to understand how powerful of an influence a past experience or set of experiences has on their decision-making.

Lessons in Intelligence: Miniature Freeman's Farm

Besides having a love of history, I've also been a gamer as long as I can remember. From wargames involving hexes and counters on paper maps to role-playing games such as Dungeons & Dragons, I spent much of my childhood creating characters, painting miniatures, and playing with friends and family.

One of the largest gaming conventions in the United States is called Historicon, which is an annual conference run by the Historical Miniature Gaming Society (HMGS) usually in Lancaster, Pennsylvania. I would often attend this convention with my eldest brother, Doug, who is also an avid wargamer. On one occasion, we signed up to play a game that re-created the 1777 Battle of Freeman's Farm from the American Revolution. We were assigned to the British and Hessians for the game and paired up against the Americans who were played by a father and younger son and another gentleman who happened to be an Air Force colonel.

FIGURE 11.2   American War of Independence miniatures made by Essex Miniatures—
Photo by Author

While almost every game is friendly between players, there is sometimes a small amount of trash talk—often in a funny or nerdy context. In this case, the Air Force colonel mentioned that as my brother and I were only a Marine lieutenant colonel and Army major, respectively, we would be outmatched by his rank along with the fact that we were just "ground guys." We cordially laughed and the turned to each other to discuss what our plan should be.

The Battle of Freeman's farm in 1777 began as a skirmish between lead elements of the British Army against a small force of American Rifleman under the command of Daniel Morgan. It quickly escalated into a full-blown battle as reinforcements moved in from both sides. Our miniature re-creation of the battle started the same way with the Air Force colonel controlling Morgan's Rifles while the father and son team brought up their reinforcements. Our Army entered the battle in two columns; my brother controlled the left while I controlled the right with several light infantry and native units at the front.

Not long into the game, I turned to my brother and told him I had figured out our opponent's decision-making process and style of play. Instead of engaging us with Morgan's Rifles as was the historical play, he was continually moving them back just out effective range of Doug's lead units, ceding valuable ground each time. Whether it was because of his background or his admiration of these Riflemen as a history buff himself, he was never going to allow his best troops adorned in the iconic white hunting shirts to take casualties. He did not want to have his unit look diminished by loss of figures on the table. Doug and

I then changed our plan so that my brother's troops would continually push Morgan's Rifles back while my light troops and Indians would move to screen and slow down any reinforcements to them. Winning combat was no longer the goal; instead we would win by taking objectives instead.

We quickly talked through our new plan and set it in motion. Over the next several turns, Doug's British and Hessian regulars continued to push back the American Riflemen while I jammed up their reinforcements on the other side of the table, sacrificing my light and native troops in the process. By the end of the time allotted for the game, the British had taken every objective but one and had ownership of almost the entire table without a lot of fighting. We were declared the winners in a decisive victory by playing the game not according to history but according to our opponents' decision-making process. While shaking hands with our opponents, my brother smiled to the Air Force colonel saying, "This is how the ground guys do it."

Knowledge

Closely related to experience and expertise is the base knowledge of a supported decision-maker. In the context of intelligence support, knowledge is not as much a measurement of how smart the decision-maker appears to be but more so their knowledge about the particular aspects related to their job. As a part of establishing communications and a working relationship with a supported customer, intelligence assets should spend time establishing how knowledgeable a customer is in three primary subjects: their organization and mission/purpose, their current situation, and the capabilities and limitations of their intelligence assets. These areas closely resemble what intelligence needs to know about the customer as depicted in Chart 11.1.

In doing so, intelligence assets may find that the customer possesses superior knowledge of a given area or, conversely, has a significant lack of understanding. While it is not an intelligence asset's purpose to tell a supported decision-maker how to do their job, it is their primary purpose to inform them about the current situation and what intelligence can and cannot do in that situation. To note, this type of assessing the customer is perception based in itself and is therefore subject to bias on the part of the observer.

With a perception of the customer's knowledge base in these three areas established, intelligence assets can then adjust their support to either take advantage of their superior knowledge or help them to overcome areas where they are perceived to be deficient.

Personality

As all customers of intelligence are human, they are also subject to personality styles, issues, and quirks in how they view the world and make decisions. This includes how they envision intelligence supporting their operation and any pronounced and persistent bias and misperceptions they may have to include social or political bias. Often, the personality quirks of an individual will be known prior to working with them. They can be picked up from reading a bio or simply passed on from someone who currently works or has worked with them in the past. Aspects of a personality may seem trivial but are extremely important in understanding the thought processes and nuances of an intelligence customer.

In learning about a customer's personality styles, it is not important to determine whether or not a customer likes cats over dogs, whether they're scared of clowns or roller coasters or something non-intelligence related. Instead, intelligence personnel should be looking for personal preferences, physical or mental handicaps, or psychological issues that are within the context of providing intelligence to them in the most effective manner possible.

For example, some customers may hate busy slides and want the main idea of a product or presentation clearly articulated at the beginning—known as BLUF (bottom-line up-front). Others may love the details and minutiae of information and want to see it all, allowing them to re-create some of the analytic work. Still others may want the bottom-line but with the details hidden in the back of the presentation with the ability to access them only if necessary. There can be quirks for or against a particular color, font, font size, or icons or animations within presentations or products. A particular writing style such as bullets versus prose may be requested. Others may want all information presented in an infographic or the ability to navigate through some of the data visualization software themselves.

Each customer is going to have different preferences, perspectives, and desires for their intelligence support, not only with the graphic or physical presentation but also with the timing and demeanor of how it is presented. This type of understanding is not critical for the conduct of intelligence but is very important in the delivery of it, especially when it is in the form of a presentation of briefing. Every personality is unique, and even knowing a customer's subtle preferences and distastes can be the difference between good and excellent intelligence support.

Lessons in Intelligence: Peer Advice

As a young U.S. Armor and then Military Intelligence officer, I regularly attended or participated in briefings and presentation at the battalion, brigade, division, and corps-level commands. Intelligence and other staff officers and soldiers routinely shared their observations and opinions of the styles and personality quirks of the various commanders we supported, along with some of their subordinate leaders and staff. Some of the best and worst advice I have both given and received included the following:

- "He can't stand slides with yellow graphics over white background."
- "He never takes notes—your slides are his notes. You'll be expected to put everything in them so he can use them when he meets with his boss later."

- "Everything will go fine until he starts relating something in the briefing to his time playing rugby. You'll need to get things back on track quickly without making it look obvious."
- "Bring water and food. You're going to be there a long time."
- "She likes to play "Stump the Chump—continually peppering you with questions until you don't have the answer to one. Don't try to challenge her questioning; just play along until you can get the hell out of there."
- "The only acceptable font is Arial and make sure your slides have no text smaller than 20pt."
- "Never say 'let me walk you through' anything. He'll take it as an insinuation that he needs hand holding and will disrupt the briefing in order to put you in your place."
- "Put out a dish of M&Ms when he comes to visit your headquarters—even if you're in the field."
- "You have 30 seconds to brief your portion and you will be timed." (I did it in 27).
- "Our commander has severe allergies. We spread hay on the ground within our TOC (Tactical Operations Center) to limit the time he can spend in it."
- "Don't let Dr. _____ present. Non-engineers won't understand a thing he is saying and if there are engineers in the crowd they will start a conversation that no one else will understand."
- "Engage mind, engage mic, engage mouth—in that order."

In one of the most unusual cases, I was getting ready to move to a unit with a new commander and had a chance to speak with a peer and friend who was a staff officer in his former unit. He told me that this commander had a habit of continually making changes to drafts of products or presentations no matter how accurate the information or perfect the grammar or spelling. This would go on for several iterations without ever getting to a product they would be happy with. To save time near the end of this drill, the staff would sometimes make two products: one with obvious mistakes for their commander to focus on and another with those mistakes already corrected as a final copy to be disseminated. This way they would be able to distract their commander from changing the trivial details once again just before the product was to go final. In other commands, these trivial changes to presentations are known as "happy to glad" or "kitty to cat" changes.

Creating a Working Relationship with the Customer

On a much more personal level, intelligence personnel must constantly work to understand customer organizations, situations, and decision-makers. There is no better way of doing this than for the intelligence leader or supervisor to develop an effective working relationship with their support organization and especially with its key decision-makers. This single person could be the organization's intelligence officer, the lead of a temporarily assigned support element, or a liaison with an intelligence asset in general support. Achieving level of trust and respect by a decision-maker should be seen as a "make or break" function for the intelligence leader.

Creating a working relationship with a customer is a two-way process. While intelligence personnel are busy learning about the various aspects of their customers, the customers are learning about their intelligence support. They need to know about their intelligence personnel, particularly key personnel within the organization or operation. Even those decision-makers with extensive experience dealing with intelligence will need to learn the specific procedures and processes of their current intelligence support. This is especially true for a new collection capability, data mining tool, or other "bleeding edge" technology that is introduced to an organization for the first time.

While getting to know their supporting intelligence assets, decision-makers are also evaluating their support. They are evaluating the effectiveness of intelligence data, tools, processes, and personnel. One of the primary measurements of intelligence effectiveness to a decision-maker includes the personal competency, knowledge, and experience of their primary intelligence point of contact—that intelligence leader or supervisor that represents the face of everything intelligence related, even for assets outside of their control.

Every great professional relationship starts with an introductory phase—that unmeasured time period where both parties are getting to know the other's capabilities and limitations. This period starts when a new decision-maker or intelligence lead joins an organization or their operation, but it can also be a part of an entirely new organization or operation with new personnel from all staff elements joining together either permanently or on an ad hoc basis. This is also the period where intelligence personnel are earning (or squandering) their decision-makers trust and respect.

For new intelligence personnel, introduction to a new organization or operation requires them to answer some immediate questions for themselves. For ongoing 24 × 7, crisis, tactical, or other surge operations, these initial questions must be answered within the first 12 to 24 hours. For a longer-term, work-day, or otherwise stable work environment, this period can extend to several days. In this way, intelligence personnel can quickly start the process of tailoring their initial processes and means to deliver effective intelligence. Critical introductory questions to be answered include the following:

CHART 11.3   Critical Introductory Questions for Intelligence Leads

Subject Area	Question
REQUIREMENTS	What kind of intelligence does the decision-maker need?
	What are the typical intelligence requirements that can be expected?
	How are requirements received and processed?
INTELLIGENCE CAPABILITIES	What are the capabilities and limitations of intelligence assets for collection, analysis, and production?

PRODUCTION AND	What types of products need to be produced on a regular basis?
PRESENTATION	What types of presentation does the customer prefer?
	What are the requirements or standards for the presentation of intelligence?
OPERATIONAL	When are standard products expected?
RHYTHM	When are standard meetings and presentations?
	Who else needs to know the results of the most recent analysis?

Answering these questions quickly and accurately will help intelligence personnel to become synchronized with their primary and secondary customers along with the rhythm and operational processes of the organization itself. Not only is the intelligence asset always in support of someone else's operation, the intelligence lead is routinely very junior to the primary decision-maker, their deputies, subordinate leaders, and the leads of other supporting staff elements. As a result, it is critical for intelligence personnel to train, adjust, and tailor their own operations to the supported or parent organization as efficiently as possible, not expect decision-makers or other supported customers to adjust to their operational ways of doing business.

Types of Intelligence Responses

Part of integrating intelligence personnel into operations is the implied requirement to understand which products are best suited for different customers, problem sets, and available intelligence capabilities. An often-cited complaint or cited deficiency of intelligence leadership is the need to improve both the written and oral communication skills of their personnel. These complaints are understandable as the intelligence profession attracts personnel from all walks of life with a corresponding wide mix of communication abilities among them.

Many intelligence personnel are simply not accustomed or comfortable with presenting or discussing their findings in a group or open forum. There are several publicly available and pay services available to assist in training personnel on writing and presentation skills, but they are most often overlooked within official training programs available to intelligence today. Even further, much of the training that is available concentrates on writing and public speaking while ignoring other skills related to presentations and required professional interactions.

Instead of repeating other sources of training for writing grammar, style, and speaking skills, a more comprehensive way of identifying the corresponding skills needed for intelligence personnel is to understand all the types of responses available. Learning each of these is easier by grouping them into different categories. In doing this, intelligence leader can more effectively identify which responses can be used along with which skills are required to deliver them effectively.

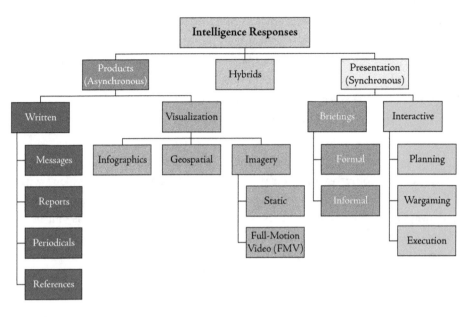

FIGURE 11.3   Types of intelligence responses

Four Required Communications Skills

As is evident from Figure 11.3, intelligence professionals must be skilled at four areas of delivering intelligence. While writing and public speaking are fairly obvious, skills in providing graphic presentations and personal communication for both one-on-one and small group interaction are also incredibly important. Each of these four skills is associated with either delivering a product or presentation of intelligence of some sort. Delivering intelligence often requires a hybrid response, i.e., creating a product and then presenting or discussing that product with decision-maker.

Intelligence professionals must therefore be proficient in all four skills, not just one or two. They may only regularly use one or two of them in one position, but throughout their career, they will be called upon to interact with the customer. Poor presentation and communications skills will most certainly undermine the credibility of the products, no matter how creative and effective the products are.

Products: Products are tangible means to deliver intelligence to a customer. They can be hard (usually paper) or soft copy and can be physically delivered by hand or transmitted electronically. Physical products are different from presentations in that they do not require the analyst to be physically presentation or linked in real time to the customer via video or voice chat. Products also have a benefit in that they can be kept and stored and therefore can be referred to again and again in the future as long as their contained information is relevant. They can also contain much more information than a customer can absorb in a briefing or wargaming session.

Written Products: Every written product requires proficiency in spelling, grammar, but there are also a wide range of required writing styles that intelligence professionals must be able to emulate. Complete sentences with the correct verb-noun agreement may be necessary for more detailed or in-depth products, but this is not necessary for all products. Some products simply require bullets instead of sentences while others require the ability to fill out a database format or annotate an included graphic or chart. Intelligence writers need to keep in mind that customers do not read their products to be entertained or to admire the author's command of the language. Succinct, simple communications are necessary to get straight to the point of a product. Written product generally fall into the following categories:

+ **Messages:** Includes simple text or hand-written messages to a decision-maker that is meant to be quick responsive and with limited focus.
+ **Reports:** A more detailed response that answers a single question or requirement with much more specificity that a simple message. Includes more deliberate writing styles and can be delivered in a standard format such as a situation report or an annex to a much larger operational plan.
+ **Periodicals:** Standard reports that are created based on a publishing schedule or timeline rather than a one-time report. As standard or formatted products, periodicals are usually updated or superseded by subsequent products.
+ **References:** An intelligence product that doesn't answer a specific requirement but is designed to provide both background and more current information for future reference by intelligence personnel or data mining tools.

Visualizations: Many intelligence customers are visual learners. Effective visualizations can convey a lot of information and do it in the context of other related information. Often, visualizations are able to show information that would be much more difficult or even impossible to achieve in a written format. Graphical products can overlay information, imagery, and geospatial data to show a more comprehensive and holistic picture of the problem set.

Mastering visualization skills requires a more artistic eye and the ability to convey required information in a way that a customer can easily absorb, understand, and use. This can be a difficult task, especially if attempting to display different types of information graphically together such layers of geospatially tagged data along with specific images of certain locations. Visualizations can be further broken down into the following:

+ Infographics—The most common type of visual presentation. Includes both text and graphics to outline subject area and can also include raw data visualizations that have been annotated for ease of explanation. Usually displayed on a slide, chart, or some other presentation software.
+ Geospatial—Georeferenced information such as an annotated map or geographically overlaid data sets. Can include multiple sources of information displayed in multiple layers, each geographically tied to an area of interest.

- Imagery (Static)—Handheld or platform-based imagery of a given subject. Often annotated for ease of presentation. Can include multispectral imagery as well as geographically tagged points of interest. Often paired with another presentation format.
- Imagery (Full-Motion Video)—Handheld or platform-based video. Can include sound or narration as well as additional graphics or annotated information.

Many written or graphical products are formatted by an organization in a way that places certain parameters or style requirements on the author. For example, most products require the author to include the main point being made at the very beginning. The common term, BLUF, is meant to remind the author not to delve into too much background or superfluous information before letting the reader know the most important piece of information that they should take away from the product in the event they forget everything else. Other mechanical requirements could include the required font or size of the text.

Presentation: Unlike products, providing intelligence through presentation is a synchronous event, meaning the intelligence analyst or officer must be physically present with the customer or linked in to their location electronically. They are usually preferred by customers in either a dynamic tactical environment where small amounts of intelligence are periodically required throughout an operation. Presentations that are recorded and stored for future playback are no longer synchronous and therefore become a product.

Presentation is also required when a portion or summary of an intelligence analytic effort needs to be disseminated to a wide audience in a short amount of time. Presentation of intelligence also allows for two-way communications to take place allowing the customer to ask questions or change the focus of intelligence on the spot. Presentations include briefings as a more structured format as well as the more dynamic interactive events that require responsiveness of appropriate knowledge and assessments.

Briefings: Presenting intelligence through an oral briefing ranges from a very structured, formal setting to more personal and either a one-on-one or small group setting. The more formal the structure or environment or the larger the audience will be for the briefing, the more one-way the communication will be.

- Formal—Formal presentations are usually conducted in a setting that requires the intelligence presenter provide an oral summary of finding to a customer. Audience can vary from a single decision-maker to a large number of people. Can be conducted in-person or remotely/virtually. Often structured in terms of format or time allotted.
- Informal—A more unstructured or ad hoc oral presentation to a given audience. Can also be conducted in-person or remote/virtually. Usually geared for conveying information in the midst of an active operation where formats and time limits are not set but extremely constrained by operational and environmental conditions.

Lessons in Intelligence:
Briefing Habits Die Hard

Like most company and field grade officers, I spent the majority of my Army career at the tactical level—from a tank and scout platoon leader for an armor battalion, transitioning to a Military Intelligence officer and getting sent right back to an infantry battalion and armor brigade. In those environments, no one referred to the delivery of intelligence as a presentation. There were briefs, key reads, intel updates, and responses to questions such as "What's your read, Deuce?" Junior officers were expected to be brief, and to the point.

After several years in this environment, I received orders to attend the U.S. Army Combined Arms Staff Services School, which had its own acronym called CAS3—pronounced "Cass-Cubed." Arriving at Fort Leavenworth Kansas for 6 weeks in the Winter of 1995, I was among a class of around 300 junior captains learning the skills required to be staff officers. We learned how to analyze events, conduct decision-matrices, and create both written and graphic correspondences in the required formats. The entire class was broken down in many smaller groups, with an attempt to intermix each of the Army branches, e.g., Infantry, Artillery, Engineer, Aviation, quartermaster. Each small group was led by an experienced Lieutenant Colonel; ours being an Armor officer, LTC Campbell, who had an impressive record during the First Gulf War.

FIGURE 11.4   Author sitting with classmates during the Combined Arms Staff Services School in early 1995

A large part of the CAS3 course involved briefings: information briefs, decision briefs, and intelligence, and operations estimates. We even briefed the daily news, weather, and sports to our classmates just to give us more time to practice presentation skills. As I had just come from an infantry battalion where I was required to brief often, I was already confident in my speaking abilities. I knew how to stand and enunciate, how to look at the entire audience, and how to move the presentation along within the time limit without any ticks, sways, or other distracting mannerisms that befall unexperienced or nervous speakers.

Unfortunately, I was shocked when I received my first set of feedback from my classmates and instructor. I received a lot of unexpected criticism that struck a nerve, mainly centered around the fact that I was speaking too quickly. I was able to get through all of the required information but spoke so fast that I ended up way under the allotted time. In some circles, this is known as "The Auctioneer" speaking style. Some of my classmates noted that I was moving through the different subtopics so quickly that they could barely keep up with all the information being thrown at them. My first reaction was that this was the way it was done during tactical operations, but I when I met with our instructor later on, I realized that there was indeed a lot of room for improvement.

LTC Campbell was sympathetic as he laid out my problem in terms that I could better understand. He reminded me that up to that point, I had spent my entire time in the Army in a combat unit. He knew from his time there that intelligence officers had to routinely deliver 20 minutes worth of information in 5 minutes of allotted time, usually in a tent or on the hood of a HMMWV, sometimes in the middle of night to group of exhausted commanders who always had other things competing for their attention. While my style of presentation was very effective in that environment, it was not effective for a more relaxed, climate-controlled office building or classroom where there was more time needed and available to absorb, analyze, and possibly follow up with additional discussion as part of the briefing.

I worked to improve my presentation skills during the rest of the course but, more importantly, learned the importance of reading my audience and adjusting my methods of delivery for the particular setting. The thousands of hours of subsequent training, teaching, executive briefings, conference panels and presentations, media interviews, and testimonies before U.S. Senate and House Committees have reinforced the importance of this lesson over and over during my career.

Interpersonal Communication: This is an often-overlooked skill for intelligence officers, but the ability to interact with decision-makers and other customers of intelligence is incredibly important. The ability to communicate effectively interpersonally inspires trust and confidence—and may be the difference between success and failure of intelligence delivery. Interpersonal skills are different from presentation skills, because they require the ability to demonstrate expertise and knowledge that goes beyond a canned set of talking points. Courteousness, professionalism, and articulateness with the ability to immediately give opinions, answer questions, and react to new ideas and directives are all part of the ability to communicate successfully with others.

A major fear for intelligence personnel working in a more interactive environment is getting caught with a question or in a situation where they simply do not know the answer or cannot accurately give "on-the-fly" analysis with confidence. Intelligence officers and liaisons are often junior to their decision-maker counterparts and yet are expected to present themselves as experts in all things intelligence. No one wants to say "I don't know" in response to a question from a decision-maker, especially one who is their boss. This is especially true if a question is asked about an area that was not deemed important before. Nevertheless, there are times when saying "I don't know—but I can find out" is the preferred answer.

Most decision-makers can also detect when someone is avoiding the fact that they don't know something by replying with a made-up answer. The skills of flexibility, responsiveness, and the ability to quickly recall information are critical to the intelligence professional. While no intelligence officer can know the answer to every question thrown at them, through experience, practice, and exposure to interactive environments, they can turn "I don't know" into "I know who does know." In time, effective interaction skills will help to create a much more responsive and respectful relationship between decision-maker and their supporting intelligence personnel.

The three primary methods of intelligence interaction include, but are not limited to, the following:

- **Planning:** Working with a team, staff, or group in preparation of upcoming operations or adjustments to current operations. Includes both one-on-one and small group communications and presentation of ideas and findings.
- **Wargaming:** Working through possible issues, courses of action, and potential outcomes of a refined plan prior to execution. Conducted in the context of the forecasted situation along with templated or expected threat responses to the plan. Requires at least two personnel, but usually conducted in a small to large group environment. The intelligence lead will represent the adversary's actions while everyone else participates in their normal roles making decisions, shaping the environment, and reacting to various events that will or could take place during the operation.
- **Execution:** Intense interaction between intelligence personnel in the midst of active and ongoing operations. Communications during execution are usually very informal as the intelligence lead is required to provide immediate responses to specific time-sensitive questions. Can involve small group or one-on-one interaction. Often made up of simple and quick intelligence inquires, requiring simple and immediate answers.

Hybrid Methods of Delivery: Almost every instance of delivering intelligence involves a mix of two or more methods. Examples can include an oral presentation of a set of charts, imagery, or full-motion video. They can also include the use of a graphic or written aid during any of the three types of interactive responses. Finally, delivery of intelligence can also include an oral presentation that has been recorded and stored for future use as a full-motion video response. Hybrid presentation skills correspondingly require the intelligence professional to be able to create a written or graphic product and then explain and answer further questions about that product in formal, informal, or interactive sessions.

Getting to know a customer's likes, dislikes, pet peeves, and tailoring products to their particular tastes take time with an element of trial and error involved. The longer that intelligence actively supports a particular customer and/or decision-maker, the more effective intelligence responses and products should be for their specific tastes.

Common Product and Presentation Elements

Intelligence products and responses are often created or crafted for a specific customer but will almost always have usefulness to a much wider audience. While the primary customer often sets specific requirements of what they want to see in a product, intelligence producers will also create and disseminate products with an eye toward greater dissemination. One of the most important questions an intelligence professional can ask themselves when creating a product or presentation is "Who else needs to know?"

In this context, intelligence producers should consider some of the universal standards and formats that are generally expected from consumers beyond the primary customer. By designing their products for a wider dissemination, common elements of writing, presentation, and organization should be considered in the creation of intelligence products. The following items to be included in most presentations and written products should be organized in the following order:

Eight common elements for intelligence products and presentations:

1. **Administrative Information:** Includes the classification (if necessary), titles and any subtitles, date and time, author, and originating organization. Can also include any specific requirement information that the product is responding to. Mostly written within the header of a written document or margins of a slide.
2. **BLUF:** Also known as an executive summary or a key read. Should only consist of a few concise statements or bulleted list. Can include several paragraphs of information if the report is a more formal or comprehensive product. Includes summarized information that provides the key analysis or judgments supported by the rest of the product in more detail. If the reader only reads and remembers one thing from this product, it should be included here.
3. **Background:** Background goes into more detail in support of the key analysis or judgment. Can include restating the requirement, an overview of the situation and environment, and a walk-through of events, i.e., a timeline. Should include

information and analysis gleaned from the preliminary analysis phase to help place the threat within the context of the environment, e.g., all or a portion of the threat map.

4. **Analysis:** A more detailed iteration of the analysis summarized in the bottom line. Includes a more detailed explanation of the analysis. Should include a walk-through of the analytic processes used in order to reach the stated conclusions. Can also include any unsubstantiated or discredited information or sources along with an explanation of why it was discounted.

5. **Next Steps:** Required for predictive analysis, meaning what is expected to take place relative to the threat in the near or far future. Often includes a time frame for the predictive analysis. For example, analysis may need to include what to expect or indicators to look for within the next 24–36 hours or 4–6 months, depending on the level of the requirement. Predictive analysis, placed within context of current situation and tied back to the requirement, can include several templated courses of action, e.g., most likely or probable, or most dangerous.

6. **Sources Used: Cite** the sources used for the analysis to include individual courses, databases, or sets of data, i.e., sources similar to an academic paper. Can use official reference formats for published works and adhere to any sourcing standards or formats within the intel organization. Can also include evaluations of sources using the different criteria listed in Chapter 5.

7. **Discussion:** Primarily included for active or collaborative products and presentations such as online products with an accompanied chat or discussion forum. Can include devil's advocacy, red-teaming efforts, or dissenting opinions if necessary. These additional sections are often included with more formal products.

8. **Final Administrative Elements:** Many formats require a reiteration of classification information as well as declassification information or authority. Can include author's name and point of contact information among other cataloging, keywords, and other meta tags associated with the product or presentation.

Often, written and product standards are implemented within different organizations. Standard Operating Procedures (SOPs) can dictate any number of parameters for authors and producers to follow. These standards will include most or all of the common elements for both operational and intelligence products. They should also consider methods and avenues for wider dissemination and accessibility of their intelligence. For the latter, the goal of supporting a wider consumer population has to balance the sensitivity, classification, and general security of the product of presentation.

Quality Control and Assurance

Creating and delivering effective intelligence requires additional measures to ensure quality. For this reason, many intelligence organizations rely on both Quality Control (QC) and Quality Assurance (QA) measures.

Quality Control (**QC**) is the act or process of checking the accuracy and overall quality of a product or service prior to delivering or disseminating intelligence. It is usually performed at the end of the Intelligence Operations Process, focusing specifically on an actual tangible product or deliverable. In some cases, QC checks can be made on a presentation by checking the actual product or by rehearsing prior to the event.

Whereas QC is product and presentation driven, QA is process driven. *Quality Assurance* (**QA**) is a term for measures that seek to ensure or improve quality throughout the entire intelligence operations and Intelligence Analysis Processes. While QC concentrates on the quality of the final deliverable, QA is much more comprehensive and looks at all of the actions, processes, and subprocesses conducted by the entire intelligence organization. As such, QA can be a periodic and can involve constant and persistent measures that can be incorporated into any part of the organization.

Depending on the size of the intelligence organization, QC and QA measures can range from being the secondary responsibility of designated personnel to the primary duty of a single person or team of persons. At the team or small group level, the responsibility for QC and QA is most often assigned as a specified or implied task of the team lead. In this manner, every product coming from that team is given a quick review by the team lead prior to delivery or dissemination. The team lead will also perform QA by periodically stepping back from operations and informally reviewing the effectiveness of the team across the various functions it performs. In this way, they can identify areas that need improvement and look for new ways to conduct their business more efficiently.

For organizations large enough to require several teams or have several divisions of teams, Quality Control and Assurance requires the creation of more formal measures. This will often involve dedicating one or more people with QC and QA responsibilities. Formalized QC and QA processes can be codified within an organization's SOPs and can include periodic or schedules reviews of any areas within the organization. Formal or semiformal reviews for quality can be conducted on collection, processing, or even the administrative and logistical processes of the organization.

Besides scheduled reviews, QA can also be conducted as needed or in direct response to an identified problem or dysfunction. For these more immediate or ad hoc reviews, the goal is to identify the root cause of a problem as soon as possible in order to mitigate and damage or further problems that result in other parts of the Intelligence Operations Process later on.

No matter the size of the intelligence organization, the designation of a Quality Assurance Manager (QAM) should also be considered. For smaller organizations, this is simply an additional duty of one of the team members. For larger organizations, this should be a full-time position that will often reside within the production management section and, in some cases, can be the actual production manager in dual-hatted role. The actual title of the QAM is not important, but the baseline responsibility of ensuring quality within each product and process throughout the organization is vital for the successful delivery of intelligence and the reputation of the organization to provide quality support to its customers.

Evaluation and Feedback

Tied directly to both QC and QA are measures that every intelligence organization must take to evaluate and receive feedback on their performance. From a QC perspective, garnering feedback is as simple as soliciting it from the customer after they've received the product or presentation. QA is distinctly different from QC in that it looks for feedback and evaluations of performance throughout the Intelligence Operations Process.

Since evaluation and feedback is conducted by people and entities, it is positioned to connect the customer, the collector, and the intelligence assets. As such, it is a form of communication itself and is conducted as a subprocess at various points during the overall process. Methods of effectively evaluating and providing feedback for intelligence operations, primarily by the customers, are discussed in more detail in Chapter 12.

Pitfalls of Delivering Intelligence

As stated throughout this chapter, delivering effective intelligence to a customer requires both an understanding the various aspects of the customer, their organization, and situation and the ability to choose and create the right product or presentation to meet their needs. Unfortunately, being able to do all of these things is not a guarantee of successful support. All intelligence professionals make mistakes or fail to adequately foresee or address an issue during the course of their work. Even the most accurate, insightful, and otherwise effective intelligence products and presentations can be doomed by mistakes or missteps made with their delivery.

TMA (Too Many Acronyms)
Dual Purpose Products
Death by PowerPoint
History of the World
Persuade v. Inform
So There I Was ...
Too Many Cooks
Slide Says This
Comic Sans
Politics

FIGURE 11.5   Ten pitfalls of delivering intelligence

The true remedy for improving and maintaining delivery of intelligence is continual experience. As everyone learns more from practice than rote memorization, experience helps to point out the subtleties of writing or presentation styles. As the intelligence professional spends more time delivering intelligence and interfacing with the customer, they will gain that valuable experience that will help them to continually improve areas of deficiency or maintain those skills that are up to standard.

With that, there are several common pitfalls in delivering intelligence that both experienced and inexperienced professionals should be aware of. The following list can be applied to both products and presentations and is not all inclusive.

1. **TMA (Too Many Acronyms):** Every line of work involving intelligence has their own language that is normal to those within it, but seemingly foreign to any outsiders or laypersons. This is often referred to as techspeak, nerdspeak, milspeak, or copspeak depending on the environment. Acronyms are routinely

used to abbreviate more complex ideas or technical jargon, but putting these into any intelligence products or presentation without proper context or explanation can quickly render an otherwise good intelligence product unintelligible. This includes using acronyms during oral presentations, where acronyms can sound similar to actual words. To make matters worse, some acronyms have more than one meaning or contain other acronyms within them. This problem can also be generational as text-based and instant messaging lexicons such as LOL, IMHO, and FAQ make their way into our daily language.

2. **Dual-Purpose Products:** Trying to deliver a presentation when a written document is needed and vice versa carries significant risks in missing the mark for the customer. Intelligence producers who do not understand the different purposes for text and graphic products are also signaling to a customer that they either don't understand the requirement or don't have an appreciation for delivering quality. Examples include presentation charts that are crammed with paragraphs of information or delivering simple diagrams or annotated imagery when a much more detailed text-based answer is required. Passing off a product designed as both a written document and a presentation may be convenient, but often ends up as a confusing hybrid.

3. **Death by PowerPoint:** Perhaps the most well-known pitfall is in overloading the customer with too much information in via presentation. Similar to the use of dual-use products, this is the tendency to cram too many ideas or items in a single chart or overloading an entire presentation with volumes of slides. Presentations are meant to present a few key ideas or concepts in a single chart, or several that are logically laid out in a presentation. Good presentations are combinations of text and graphics that are concisely organized and can be easily followed with the right amount of information. Bombarding the customer with entire operational plans or complex technical concepts in a presentation will ensure that they will miss key ideas, become bogged down in details, or simply lose interest.

4. **History of the World, Volume 1:** Intelligence products lacking conciseness that include too much superfluous, background, or supporting information as its main feature is of little use to a customer. Information that should normally be included only as backup can often obscure the bottom line and force the customer to do the extra work of sifting through it in order to find the key points that they really need. Akin to death by PowerPoint, intelligence producers who do not focus their products or presentations on the key ideas and concepts as a priority will lead their customers into thinking they don't actually understand what information is key in the first place. Even for those customers who specify they'd like to see all the details, organizing the less important pieces of information to backup slides or sections is critical for a ensuring the main assessments aren't lost in the chaff.

5. **Persuade Versus Inform:** Even well-written products and expertly delivered presentations are often betrayed by analysis that attempt to persuade a customer

instead of informing them. This occurs when an intelligence analyst or producer feels the need to change the mind of their customer toward their own perspective rather than let their customer make informed unfettered decisions. Intelligence products and presenters that attempt to persuade a customer will tend to leave out facts that may be contrary to their argument or indicate a different possibility. For customers to trust their intelligence support, they must be confident they are being presented with all the facts instead of one-sided talking points.

6. **So There I Was …:** Intelligence personnel, like their customers, develop experience and expertise in a variety of areas throughout their careers. Combined with ego, this experience can turn into a need to draw attention to themselves or display a condescending attitude, especially during presentations. References to themselves can be both blatant and subtle. No matter how much a Subject Matter Expert (SME) or experienced intelligence professional may think they are, making a product or presentation about themselves more than the subject at hand risks both the quality of the analysis and—in the long run—the customer's trust. The customer doesn't care about the analyst's trials and experiences; it is only that the product is trustworthy.

7. **Too Many Cooks:** While diversity of opinion is incredibly important during the Intelligence Analysis Process, including too many authors or presenters in delivery of intelligence risks the loss of a unified voice. Differing opinions are welcome in analysis, but they must be worked through prior to delivery. There are several group analytic techniques such as Devil's Advocacy and Group A/B Analysis that provide for a structured approach to this. Allowing differing opinions or delivery styles to persist in the delivery of intelligence will often lead to a conflicted or convoluted product or presentation. In the end, the customer will be forced to decide between the differing opinions when their intelligence asset couldn't say with confidence which was correct.

8. **Slide Says This:** A lack of speaking confidence or presentation skills can lead presenters of intelligence to fall back on parroting information from slides instead of standing on their own knowledge and expertise. Some of the poorest presenters simply read from slides line by line—bullet and paragraph. Hiding behind a presentation, no matter how well it is as a product, tells the customer that the presenter lacks the expertise or confidence in their own presentation abilities. Implicitly, it will also signal to the customer that there may be a lack of confidence in the analysis itself.

9. **Comic Sans:** Today's presentation documentation technology gives intelligence personnel new and unique ways to present their analysis in interesting, eye catching, and memorable ways. Unfortunately, many products and graphics presentations can be muddled by too many animations or cute fonts. A rule of thumb for creating intelligence products should be: *Just because you have the ability to include dozens of fonts or animations doesn't mean you need to include all of them.* These visual tricks are meant to highlight key points, but too many

are just distractions. This includes bullet points, slide transitions, texture, and imbedded imagery.

10. **Politics:** Political bias in an anathema to good intelligence and yet it frequently can find its way into an intelligence product or presentation. Every intelligence professional has a political opinion, perception, or bias; it cannot be eliminated. Instead, intelligence producers must use QC and QA measures to actively eliminate bias prior to delivery of intelligence. Politically biased products may contain accurate information but be betrayed how they are skewed to support a particular political bent. Even a subtle joke or reference to a politically charged topic during presentation will signal to a customer that their support may be skewed by a set of presumptions on the part of the analyst or presenter. A key method to combat this is to ensure reviews of materials are conducted by people with a different perspective or background of the original author.

All these pitfalls are largely the result of an intelligence producer losing focus or straying from the original purpose of their analysis—that is to provide support to a customer as articulated by their requirements and specifications. Intelligence products and presentations that are organized, concise, and well written are deemed so because they stayed true to the needs of the customer without extraneous opinions, arguments, or agendas.

Summary

As already demonstrated, a lot of effort goes into providing intelligence to the customer. It involves the work of many people, working in several different areas to deliver effective responses to customer requirements. The actual delivery of that intelligence is an often overlooked but critical part of the Intelligence Operations Process. Even the most expert, accurate, and timely analysis that is poorly delivered is going to be seen as ineffective and unhelpful. While constantly working to improve collection, processing, and analytic skills, intelligence personnel must also work to improve their ability to produce and deliver outstanding products and presentations.

Key Summary Points

1. Delivering intelligence is not part of the Analysis Process, but is a critical and often overlooked part of the Intelligence Operations Process
2. Delivering intelligence effectively to a customer requires understanding three critical aspects of the customer: The Supported Organization, The Current Situation, and the Decision-Maker themselves.
3. There are several methods for delivering intelligence, each associated with one of four critical skills that intelligence professionals must possess to be effective.

4. Intelligence professionals must always be aware of the eight common elements of intelligence products and presentations, but they must also be aware of many of the common pitfalls that increases the risks of an ineffectively delivery.

Discussion Questions

+   In understanding a supported decision-maker, what are some aspects of them that should be considered besides those areas listed in this chapter?
+   Which intelligence products are best suited for the military, commercial, and law enforcement environments, respectively? What are the major differences between these environments that should be considered when developing products?
+   Considering today's technology, what new ways of delivering intelligence can we foresee in the near future?
+   Are there any additional pitfalls worth noting for new intelligence personnel not listed in this chapter?

Chapter 12

Intelligence Design–Supporting Operations

- ▸ After completing this chapter, you will be able to:
- ▸ Be familiar with many of the important operations that support the Intelligence Operations Process, but are not necessarily part of it.
- ▸ Understand the difference between levels of operation and levels of analysis along with planning considerations related to each.
- ▸ Be familiar with the key concepts related to various supporting operations, including personnel manning, security, communications and situational awareness, collection, training and education, and customer support.

Supporting the Intelligence Operations Process

Understanding and using the Intelligence Operations Process comes with the understanding that it is not the sole process taking place within the organization or center. Surrounding and in support of the Intelligence Operations Process are several crucial operations and functions. Financial operations ensure the costs for intelligence people, facilities, and materials are paid. Personal, physical, and information security operations, respectively, protect people as well as the facilities and intelligence related data and information involved. Recruitment, advancement, education, and training of personnel find the right people for the job and professionally develop them once they are on board.

Supporting operations are often overlooked in intelligence studies as many of their functions are not intelligence-specific. Many of these operations are also not conducted by intelligence personnel. In the largest intelligence organizations, personnel with specialties such as human resources, financial and logistics, and IT personnel among other career areas will run operations alongside the main effort.

Supporting operations are required to operate at the same peak efficiency as the Intelligence Operations Process. If there is a dysfunction or breakdown in any of these supporting processes, the ability of the organization to provide intelligence support eventually ceases along with it. An often-used statement related to logistics as a support operation is that amateurs talk about tactics, but professional study logistics.[1] Intelligence Operations Process may be the tip of the arrow, but it's completely ineffective without the shaft, fletching, and bow all working together as one.

Similar to the Intelligence Operations Process, supporting operations within an intelligence organization involve the same four common elements: data, tools, people, and processes. While the makeup of each of these is unique to a specific organization, they do have some of the same patterns and similarities across organizations that share similar missions, purposes, and operating environments.

Planning Considerations for Intelligence and Supporting Operations

There are several significant characteristics somewhat unique to intelligence operations that require careful consideration of those planning and performing their support. These characteristics can be considered variables that will set the parameters or change a supporting operation depending on their status. Support operations from personnel manning, security, or collection and requirements management can be vastly different depending on the level of operation, levels of analysis performed, and the associated relationship of the intelligence organization to the customer.

Planning Consideration: Levels of Operation

Planning the necessary actions to support intelligence operations requires understanding several operational aspects of both the customer and their organization. The most important of these is the level at which the customer/decision-maker and supporting intelligence organizations operate. Whether the customer is operating at the strategic, operational, or tactical level, intelligence support must tailor their organization, business rhythm, and customer relationship to that level.

In plain terms, *strategic*-level customers conduct their planning and operations to achieve long-term overarching goals and objectives. They often include decisions and events of national or international importance and will encapsulate several operational and untold numbers of tactical operations. Most national intelligence agencies are found at the strategic level as are security and competitive intelligence functions within large multinational corporations. Any customer planning that requires looking out months to years into the future requires the support of strategic-level intelligence.

---

1   This quote is attributed to U.S. Army General Omar Bradley, U.S. Marine Corps General Robert H. Barrow, and the Israeli military historian and theorist Martin van Creveld.

At the lowest level, *tactical*-customers are usually leaders that are responsible for decisions and events that have local and more immediate outcomes. This is the level where events happen, targets are affected, arrests are made, and combat occurs. This level differs from the strategic level as it includes individual and small group actions instead of overarching campaigns. Tactical operations are usually supported by small teams of intelligence personnel and are focused in real-time or near real-time information with predictive analysis measured in minutes, hours, and, maybe, a few days forward at the most.

The *operational*-level customers of intelligence are situated in-between strategic and tactical operations. From a planning standpoint, their operations can encapsulate several tactical operations or be itself a minor campaign within an overall strategy such as security along a shipping line or a reduction in drug crimes within a large metropolitan area. Customers here are not as concerned about what's around the next corner or hill, but they are concerned about how many corners and hills they must traverse and who is trying to thwart their efforts. Intelligence teams in support at this level are somewhat larger than their tactical counterparts and can consist of standalone units or task forces. They can even include interagency participation, but very few of them operate with complete independence. Operational-level intelligence can also include ad hoc or temporary teams of experts, aka tiger teams, assigned to address a specific area within the operation such as concentrative on a particular drug lord or cartel within a war of drugs. Predictive analysis is measured in days and weeks, but rarely more than 180 days.

Intelligence operations have several distinct variables depending on the level of operations they normally work within. From the types of products that are normally requested to the types of intelligence organizations that are needed to service those requests, intelligence organizations will find some distinct planning and management challenges at each level. For example, intelligence organizations at the strategic level are obviously more robust, expensive, and require numerous divisions and subdivisions for each of the require specializations. Tactical-level intelligence requires small, agile, and flexible teams that are able to handle all their tasks with a handful of men. A few very broad-based characteristics for each level are listed in Figure 12.1.

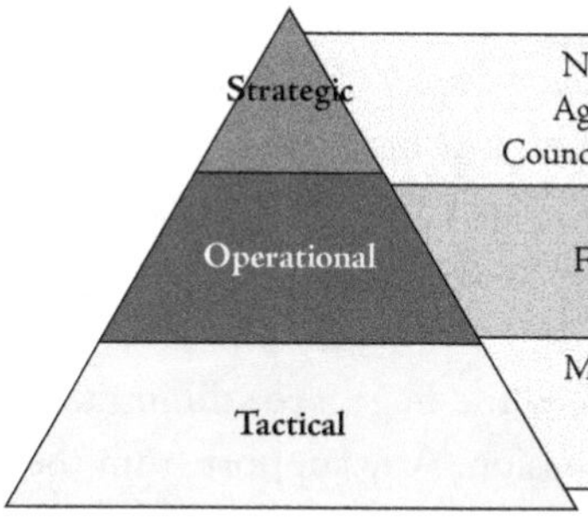

	Quantity of Responses	Types of Intelligence Organizations	Product Examples	Level of Detail/ Specialization
Strategic		National and Defense Intel Agencies, National Security Council, Service Level Agencies	National Intelligence Estimates, Presidential Decision Briefs	High
Operational		Joint Intel Centers, Fusion Centers, Joint Intel Task Forces,	Threat Profiling, Indications and Warnings, Ops Intel Estimates	Medium
Tactical		Military Intelligence Units, Tactical Intel Cells and Investigative Teams	Tactical Intel Estimates, Name Vetting, High Value Target and Person Lists	Low

FIGURE 12.1   Intelligence and levels of operations

Planning Consideration: Width and Depth of Analytic Support

Because of the size and complexity of their operations, intelligence support for customers at strategic and operational levels requires higher levels of detail and specialization. For example, a customer' request for intelligence relating to an adversary's nuclear weapons development program requires analysts who possess subject matter expertise that can be dedicated to answer the customer's specific technical questions. Individuals working within a federal level agency can be assigned such niche topics as a single terrorist group or gang, the financial structure of a drug cartel, or the various communications emanating from a particular country or region. This is possible because of the environment that strategic-level intelligence organizations offer.

The robust and specialized intelligence of this sort highlights an important distinction between the types of intelligence organizations. Not only must planners understand the normal depth of analysis that is routinely expected from their intelligence assets, they must also understand the width expected of the entire organization as a whole, i.e., the number and variety of topics that must be covered with both collection assets and analytic expertise. An organization or team, e.g., that is primarily responsible for creating a daily read file or executive summaries, would be known as having mile-wide, inch-deep coverage. Conversely, a small team of a few analysts that specialize in the inner workings and detailed decision-making processes of a single group would be seen as having inch-wide, mile-deep responsibilities.

The largest intelligence organizations, such as the Central Intelligence Agency (CIA), Defense Intelligence Agency (DIA), National Geospatial-Intelligence Agency (NGA), and National Security Agency (NSA) are in effect, consolidations of a huge number of intelligence specialists and subject matter experts. As individuals, analysts working in these environments are expected to have mile-deep depth while the agency as a whole is expected to have global, i.e., mile-wide coverage. Within strategic-level organizations, consolidating resources and expertise within a single agency or within several federated agencies helps to conserve these resources and centralize control of assets.

With the ability to consolidate personnel and resources at the highest levels, strategic level organizations have the ability to provide not only intelligence to national decision-makers as their primary mission but also varying levels of support to customers at the operational or even tactical level. This is a trend that has become more pronounced since 9/11 as strategic-level organizations shift resources and assets, dedicating them to reinforce operational or tactical operations for the most high-priority missions and customers. In some instances, providing remote or even physical co-location of assets with the lower-level customer is also possible, providing national-level capabilities straight to the tip of the spear.

Unfortunately, the few strategic-level organizations, while huge, are still limited in their ability to support every tactical or operational mission. Any support from these agencies to a lower-level organization is highly restricted and prioritized according to the urgency of the mission and available resources. As detailed in Chapter 3, the limits to strategic-level intelligence in providing substantive support on everything to everyone has led many tactical-, operational-, and even other strategic-level customer to create their own intelligence asset within their own organization.

At the other end of the spectrum, tactical intelligence teams must rely on a few personnel to have a general understanding of a lot of different threat aspects. Tactical intelligence responses are much more informal and therefore much more numerous than responses at higher levels. Time and resources that can be committed to quality-control measures is extremely limited. Intelligence responses can range from simple products such as an Intelligence Estimate and can also be satisfied by quick verbal answers to questions. Tactical intelligence also requires frequent, if not constant, contact with the customers and decision-makers they support. As tactical operations are on 24 hours a day, so is the required intelligence support.

Lower-level intelligence organizations cannot normally support analysis at the higher levels. Tactical intelligence teams are not manned, equipped, or usually experienced enough to support strategic-level decision-makers. As they are usually part of the supported organization, their primary customer is their owning organization first with almost no capability left over to support anyone else.

Raw information and intelligence collected at lower levels is routinely sent higher, but usually incorporated into a strategic-level product by someone at that level. Intelligence at higher levels is much more easily designed to filter down their finished products. As this type of intelligence is designed to assist many tactical intelligence teams, they will not be tailored to the exact specifications of each unit or decision-maker's request.

Customer Relationships Relative to the Level of Operation

As noted in Chapter 3, the rapid and continuing expansion of intelligence into other sectors of our society, i.e., law enforcement, state and local government, and the commercial sector is resulting in the proliferation of tactical-level intelligence teams. More and more decision-makers who have identified the need to understand and counter their own threats have turned to creating small- to mid-sized intelligence teams that answer their requirements as their top or only priority.

Because of their size and relatively limited capabilities to sustain themselves, intelligence teams at the tactical level are almost always an organic part of the organization they support and therefore are much more numerous than their strategic-level siblings. In the U.S. Army alone, there is an intelligence organization, however small, within each division, brigade, and battalion. Some combat companies or special operations teams can include even smaller intelligence elements of only one or two personnel within them.

Being an organic part of the supported organization requires that intelligence is almost exclusively conducted to satisfy internal requirements. This is also known as being in direct support, but in the case of an organic intelligence asset, this is a permanent relationship. In return, the support organization takes care of most, if not all, of the supporting operations, e.g., personnel, security, sustainment and logistics, and communications. For the most part, tactical intelligence teams are part of their supported organization, because it frees up personnel to concentrate their limited capabilities to support to their key decision-makers.

Going from tactical to operational to strategic intelligence support requires exponentially higher amounts of resources in terms of collection and processing systems along with dedicated subject matter expertise. Besides analysis, almost every aspect of running an intelligence operation at the strategic level from quality control, budget, human resources, legal, to public affairs requires extensive resources, management, and oversight. The larger and more autonomous an intelligence organization becomes, the more they are therefore responsible for providing these supporting operations in order to function effectively.

Strategic-level organizations having robust capabilities can provide both direct and indirect support to multiple customers simultaneously. Indirect support is a relationship where the supporting intelligence organization is conducting collection and analysis that a customer can use for decision-making, but they are not subordinate or specifically answerable to that customer's requirements.

As organizations get to the size requiring thousands of personnel, the primary function of intelligence must remain the priority and not get overwhelmed by supporting processes. This may seem like a relatively straight forward, but just as intelligence personnel can lose sight of the fact that everything they do is in support of a customer, support personnel can likewise lose sight that the primary mission of their area is to support intelligence and ensure it continues to work effectively for the customer. The true sign of a successful supporting function within an intelligence organization is when it is not noticed; i.e., intelligence personnel can concentrate on working the Intelligence Operations Process without fear of some part of it breaking down due to inoperable communications, logistics, or lack of security.

Planning Consideration: Levels of Analysis

Similar to levels of operation, intelligence managers should also understand the different levels in which their organization primarily conducts analysis. These levels are distinctly different from the levels of operation and are much more fluid in terms of analytic processes. Analysis can be conducted at the micro, macro, or global levels.[2] The initial level of which and analyst works is usually dictated by the requirement.

Micro-level analysis involves focusing on a single entity, e.g., a node, person, or event along with the entities that can be directly or indirectly associated to that event. Requirements calling for micro-level analysis could ask for information related to a key individual such as a faction leader, CEO, or politician with products that look like tailored biographies or summaries of specific events.

---

2   These different levels of analysis were first noted in 1999 by Dr. Eileen Preisser, a senior intelligence scientist working within the Information Dominance Center (IDC) run by what was then called the U.S. Army's Land Information Warfare Activity or LIWA. It was used extensively during several analysis programs in support of both Counterterrorism and Counterintelligence missions during her tenure there.

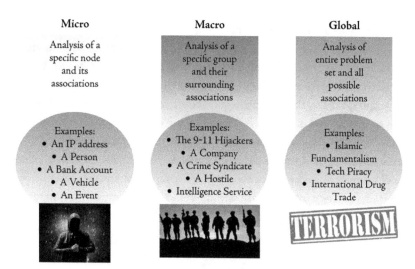

Micro	Macro	Global
Analysis of a specific node and its associations	Analysis of a specific group and their surrounding associations	Analysis of entire problem set and all possible associations
Examples: • An IP address • A Person • A Bank Account • A Vehicle • An Event	Examples: • The 9-11 Hijackers • A Company • A Crime Syndicate • A Hostile Intelligence Service	Examples: • Islamic Fundamentalism • Tech Piracy • International Drug Trade

FIGURE 12.2   Levels of intelligence analysis

Macro-level analysis is similar to micro-level analysis but focuses on a single organization or even a loosely tied group of individuals instead of a single entity or person. It can also be focused on a series of related events such as a string of crimes or actions and events related to that single group. Threat Profiling is most closely related to macro-level analysis as it organizes and assists in prioritizing other analytic techniques to answer requirements about threat groups as opposed to individuals.

Global-level analysis is somewhat different from the other two levels because instead of people or groups, it focuses on trends, possible patterns, or idiosyncrasies related to an entire problem set. Global analysis answers requirements that transcend one individual or threat group. Intelligence requirements that involve global-level analysis include looking at phenomenon such as international human trafficking, the radical Islamic terror groups in the Maghreb, or the contraband weapons trade on the dark web.

There is no straight correlation between the level of the operation and any corresponding level of analysis. Depending on the level of the supported operation, the level of analysis will routinely shift or jump back and forth from one level to another and back again. Analysts who begin their work answering requirement at one level may find that they need to jump up or down levels multiple times during the Intelligence Analysis Process. By jumping levels during the analytic process, even if momentarily, analysts can gain a different perspective or identify and explore a previously unrevealed facet outside of their requirement that could affect the customer's operation.

For example, a micro-level requirement asking for the biography and potential decision-making processes of a prominent drug-cartel leader would require preliminary analysis into the group they head up. This would require analysts to jump to the macro level in order to get a better understanding of the entire group. Even further, initial returns may require a further jump to the global level when the analyst decides that they need a better understanding of the overall activities of Central America cartels altogether.

Conversely, analysis at the global level could identify a previously unknown group or individual that the analyst decides should be looked into or "drilled-down." Jumping down to the micro level would then allow the analyst to get a better understanding of who this person is and how they would affect the operation.

In a very general sense, the higher the level of operations, the more flexibility there will be to jump from one level of analysis to the next during the analysis process. Lacking any amount of real flexibility in their environment, intelligence teams at the tactical level are almost exclusively focused on macro-level analysis. Their requirements are centered on the immediate threats to the supported organization often amidst 24-hour, fast-paced, and often dangerous or intentionally lethal. As more and more specialization occurs at the operational and strategic levels, a correlating ability of an intelligence effort to jump from one level to another during analysis is more frequent. This can happen both concurrently and multiple times during the analysis process.

Understanding the amount of flexibility an intelligence asset has in moving from one level of analysis to another should be important to managers who need to ensure their personnel are working effectively for the right level of operation. Gaining a different perspective on a problem or identifying a new area of concern is a valuable method in analysis, but in spending too much time working outside of what the requirement asks for can consume valuable time and resources.

This phenomenon is termed "Going down the Rabbit Hole" in analysis. It occurs at the tactical level when analysts spend too much time indulging their interest in the history and strategic considerations of a problem set instead of answering their assigned requirements directly. Conversely, analysts working at the strategic level who have a habit of identifying and then drilling down into one unrelated area after another are also burning limited time and resources available.

Analysts are trained to routinely and effectively follow where the information takes them, but experienced analysts and supervisors of more junior analysts need to be able to identify when there is time or resources available to explore other levels of analysis. More importantly, they must also understand when it is not useful or constructive. They will then need to guide or direct their analysts back to the pertinent requirements at hand.

Planning and Organizing Support to Intelligence Operations

Taking each of these important considerations into account, intelligence leaders, and managers at all levels of operations and analysis can more effectively identify both the implied and specified tasks within their organization and plan and manage effective supporting operations. The most logical way to present some of the most important supporting operations is to do so in the same manner the U.S. military designates staff elements within their command structure: 1 = Personnel, 2 = Intelligence and Security, 3 = Operations, 4 = Logistics, 5 = Civil/Public Affairs, 6 = Communications, 7 = Information Operations.

Some of these areas do not directly apply or relate to support operations within intelligence organizations such as operations (redundant) and information operations (not applicable), but this method serves as a standardized set of broad categories to help planners approach their management of all their required supporting operations. While each intelligence organization will have unique circumstances and parameters for supporting their own operation, a few of the most important support operations are worth noting.

Personnel Manning

Many personnel considerations are discussed in detail in Chapter 7 including skillsets based upon size and specialty of an organization. With these considerations in mind, management of intelligence personnel requires plans and operations in order to recruit, schedule, maintain, and professionally grow a qualified workforce. Each has some unique considerations depending on the mission and needs of the organization.

Business Hours Versus Continuous Operations

At all levels of operation, intelligence is primarily a continuous operation. Events at the tactical and operational levels have no downtime as their customers rely on up to the minute analysis at all hours of the day and week. Intelligence is also conducted continuously at the strategic level in centers conducting constant collection, monitoring, and on-call analysis in support of both lower level operations and crisis situations. Intelligence in support of continuous operations could include combat or crisis scenarios as well as a variety of monitoring requirements of various network security or incident watch centers.

Operating during normal business occurs for analysis that is not as time sensitive and fulfills more routine or in-depth requirements. Intelligence operating at business hours is normally in an office environment creating products such as daily reports, national intelligence estimates, or other products containing macro- and global-level analysis. Intelligence created during business hours involves events and information that is more persistent and not subject to significant hourly changes.

No matter the hours of operation, personnel have to sleep. Human factors such as eating, sleeping, exercise, family, training, vacation, etc. all have to be accounted for in personnel management. Depending on the situation, some of these issues can be disregard for limited periods of time but have to be taken into account eventually. For example, in a tactical environment, personnel can go without sleep for extended periods but soon start to lose their mental capacity to accurately perform even some of the basic cognitive functions. The requirement to eat or take short breaks is on an even tighter timeline.

While a successful manning plan will often go unnoticed, a dysfunctional or broken plan will be glaring and result in problems in several other aspects, including performance, quality, and morale. Providing effective personnel support requires an understanding of the mission and the environment, but it also requires planning and active management of personnel throughout daily and crisis periods.

Creating a manning plan, intelligence managers must start with the individual position and how often needs to be filled. A majority of manning requirements fit into the following five categories with a few exceptions:

- **Normal Business Operations:** Positions are usually filled 8 hours a day, 5 days a week. Barring replacement requirement for critical leadership positions, these can be filled indefinitely by a single person.
- **Extended Hours:** Required for heavier than usual influx of requirements, increasing hours from 8 per day up to 12. Can also increase days per week to 6 or 7 days. Still only filled with a single person per position but can be sustained for weeks to a few months at most. Deployed environments can extend this time frame further, but personnel will eventually need to be rotated out or go back to a normal schedule after several months.
- **Surge Periods:** Used for extended crisis situations where a single position needs to be filled for up to 12 hours a day, 7 days a week. Carries the option to have two persons fill one position, each working 12-hour shifts for a constant fill. Sustainable for only a few weeks within an office environment, or for up to a few months in a deployed environment within planned breaks and downtime during lulls in operational tempo.
- **Tactical Fill with Overlap:** Except for basic human needs, a position in this environment is constantly filled except for sleep. Can be sustained by a single person per position for a few weeks at most without breaks or for several months with significant downtime factored in periodically. Can also be filled by two person working 8–12 hours a day for a longer period of time similar to a surge period.
- **Constant Fill:** Used for positions that require continuous manning 24 hours a day. If only one person works 24 hours a day, they are no longer effective as analysts after a single day and usually mentally exhausted for a while afterward. Manning a 24-hour position indefinitely requires four people working 40 hours per week with one person working an additional 8 hours once every 4 weeks. Building in overlap, vacation, training, and other administrative requirements can bump the assigned number up to five people per position.

Each of these categories for manning can be adapted and tailored. Caveats and exceptions to manning plans are numerous. Most tactical environments by their very nature involve continuous operations. Strategic environments can call for either continuous operations, such as a watch or incident center, or operate along normal business hours. Planning for personnel manning must take into account the numerous differences between operating on a 24-hour versus an 8-hour basis.

Deployed environments allow for extended hours since personnel don't need to take much time for personal lives—but the drawbacks are numerous in terms of sustainment. Planning factors include requirements for human factors such as sleep, food, shelter and physical security. In addition, manning must take into account experience, rank, experience, and qualifications of personnel as well as the skills required to deliver intelligence through products or presentation.

Operational Security

The security of an intelligence operation is an ongoing requirement. In many areas of society, operational security is simply known as OPSEC, which covers the protection of a mission or organization from the prying eyes of their threats. In a basic sense, security means the protection of the operation along with the people, facilities, and information used to conduct intelligence.

For smaller intelligence teams, security requires coordination with their parent or supported organization and using the team's very limited resources to contribute to the overall security of that organization. For larger organizations and agencies, security involves detailed planning and the dedication of an extensive amount of resources to secure vital areas. Like other supporting operations, effective security measures are unobtrusive and allow intelligence operations to continue without hindrance or disruption. The best security programs quite often go unnoticed by those who benefit from it.

No matter the level, security planning and management involves protective measures in three major areas, all of which require varying levels of time and resources committed to them:

CHART 12.1   Areas of Security for Intelligence Planning

Type of Security	Description
PHYSICAL SECURITY	Involves the creation and operation of a secure physical space for intelligence operations to be conducted. Includes facility security, barriers, active and passive protections, and safeguarding of classified, proprietary, or otherwise protected information. Also involves dedicated security personnel, which usually requires armed and trained specialists.
PERSONNEL SECURITY	Involves clearances, permissions, and background investigations into the personnel who will be entrusted with collecting, storing, and using classified and protected information as well as working on classified or protected operations. Requires extensive coordination with personnel management experts as well as with external organizations with investigative capabilities.
INFORMATION SECURITY	Involves the direct protection of classified or protected information. Can include physical or hard copy information protection, but more and more is associated exclusively with protection of networks, databases, and servers where information resides in digital form.

Most security plans are comprehensive in that they have to cover all three areas adequately. This may seem simple enough, but every security plan is subject to competing interests within the organization. Security is not the primary mission or function of an intelligence organization, but it is doomed to fail in all other aspects if security is inadequate. Security plans must take into account the follow specific considerations:

1. **Security Requires Intelligence and Counterintelligence Support:** Just as a decision-maker requires intelligence to counter and defeat their threats, planners must also understand the threats to the security of the intelligence operation. Counterintelligence experts can cover many of three areas that need protection and must be supported with collection and analysis of the threats they must protect against.

2. **Security Must Always Be Successful:** Those who wish to attack, harm, hack, degrade, steal, or otherwise defeat an organization only have to defeat their security one time in order to be successful. Security forces and planning must continually look at potential avenues of attack from all types of threats using imagination, lessons learned, and analysis of the threat in terms of profile elements. Security cannot be everywhere at all times, so using the profiles of their various threats, planners must be able to identify critical areas where their limited resources must be applied.

3. **Excessive Security Can Hamper Operations:** Security plans must strike a balance between protecting operations and hampering them to the point that they ineffective. Planners must ensure their security plans are not self-defeating, being so burdensome that personnel spend more time working with required security processes than actually doing the work assigned to them. Under this and many other competing requirements, security planners have to consider the secondary and tertiary effects on the operation they are supposed to protect.

4. **Security Personnel Planning:** Security plans, especially for ad hoc or crisis situations, can often require increasing the number of security personnel in given areas. As organizations simply can't hire qualified security personnel for short periods of time, they will either have to borrow from another or higher organization or temporarily assign their other personnel to the job. The latter will always result in reduced capabilities where these personnel were pulled from. Overall personnel manning plans for intelligence operations must always take into account the drain on personnel that security plans require to be successful.

5. **Actions Before, During, and After Security Compromise:** Just as organized threats include actions required leading up to, during, and after a breach of an organization, security plans must include the same. The goal of security planning is not only to stop any attacks or breaches, but they must also be designed to thwart, disrupt, or discourage threats beforehand. Security plans must also include measures to be taken immediately after a successful breach in order to stop the attack and mitigate the damage as quickly as possible. Further on, security plans must also include immediate measures that must be taken to quickly recover. Getting operations back to normal, mitigating the loss of data, and shoring up network defenses are part of longer term plans, and also require a substantial amount of resources for planners to consider.

6. **Include a Plan for Insider Threats:** The damage caused by an insider, those either causing accidents or acting with malicious intent from inside an organization can be just a devastating to operations as an external threat or intrusion. Insiders are already behind many of the security walls meant for external threats. The same efforts taken to provide an open and unfettered work environment to personnel will always be vulnerable to intentional and unintentional disruption. Planners must include personnel security, not just as a program that provides clearances for individuals to access the work environment but as a means to monitor and identify potential risks as an ongoing requirement.

7. **Include Periodic Testing and Assessment of Security:** Even the best security plans on paper will be ineffective if they only rely on passively monitoring entry points, security clearances, and network firewalls. Active security requires much more effort and assigned resources. Active security includes periodic checks and vulnerability assessments into their overall plan. Testing of security plans through both a black hat (threat) and white hat (consultant) perspective will reveal many risks, weaknesses, and outright vulnerabilities that can never be identified by planning alone. Often, an organization will need to coordinate with external subject matter expertise for periodic support.

8. **Avoid Competing and Conflicts of Interest:** Security plans and personnel are under a tremendous amount of pressure from competing interests within their organization. Supervisors don't like burdensome regulations, and personnel will routinely subvert security policies and directives to make easier work. Planners must be constantly aware of these competing interests. They must also ensure their personnel, and plans are able to withstand pressure from above and subversion from below. To help set up a semi-autonomous environment for security personnel in larger organizations, full-time security personnel are often placed within their own section, not beholden to an intelligence operations chief or similar midlevel supervisor.

Supporting Operations: Communications and Situational Awareness

Intelligence analysts, especially those working deep within the catacombs of an intelligence center, often refer to themselves as mushrooms. In general terms, it means they are kept in the dark both literally and figuratively and fed manure (and other associated terms) every so often. The underlying cause of this perception is a persistent lack of and misunderstanding of both leadership and management within some intelligence leaders at every level. Intelligence draws in people of all stripes, some of which are able to rise to leadership positions through skills and expertise, but not necessarily through leadership or management skills.

Among the other desirable attributes of an effective leader are those associated with communications, i.e., keeping people informed and aware of what's happening around them. It is strongly tied to a critical requirement of all leaders to take care of their people. From the first-line supervisor to the director level and beyond, leadership and effective management are the tools to take care of people. Intelligence personnel work harder, have higher morale and retention, and show more innovation, imagination, and inspiration if they possess a working understanding of the organization's mission and vision as conveyed by effective leadership.

Intelligence personnel require an understanding of the issues and challenges that affect them on a day-to-day basis. This includes those items that will have both a direct and indirect effect on them as well as situations that will require them to react or adjust to changes. Having a high degree of situational awareness in this manner becomes an implied and ongoing support requirement of intelligence leadership at every level.

There are several tools or avenues available to the intelligence supervisor, given the characteristics of the work environment and level of operation. The ability to communicate information for situational awareness differs highly between 24-hour tactical operations and regular work hours in an office environment. Information can be delivered as a read-file, web-posting, or presentation for those personnel working remotely or during nonstandard hours, but the best method of instilling a situational awareness in personnel is in person.

Situational awareness briefings or products can be formal or informal and are often given different names. More formally, these meetings are often called Battle Update Briefs (BUBs) for military personnel or roll-call for law enforcement. They can also be called shift-change briefs during a period of overlap between outgoing and incoming personnel within a 24-hour operation. The most informal method practiced is often called a stand-up meeting, where personnel will actually stand within a small designated area. This last method implies a meeting so short that there no need to sit for it.

Every organization will have the format that best fits the needs of their mission and situation. Some can be standardized to the point that they are codified within a Standard Operating Procedure (SOP). No matter the format, there are several topics that can be covered including the following.

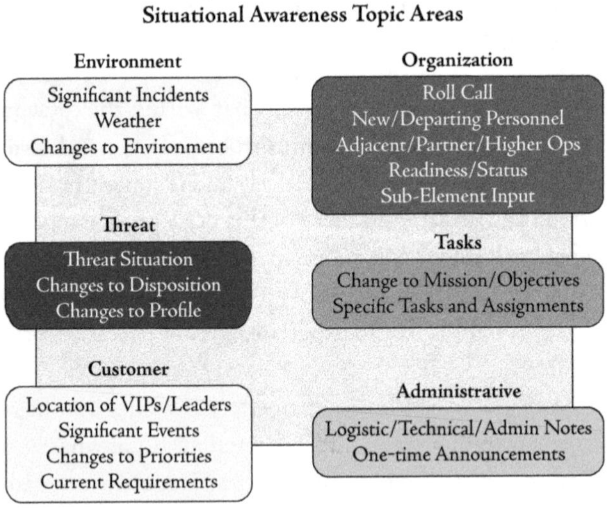

Situational Awareness Topic Areas

FIGURE 12.3   Situational awareness topic areas

With the variety of topics available, it is important to understand that update briefings are not meant to be long and drawn out nor free-for-alls in terms of who speaks or presents. They are conducted in an orderly and often standardized process by experienced individuals—usually by the organization's leadership or by someone such as a designated briefer or facilitator who is able to include input from leadership. If there is a topic of coordination or contention between two attendees, they are usually asked to continue their discussion afterwards so as not to tied everyone else up listening to them.

Supporting Operations: Assigning Tasks and Responsibilities

Members of an intelligence team are all individual contributors to the accomplishments and success of the team. In turn, each team combines their efforts with the rest of their organization to provide intelligence support to customers. As explored in Chapter 7, intelligence organizations make specific use of different intelligence specialties and areas of expertise. Managers place these people within a structure that provides the most effective way for them to work.

Creating an efficient work environment for intelligence operations requires both leadership and management skills. While leadership is focused on fostering a positive climate, motivating personnel, and emphasizing a unity of effort in moving the organization forward, management skills are focused on the running of the organization and ensuring all the different pieces of it are working together in a synchronized manner. One of the critical aspects of organizational management is in assigning duties and responsibilities to personnel.

Every intelligence position should have well-written and concise duties and responsibilities assigned to them. These duties and responsibilities define the job and are frequently used as job descriptions for vacancies and resumes for those who currently work or have previously worked that position. It can be a written paragraph or a simple bullet list of the details of the areas that position is responsible for.

This list will usually comprise both duties, in the form of specified individual tasks, as well as responsibilities that are more general in nature. Within their responsibilities are many implied tasks that the holder of the position must identify and prioritize themselves. While tasks are usually included for simple and limited functions, responsibilities assign parameters, giving the holder the freedom to develop their own plans and courses of action on how best to carry them out.

In the U.S. Army, the duties and responsibilities for both individuals and units are codified by a Mission Essential Task List (METL). Similarly for the Navy and Marine Corps, these lists of both individual and collective tasks are called Naval Tactical Task List (NTTL) and Marine Corps Tasks (MCTs), respectively.

Whether they are new to an already up and running organization or creating a new intelligence team from scratch, managers must ensure that their personnel are working in a manner that is synchronized with the team and that their team or teams are in tune with the mission, vision, and goals of the higher organization. As shown in Figure 12.4, both individual and collective tasks should be tied into a higher organization's areas of responsibility in a way intelligence personnel are focused on the same requirements and missions of the team. This may seem self-evident for intelligence operations, but disconnects between individual and team priorities of work within an organization can often be attributed to problems in either defining or adhering to assigned tasks and responsibilities.

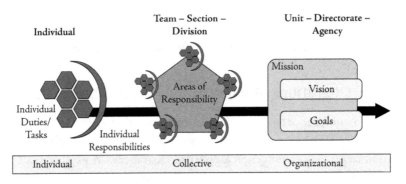

FIGURE 12.4   Task and responsibility relationships

Assigning tasks and responsibilities to the individual positions, teams, or other organizations within their area of responsibility provides the following benefits to intelligence managers:

1. **Unity of Effort:** Assigning tasks allows managers to more easily ensure the work of their personnel is effectively tied into their higher organization—be it a parent unit, directorate or agency. This will help the intelligence manager to identify disconnects, gaps in required responsibilities, and, perhaps more importantly, where redundancy occurs.

2. **Reduce Risk and Waste:** Managers must also ensure that tasks and responsibilities are clearly understood by all their personnel and adhered to during everyday operations. Depending on the organization, they should also be revisited and updated on an annual or semiannual basis.

3. **Identify the Right Balance for Subordinate Work Priorities:** Managers can more easily balance between these two types of assignments—tasks versus responsibilities for each of their personnel. A job description heavily weighted with tasks over responsibilities has very little flexibility or autonomy, and therefore is normally associated with new, entry-level, or lower ranking positions. On the other hand, merely assigning tasks to a person without tying them to overall responsibilities or contributions to the team can be demeaning, showing a lack of trust or indication of micro-management, especially for higher-level positions.

4. **Codify Positions, Not Persons:** Duties and responsibilities should be developed for a position, not a person. Every individual has a unique set of skills and experience, but people change positions quite frequently. Understanding and working with the job descriptions for a position is a much more stable approach and not reliant upon the ability of a particular person to work that position from one day to the next.

Lessons in Intelligence:
Resolving Personal Conflicts

As a program and portfolio manager for intelligence training while working for Lockheed Martin, I was experiencing the rapid growth of my primary contract—to provide training to the U.S. Army Intelligence & Security Command in which I managed their training program called Foundry. Starting with 7 instructors in 2002, we doubled in size twice, expanding to 14 instructors the next year and to about 30 instructors the following year.

While this was a result of the success of our instructors training Army intelligence soldiers and other DoD personnel, these two expansions also led to many management and leadership problems among our ranks.

One of the most significant problems was the increase in personal conflicts between my managers. As both leaders of instructor teams and continuing to train as senior instructors themselves, I found that interpersonal relations between several of them were growing more and more strained. Incidents were occurring where one manager was stepping into the others' areas, while another would take it upon themselves to provide quality control for other instructors' work, no matter whose team they were on. Arguments took place and tempers flared on several occasions. After giving some time and room for a few of the managers to work out their differences to no avail, I began looking into the root cause of the problem myself.

I quickly hypothesized that the problem most likely lay in a general lack of understanding of who was responsible for what amidst all the recent growth that had taken place. To combat this, I waited until our next team meeting to give all my instructors a homework assignment. Each instructor was required to list out their current duties and responsibilities as they saw them. I told them to list everything they could think of in a bullet format and that there were no wrong answers. From there, I would evaluate and edit each so that all similar positions would be the same with the exception of assignments of side or additional duties for many of the senior personnel.

Just as I had suspected, as the lists came in, I saw that many of the senior instructors/team leads had conflated what they thought they were responsible for. A few of them were taking responsibility for many areas that were actually the responsibility of my technical and training managers. While this showed great initiative that I didn't want to squelch, it also resulted in most of the personnel problems within the team. After rewriting each of them and re-issuing each person's duties and responsibilities to the entire team, I spent the next several days repairing both the bruised egos and initial confusion that I knew would result. After a few weeks, the problems lessened and interpersonal conflicts decreased by a significant amount.

Supporting Operations: Intelligence Collection Operations

Collecting data and information about threats plays a critical part in supporting intelligence operations. While there are numerous sources that can be available to help satisfy intelligence requirements, someone or something has to actually obtain that information for analysis. Of all the other supporting operations for intelligence, collection is the most extensive. It involves its own set of organizations, collection platforms, and plans with funding levels that far surpass all the other steps of the Intelligence Operations Process. Collection operations run concurrent to analysis and production and is driven by both specific and general or indirect requirements.

As previously discussed, intelligence customers pass their requirements to their supporting intelligence asset or organization. If the customer owns their own intelligence asset; e.g., it is within the organization they command, manage, or control, they task that asset. If they do not own the asset such as if it was at a higher echelon or external to their organization altogether, support must be requested and managed in turn by the owner receiving the request. Some organizations will have their own collection capabilities such as those within the military, security, or law enforcement, i.e., government communities. Others do not, especially within the commercial environment.

For collection management purposes, it is important to note that all collection assets have different characteristics broadly categorized according to three criteria. They are either cyber or in the real world, are technical or human based, and can either be constant or periodic in obtaining data or information. A cyber-based collection tool such as a search engine or bot will be technical and provide information on a periodic basis meaning each search reveals results one time per search. A reconnaissance satellite is a real-world collection asset, is technical by nature, and can either produce one-time imagery or constantly stream captured communications or other signatures as it never needs rest.

There are two obvious exceptions to these characteristics: Cyber collection cannot be human, and human collection cannot be constant. Cyber collection using data mining tools are used by analysts, but exclusively use algorithms and other computer code to work. Humans, on the other hand, cannot stream data into an intelligence center, no matter how fast they can transmit reports or data.

Evaluating each collection asset according to the three criteria along with their exceptions results in only five broad categories of collection assets for a collection manager to consider in their planning efforts.

This is a basic portrayal of collection assets by the three functional criteria that can be further broken down into additional subcategories. For example, the technical categories can further be subdivided into cyber, ground, aerial, or orbital collection assets. Even further, aerial collection assets can be subdivided themselves into manned and unmanned, government or commercial, and military or nonmilitary platforms, each carry more refined characteristics for collection managers to consider.

One of the reasons why cyber collection is different from other technical collection assets is that in cyber collection, the primary means of obtaining relevant information has already been collected or is constantly being collected from the generating source.

This is a significant distinction in determining how best to gather information for a particular requirement or problem set, especially by intelligence organizations that rely on data mining and visualization tools.

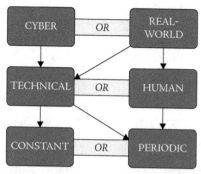

Collection Category	Examples
Cyber – Tech - Constant	Network monitors, Sniffers, spyware
Cyber – Tech - Periodic	Search engines, Web-crawlers, hacking
Real-World – Tech - Constant	Signal Interceptors, RADAR, Ground Sensors
Real-World – Tech - Periodic	Aerial & Satellite Imagery, Open-Source Publications
Real-World – Human - Periodic	Spies, Social Engineering, Hand-held Imagery

FIGURE 12.5   Intelligence collection asset categories

If data/information has already been collected, it is simply a matter of gaining access to it, running specific queries related to the problem set and then working with the results. Very little coordination, tasking, and management are needed if the intelligence analyst can easily access information through a simple search engine or some method run from their workstation.

However, if the information needed is not readily available, it then must be obtained either through tasking collection assets or requesting support the information from an outside supporting organization. If the latter, that organization receiving the request will manage it among their other requirements, and if they can fulfill, it will determine whether they can query their own databases or task someone/something to collect it.

A collection operation requires two primary types of management. First is the management of the requirements themselves—how they are received, evaluated, prioritized, catalogued, tracked, assigned, and fulfilled. Second is the management of collection operations or how the information is actually gathered—which assets are able and available to collect it and any operational planning associated with the collection such as weather, movement, logistic support among them. These two areas of management become more pronounced and distinct from each other in larger organizations. In the largest organizations or agencies, entire divisions or directorates are devoted to one or the other. Whether these are full-time or part-time jobs, they are critical responsibilities and must be assigned to one or more people. Some collection operations, such as major military commands or regional fusions centers, are so large that they require an entire team of personnel often dividing responsibilities between two or more different people.

Collection management requires detailed planning and prioritization of intelligence requirements according the available assets owned by an organization. Available assets are assigned based on the importance of the requirement as relayed by either the customer or the overall intelligence manager. Collection management also requires good and uninterrupted communications with the customer or those who handle their requirements so as to understand both the purpose and the effectiveness of what was collected.

Supporting Operations: Professional Development through Education and Training

An effective long-term intelligence operation requires more than just bringing people into an operation and having them perform their work day after day, year after year. It also requires taking care of people beyond providing a safe, secure, and workable environment or adequate pay and compensation for work conducted. An effective intelligence organization must continually be allowed to grow their people, improve their skills, and have them learn new skills for both their professional and personal fulfillment. The primary avenues of doing this are to provide education and training as part of an overall professional development plan.

Education

From an intelligence operations perspective, *education* is any type of learning that is directed toward an academic degree of some level to include undergrad, graduate, and postgraduate levels. It also includes academic credit that confers a certificate of some sort, but it should also be part of achieving one of the aforementioned degrees.

Education is viewed as a foundational requirement for most intelligence positions within an organization. Position descriptions for those seeking to fill them will include within their requirements both a relative level of degree and years of experience. For example, a vacancy for a senior intelligence analyst position is often advertised as requiring either a bachelor's degree and eight years' experience or a master degree and four years' experience. While there are a handful of intelligence-specific degrees currently offered by colleges and universities, intelligence is a profession that relies on a wide variety of degrees, from accounting to geography and from psychology to computer science.

While intelligence organizations will routinely demand certain levels of higher education for their positions, the time and costs required to obtain a degree prohibits all but the largest organizations from providing education directly for their personnel. Providing tuition to full-time students is an enormous financial burden for any organization. Full-time students are also not able to work a full-time intelligence job while they are in school. This combination of tuition costs and loss of productivity is simply not affordable to all but the highest levels of the U.S. Intelligence Community. Schools and educational programs provided directly by organizations such as the National Intelligence University or Naval Post-Graduate School within the U.S. Department of Defense are relatively small, highly competitive, and require a significant commitment to those able to attend them. They are also run in the interests of what the government needs in its people, not the greater intelligence market.

Much more common is where organizations, both within the government and commercial sector, provide tuition assistance for their personnel to pursue an education on their own time. These programs often require a degree plan from the student, i.e. showing how a course is part of a student's path to obtain a degree. Many paying organizations will reimburse the student/employee based upon how well they did in each course. Some will also require a commitment to stay with their organization for a time after completion.

For the vast majority if intelligence personnel, education is a personal choice and an individual endeavor. Each path taken is unique to the individual and therefore is seen not as a rank but as a show of both commitment and possession of a baseline of knowledge. This baseline is important, but only when combined with a proven record of experience and a demonstrated ability to take on increasing responsibilities.

Training

While education is focused on learning and increasing knowledge, **Training** is focused on learning skills and applying knowledge at the right time and in the right places. Training takes much less time and resources than education and can be focused and tailored toward the specific skills an organization deems important. While learning is still an individual function, training can be conducted to instill both individual and group skills. Many people can be trained on the same skill at once, such as how to conduct a specific analytic technique or operate a piece of equipment or software.

Training differs markedly from education in that groups of people can also be trained as a team, with each person learning an individual skill as part of a group's actions such as how to conduct a group analytic technique or operate equipment that requires an entire crew.

For these reasons, intelligence organizations are more involved in training their personnel than in their education. Training can consist of complex programs involving full-time instructors and administrative personnel, but it can also be as simple as an ad hoc or informal session involving a handful of people trained by a more experienced member of a team. Training is a constant requirement of an effective organization as the need for training goes far beyond initial training for new personnel. It involves understanding the tasks and responsibilities of intelligence personnel as well as the skills necessary to complete them in an efficient manner. In creating a new training program or in reviewing a current training program, intelligence managers must consider several related areas.

Funding and Resourcing

Training requires resourcing. Expertise must be captured and presented in an objectifiable and repeatable way. Personnel must be designated as instructors or admin/support personnel depending on the size of the training program. Space must be allocated and reserved for training. Training materials and equipment must be created or purchased. Committing to training from a resource and financial perspective can become quite extensive depending on the type of training required as well as the environment used. It is one of the reasons why training is often seen as a necessary when budgets are plenty, but one of the first of the supporting operations to be eliminated when budgets are tight.

If an organization places a priority on the training of their personnel, that priority must be shown in the commitment of resources. This includes costs for instructor labor and allocation of materials and learning platforms. They must also invest in both physical and virtual training spaces depending on their requirements. Resources must be managed as diligently as any other budget and funding requirements, often with the ability to show the results of training in a tangible manner to those in leadership, i.e., those who are paying for the training.

Learning Environments

With the introduction of information technology into the classroom over the past decades, learning has been able to escape the classroom entirely. Training programs can now adapt different types of learning environments based on learning requirements. From the use of avatars to Massively Multiplayer Online (MMO) environments, training developers and instructors have many tools and avenues to reach different types of learners.

As shown in Figure 12.6, intelligence managers must determine the training environment that best fits both their learning objectives and the resources available. These two primary drivers determine which of the learning environments (or a combination thereof) provides the most efficient way to training and development their personnel. Each of these learning environments offers unique benefits as well as issues that must be adequately addressed:

Levels of Training and Certifications

Each intelligence organization is going to have a mix of different personnel with different levels of experience and areas of expertise: new and senior analysts, first-line supervisors, collection managers, technical integrators, production specialists, support and administrative personnel, and mid- to senior-level leadership. A training program will need to fulfill the needs of each in a cost-efficient manner. One simple method is to provide foundational level training for all new personnel no matter their station or rank, and then build upon that initial training with more advance and specialized courses required for different positions within the organization.

One of the more recent trends in intelligence training is in certifications, both within the government and commercial sectors. Certifications are similar to education degrees in that they signify a commitment to achieve them, but unlike degrees, training certifications are based on applied knowledge and experience. Personnel with credentials in the various intelligence-related certifications now available have demonstrated that they possess a baseline of knowledge and/or experience. For intelligence managers, certifications can

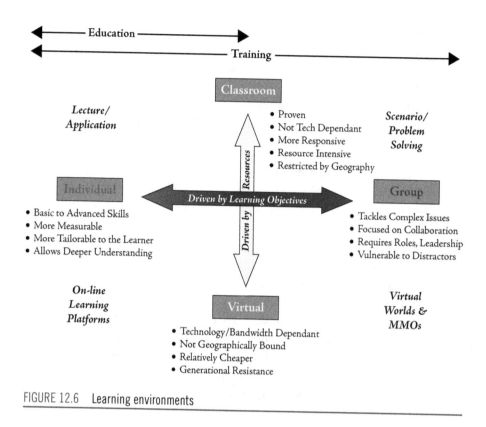

FIGURE 12.6   Learning environments

be required for employment and therefore act as a screening system for new personnel, but they can also be used to help focus training objectives toward a tangible goal for current personnel.

Internal or External Training

Managing a training program will ultimately require a decision on whether or not to turn to external resources for assistance. Just as in determining the most efficient learning environment, intelligence managers must consider whether or not they have the authority and resources to meeting their training requirements using their own resources. Quite often, organizations may have adequate funding but lack the ability to secure dedicated training space or systems internally.

Internal training teams are usually used by the larger organizations where the training requirement is large enough to keep training personnel gainfully employed all the time. When they are not conducting instruction, they are still getting paid. Larger organizations are able to take advantage of this downtime by tasking their instructors with training development and improvements, instructor certifications, administration, and travel requirements.

External training providers can provide qualified personnel, expert instructions, and even their own venues as in classrooms or learning platforms for instruction. External training providers can be a more expensive option, but not when considering how cost-prohibitive classrooms, information systems, and instructor expertise can be, especially in smaller organizations.

External training allows for a somewhat cost-effective approach for smaller organizations but we find that the training they purchased was originally designed for someone else. In purchasing external training, there are generally three options, ranked from least to most expensive and least to most tailored toward the purchaser's requirements:

1. **Courses off-the-shelf:** Purchasing seats in already created courses will provide adequate training on many intelligence-related subjects but will not necessarily be tailored to the data, software tools, or specific problem-sets of the organization. On the other hand, students will be able to gain differing perspectives when they attend courses with students from other intelligence organizations.

2. **Modularized Training:** Training providers that have a wide variety of courses available can be approached to build a course or set of courses using individual blocks of instructions. There will be additional costs for this modularized approach, but it allows for more tailoring to the learning requirements of the organization. If possible, purchasers are able to build their own courses, by selecting from a menu of already built blocks of instruction and having the trainer integrate these blocks into a somewhat tailored course for their needs.

3. **Built from Scratch:** This is the most expensive option for external training as it requires the creation of courses specifically geared for the paying organization—their mission, data, tools, problem sets, and individual skill levels. It is the most labor intensive on the part of the developer and limits the ability to export that training to other organizations that may otherwise benefit from more generally applied instruction.

Lessons in Intelligence: Persistent Costs of Training

My time as a program manager for intelligence training as a defense contractor started out small in 2002. After I gave a walk-in, unsolicited proposal to a few mid- to senior-level managers within the U.S. Army Intelligence and Security Command (USAINSCOM or just INSCOM), I was awarded a modest contract and able to create a team of seven instructors tasked with creating training for intelligence analysts working within INSCOM's Intelligence Operations Center (IOC). We created a single class within a few weeks but quickly realized that several others would be needed for a more comprehensive training program. As our courses grew more popular and spread by word of mouth, INSCOM leadership doubled the size of our contract to 14 instructors and support personnel, asking us to take our courses out on the road to their various commands and units around the world.

One senior leader within the INSCOM IOC was critical of my training program from the start. He would often disparage myself or my team members in staff meetings or throw off-handed comments as he recognized us in the hallways of the headquarters building. One of his chief criticisms was that a majority of his personnel receiving our training were contractors like us. He was very vocal in stating that he didn't feel that the government should be paying for us to train other contractors. In his mind, our training was a waste of money as contractors should come to the job already trained.

After several weeks of his passive-aggressive behavior, he finally crossed the line with a comment and accusation against our program in a fairly high-level meeting. As the manager in charge of all analysts working within the IOC, he stated he would no longer allow contractor personnel to attend our training, and tell their respective companies that their people would have to get training on their own. My own training manager, who himself was a Colonel in the Army Reserves, was in that meeting. He recounted to me later what happened when he pulled this IOC manager aside after the meeting.

In a soft-spoken and logical manner, my training manager laid out the consequences of his declaration. He let the IOC manager know that while he may think he was saving money in the long run, changing the skill requirements for all contractor personnel would require the government to rewrite the requirements of each contract involving personnel within the center. The companies who provided the analysts, more than 70% of the workforce, would then be able to charge a higher rate for the personnel in order to recoup the costs of the new skill requirements. If there was a sudden vacancy, there would also have to be a delay of up to three weeks in finding a replacement as they would need to be trained prior to starting.

One way or another, the government would be paying for training either internally or externally. If not, the IOC manager pulling his contractors from our courses would have to personally take responsibility for any consequences that resulted from using untrained personnel within the center. As the conversation ended shortly thereafter, the IOC manager backed-down from his declaration as he neither had the authority to make contractual changes, nor did he have the fortitude to take the risks as explained to him.

Buttonology Versus Application

In an environment surrounded by technology, intelligence managers have to ensure the focus of training remains on the analyst and not on technology. Often, data mining tools developed by engineers are accompanied by training developed by those same engineers and is therefore focused on the engineering aspects of the tools, not the end user. In simple terms, analysts need to know how to drive the car, not just how the engine works. Analysts can train on tools and visualization every aspect of a tool's functions, i.e., "buttonology," but if they're never trained on how to use the technology within their problem sets or mission requirements, their training will be ineffective. Teaching buttonology, instead of applied skills, is part of a larger potential pitfall set that many instructors have a tendency to fall into, i.e., training what they know and what experience they have versus what the students need to learn.

Reviewing both internally and externally developed training, intelligence managers must pay particular attention to the learning objectives of a course and how well the lesson plans and materials align with those objectives. They must also look to ensure that three fundamental components are present in any training: (1) definable learning activities that are tied directly to (2) learning objectives or outcomes that include (3) methods to measure the effectiveness of the training.

This most effective way to do this is to either attend training themselves or conduct post training interviews and discussions with qualified personnel who have attended training. They can also review the coursework materials, but they must do so with knowledge of what type of training is needed for their organization. The ultimate goal of either creating training material internally or purchasing it externally is that it trains intelligence personnel in skills that can be applied to their work environment, using their tools and data, to emulate their customers' requirements.

Supporting Operations: Customer Support

Restating the argument made at the beginning of this book, the ultimate purpose of intelligence is to support a customer. Every action taken in intelligence operations, whether in the areas of collection and analysis, production and delivery, or administrative and logistics, is all conducted to support a customer. Everything part of the Intelligence Operations Process is in control of intelligence personnel except one—the customer themselves.

As outlined in the Intelligence Operations Process in Chapter 8, the supported customer plays a critical role, both as the requestor and recipient of intelligence analysis. They are both the driver of what intelligence personnel need to work on and the evaluator of what is delivered or presented to them as a result of the process. This makes their participation a critical part of intelligence's success or failure and yet much of their participation is outside of the control of intelligence personnel.

Unfortunately, no matter how effective, accurate, or otherwise outstanding an intelligence organization or operation is, customers can still make mistakes and errors. Indeed, many of worst decisions in history were made not because of faulty intelligence but because a decision-maker, using good intelligence, failed to make the right decision anyways. As it is not the job of intelligence to influence or persuade a decision-maker. It is the job of intelligence to ensure that customers make decisions with the most accurate, timely, and comprehensive information and knowledge about their threats as possible.

Doing this comes with the implied requirement that the intelligence professional establish themselves as a credible and reliable professional and, in many cases, personal asset. This is a difficult proposition simply because the intelligence officer and analyst will almost always be junior to their customers in terms of rank, position, and experience.

Intelligence personnel will also have a significant difference in skills and experience than their customers. The perception that intelligence is something that just happens behind a magical door and is conducted by nerds and geeks will always persist. To combat these differences and perceptions, intelligence managers must seek out ways to bring the customer into their operations process as an active and cooperative participant.

An effective method to do this is to show, explain, train, and involve the customer in the different parts of the specific methods and processes used to support them. Many customers will already have experience with intelligence in general or doctrinal terms, so it will be important to provide answers to the following questions specific to their supporting intelligence asset:

+ Who is working to support them along with their knowledge and experience?
+ What are the capabilities and limitations of their intelligence assets?
+ Where do they fit into the process and their role as a customer?
+ What are the time tables and expectations for different types of requirements?
+ How does their supported intelligence actually conduct their work for them?

Similar to methods used to deliver intelligence, answering these questions can be done through either product or presentation. A simple guide can be published online, soft-copy, or hard-copy to various levels of customers, outlining the various data, tools, people, and processes that make up their intelligence support. As shown in the example in Figure 12.7, presenting a process to non-intelligence personnel will still mirror the Intelligence Operations Process but will help to explain it in ways that is relevant to

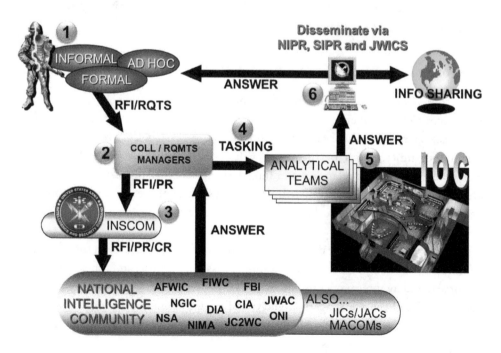

FIGURE 12.7   Example of intelligence process presented for customers

them. The following chart was prepared in 1999 to brief visitors and leaders within the Army's Land Information Warfare Activity (LIWA) on how their intelligence branch would support their requests.

In presenting this process, customers and other supported personnel were able to learn that requirements (1) were received by the intelligence branch by the collection/requirements managers who (2) evaluated it to determine the branch's ability to answer it in house or (3) send it up through higher headquarters (INSCOM). Often, it would then go to the appropriate agency within the National Intelligence Community as a request. Upon receiving the answer or if the branch could simply answer the requirement themselves, it was then assigned (4) to one of the branch's analytic teams. The teams would then create a final product (5) for review before sending it out (6) to both the customer and the rest of the intelligence community through various classified networks.

Without bogging customers with the internal details of how the Intelligence Operations Process works, it is instead presented with a focus on how a customer would be supported. Other important items can be added to a presentation like this, including: What is needed within requirement request for the best results, what products can and cannot be created, and how long the customer should expect to receive a response or product in return. Several methods and approaches can be used to ensure that the customer is familiar with their intelligence asset. The more effective intelligence personnel are at informing their customers about how they work, the better the working relationship will be in providing intelligence overall. Customer support, along with all of the other supporting operations of intelligence, is geared toward one primary purpose and that purpose should be displayed on a large banner within every intelligence center: Intelligence Is for the Customer.

Summary

While this chapter highlights several of the most critical supporting operations, intelligence professionals will encounter many more aspects and issues in the course of their day-to-day operations. These can include financial, contracting, legal, human resources, equal opportunity, ethics, performance evaluations, intelligence oversight, environmental, logistics, public relations, and interpersonal relationship issues among many others. Handling these effectively will not ensure success of the overall operation, but the inability to understand, work, or mitigate the problems they can present is an almost guarantee of failure.

The key to navigating these different areas along with those outlined in this chapter is to understand and stay focused on the primary mission, purpose, and functions of both the current and long-term operations. Every issue will be as unique as the organization it occurs in. Intelligence managers should therefore devote time and effort to train their personnel as well as themselves through research, coordination with associated experts, and exposure to these facets as they occur.

Key Summary Points

+ Effectively conducting intelligence operations requires the successful conduct of many supporting operations. Many of these operations are not considered part of the primary function of an intelligence organization and are also not necessarily conducted by intelligence personnel.
+ Providing support to intelligence operations requires considerations related to both the level of operations and the level of analysis routinely conducted by the organization.
+ Supporting operations include, but are not limited to, personnel manning, security, communications and situational awareness, collection, education and training and customer support. It can also include many other processes and facets that must be understood and considered.

Discussion Questions

+ Besides the levels of operation and levels of analysis, what other major environmental or mission-related factor should be considered for intelligence operations? Why?
+ What are some of the ways that intelligence training and education programs can best take advantage of emerging technologies for more effective learning? Are some better suited for one or the other?
+ What are some of the ways that customers of intelligence, who are not familiar with their supporting intelligence assets, are hindered in their decision-making? What are some of the most effective methods to mitigate this?

Figure Credits
Fig. 12.2a: Copyright © 2016 Depositphotos/ra2studio.
Fig. 12.2b: Copyright © 2015 Depositphotos/roxanabalint.

Index

D

data and information
  functionality, 119
  management, 79–80
  mapping open sources,
    111–113
  media bias and accuracy,
    113–114
  mining and visualization
    tools, 120
  raw and refined materials,
    102–104
  reliability, 108–111
  right selection of, 104–105
  security, 105–108
dataflow, 92
data mining, 120, 123–144
  arguments against, 125–128
  as inquiry, 123–124
  considerations, 133–134
  foot printing, 138–143, 140
  intelligence oversight,
    128–130
  operational capabilities,
    131–133
  purpose of, 131
  tools, 135–138, 137
  water flow charting,
    142–144, 143

data pipes, 92
data stream, 92
Davis, Jack, 6
Dayton, Elias, 43
decision-makers, 261–266
  experience and expertise,
    262–263
  knowledge, 265
  leadership style, 262
  personality, 265–266
Defense Intelligence Agency
  (DIA), 51
delivering intelligence
  communications skills
    required for, 270–276
  creating and delivering
    response, 257–259
  current situation, 260–261,
    261
  decision-makers, 261–266
  pitfalls of, 279–282
  product and presentation
    elements, 276–277
  quality control and
    assurance, 277–279
  supported organization,
    259–260, 260
  types of responses, 269, 270

understanding customer,
    259, 259–267
  working relationship with
    customer, 267–269
demographics of threat
  profiling, 236–238
Desert Shield, 26
detailed analysis, 197.
  See also threat profile/
  profiling
  defined, 241
  methods for, 229, 229–230
  overview, 276–277
  tool and techniques,
    228–229
Director of National
  Intelligence (DNI), 44
discovery analysis, 115
diversity
  intelligence community, 68
  personnel manning,
    162–164
Donovan, William J., 50–51
drivers of intelligence
  operations, 82–84
Drug Enforcement
  Administration, 51
dual-purpose products, 280

E

education, for intelligence
  personnel, 170, 171,
    304–305
Elder, Linda, 109–110
empowerment, of
  intelligence personnel,
    170–171

leadership, 170–171
professional development.
  See professional
  development
training. See training
engagement, of intelligence
  personnel, 169–170

environment
  information, 211
  physical, 209–210
  preliminary analysis, 206,
    209–213
  sociopolitical, 211
Executive Order 12333, 57, 69

F

Family Education Rights and
  Privacy Act (FERPA), 107
financial operations, 285
First Gulf War (1990–1991),
  24–28

media coverage, 26
foot printing, data mining,
  138–143
formal requirements
  implied, 189–190

specified, 189
full-motion video, 272
Full Spectrum Dominance, 30
functionality, of data and
  information, 119

G

game table configuration,
  94–95
geospatial intelligence
  (GEOINT), 11, 117–118,
  271

global-level analysis, 291
goals, threat group, 233–236
  association with targets,
    242–243
  identifying, 217–218

"Going down the Rabbit
  Hole,", 292
GOTs tools, 135,
  136
guerrilla warfare, 34

H

Hackett, John, 28
Hale, Nathan, 45
Hanks, Tom, 9
Hanson, Robert, 54
Hayden, Sterling, 151

Health Insurance Portability
  and Accountability Act
  (HIPAA), 107
hierarchy of needs (Maslow),
  166, 171

Historical Miniature
  Gaming Society (HMGS),
  263
Historicon, 263
Hudson, Rex A., 236–237

human intelligence (HUMINT), 11, 54, 118
human support, 157–158

Hussein, Saddam, 24, 31, 32, 53–54, 58, 61. *See also* First Gulf War (1990–1991)

hybrid intelligence center, 97–98
hybrid methods of delivery, 275–276

I

imagery intelligence (IMINT), 118, 272
implied requirements
  formal, 188–189
  informal, 190
inequality, rule of, 39
infographics, 271
informal requirements
  implied, 190
  specified, 188
information. *See* data and information
information environment, 211
information technology, 13
insider threats, 296–297
intelligence
  as art *vs.* science, 12, 12–14
  as business, 3, 8–9
  as profession, 1–2, 9–10
  defining, 2–5
  disciplines, 10–12, 11
  evolution, 48–49
  history, 45–47
  purpose, 3, 5–6
  requirements.
    See requirements
  roles, 6–7, 8
  rules, 16–19
intelligence analyst, 158
Intelligence and Security Command (INSCOM), 147
intelligence centers. *See also* intelligence operations
  analysis, 87, 88
  collaboration, 87, 88–89
  core components and, 98–99
  data and information management, 92–93
  functions, 87–89
  game table configuration, 94–95
  hybrid configuration, 97–98

office operations, 89, 89–90
physical layout, 84–86
pod configuration, 96
presentation, 87, 88, 89
security, 84–85
tactical operations, 90–91
theater configuration, 93
types, 92
virtual configuration, 97
intelligence chief, 156–157
intelligence community, 43–71
  as diverse and expansive, 68
  bottom-up approach, 44, 71, 71–72
  collection systems, 53
  mapping, 69–72
  overview, 44–45
  requirements overloading structure of, 65–66
  top-down approach, 44
intelligence operations. *See also* intelligence centers; supporting operations
  challenges to, 77–81, 78
  drivers of, 82–84
  integrating processes into, 177–179
  levels of, 286–287, 287
  mission and purpose, 81–82
  overview, 276–277
  pillars of, 98–99
intelligence oversight regulations, 129–131
intelligence personnel, 145–172, 171, 305
  as critical component, 146–147
  building team, 152–158
  business hours *vs.* continuous operations, 293–295

career path and selection, 150–154
college graduates as, 150
diversity in, 162–164
IT personnel as, 149–150
law enforcement personnel as, 149
manning plans, 158, 160
military and, 148–149
organizational structure, 159–161, 161
tasks and responsibilities, 299–301, 300
work environment, 164–172
intelligence process
  analysis. *See* analysis
  as never-ending process, 179
  communication models, 183–185, 184
  criticisms, 181–183
  integrating, 269–271
  operational practice, 185, 185–188
  overview, 276–277
  requirements.
    See requirements
  rules for, 177
  team building and, 152–154, 153
intelligence quotient (IQ), 3
International Association for Law Enforcement Intelligence Analysts (IALEIA), 48
interpersonal communication, 274–275
interrogation companies of U.S. Army, 55–56
Iran–Contra affair, 54
Islamic fundamentalist terror groups, 220, 220–221
IT personnel as intelligence personnel, 149–150

J

Japanese attack on Pearl Harbor, 49, 50

Joint Surveillance Targeting Attack Radar System (JSTARS), 26

K

Kennedy, John F., 21

kill/death (KD) ratio, 22

knowledge of customers, 267

L

labor calculations, 155, 155–156

Land Information Warfare Activity (LIWA), 126

Langer, William L., 50

Law Enforcement Intelligence Unit (LEIU), 48
law enforcement personnel as intelligence personnel, 149
leadership
    intelligence personnel, 107–108
    Maslow's hierarchy, 167, 171

M

macro-level analysis, 291
mainstream media, 111–112
management skills, 299
Maslow, Abraham, 167
    hierarchy of needs, 167
measurements and signature intelligence (MASINT), 11
media
    aggregate sites, 112

N

National Geospatial Agency (NGA), 11
National Geospatial-Intelligence Agency (NGA), 51, 288
National Imagery and Mapping Agency (NIMA), 53
National Intelligence Community, 11

O

objectives, threat group, 224–226
    association with targets, 242–243
    identifying, 217–218
Office of Strategic Services (OSS), 49–51
Officer of the Director of National Intelligence (ODNI), 57, 69
open-source intelligence (OSINT), 11, 116

P

Paul, Richard, 109–110
Pearl Harbor, Japanese attack on, 49, 50
periodicals, 271
personality style, 265–266
personnel
    intelligence. See intelligence personnel
    security, 296
Peters, Ralph, 65, 66
physical environment, 209–210

threat group, 240–242, 242
leadership style, 262
learning environments, 306, 307
learning, intelligence as, 18
Lee, Robert E., 46
levels of operation, 286–287, 287

bias and accuracy, 113–114
    mainstream, 111–112
    mapping, 111–112
messages, 271
methods of operation (MO), of threat group, 246–249
Mexican–American War, 47
micro-level analysis, 290, 291
Microsoft, 52

National Intelligence Estimate (NIE), 64
National Photographic Interpretation Center (NPIC), 51
National Reconnaissance Office (NRO), 51, 53
National Security Act of 1947, 51
National Security Agency (NSA), 11

open sources
    aggregate sites, 112
    bias, 113
    social media sites, 113
operational capabilities of data mining, 131–133
operational-level customers, 287
operational security, 295, 295–297
Operation Iraqi Freedom, 31

Platoon Kill Battalion (PKB), 30
pod-type intelligence center, 96
political bias, 282
politics, intelligence and, 18
predictive analysis, intelligence as, 17
preliminary analysis, 196–197
    adjustments of strategy, 223–224, 224

customer relationships relative to, 289–290
Liang, Qiao, 33
link analysis, 229
Lockheed Martin, 15
lower-level intelligence organizations, 289

Military Information Division, 47
military personnel, as intelligence personnel, 298–299
modularized training, 308
Morgan, Daniel, 264
motivations, threat group, 233–236

9/11 attacks, 31, 130
Negroponte, John, 51
Network Centric Warfare, 30
Nixon, R., 49
North Atlantic Treaty Organization (NATO), 28
Northern Alliance. See Afghan United Front
Northrop-Grumman, 15

operations. See intelligence operations
operations, intelligence as, 18. See also intelligence operations
organizational structures
    intelligence personnel, 160–162, 161
    threat group, 237–240, 239
Otero, Vanessa, 113
    chart created by, 113–114, 114

analyzing requirement, 206–208
defining, 202–203
defining the area of interest, 220–222
environment, 209, 209–213
identifying threat goals and objectives and courses of action (COA), 217–220
identifying threats, 212–213
objectives of, 204–205
overview, 201–202

CPSIA information can be obtained
at www.ICGtesting.com
Printed in the USA
LVHW062006261122
733825LV00002B/4

9 781516 523580